Henryk Pietras SJ

Council of Nicaea (325)

Religious and Political Context, Documents, Commentaries

G&BP
GREGORIAN & BIBLICAL PRESS

Permissu Superiorum

Traduzione a cura di Marcin Fijak

© 2016 Gregorian & Biblical Press
Piazza della Pilotta 35, 00187 - Roma
www.gbpress.org - books@biblicum.com

© 2022 ristampa

ISBN 978-88-7839-329-5

ABBREVIATIONS

BLE	Bulletin de Littérature ecclésiastique, Toulouse 1899-
CanApost	Canones Apostolorum
CanPG	Canones Patrum Graecorum
ConstApost	Constitutiones Apostolorum
CSEL	Corpus Scriptorum Ecclesiasticorum Latinorum, Wien 1866-1986
CTh	Codex Theodosianus
DSP	Dokumenty Soborów Powszechnych, układ i oprac. A. Baron, H. Pietras SJ, Wydawnictwo WAM, Kraków 2001-2003
GCS	Griechischen Christlichen Schriftsteller, Leipzig – Berlin 1897-
h.e.	Historia Ecclesiae (Eusebius of Caesarea, Philostorgius, Socrates Scholasticus, Sozomen, Theodoret of Cyrrhus)
JThS	Journal of Theological Studies, London 1899-
NDPAC	Nuovo Dizionario Patristico e di Antichità Cristiane, Marietti, Casale Monferrato 2006
PG	J.-P. Migne, Patrologia Graeca, 1857-1886
PL	J.-P. Migne, Patrologia Latina, 1844-1864
POK	Pisma Ojców Kościoła, Poznań 1924-
PSP	Pisma Starochrześcijańskich Pisarzy, Warszawa 1969-
SCh	Sources Chretiennes, Paris 1941-
SCL	Synodi et Collectiones Legum I-VI, red. A. Baron, H. Pietras SJ, Wydawnictwo WAM, Kraków 2006-2011
SEA	Studia Ephemeridis „Augustinianum", Roma 1967-
v.C.	Vita Constantini
VoxP	Vox Patrum, Lublin 1981-
ZAC	Zeitschrift für Antikes Christentum, Berlin 1997-
ZN UJ	Zeszyty Naukowe Uniwersytetu Jagiellońskiego, Kraków
ZKG	Zeitschrift für Kirchengeschichte, Stuttgart 1876-
ŹMT	Źródła Myśli Teologicznej, Kraków 1996-

PREFACE

What is the aim of this book?

In 2001, I began publishing articles dedicated to the First Ecumenical Council. The first one was an article in Italian published in "Gregorianum," which was concerned with the reasons for summoning the Council.[1] Of course, I had known scholars' views and works on the subject, including my professors, with such notable figures as Professor Manlio Simonetti, whose book *La crisi ariana nel IV secolo*[2] helped to direct historiography onto the tracks which it has been unable to leave to this day. His book is an outstanding achievement, very sophisticated and written with a maximum of scholarly diligence. It encompasses a long stretch of history and will surely continue to remain, in its entirety, an unsurpassed work for many years to come. With respect to the issues such as the origin of Arianism and the Council of Nicaea, it is based, however, on the assumption that the great historians of the fifth century, i.e., Socrates, Sozomen, Theodoret of Cyrrhus, are right. As for me, I have come to doubt this particular claim. An incentive to write the above-mentioned first article came almost as an accident. Namely, I read with a great interest, and for reasons I cannot remember now, two books dealing with sea journeys in the Roman and medieval times.[3] At the same time, I have realized that the Emperor Constantine received the news of the theological dispute between Arius and Bishop Alexander, and of the whole turmoil caused by the controversy, too late to be able to summon the bishops from near and far in order to deliberate on the issue. The letters of invitation could not have possibly reached the addressees sufficiently in advance to enable their arrival at Ancyra or Nicaea for a synod to be held in June 325; as we shall see, the venue of the synod was most probably changed at the last moment. Therefore, it was necessary to find a different reason for such a solemn invitation. I posited, in the aforementioned article, that the reason may have been simply (no more, no less) the twentieth anniversary of Constantine's rule. I also arrived at a conclusion that Eusebius of Caesarea was the author whose accounts of the beginnings of Arianism and

---

[1] *Le ragioni della convocazione del Concilio Niceno da parte di Costantino il Grande. Un'investigazione storico-teologica*, in *Gregorianum* 82/1 (2001), 5-35.

[2] *La crisi ariana nel IV secolo*, SEA 11, Roma 1976.

[3] *La navigazione mediterranea nell'Alto Medioevo*, „Settimane di Studio" 25, 11-20 aprile 1977, Centro Italiano di Studi sull'Alto Medioevo, Spoleto 1978 and R. Chevallier, *Voyages et déplacements dans l'Empire Romain*, Armand Colin, Paris 1988.

the First Council are the most cohesive. A number of later historians had drawn on, and modified, much of his account; as we will see in the course of our discussion, they had most likely given credence to the interpretation imposed by Athanasius. In consequence, I began to examine the problem as based on the relevant sources and attempted to keep away from certain clichéd explanations.

In my subsequent article, I was concerned with the origins of the so-called "Arian controversy."[4] I had undertaken to discuss Arius' letter to Alexander, with the creed stated by the former, and Alexander's letter in which he had informed the bishops about the condemnation of Arius and clarified his position on the issue in question. Upon closer analysis, I concluded that the controversy over Arius was fundamentally a Christological one, though with Trinity-related implications. It appears that Arius had been unable to accommodate the question of Christ's obedience, which Paul of Tarsus describes as His merit, in a counter-analogy to Adam's disobedience. For if this obedience can be understood in terms of merit, it signifies that Christ's disobedience would have been at least theoretically possible, which would have constituted an alteration. Yet since the Divine Nature does not allow for any change, hence the conclusion that the Son's nature is created. To tell the truth, the resolution of this particular dilemma would become possible only at a much later date, when the Church ultimately stated the position against the view of only one – divine – will in Christ and specified that the human and divine wills had existed in Christ as equally true. However, it would be officially formulated only at the Third Council of Constantinople (680). In the fourth century, no one had yet come across such a distinction and the dilemma had turned into a spark igniting the following controversy: Arius' deliberations on the obedience of Jesus led him to believe that the Son of God could not have a divine nature, while his opponents' deliberations on the Son's divine nature led them to believe that He is immutable and they were not able to explain the question of Jesus' obedience. In effect, more general principles were referred to.

The beginning of the controversy had coincided with the Emperor Constantine's letter to Alexander and Arius (autumn of 324); most probably, only then did he get to know about the problem. I discussed the issue of the letter in another study.[5] In consequence, I became more firmly convinced that Arianism had not been the reason behind the council, as the Emperor did not pay very much attention thereto. He regretted public contentions occasioned by the dispute, yet he considered their cause as insignificant.

---

[4] *Początek „kontrowersji ariańskiej"*, in ZN UJ, *Studia Religiologica* 39, Kraków 2006, 57-79.

[5] *List Konstantyna do Aleksandra i Ariusza a zwołanie Soboru Nicejskiego*, VoxP 26 (2006) vol. 49, 531-547 (published 2007).

The next thing I had to put under serious consideration was to find out the origin of such a profound and widespread conviction of the anti-Arian nature of the Council and its decisions. It turned out that everything had begun with some post-synodal epistles: Constantine's letter to the Church of Alexandria and the Council Fathers' letter to the same Church. The both are known from Socrates' *History* and their authenticity had never been questioned, even though Eusebius makes no mention of them at all. What was written there was accepted as patently obvious. What is the most striking thing, however, is that their contents are significantly different from the evidence present in some other, unquestionably authentic, letters. I am talking about Constantine's letter to all churches (stating the decisions affirmed at the synod, with no reference to Arianism) and Eusebius' letter to his church (on the same subject, also with the emphasis on different points). In addition, the authenticity of Eusebius' epistle was confirmed by Athanasius of Alexandria, the most outspoken anti-Arian of all, who had cited the said letter in its entirety and thus preserved it for posterity. The results of those findings and examinations can be found in an article published in Polish and Italian (2008).[6]

Simultaneously, I continued work on publishing the synodal documents of the ancient Church as part of the series "Synodi et Collectiones Legum" with my friend Arkadiusz Baron, Professor of the Papal Academy of Theology (now the Papal University of John Paul II). The project involved the tasks of reading the documents (several times), comparing, examining, and editing them. My efforts resulted in the observation that in the course of 25 years after the Council no one was actually eager to adhere to the Creed adopted there; hence, a number of new creed versions were formulated at various synods and submitted for the Emperor's approval, to substitute for the original one.[7] Likewise, the question of Arius did not produce much of an uproar, either. The actual problem in the East and West centred on the figure of ... Bishop Athanasius of Alexandria, removed from his See for, generally speaking, administrative reasons, yet preferring to represent himself as a victim of religious persecution and calling all his opponents "Arians," no matter how hard they would try to deny it. We know him as Athanasius the Great, a figure of extraordinary fortitude. The labels he had used became widely adopted and influenced the perspective of later historians.

In this book, I have undertaken to deal with the subjects discussed in the aforementioned articles. Although this present attempt is essentially a

---

[6] *Lettera di Costantino alla Chiesa di Alessandria e Lettera del sinodo di Nicea agli Egiziani (325) – i falsi sconosciuti da Atanasio?*, in *Gregorianum* 89, 3 (2008), 727-739.

[7] Cf. H. Pietras, *Spór o wyznanie wiary w IVw.*, in *Teologia Patrystyczna* 4 (2007), 35-50.

brand-new effort, I do not pretend to claim I have not "plagiarized" myself on certain points. In the course of my work, I also found a number of inaccurate, or even incorrect, statements in those earlier articles. Therefore, I would like to take this opportunity to dissuade the reader from paying much attention to them. My present perspective is somewhat different and more comprehensive. I should also note that on several particular points I have taken a different opinion, while in many others I have added more detail.

In my intention, this book is to be a discussion of the relevant sources. For this reason, all the documents herein are cited in Greek, with their corresponding English renditions, in order to substantiate my analysis.

At the same time, I would like to make a pre-emptive response to the following possible charge: if the author believes that the Arian controversy was not the reason for summoning the Council or even the main theme of the proceedings, why discuss it at so much length, instead of beginning to deal with the Council itself?

I would offer the following reply: it is not because of any initial assumption on my part, but due to the results of my analysis of the documents relevant to the controversy. As I do not want my words to be taken for granted, I believe it is necessary to have a closer look at the whole process leading to these particular conclusions. I have written this book in order to revisit the sources on the Council of Nicaea and submit my discussion to the judgement of those more insightful than me, as I realize I might have overlooked some points of significance, which everybody, except me, is perhaps aware of. In addition, it is also intended to revise the present views on the subject which can be found in all the history textbooks.

At this point I would like to thank Fr. Norman Tanner S.J. who was the first to believe me that it could be like that .

INTRODUCTION

An Outline of Christological Disputes Prior to the Arian Controversy

It is not my intention now to present an extensive discussion of the Christology before Arius. At this point, I think it is more useful to offer an overview, several pages long, with no reference to specific sources, which may serve as a starting point for further analysis. As each term used herein would have entailed dozens of annotated bibliographical items, I have decided to take a "zero option." After all, the Christological controversies are not what this book sets out to explore.

Christological disputes had been a constant companion of the Christian faith from the beginning. We know that the early generations of Christians had already witnessed the emergence of the view known as *Docetism*, reducing the humanity of Jesus to the role of a phantasm, an entity whose existence is not real, even though many people may actually believe it is. A rival view, directly opposite to *Docetism*, was represented by the *Ebionites* ("the poor"), who were Christians of Jewish origin, simple in spirit and dedicated to the belief in Jesus Christ's humanity. However, they did not dare to go any further, unable to reconcile the monotheistic faith with the recognition of Christ's deity.

Throughout the second century, in a period of the rapid growth of Christianity, various conceptions relating to Jesus Christ came into existence. Although many of them proved to have been headed down a dead-end street, they had originated from genuine and sincere efforts to search for the truth.

Attempts were made within the Church to maintain the faith in one God and, simultaneously, in the deity of the Father, the Son, and the Holy Spirit, which appeared to be a daunting endeavour from the logical point of view. It is therefore no surprise that certain attempts were undertaken to simplify the complicated reasoning. One of them was the *Monarchian* view, defending the oneness of God by assuming that Father, Son, and Holy Spirit are only three ways in which one and the same God reveals Himself. From the historical and philosophical perspective, *Monarchianism* is also known as *Modalism* (*modus* - "mode," "manner"). A prominent advocate of this view was Sabellius, hence the movement was called *Sabellianism*. *Monarchianism* had also existed in its *Adoptionist* form. The followers of this view believed that the true Son of God is solely Jesus born of Virgin Mary and adopted by God as His son. The monotheistic faith was thus preserved, though still at the expense of the Son's real existence (*Modalism*) or his deity (*Adoptionism*).

The most significant proponent of this particular Christological conception was Paul of Samosate, Bishop of Antioch, condemned by several synods in the years 264-268. It is notable that his name appears in one of the Nicene canons and will continue to be a bogey man as well as a point of reference and comparison throughout the fourth century: to prove the presence of similarities between a person's views and Paul's teachings meant that the incriminated individual would be certainly considered as a heretic.

Ultimately, it had taken many centuries of theological disputes to give a more precise and clearly defined shape to discussions on matters of the faith.

Gnosticism constituted an important intellectual contribution to those disputes. This philosophical and religious movement, influenced by the Persian dualistic teachings, the belief in the good and the bad god, the primacy of spirit over matter, predestination to salvation or annihilation, had also formed its own myths relating to Christ. Although the Gnostic movement was divided into a great variety of schools and groups, their teachings on Christ can be generally described as follows: He combines in Himself being an Only-Begotten Son of the Good God, a First-Born of the spiritual world, as well as a Messiah, endowed with the psyche (but not the spirit), who is the Creator's Son, subordinate to God the Father. As his humanity was ostensible (which tallies with the Docetic view), he could not have died in reality, and he had only assumed the appearance of death. He was not a saviour in actual fact, as he had come to find the people destined to be saved and to make them realize that destiny.

Roughly in the mid-third century, the two bishops, Dionysius of Alexandria and Dionysius of Rome, exchanged their noteworthy correspondence. It stemmed from something we could call a "citizen's notification of a suspected criminal act." A certain group of the faithful within the Church of Alexandria expressed outrage at their bishop who had allegedly referred to the Son of God in such terms as if he intended to diminish, or even deny, His deity, saying that He was the work of God, a creation, etc. There were some grounds for the indignation, if only to a certain extent. Since the very beginning of the existence of the Church, it had been customary to apply the Biblical teachings on the Divine Wisdom to Christ. In the Book of Proverbs, the Divine Wisdom says: "The Lord created me at the beginning of his work, the first of his acts of old" (Proverbs 8:22). Therefore, one could possibly ponder on the sense of it all, but it was impossible to deny it. Moreover, Dionysius of Alexandria referred to the Father, the Son, and the Holy Spirit as three hypostases, i.e., three existing Entities. It was completely uncontroversial in the East, but in the West it had a semblance of a blasphemy. The "notice" sent to Rome resulted in a synod as well as a letter dispatched to Alexandria, critical of this particular view of referring to God. The fundamental problem consisted in rendering the Greek term *hypostasis* into the Latin *substantia*, and the latter was usually regarded as a generic, not individual, entity. Therefore, although the Greek assertion of the existence of the three hypostases of the Trinity did not amount to anything more than accentuating the veracity of the existence of the Father, the Son, and the Holy Spirit (contrary to the above-mentioned Modalists), it became a heretical claim in its Latin rendering, stating the existence of the three separate divine substances, i.e., briefly speaking, of three Gods. It is the first case ever of a theological dispute between the East and West caused by a linguistic misunderstanding. Each party continued to abide by their side of the issue, but the root of the problem, giving rise to further disputes, remained.

By the turn of the third and fourth centuries, the distinction between the Alexandrian and Antiochene theologies had become evident.

The Alexandrian theology owed its identity to the origins rooted in the deliberations of the Alexandria-based Hellenized Jews, led by Philo of Alexandria. Active in the early first century AD, he endeavoured to explain the Scriptures in terms of the Greek philosophy, especially that of Platonic provenance. This strain of philosophy is essentially a "descending" one: humans are souls descended from the world of idea and temporarily attached to matter, yet their destiny is to return to where they had come from. From God (i.e., "from above") comes everything else, while the sense of the Scriptures is divine, spiritual, extending beyond the literal meaning. Christians had taken over that specific mentality, adding Jesus Christ to the equation. In accordance with the general concept of "descending," Christ is perceived as the Son of God who had descended upon the earth and entered the human body, thus becoming a man.

The Antiochene view was different. The beginnings of that theological school of thought were more closely linked to the activity of rabbis (or, to put it more generally, Palestinian Jews). They adhered to the view that signs of God's special favour could be found in someone's ascent to, not descent from, heaven (as the descent might point to an angel, at the most). Their theology had thus become an "ascending" one. Such celebrated figures were Elijah, who was taken up to heaven, as well as Enoch, Melchizedek, and Isaiah. The Jews held the Scriptures to have been divinely inspired in the literal sense, as if having been written in sacred letters. Therefore, they did not feel they needed to pursue any spiritual allegories. In the case of Jesus Christ, as a consequence, they reckoned it was more important that He was a man who had risen from the dead and ascended to heaven than the view that He was a Son of God who had descended upon the world. In its extreme form, this view may have morphed to the *Adoptionist* doctrine, like that of Paul of Samosate, or, alternatively, it could have been orthodox.

These two approaches to theology, "ascending" and "descending," can exist without coming into conflict ... unless they do happen to collide, which would continue to occur even as late as the fifth century. The two disparate modes of approaching theological issues were evidently present in the background of the disputes between the bishops of Alexandria and Antioch, with such notable examples as Theophile and John Chrysostom, Cyril and Nestorius, Dioscorus and Flavian. Moreover, the Antiochene school of exegesis situated itself in opposition to the tradition of the Alexandrian theology. Well, people may be sometimes so stubborn and opinionated.

Throughout the book, and especially in the documents I have examined, much of this human obstinacy and contrivance can be found. But God's writing runs straight even along curved lines.

I have basically used the commonly available renditions for the purpose of this book. At certain points, however, I took the liberty of making some slight revisions, as some alternatives, either synonymous expressions or whole phrases, were necessary from the thematic perspective. It is my hope that the Greek text itself shall justify my choice sufficiently. All sources of the citations are stated in Bibliography.

I

FROM THE BEGINNING OF THE "ARIAN CONTROVERSY" TO THE CONDEMNATION OF ARIUS (*CA.* 323)

It is generally assumed that the dispute between Bishop Alexander and presbyter Arius took place at Alexandria in *ca.* 320-322.[1] According to history textbooks, it followed from their discussion that Arius did not believe in the eternal existence and deity of the Son of God. In consequence, Arius and his followers were condemned by a specially convened synod, and Alexander sent the notification of the fact to the bishops in the other provinces of the Empire. In response to the situation, the Emperor Constantine sent Bishop Hosius with a special letter addressed to Alexandria, on a mission to disarm the conflict that was to have spread over the entire Church by that time. It took place after the Emperor's return to Nikomedia, following his campaign against Licinius, i.e., at the end of September 324, at the earliest. As Hosius' efforts brought no results, he returned to Nikomedia, informed the Emperor that the dispute had turned into a serious controversy over the Trinity, more dangerous to the unity of the Church than it had appeared before, and suggested summoning a synod of bishops of the entire Church.[2] Constantine is said to have sent letters to the bishops, inviting them to Ancyra (present-day Ankara). In the following spring, however, he decided to change the location and settled for Nicaea, where he had a palace as well. Besides, the distance between the city of Nicaea and Nikomedia, the place of the Emperor's residence, was much shorter. The bishops were to assemble there in July 325 in order to condemn Arius and formulate a new, explicitly anti-Arian, creed. The council had also dealt with the issues such as the date of Easter as well as formulated twenty canons that were to normalize the disciplinary practice of the Church. There is no doubt about these things and this is how we could put it in a nutshell. Details of the story can be found in all the publications relevant to the subject.[3] The problem

---

[1] Cf. L. Ayres, *Nicaea and Its Legacy, an Approach to Fourth-Century Trinitarian Theologies,* Oxford Univ. Press, 2004, 15-16, dates it back to 318, but also allows 322.

[2] As it is related, on the basis of the fifth-century sources, by, among others, the renowned Russian byzantinologist of the pre-Revolution period Aleksander Wasiliew (1867-1953), in his *History of the Byzantine Empire,* vol. 1, ch. 2: "The Empire from Constantine the Great to Justinian", Madison 1928 (trans. from Russian); cf. the phrase *tout le monde* therein.

[3] Cf., e.g., the fairly recently published work: A. Kotłowska, *Obraz dziejów w „Chronici Canones" Euzebiusza z Cezarei,* Poznań: Wydawnictwo Poznańskie 2009, 53-55.

is that if we take a closer look and investigate the issue further, it does not appear very likely.

A few years ago, De Decker suggested it all may have happened shortly after the so-called Edict of Milan (313), yet this is only a supposition based on the information that there had been a number of letters by various bishops dealing with the issue.[4] It does not seem very convincing especially because the controversy would have become then a "worldwide" one and there would have been no way to account for the state of Constantine's knowledge of the situation, as evident in the letter to Alexander and Arius (obviously, he had not formulated the contents of the letter himself, as it was the task of his advisors in religious matters).

Difficulties with determining the beginning and the key point of the dispute arise from the fact that the extant records are later than the events in question, while the epistles left by those concerned with the issue cannot be dated with accuracy. Historiography[5] gives credence to Socrates, who presents the following account of the origin of the controversy:

καί ποτε παρόντων τῶν ὑπ' αὐτῷ πρεσβυτέρων καὶ τῶν λοιπῶν κληρικῶν, φιλοτιμότερον περὶ τῆς ἁγίας Τριάδος, ἐν Τριάδι μονάδα εἶναι φιλοσοφῶν, ἐθεολόγει. Ἄρειος δέ τις πρεσβύτερος τῶν ὑπ' αὐτῷ ταττομένων, ἀνὴρ οὐκ ἄμοιρος διαλεκτικῆς λέσχης, οἰόμενος τὸ Σαβελλίου τοῦ Λίβυος δόγμα εἰσηγεῖσθαι τὸν ἐπίσκοπον, ἐκ φιλονεικίας κατὰ διάμετρον εἰς τὸ ἐναντίον τῆς τοῦ Λίβυος δόξης ἀπέκλινε, καὶ ὡς ἐδόκει, γοργῶς ὑπαπήντησε πρὸς τὰ παρὰ τοῦ ἐπισκόπου λεχθέντα·	[Bishop Alexander] attempted one day in the presence of the presbytery and the rest of his clergy, to explain, with perhaps too philosophical minuteness, that great theological mystery—the Unity of the Holy Trinity. A certain one of the presbyters under his jurisdiction, whose name was Arius, possessed of no inconsiderable logical acumen, imagining that the bishop was subtly teaching the same view of this subject as Sabellius the Libyan, from love of controversy took the opposite opinion to that of the Libyan, and as he thought vigorously responded to what was said by the bishop.

---

[4] D. De Decker, *Eusèbe de Nicomédie, pour une réévaluation historique critique des avatars du Premier Concile de Nicée*, in *Augustinianum* 45 (2005), 112.

[5] Among the Polish publications on the subject, his views are discussed in brief by, e.g., J. Gliściński, *Współistotny Ojcu*, Łódź: Diecezjalne Wydawnictwo Łódzkie 1992, 21ff.

καὶ φησὶν, "εἰ ὁ Πατὴρ ἐγέννησε τὸν Υἱὸν, ἀρχὴν ὑπάρξεως ἔχει ὁ γεννηθείς· καὶ ἐκ τούτου δῆλον, ὅτι ἦν ὅτε οὐκ ἦν ὁ Υἱός· ἀκολουθεῖ τε ἐξ ἀνάγκης, ἐξ οὐκ ὄντων ἔχειν αὐτὸν τὴν ὑπόστασιν".

'If,' said he, 'the Father begat the Son, he that was begotten had a beginning of existence: and from this it is evident, that there was a time when the Son was not. It therefore necessarily follows, that he had his substance from nothing.[6]

Notably, several more details can be found in Sozomen's work, as based on the historian's own sources. Thus, Arius had reportedly asserted that:

τὸν υἱὸν τοῦ θεοῦ ἐξ οὐκ ὄντων γεγενῆσθαι, καὶ εἶναί ποτε ὅτε οὐκ ἦν, καὶ αὐτεξουσιότητι κακίας καὶ ἀρετῆς δεκτικὸν ὑπάρχειν καὶ κτίσμα καὶ ποίημα καὶ ἄλλα πολλά, ἃ λέγειν εἰκὸς τὸν τούτοις συνιστάμενον εἰς διαλέξεις προϊόντα καὶ τὰς κατὰ μέρος ζητήσεις.

the Son of God was made out of that which had no prior existence, that there was a period of time in which he existed not; that, as possessing free will, he was capable of vice and virtue, and that he was created and made: to these, many other similar assertions were added as he went forward into the arguments and the details of inquiry.[7]

It follows from this account that the controversy was to have concerned not so much the mystery of the Trinity as the Son of God Himself: namely, that He is created, not eternal, and that He can choose virtue or vice. Socrates states that Arius had put forward a thesis even contrary to Sabellius' teachings. The latter had asserted that there was no real hypostatic difference between the Father and the Son, that there is only one God in one hypostasis or essence, but He reveals Himself in various ways and we call these ways the Father, the Son, and the Spirit *sine fundamento in re*. The apprehension of falling into Sabellianism had reputedly induced Arius to opt for such a radical distinction between the Father and the Son that he even went so far as to deny that the Son's deity was identical with the Father's.

The Church of Alexandria had already been faced with a similar problem. About the year 260, Bishop Dionysius had run afoul a certain group of the faithful by referring to the Father, the Son, and the Spirit in some terms which had apparently suggested that the persons of the Trinity are so distinct and distinguishable that it gave the appearance of tritheism.[8] It seems there was an ever-present fear of Sabellianism and tritheism in

[6] Socrates, *h.e.* I, 5 (NPNF 2,2).

[7] Sozomen, *h.e.* I, 15 (NPNF 2,2).

[8] Cf. H. Pietras, *Jedność Boga, jedność świata i jedność Kościoła. Studium fragmentów Dionizego Aleksandryjskiego*, Kraków: Wydział Filozoficzny TJ, 1990, Ch. II.

Alexandria. Incidentally, there were grounds for such attitudes, while various pronouncements on the Trinity would be appraised on the basis of a distance, so to speak, from one of the two extremes.

In the early phase of the controversy, Arius appears to occupy the position of a successor to Bishop Dionysius' views, whereas Alexander takes the place of the worried opponents. It is then no surprise that Arians would attempt to make use of Dionysius' writings later on in order to substantiate their teachings. It would be vehemently opposed by Athanasius, as we shall see repeatedly further on.

Let us recall that Origen had also considered the Sabellians as a cause for concern, and this may have been the reason why he had steered clear of using the notion of *ousia* in the sense of the deity of the Trinity, but he would consistently refer to three hypostases, and sometimes referring separately to the *ousia* of the Father and the *ousia* of the Son. At any rate, the dispute mentioned by Socrates fits in with the character of theological debate in Alexandria and is no surprise at all.

It appears to follow from Sozomen's subsequent words that the exchange in question, though vehement, had not yet caused any permanent controversy between Arius and the bishop. However, some people in Alexandria were scandalized by Arius' statements and Alexander's tolerance thereof. They made a formal protest and provoked a debate, in which, nonetheless, Alexander acted as an arbitrator, not a party. Therefore, the dispute had actually involved Arius and a certain vaguely defined "pressure group," which would correspond with Constantine's statement from the aforementioned letter, saying that a scholarly debate on particulars had caused discord in the entire Church of Alexandria. We shall examine the said letter further on.[9]

According to Sozomen's sources, the dispute had proceeded as follows:

ὡς δὲ συμβαίνειν φιλεῖ περὶ τὰς ἔριδας τῶν λόγων, ἑκάτερος ἐπειρᾶτο νικᾶν. συνίστατο δὲ Ἄρειος μὲν τοῖς παρ' αὐτοῦ εἰρημένοις, οἱ δὲ ὡς ὁμοούσιος καὶ συναΐδιός ἐστιν ὁ υἱὸς τῷ πατρί. συνεδρίου δὲ πάλιν γενομένου τοσαύτας διαλέξεις ἀνακινήσαντες οὐ συνέβησαν ἀλλήλοις.	But it happened on this occasion, as is generally the case in a strife of words, that each party claimed the victory. Arius defended his assertions, but the others contended that the Son is consubstantial and co-eternal with the Father. The council was convened a second time, and the same points contested, but they came to no agreement amongst themselves.

[9] See Ch. 3.

ἀμφηρίστου δὲ τῆς ζητήσεως ἔτι δοκούσης εἶναι πέπονθέ τι καὶ Ἀλέξανδρος τὰ πρῶτα πῇ μὲν τούτους πῇ δὲ ἐκείνους ἐπαινῶν. τελευτῶν δὲ τοῖς ὁμοούσιον καὶ συναΐδιον εἶναι τὸν υἱὸν ἀποφαινομένοις ἔθετο· καὶ τὸν Ἄρειον ὁμοίως φρονεῖν ἐκέλευσε τῶν ἐναντίων λόγων ἀφέμενον. ἐπεὶ δὲ οὐκ ἔπεισεν, ἤδη δὲ πολλοὶ τῶν ἀμφ' αὐτὸν τῶν ἐπισκόπων καὶ τοῦ κλήρου λέγειν ὀρθῶς τὸν Ἄρειον ἐνόμιζον, ἀπεκήρυξε τῆς ἐκκλησίας αὐτόν τε καὶ τοὺς συμπράττοντας αὐτῷ περὶ τὸ δόγμα κληρικούς.

During the debate, Alexander seemed to incline first to one party and then to the other; finally, however, he declared himself in favor of those who affirmed that the Son was consubstantial and co-eternal with the Father, and he commanded Arius to receive this doctrine, and to reject his former opinions. Arius, however, would not be persuaded to compliance, and many of the bishops and clergy considered his statement of doctrine to be correct. Alexander, therefore, ejected him and the clergy who concurred with him in sentiment from the church.[10]

Alexander had not been entirely convinced that Arius had been certainly wrong and his opponents right. As for the latter, it was said that they had firmly supported referring to the Son as consubstantial with the Father. There are traces of a dispute on the legitimacy of pronouncing the consubstantiality of the Father and Son in the correspondence between Dionysius of Alexandria and Dionysius of Rome, known primarily from the brief work *De sententia Dionysii* by Athanasius.[11] At that time as well, that is, about 260, some faithful in the Church of Alexandria were reportedly scandalized by, among other things, their bishop's evasion of this term.[12] Roughly sixty years had passed and the same problem recurred again, with the presbyter Arius, not the bishop, as the main culprit. As regards Dionysius, he went on to defend himself as follows:

κατ' ἐμοῦ ψεῦδος ὄν, ὡς οὐ λέγοντος τὸν Χριστὸν ὁμοούσιον εἶναι τῷ θεῷ.

the charge they allege against me is untrue, namely, that I denied Christ to be of one essence with God.

[10] Sozomen, *h.e.* I, 15 (NPNF 2,2).

[11] Athanasius, *De sententia Dionysii*, ed. H. G. Opitz, *Athanasius Werke. Urkunden zur Geschichte des arianischen Streits 318-328*, II/1, Berlin: W. de Gryter, 1934, 46-67. Our argument can be found at *Sent* 18, 1. It has been hypothesized that the entire work of Athanasius is a kind of artifice: the Eusebians would have allegedly drawn up a false collation of excerpts from Dionysius in order to substantiate their theses, and Athanasius responded in the same manner (Uta Heil (ed.), *Athanasius von Alexandrien, De sententia Dionysii*, Patristische Texte und Studien 52, Berlin–New York Walter de Gruyter, 1999). I think this hypothesis is rather unconvincing.

[12] Cf. H. Pietras, *Jedność Boga, jedność świata...*, 55.

εἰγὰρ καὶ τὸ ὄνομα τοῦτό φημι μὴ εὑρηκέναι μηδ᾽ ἀνεγνωκέναι που τῶν ἁγίων γραφῶν, ἀλλά γε τὰ ἐπιχειρήματά μου τὰ ἑξῆς, ἃ σεσιωπήκασι, τῆς διανοίας ταύτης οὐκ ἀπάδει. καὶ "γὰρ ἀνθρωπείαν γονὴν παρεθέμην δῆλον ὡς οὖσαν ὁμογενῆ, φήσας πάντως τοὺς γονεῖς μόνον ἑτέρους εἶναι τῶν τέκνων, ὅτι μὴ αὐτοὶ εἶεν τὰ τέκνα, ἢ μήτε γονεῖς ἀναγκαῖον ὑπάρχειν εἶναι μήτε τέκνα. [...] οἶδα δὲ καὶ μέμνημαι πλείονα προσθεὶς τῶν συγγενῶν ὁμοιώματα· καὶ γὰρ καὶ φυτὸν εἶπον ἀπὸ σπέρματος ἢ ἀπὸ ῥίζης ἀνελθὸν ἕτερον εἶναι τοῦ ὅθεν ἐβλάστησε, καὶ πάντως ἐκείνῳ καθέστηκεν ὁμοφυές. καὶ ποταμὸν ἀπὸ πηγῆς ῥέοντα ἕτερον σχῆμα καὶ ὄνομα μετειληφέναι· μήτε γὰρ τὴν πηγὴν ποταμὸν μήτε τὸν ποταμὸν πηγὴν λέγεσθαι καὶ ἀμφότερα ὑπάρχειν καὶ τὴν μὲν πηγὴν οἱονεὶ πατέρα εἶναι, τὸν δὲ ποταμὸν εἶναι τὸ ἐκ τῆς πηγῆς ὕδωρ.

For even if I argue that I have not found this word nor read it anywhere in the Holy Scriptures, yet my subsequent reasonings, which they have suppressed, do not discord with its meaning. For I gave the example of human birth evidently as being homogeneous, and saying that certainly the parents only differed from their children in not being themselves the children, else it would follow that there was no such thing as parents or children. [...] But I know, and recollect, that I added several similitudes from kindred relations. For I said that a plant, sprung from a seed or root, was different from that whence it sprung, and at the same time entirely of one nature with it: and that a stream flowing from a well receives another form and name,— for the well is not called a river, nor the river a well,—and that both existed, and that the well was as it were a father, while the river was water from the well.[13]

It can be seen that consubstantiality, in Dionysius' view, is equivalent to the sameness of nature in the generic sense: from that perspective, children are not different from their parents, except that they are not parents. Apparently, he also asserts that the significance of this notion is associated too closely with the begetting specific for humans and animals to apply it to God, especially as it cannot be found in the Scriptures and, as such, is not necessary. But who were the adversaries of Dionysius and those of Arius? According to Simonetti, they were Monarchians influenced by Sabellius, in whose view the Father, the Son, and the Holy Spirit constitute the oneness undivided into persons and hypostases. It is difficult to say, but it is possible that their views had not been as radical as those of Sabellius.[14]

---

[13] Athanasius, *De sententia Dionysii*, 18 (NPNF 2,4); cf. H. Pietras, *Jedność Boga, jedność świata i jedność Kościoła*, 90.

[14] M. Simonetti, *Aspetti della cristologia del III secolo: Dionigi di Alessandria*, in *Bessarione*, Quaderni di Academia Cardinalis Bessarionis 7, Herder, Roma 1989, 52ff. Cf. H. Pietras, *L'unità di Dio in Dionigi di Alessandria*, in *Gregorianum* 72 (1991), 485ff.

According to Sozomen's mention, Arius professed the possibility of Christ's choice of virtue or vice, which would signify, in his opinion, that the Son's nature is different from that of the Father, who is unchangeable by nature. Likewise, he could not have agreed to consubstantiality, which in itself encompassed the sameness of the two natures.

Let us note it also follows from this account that Alexander attempted to weigh his words with great caution and did not show much enthusiasm for the view held by those participants in the debate who had upheld the concept of consubstantiality, in a similar way to those who had complained, sixty years before, to Dionysius of Rome about Dionysius of Alexandria, saying that the latter did not want to use this word, as we have just noted. Therefore, he did his best to be cautious, but eventually he sided with those who had advocated speaking of consubstantiality. It is worth having a closer look at the wording of the sentence: "He gave his support to those who professed that the Son of God is consubstantial," not to professing that He is consubstantial. This is a fairly conspicuous difference, explaining in part why the participants of the Council of Nicaea, including Alexander, had a notable aversion to the term "consubstantial," as we shall see further on (cf. Chapter 2). In Alexander's letters, the term is not mentioned at all; his position is stated and explained very well with no recourse to the word.

The very core of the controversy appears to be represented, from the perspective of over thirty years, by Athanasius in his first letter to Serapion. The author makes reference to the Arians in the context of the dispute over the deity of the Holy Spirit:

Οἱ μὲν γὰρ Ἀρειανοί, καίτοι τὴν ἔνσαρκον παρουσίαν τοῦ Λόγου καὶ τὰ δι' αὐτὴν εἰρημένα μὴ νοήσαντες, ὅμως ἐξ αὐτῶν πρόφασιν λαβόντες εἰς τὴν ἑαυτῶν αἵρεσιν, καὶ οὕτως ἠλέγχθησαν θεομάχοι καὶ ὡς ἀληθῶς ἀπὸ γῆς κενολογοῦντες.	The Arians, having misunderstood the incarnate presence of the Word and the things which were said in consequence thereof, took from them an excuse for their heresy and were condemned as enemies of God and as speaking things which are in truth idle and earthly.[15]

The Italian edition[16] suggests that "earthly" alludes to John 3:31: " (...); the one who is from the earth belongs to the earth, and speaks as one from the earth." (where, nonetheless, it is expressed as ἐκ τῆς γῆς). Possibly, Athanasius is rather concerned with the differences in the approach to

---

[15] Athanasius, *ep. Serap.* I, 3 (in: *The Letters of St. Athanasius Concerning the Holy Spirit*, C.R.B. Shapland (trans.), The Epworth Press, London 1951).

[16] E. Cattaneo, Collana di testi patristici 55 (1986), *ad loc.*

Christ's deity which are peculiar to Alexandria and Antioch: the Alexandrian theology speaks of the descent of the Logos upon the earth, whereas the Antiochene school opts for the reverse view ("from below"), beginning from the humanity of Christ, which may give rise to such questions as those at the core of Arius' position.

Demonstrating Arius' view as firmly rooted in the Antiochene tradition in the letter to Serapion, a bishop who was thoroughly "Egyptian," may be also a rhetorical shortcut alluding to the views espoused by Paul of Samosate. Athanasius' letters to Serapion, concerned with the Holy Spirit, were written at the turn of the 350s and 360s, thus the author may have actually had a volume of the *Church History* by Eusebius of Caesarea. It looks as though he might have used citations from this work. Eusebius cites a synodal letter from Antioch (dated 268 or 269). Among other things, he refers to Paul in the following excerpt:

For to anticipate something of what we shall presently write, he is unwilling to acknowledge that the Son of God has come down from heaven. And this is not a mere assertion, but it is abundantly proved from the records which we have sent you; and not least where he says 'Jesus Christ is from below.'[17]

There was much apprehension about Paul's views, as attested by a mention of his followers in canon 19 of the Council,[18] as well as the entire book *De ecclesiastica theologia* by Eusebius, aimed at Marcellus of Ancyra, in which a comparison to Paul is made in terms of an invective.[19]

This statement of Athanasius is treated as one of the arguments for Arius' Antiochene education. However, if this is primarily a rhetorical statement, the argument does not appear to have been very solid, especially in view of what we have already noted before, i.e., the predominantly "Alexandrian" character of the whole dispute.

Alexander's situation in the course of the contention was not an easy and simple one. From his perspective of over a hundred years, Sozomen thought that something wrong must have befallen to Alexander, as he had been hesitant about clearly acknowledging that Arius' critics were right. It would have been difficult to explain it with his purely diplomatic approach to the issue. As we have seen, he had disliked speaking of consubstantiality, either, considering that it gave him some material associations, just as it had previously been the case with Dionysius of Alexandria and Origen

---

[17] Eusebius of Caesarea, *h.e.* VII, 30, 11 (NPNF 2,1); cf. Council of Antioch (268/269), SCL 1, 46.

[18] Cf. Ch. 5.

[19] Cf. J. Słomka (ed.), *Marceli z Ancyry. Fragmenty zachowanych pism (1-35)*, in *Vox Patrum* 32-33 (1997), 439-450.

(notably, the latter had used the term only once, in reference to a corporal emanation which may be an image reflective of the Son's descent from the Father, but not referring directly to the Trinity.[20] If we also take into account Epiphanius' information to the effect that Melitius had reportedly taken a stand against Arius,[21] we can surmise that the bishop had not been inclined to recognize that the man who had caused him so many problems in the Church was right. The further developments make it clear Alexander had not acknowledged that Arius was right.

Perhaps in hopes of reaching a final settlement of the matter, Alexander convened a synod at which as many as one hundred bishops were to pronounce their opinion on the contested issue. Arius prepared a written statement of his views, which is, apparently, the first of his known and attested letters.[22] Later on, we will also have a look at Arius' letter to Eusebius of Nikomedia that some scholars consider to be the first one.[23] However, in view of the character of the letter addressed to Alexander, I think that the reverse order is more likely. This particular letter is known in the versions preserved by Athanasius and Epiphanius. As far as the text itself is concerned, the differences are very slight, with no significance for the overall theological content. It is clearly evident, nonetheless, that the two versions are independent of each other. Athanasius specifies the addressee of the letter, while Epiphanius cites the signatures of Arius' supporters that are omitted by Athanasius. Let us follow the majority of the writers and focus on Athanasius' version of the letter, supplementing it with the conclusion from Epiphanius' version. The letter and a commentary are as follows:

Arius, *A Letter to Alexander*[24]

1. Μακαρίῳ πάπᾳ καὶ ἐπισκόπῳ ἡμῶν Ἀλεξάνδρῳ οἱ πρεσβύτεροι καὶ οἱ διάκονοι ἐν κυρίῳ χαίρειν.	Blessed Pope and Bishop, Alexander, the Presbyters and Deacons send health in the Lord.

[20] Origenes, *fr. in Hbr*, as cited by Pamphilus in his *Apology for Origen.*

[21] Epiphanius, *Panarion* 69, 3 (ed. K. Holl, vol III, Leipzig 1933, 154).

[22] Thus also W. Löhr, *Arius Reconsidered* (part 2), in ZAC 10 (2006), 121-129. According to Manlio Simonetti, Arius wrote the letter in exile, perhaps following the suggestion of Eusebius of Caesarea (M. Simonetti, *Il Cristo II*, Arnaldo Mondadori Editore 1986, 74). Cf. also my commentary below the letter.

[23] In addition to Simonetti above, cf., e.g., Ch. Stead, *Arius in Modern Research*, in JThS 45 (1994), 24.

[24] Arius, *A Letter to Alexander*, in: Athanasius, *De Synodis*, 16 (NPNF 2,4); Epiphanius, *Panarion* 69, 7-8 (in: *The Panarion of St. Epiphanius, Bishop of Salamis*, P. Amidon (trans.), OUP, New York – Oxford 1990); M. Simonetti, *Il Cristo* II, 76-79.

2. Ἡ πίστις ἡμῶν ἡ ἐκ προγόνων, ἣν καὶ ἀπὸ σοῦ μεμαθήκαμεν, μακάριε πάπα, ἔστιν αὕτη οἴδαμεν ἕνα θεόν, μόνον ἀγέννητον, μόνον ἀίδιον, μόνον ἄναρχον, μόνον ἀληθινόν, μόνον ἀθανασίαν ἔχοντα, μόνον σοφόν, μόνον ἀγαθόν, μόνον δυνάστην, πάντων κριτήν, διοικητήν[25], οἰκονόμον, ἄτρεπτον καὶ ἀναλλοίωτον, δίκαιον καὶ ἀγαθόν, νόμου καὶ προφητῶν καὶ καινῆς διαθήκης τοῦτον θεὸν γεννήσαντα υἱὸν μονογενῆ πρὸ χρόνων αἰωνίων,

Our faith from our forefathers, which also we have learned from thee, Blessed Pope, is this: We acknowledge One God, alone Ingenerate, alone Everlasting, alone Unbegun, alone True, alone having Immortality, alone Wise, alone Good, alone Sovereign; Judge, Governor, and Providence of all, unalterable and unchangeable, just and good, God of Law and Prophets and New Testament; who begat an Only-begotten Son before eternal times,[25]

In his acceptance of the Son's having been begotten before eternal times, Arius clearly rejects the views put forward by Paul of Samosate and concurs with the commonly accepted teaching on [the Son] "begotten before all ages." Let us note that this ambiguous formula remains in the creeds.

δι' οὗ καὶ τοὺς αἰῶνας καὶ τὰ ὅλα πεποίηκε, γεννήσαντα δὲ οὐ δοκήσει, ἀλλὰ ἀληθείᾳ· ὑποστήσαντα ἰδίῳ θελήματι ἄτρεπτον καὶ ἀναλλοίωτον

through whom He has made both the ages and the universe; and begat Him, not in semblance, but in truth; and that He made Him subsist at His own will, unalterable and unchangeable;

As we have already seen, in Sozomen's view, Arius asserts that the Son is characterized by being able to choose vice or virtue.[26] It is here confirmed by Arius himself in the previous sentence, where he states that the Father is the only one who is unalterable and unchangeable, while in the following one, as if in contradiction to himself, he says that the Son is made unalterable and unchangeable. Various interpretations may prove misleading and imply that, according to Arius, the Logos cannot change under any circumstance, that is, the immutability of the Father and the Son is the same. In fact, it is not like that. As we have seen in Sozomen's account, Arius held that Christ was free and thus able to choose good or evil. For the purpose of making the immutability more specific, it was added whether it was *de facto* (i.e., it exists, but, at the same time, it might not) or derived of the nature itself. Arius went on to explain this view in more detail. In his principal work *Thalia*, preserved in several fragments only, he wrote in reference to Christ:

[25] To cite Epiphanius: μόνον κριτὴν πάντων διοικητὴν.
[26] Cf. Sozomen, *h.e.* I, 15.

And since He is by nature changeable, and only continues good because He chooses by His own free will, He is capable of being changed, as are all other things, whenever He wishes. And therefore God, as foreknowing that He would be good, gave Him by anticipation that glory which He would have obtained afterwards by His virtue; and He is now become good by His works which God foreknew.[27]

Let us notice that the analogical argumentation would be applied in reference to the Immaculate Conception of the Virgin Mary: God had foreseen Her obedience and bestowed His grace earlier on Her, which Her Son was to come to deserve. Such a conception of immutability – willingly accepted, not derived of nature, may have arisen from contemplations over the obedience of Christ. If, theoretically speaking, Christ could not have been disobedient towards the Father, then His obedience had not been a merit He had deserved, but merely a necessity. On the contrary, Paul of Tarsus writes that Christ had become obedient to His death and therefore God exalted Him above all else.[28] Thus, if the obedience as a merit, as well as all the other human qualities of Jesus, were simply referred to the Son of God as the sole subject, the Son of God must perforce appear as alterable and changeable, even if in theoretical terms only.[29] The solution to this problem would be found only 350 years later, at the Third Council of Constantinople (680-681), the bishops would define the existence of the human and the divine will in Jesus, which, albeit two, are concordant with one another.[30] Such a decree would have possibly prevented Arius from having formulated the teaching of the natural mutability of the Son of God (i.e., as a result, of His non-divinity), which he had inferred from Jesus' deserving obedience. At that time, however, no one had thought of such a distinction as yet.

κτίσμα τοῦ θεοῦ τέλειον, ἀλλ᾽ οὐχ ὡς ἐν τῶν κτισμάτων· γέννημα	perfect creature of God, but not as one of the creatures; offspring,

Arius understands speaking of the Son's being created as tantamount to speaking of His being begotten. It may have been due to his understanding of Proverbs 8:22ff: (22) "The Lord created me (*ektisen*) at the beginning of his work, the first of his acts of old. (23) Ages ago I was set up (*ethemeliosen*), at the first, before the beginning of the earth. (24) When there were no depths I was brought forth [literally: 'made'] (*poiesai*), when there were no springs abounding with water. (25) Before the mountains had been shaped,

---

[27] Athanasius, *A Letter to the Bishops of Egypt and Libya* 12 (NPNF 2,4); PG 25, 564B-565C.

[28] Cf. Ph 2:9.

[29] Cf. H. Pietras, *Początki teologii Kościoła* III, 3.1.5 [32], WAM 2007.[2]

[30] Cf. DSP 1, 309-323.

before the hills, I was brought forth (*genna*)." It was generally taken as the Wisdom speaking of herself. Therefore, the use of all the terms such as "created," "set up," "made," "brought forth," was justified in reference to the Son's descent from the Father. They all point to the Son's inception. Indeed, even though Origen had argued at length that it was the causality, not any beginning in time, his deliberations had clearly failed to convince everybody.

Let us note it is not obvious at all that Arius considered the text of Proverbs 8:22ff as so significant as it may seem. There are very few known allusions or references to this excerpt: herein (though barely hinted at) and in a letter to Eusebius of Nikomedia (5).[31] Not many for such a pivotal text, even if we take into account the scarcity of the extant sources.

ἀλλ' οὐχ ὡς ἓν τῶν γεγεννημένων (3.) οὐδ' ὡς Οὐαλεντῖνος προβολὴν τὸ γέννημα τοῦ πατρὸς ἐδογμάτισεν,	but not as one of things begotten; nor as Valentinus pronounced that the offspring of the Father was an issue;

In effect, Arius renounced any form of contemplating the Son's descent from the Father that would depart from the letter of the Scriptures. Thus, he could not accept talking about emanation, as the term denoted something coming out of something else, like, for instance, steam out of water. With regard to God, it would have signified a certain diminishing of the Divine monad. Incidentally, let us also recall that Tertullian raised no objections against making use of the term, for which he would offer the following justification:

"If any man from this shall think that I am introducing some προβολή – that is to say, some prolation of one thing out of another, as Valentinus does when he sets forth Æon from Æon, one after another – then this is my first reply to you: Truth must not therefore refrain from the use of such a term, and its reality and meaning, because heresy also employs it. The fact is, heresy has rather taken it from Truth, in order to mould it into its own counterfeit. Was the Word of God put forth or not? Here take your stand with me, and flinch not. If He was put forth, then acknowledge that the true doctrine has a prolation; and never mind heresy, when in any point it mimics the truth."[32]

Tertullian could have said those things indeed, as he considered God's substance to be corporal. On the contrary, Arius had clearly evaded any material conception of a divisible God.

---

[31] See Ch. 2.

[32] Tertullian, *Against Praxeas* 8 (ANF 3).

οὐδ' ὡς Μανιχαῖος μέρος ὁμοούσιον
τοῦ πατρὸς τὸ γέννημα εἰσηγήσατο,

nor as Manichæus taught that the
offspring was a portion of the Father,
one in essence;

The theological system of Mani is very complicated and abstruse in a typically Gnostic way. However, he makes reference to emanations as well, just as the Valentinians would; likewise, in all probability, he made use of the notion of consubstantiality. In Mani's view, however, God was not corporal (material), therefore Arius rather infers the meaning from the very usage of the notion of consubstantiality, in accordance with his own teachings. It appears that he makes an inseparable association between consubstantiality, on the one hand, and emanation as well as corporality, on the other. That is why he rejects them all *en bloc.* The numerous works drawing much on Prof. Manlio Simonetti tend to reiterate his view that the concept denoted by *homoousios* had primarily a Monarchian, and more or less orthodox, overtone. From the text in question, and the subsequent debates on this particular term, it follows that the real cause for alarm was its material connotation.

As we have noted before, Dionysius of Alexandria disliked the use of the term "consubstantial" and associated it with the notion of homogenesis, used to describe the generic identity of parents and children. Perhaps, it is another thing where Arius attempts to imitate him. In his view, however, begetting children may appear as a bad example for representing the Father's relation with the Son, as giving birth constitutes a certain change, whereas at the beginning of that letter Arius makes it clear that the Father is unalterable and unchangeable. Other instances described with the use of the notion of consubstantiality had the same flaw as well: there was always something coming out of something else, that is, there may have always existed the suspicion of a mutability being imparted to God, and Arius had seen no place for anything like that in the spiritual God. Let us remember that Origen could not see such a possibility, either.[33]

οὐδ' ὡς Σαβέλλιος τὴν μονάδα διαιρῶν
υἱοπάτορα εἶπεν,

or as Sabellius, dividing the Monad,
speaks of a Son-and-Father;

According to Sabellius, there exists only one Divine hypostasis, revealing as either the Father or the Son. Consistently, the Holy Spirit ought to enter into the equation, even though the Christological deliberations were limited to the relationship Father-Son. Thus, the Son would not really exist as separate from the Father, which Arius had rightly denied.

[33] Cf. H. Pietras, *Argumentacja filozoficzna za wiecznością Syna Bożego u Orygenesa,* in: *Ojcowie Kościoła wobec filozofii i kultury klasycznej. Zagadnienia wybrane,* eds. F. Drączkowski, J. Pałucki, M. Szram, Polihymnia, Lublin 1998.

οὐδ' ὡς Ἱέρακας λύχνον ἀπὸ λύχνου ἢ ὡς λαμπάδα εἰς δύο,

nor as Hieracas, of one torch from another, or as a lamp divided into two;

Possibly, Arius makes reference to a contemporary Egyptian monk, who is also mentioned by Epiphanius.[34] He was said to have been a radical follower of Origen; as it is, we do not know why he would have made such a statement. In turn, Justin agreed with the view comparing the Son's descent from the Father to the flame of one torch coming from the other.[35] Arius disapproves the suggested sameness of the nature of the two torches, which may have hinted at an ungodly conception of the existence of two gods.

οὐδὲ τὸν ὄντα πρότερον ὕστερον γεννηθέντα ἢ ἐπικτισθέντα εἰς υἱόν,

nor that He who was before, was afterwards generated or new-created into a Son,

Referring to stages of the existence of the Logos had been probably a borrowing from the views of Philo of Alexandria[36] and fairly common among the "philosophical" Fathers, such as Justin, Tertullian, Clement of Alexandria. Such a view could not have been possibly reconciled with Arius' theological mindset, as the acceptance of the Logos' perpetual existence, just as that of God the Father, would have necessarily entailed the acknowledgement, in Him, of the Divine nature, identical with that of the Father. This, in turn, ran counter to his theory of the possibility of changes in Christ, changes in the sense of being able to choose right or wrong: as God was, by definition, recognized as unalterable. It does not appear likely, therefore, that Arius' theological thought had been somehow influenced by the philosophers, especially those of Neo-Platonic persuasion.

ὡς καὶ σὺ αὐτός, μακάριε πάπα, κατὰ μέσην τὴν ἐκκλησίαν καὶ ἐν συνεδρίῳ πλειστάκις τοὺς ταῦτα εἰσηγησαμένους ἀπηγόρευσας,

as thou too thyself, Blessed Pope, in the midst of the Church and in session hast often condemned;

There is no reason to question this statement, as Arius only cited the teachings that had already been commonly regarded as wrong.

---

[34] Epiphanius, *Panarion* 67.

[35] Justin, *A Dialogue with Trifon* 128, 4.

[36] Cf. Philo of Alexandria, *De Opificio Mundi* 19; H. Pietras, *Początki teologii Kościoła*, 157ff.

ἀλλ᾽ ὥς φαμεν θελήματι τοῦ θεοῦ πρὸ χρόνων καὶ πρὸ αἰώνων κτισθέντα καὶ τὸ ζῆν καὶ τὸ εἶναι παρὰ τοῦ πατρὸς εἰληφότα καὶ τὰς δόξας, συνυποστήσαντος αὐτῷ τοῦ πατρός. (4.) οὐ γὰρ ὁ πατὴρ δοὺς αὐτῷ πάντων τὴν κληρονομίαν ἐστέρησεν ἑαυτὸν ὧν ἀγεννήτως ἔχει ἐν ἑαυτῷ· πηγὴ γάρ ἐστι πάντων.

but, as we say, at the will of God, created before times and before ages, and gaining life and being from the Father, who gave subsistence to His glories together with Him. For the Father did not, in giving to Him the inheritance of all things, deprive Himself of what He has ingenerately in Himself; for He is the Fountain of all things.[37]

Arius reiterates the Biblical phrases and makes it clear that it should be construed in the sense that the Divine monad remains intact and undiminished.

The phrasing "before times and before ages" is very complex in its semantics. It communicates that the Son does not belong to the world of the created beings that were brought forth in time. Apparently, a possible explanation can be found in *De Opificio Mundi* by Philo of Alexandria. He assigns the creation of the Logos, as that of the "mental world," to the first day of the creation, i.e., "at the beginning," which should be construed in the sense of number, not time.[38] Time was created later on and changes could therefore have arisen only upon the creation of time. The Logos is created on "day one,"[39] not the first day, as He does not as yet belong to the time that entails changes. The "temporal" creation begins on the second day, when the visible skies are created. If these theories are treated as a background to Arius' deliberations, it can be seen quite clearly that the creation of the Son does not have any impact on the immutability of the Father, as it had been made before time, with which any change is necessarily connected. Likewise, the Father has not brought anything out of Himself, as the Son has come into existence "at the will of God," that is, as if by His order.

ὥστε τρεῖς εἰσιν ὑποστάσεις <πατὴρ υἱὸς καὶ ἅγιον πνεῦμα.>[40] καὶ ὁ μὲν θεὸς αἴτιος τῶν πάντων τυγχάνων ἔστιν ἄναρχος μονώτατος, ὁ δὲ υἱὸς ἀχρόνως γεννηθεὶς ὑπὸ τοῦ πατρὸς καὶ πρὸ αἰώνων κτισθεὶς καὶ θεμελιωθεὶς οὐκ ἦν πρὸ τοῦ γεννηθῆναι, ἀλλὰ ἀχρόνως πρὸ πάντων γεννηθεὶς μόνος ὑπὸ τοῦ πατρὸς ὑπέστη.

Thus there are Three Subsistences. And God, being the cause of all things, is Unbegun and altogether Sole, but the Son being begotten apart from time by the Father, and being created and founded before ages, was not before His generation, but being begotten apart from time before all things, alone was made to subsist by the Father.

[37] Epiphanius: <τοῦ> τὸ ἀγένητον.

[38] Philo of Alexandria, *De Opificio Mundi* 24-27.

[39] Philo of Alexandria, *De Opificio Mundi* 35.

[40] See Epiphanius.

It is worth recalling that speaking of the creation, or the begetting, of the Son before time, but at a certain definite moment, nonetheless, had been very common in the ancient Church. It was only Origen who had made the logical reasoning to assert that the Son was co-eternal with the Father.[41] Arius upholds Origen's thesis of the three hypostases, without following his line of argumentation throughout. It is notable, however, that he makes a very clear statement of his views with respect to the creation (begetting) of the Son beyond time, not at the beginning thereof: the Son is *achronos*, he has nothing in common with time. It would imply then that Arius did not want to speak (at least at that particular moment) of the time that might have existed prior to the creation of the Son. Still, he goes on to say that the Father is God before the Son, thus introducing the concept of time into his discussion.

οὐδὲ γάρ ἐστιν ἀίδιος ἢ συναίδιος ἢ συναγέννητος τῷ πατρί, οὐδὲ ἅμα τῷ πατρὶ τὸ εἶναι ἔχει, ὥς τινες λέγουσι τὰ πρός τι	For He is not eternal or co-eternal or co-unoriginate with the Father, nor has He His being together with the Father, as some speak of relations,

This is, possibly, in reference to the Father-Son relation, which, according to Origen and Dionysius of Alexandria, clearly points to the both of Them being co-eternal.[42] They stress that there can be no Father without His issue, nor can the issue exist without Father. Thus, by virtue of the immutability of God as the Father, the said relationship must be eternal. In Arius' view, it is precarious as it introduces duality instead of singularity.

As we have seen at the end of item 3 above, the Father exists with the Son: συνυποστήσαντος αὐτῷ τοῦ πατρός. But now it is also said that the Son "has no existence with the Father:" οὐδὲ ἅμα τῷ πατρὶ τὸ εἶναι ἔχει. How can it all be reconciled? What sense must Arius have assigned to the specific terms in order to avoid contradiction? It appears that the difference consists in determining the subject which exists *with*: the Father exists *with* the Son (αὐτῷ), but the Son does not exist *with* the Father (here, another *dativus*: τῷπατρί). This is not merely a tautological subtlety. The Father has been with the Son since always, meaning since He had come into being, that is, before time (on "day one," in Philo's words), while the Son cannot have been with the Father since always, because, in that case, He would have been eternal, and, as Arius asserts, He is not. The case in point, as he argues, is that the

---

[41] Cf. H. Pietras, *Argumentacja filozoficzna za wiecznością Syna Bożego u Orygenesa*, in: *Ojcowie Kościoła wobec filozofii i kultury klasycznej*, 89-97.

[42] Cf. Origenes, *De Principiis* II, 2, 1; Dionysius, in: Athanasius, *De sententia Dionysii* 15, 1.

Father's relation to the Son is totally different from the Son's relation to the Father. In his commentary on this statement, Professor Simonetti[43] supposes that this may have been a reference to Origen's theory. The latter writes that the Son must be, logically speaking, co-eternal with the Father and have an existence with Father (as based on the Father's relation to the Son, which, as he argues, must be eternal, for otherwise it would imply a change in God).[44] Arius does not set out from an analysis of the relation, nor does he arrive at any analysis. He does not recognize one relation between the Father and the Son, or the two relations represented as one reflecting the other as if in a mirror image, but asserts that there exist two very dissimilar relations, with no symmetry between them.

δύο ἀγεννήτους ἀρχὰς εἰσηγούμενοι, ἀλλ' ὡς μονὰς καὶ ἀρχὴ πάντων, οὕτως ὁ θεὸς πρὸ πάντων ἐστί. διὸ καὶ πρὸ τοῦ υἱοῦ[45] ἔστιν, ὡς καὶ παρὰ σοῦ μεμαθήκαμεν κατὰ μέσην τὴν ἐκκλησίαν κηρύξαντος. '5. καθὸ οὖν παρὰ τοῦ θεοῦ τὸ εἶναι ἔχει καὶ τὰς δόξας καὶ τὸ ζῆν καὶ τὰ πάντα αὐτῷ παρεδόθη[46], κατὰ τοῦτο ἀρχὴ αὐτοῦ ἐστιν ὁ θεός. ἄρχει γὰρ αὐτοῦ ὡς θεὸς αὐτοῦ καὶ πρὸ αὐτοῦ ὤν.

introducing two ingenerate beginnings, but God is before all things as being Monad and Beginning of all. Wherefore also He is before the Son; as we have learned also from thy preaching in the midst of the Church. So far then as from God He has being, and glories, and life, and all things are delivered unto Him, in such sense is God His origin. For He is above Him, as being His God and before Him.

It can be seen that Arius cannot speak of the Father as the cause of the Son's existence without introducing a chronological order. Yet, notably, Arius' chronology looks very much like that of Philo. There has existed the eternity of God, "day one" of the creation of the Logos and the time beginning from the number two (on the "second day"). From the perspective of time, the Son is everlasting, in the sense existing before ages (as we can see in various creeds), but from the perspective of eternity, He has His "origin," strictly speaking, "before all ages."

Alexander did not depart from orthodoxy, of course, by asserting that God is before all, also before the Son. Origen's teachings were similar in this regard and I believe this is no reason for accusing him of subordinationism. He had elaborated on that particular view further, many times referring to spiritual nourishment and that everything in existence, except for God the

---

[43] M. Simonetti, *Il Cristo* II, 550.

[44] Cf. H. Pietras, *Argumentacja filozoficzna...*

[45] Epiphanius: πρὸ τοῦ Χριστοῦ.

[46] Epiphanius: παρασχόντος.

Father, needs the nourishment to exist, including the Son.[47] The Father "nourishes" the Son by imparting His substance to Him. Since the real substance (*ousia*) of God is the Wisdom,[48] the Son is thus rightly called the Divine wisdom.

This is what Arius had overlooked in Origen's teachings or, possibly, he had not been able to imagine a spiritual nourishment in which the nourished one has gained with no effect at all upon the one who nourishes. He had also denounced speaking of a relation, apprehensive of acknowledging the one between the Father and the Son as eternal, for in that case it would have signified speaking of two ingenerate causes.

Therefore, we could perhaps venture a supposition that Arius' most serious problem was the inability to conceive of the descent of the Son from the Father other than through creation, with the simultaneous dependence on the reliability of that conception.

εἰ δὲ τὸ "ἐξ αὐτοῦ" καὶ τὸ "ἐκ γαστρὸς" καὶ τὸ "ἐκ τοῦ πατρὸς ἐξῆλθον καὶ ἥκω" ὡς μέρος αὐτοῦ ὁμοουσίου

καὶ ὡς προβολὴ ὑπό τινων νοεῖται, σύνθετος ἔσται ὁ πατὴρ καὶ διαιρετὸς καὶ τρεπτὸς καὶ σῶμα κατ' αὐτοὺς καὶ τὸ ὅσον ἐπ' αὐτοῖς τὰ ἀκόλουθα σώματι πάσχων ὁ ἀσώματος θεός. <ἐρρῶσθαί σε ἐν κυρίῳ εὔχομαι, μακάριε πάπα. Ἄρειος, Ἀειθάλης, Ἀχιλλᾶς, Καρπώνης, Σαρματᾶς, Ἄρειος, πρεσβύτεροι· διάκονοι Εὐζώϊος, Λούκιος, Ἰούλιος, Μηνᾶς, Ἑλλάδιος, Γάϊος· ἐπίσκοποι Σεκοῦνδος Πενταπόλεως, Θεωνᾶς Λίβυς, Πιστός· ὃν κατέστησαν εἰς Ἀλεξάνδρειαν οἱ Ἀρειανοί.>

But if the terms 'from Him,' and 'from the womb,' and 'I came forth from the Father, and I am come',[49] be understood by some to mean as if a part of Him, one in essence or as an issue, then the Father is according to them compounded and divisible and alterable and material, and, as far as their belief goes, has the circumstances of a body, Who is the Incorporeal God. <I pray for your health in the Lord, blessed Pope. Arius, Aeithales, Achillas, Carpones, Sarmatas, Arius, presbyters. Deacons: Euzoius, Lucius, Julius, Menas, Helladius, Gaius. Bishops: Secundus of Pentapolis, Theonas the Libyan, and Pistus whom the Arians ordained for Alexandria.>

The expression used in this passage reveals that Arius conceives of discussing consubstantiality as presupposing corporality, as only a body can consist of parts.

[47] Cf. Origenes, *CIo.* XIII, 33, 203 - 34, 225.

[48] Cf. Origenes, *exc. in Pr.*, PL 17, 185; cf. H. Pietras, *Pojęcie Bożej substancji absolutnej u Orygenesa – próba ujęcia*, ZN UJ MCCXLVI, in *Studia Religiologica* 33 (2000), 127-140.

[49] *1 Cor.* 8:6; *Ps.* 109:3; *Jo.* 8:42.

Arius' reluctance to fall into speaking of consubstantiality or emanation in describing the Son's descent from the Father, i.e., to evade the risk of the concepts becoming too "corporal," are the same as those of Origen, when he had objected to the custom of interpreting Ps 44:2 ("The beautiful word flows out of my heart"), in this particular way.[50] Origen is aware of the fact that this verse is commonly construed as referring to God the Father, who brings the word out of Him. However, he does not apply it directly to the Son and is definitely wary of embracing the Divine reality in a corporal, material way:

It is very strange to suppose that the heart is a part of God, similar to the heart in our body. But we must remind them that as God's hand, and arm, and finger are mentioned, we do not attach our understanding to the literal sense, but examine how we should understand these expressions correctly and in a manner worthy of God, so also must we take God's heart to be his intellectual and purposeful power concerning the universe.[51]

In this way, he goes on to say, the Father does not want to retain the words of the truth for Himself and "exhales them," thus creating their reflection in the Word.[52] Further on in his commentary, Origen writes that it should not be understood as spoken by God the Father, as the words may be attributed to one of the prophets. It can be seen then that Arius was not the only one who was uneasy about the corporeal conception of God.

All the followers of Arius, who had signed the letter, and Arius himself, had been excluded from the Church by Alexander, as communicated in Alexander's letter to all the bishops, to be discussed a bit further on. These particular names all attest, in my opinion, to the fact that the letter had been written prior to the condemnation, not afterwards. Otherwise, dispatching the letter and inserting the signatures in the same sequence would have appeared as an audaciously vexing to Alexander. Besides, it is not very likely that after their exclusion from the Church all of them had travelled together to the same places, let alone that it is not certain at all whether they had ever departed from Alexandria together. As we have seen before, Arius and Alexander would be, later on, the addressees of the Emperor's letter, which means that Arius must have presumably returned there despite being excommunicated.

Although it is likely that Alexander had indeed copied the names of those to be condemned from Arius' letter (in exactly the same sequence in which they had imprudently signed their names), it must be noted that it is

---

[50] *Ps* 44:2.

[51] Origenes, *CIo* I, 38, 281-282 (in: *The Fathers of the Church*, The Catholic University of America, Washington 1989, vol. 80).

[52] Origenes, *CIo* I, 38, 283.

necessary to assume the existence of those signatures below the contents of the letter. As I have already mentioned before the discussion of this letter, we know their names from the version cited by Epiphanius. To be honest, let us notice that, theoretically speaking, Epiphanius could have inserted those names there by copying them from Alexander's letter. In my opinion, it is not very likely, but we cannot rule it out altogether.

On *Thalia*

It appears that at about the same time as the events and letters in question, or perhaps at some earlier date, prior to the outbreak of the controversy, Arius had composed his *Thalia* ("Feast"). Written in verse, it probably aimed to serve the purpose of propagating his teachings. The original text is lost, but a large fragment of the work can be found in Athanasius' *De Synodis Arimini in Italia et Seleuciae in Isauria*.[53] The extant text looks like a collection of citations rather than a homogenous fragment. It is presented below without any commentary, as a poetic illustration of the contents of those letters. I think it does not seem very likely that the text had been composed in a later period by one of the imitators of Arius, and that Athanasius would have made such a glaring error, although it should be noted that Charles Kannengiesser's doubts are not unjustified.[54]

Αὐτὸς γοῦν ὁ θεὸς καθό ἐστιν ἄρρητος ἅπασιν ὑπάρχει.	God Himself then, in His own nature, is ineffable by all men.
ἴσον οὐδὲ ὅμοιον, οὐχ ὁμόδοξον ἔχει μόνος οὗτος.	Equal or like Himself He alone has none, or one in glory.
ἀγέννητον δὲ αὐτόν φαμεν διὰ τὸν τὴν φύσιν γεννητόν·	And Ingenerate we call Him, because of Him who is generate by nature.
τοῦτον ἄναρχον ἀνυμνοῦμεν διὰ τὸν ἀρχὴν ἔχοντα,	We praise Him as without beginning because of Him who has a beginning.
ἀίδιον δὲ αὐτὸν σέβομεν διὰ τὸν ἐν χρόνοις γεγαότα.	And adore Him as everlasting, because of Him who in time has come to be.
ἀρχὴν τὸν υἱὸν ἔθηκε τῶν γενητῶν ὁ ἄναρχος	The Unbegun made the Son a beginning of things originated;

[53] Arius, *Thalia*, in : Athanasius, *De Synodis* 15 (NPNF 2,4).

[54] Ch. Kannengiesser, *Les „Blasphèmes d'Arius" (Athanase d'Alexandrie, De Synodis 15): un écrit néoarien*, *Mémorial Festugière. Antiquité païenne et chrétienne*, éd. E. Lucchesi, H.D. Saffrey, Genève 1984, 143-151.

καὶ ἤνεγκεν εἰς υἱὸν ἑαυτῷ τόνδε
τεκνοποιήσας,
ἴδιον οὐδὲν ἔχει τοῦ θεοῦ καθ'
ὑπόστασιν ἰδιότητος,
οὐδὲ γάρ ἐστιν ἴσος, ἀλλ' οὐδὲ
ὁμοούσιος αὐτῷ.
σοφὸς δέ ἐστιν ὁ θεός, ὅτι τῆς σοφίας
διδάσκαλος αὐτός.
ἱκανὴ δὲ ἀπόδειξις ὅτι ὁ θεὸς ἀόρατος
ἅπασι,
τοῖς τε διὰ υἱοῦ καὶ αὐτῷ τῷ υἱῷ
ἀόρατος ὁ αὐτός.
ῥητῶς δὲ λέξω, πῶς τῷ υἱῷ ὁρᾶται ὁ
ἀόρατος·
τῇ δυνάμει ᾗ δύναται ὁ θεὸς ἰδεῖν·
ἰδίοις τε μέτροις
ὑπομένει ὁ υἱὸς ἰδεῖν τὸν πατέρα, ὡς
θέμις ἐστίν.
ἤγουν τριάς ἐστι δόξαις οὐχ ὁμοίαις,
ἀνεπίμικτοι   ἑαυταῖς   εἰσιν   αἱ
ὑποστάσεις αὐτῶν,
μία τῆς μιᾶς ἐνδοξοτέρα δόξαις ἐπ'
ἄπειρον.
ξένος τοῦ υἱοῦ κατ' οὐσίαν ὁ πατήρ,
ὅτι ἄναρχος ὑπάρχει.
σύνες ὅτι ἡ μονὰς ἦν, ἡ δυὰς δὲ οὐκ
ἦν, πρὶν ὑπάρξῃ.
αὐτίκα γοῦν υἱοῦ μὴ ὄντος ὁ πατὴρ
θεός ἐστι.
λοιπὸν ὁ υἱὸς οὐκ ὢν ὑπῆρξε δὲ
θελήσει πατρῴᾳ
μονογενὴς θεός ἐστι καὶ ἑκατέρων
ἀλλότριος οὗτος.
ἡ σοφία σοφία ὑπῆρξε σοφοῦ θεοῦ
θελήσει.
ἐπινοεῖται   γοῦν   μυρίαις   ὅσαις
ἐπινοίαις πνεῦμα, δύναμις, σοφία,
δόξα θεοῦ, ἀλήθειά τε καὶ εἰκὼν καὶ
λόγος οὗτος.
σύνες ὅτι καὶ ἀπαύγασμα καὶ φῶς
ἐπινοεῖται.
ἴσον μὲν τοῦ υἱοῦ γεννᾶν δυνατός
ἐστιν ὁ κρείττων,
διαφορώτερον δὲ ἢ κρείττονα ἢ
μείζονα οὐχί.

and advanced Him as a Son to Himself by adoption.

He has nothing proper to God in proper subsistence.

For He is not equal, no, nor one in essence with Him.

Wise is God, for He is the teacher of Wisdom.

There is full proof that God is invisible to all beings;

both to things which are through the Son, and to the Son He is invisible.

I will say it expressly, how by the Son is seen the Invisible;

by that power by which God sees, and in His own measure,

the Son endures to see the Father, as is lawful.

Thus there is a Triad, not in equal glories.

Not intermingling with each other are their subsistences.

One more glorious than the other in their glories unto immensity.

Foreign from the Son in essence is the Father, for He is without beginning.

Understand that the Monad was; but the Dyad was not, before it was in existence.

It follows at once that, though the Son was not, the Father was God.

Hence the Son, not being (for He existed at the will of the Father),

is God Only-begotten, and He is alien from either.

Wisdom existed as Wisdom by the will of the Wise God.

Hence He is conceived in numberless conceptions: Spirit, Power, Wisdom, God's glory, Truth, Image, and Word.

Understand that He is conceived to be Radiance and Light.

One equal to the Son, the Superior is able to beget;

but one more excellent, or superior, or greater, He is not able.

θεοῦ θελήσει ὁ υἱὸς ἡλίκος καὶ ὅσος ἐστίν,

At God's will the Son is what and whatsoever He is.

ἐξ ὅτε καὶ ἀφ' οὗ καὶ ἀπὸ τότε ἐκ τοῦ θεοῦ ὑπέστη,

And when and since He was, from that time He has subsisted from God.

ἰσχυρὸς θεὸς ὢν τὸν κρείττονα ἐκ μέρους ὑμνεῖ.

He, being a strong God, praises in His degree the Superior.

συνελόντι εἰπεῖν τῷ υἱῷ ὁ θεὸς ἄρρητος ὑπάρχει·

To speak in brief, God is ineffable to His Son.

ἔστι γὰρ ἑαυτῷ ὅ ἐστι τοῦτ' ἔστιν ἄλεκτος,

For He is to Himself what He is, that is, unspeakable.

ὥστε οὐδὲν τῶν λεγομένων κατά τε κατάληψιν συνίει ἐξειπεῖν ὁ υἱός.

So that nothing which is called comprehensible does the Son know to speak about;

ἀδύνατα γὰρ αὐτῷ τὸν πατέρα τε ἐξιχνιάσει, ὅς ἐστιν ἐφ' ἑαυτοῦ.

for it is impossible for Him to investigate the Father, who is by Himself.

αὐτὸς γὰρ ὁ υἱὸς τὴν ἑαυτοῦ οὐσίαν οὐκ οἶδεν,

For the Son does not know His own essence,

υἱὸς γὰρ ὢν θελήσει πατρὸς ὑπῆρξεν ἀληθῶς.

for, being Son, He really existed, at the will of the Father.

τίς γοῦν λόγος συγχωρεῖ τὸν ἐκ πατρὸς ὄντα αὐτὸν τὸν γεννήσαντα γνῶναι ἐν καταλήψει;

What argument then allows, that He who is from the Father should know His own parent by comprehension?

δῆλον γὰρ ὅτι τὸ ἀρχὴν ἔχον, τὸν ἄναρχον, ὡς ἔστιν, ἐμπερινοῆσαι ἢ ἐμπεριδράξασθαι οὐχ οἷόν τέ ἐστιν.

For it is plain that for that which has a beginning to conceive how the Unbegun is, or to grasp the idea, is not possible.

These utterances are certainly profound. Yet, nevertheless, it would be perhaps an exaggeration to ascribe such a brilliance to them that would, as Charles Kannengiesser notes, even alienate Arius from other theologians and make it difficult even for Eusebius of Caesarea to understand what he really meant.[55]

There will be certainly more clarity in discussing the relevant issues as they are expressed in the letters and other documents, so let us now revert to the synod summoned by Alexander. We have no information concerning the course of the synodal proceedings or any positive reception to Arius' epistle. In all likelihood, however, the response was unfavourable, as all the

---

[55] CH. Kannengiesser, *Alexander and Arius of Alexandria: the last ante-Nicene theologians*, *Homenaje P. Antonio Orbe*, ed. E. Romero-Pose, Santiago de Compostela 1990, 391-403; *Arius and Athanasius: two Alexandrian Theologians*, Variorum, London 1991, art. IV.

signatories had been excluded from the communion of the Church.[56] Lewis Ayres notes that Arius had been excommunicated because he refused to sign the *credo* presented by Alexander.[57] I cannot say anything about the existence of such a creed. Obviously, the Church of Alexandria must have relied on a certain creed, yet there is no reason to suppose that it would have been much different from those in use elsewhere, and formulated in so much detail as to make it problematic for any Christian to sign.[58]

A veritable epistolar war ensued from the excommunication. According to contemporary historians, Arius had addressed a letter to Eusebius of Nikomedia (see Chapter 2), in hopes of obtaining his support. In consequence, Eusebius undertook to defend Arius and wrote a number of letters to various influential figures in the Church. One of them, addressed to Paulinus of Tyr, will be discussed further on. Some of the bishops had agreed with Arius' stance and defended him in their letters to Alexander, while the others, on the contrary, acknowledged that the bishop was right and confirmed his position. On his part, Alexander did not waste time and sent out a reputedly great number of letters in order to secure more support. Epiphanius writes[59] of a *dossier* comprising 70 documents, of which only two have survived: a post-synodal encyclical (cf. Ch.2) and a letter to Alexander of Byzantium. However, this number may be possibly a certain misrepresentation. We do know that there was a contemporary custom of collecting both received and dispatched letters. Since the first letter was an encyclical addressed to all the bishops, it was sufficient to rely on just one, but replicated in many copies. Subsequently, Alexander would have received many letters in response, from those who had supported him or Arius. Those circumstances may account for the sizable body of the collected documents.

Epiphanius states[60] that Arius left Alexandria and went to Caesarea to meet with Bishop Eusebius. Some time thereafter, according to Sozomen's account, he addressed letters to Bishop Paulinus of Tyr, Eusebius of Caesarea, and Patrophilus of Scythopolis, requesting that he and his adherents could continue to serve as presbyters in their churches. Sozomen describes this appeal as follows:

---

[56] Socrates, *h.e.* I, 6. Cf. below.

[57] L. Ayres, *Nicaea and Its Legacy, an Approach to Fourth-Century Trinitarian Theology*, Oxford Univ. Press, 2004, 17.

[58] For a general view of this subject, cf. L. Ayres, *Nicaea and Its Legacy*, 85-88.

[59] Epiphanius, *Panarion* 69, 4.

[60] Epiphanius, *Panarion* 69, 4.

εἶναι γὰρ ἔθος ἐν Ἀλεξανδρείᾳ 'καθάπερ καὶ νῦν ἑνὸς ὄντος τοῦ κατὰ πάντων ἐπισκόπου τοὺς πρεσβυτέρους ἰδίᾳ τὰς ἐκκλησίας κατέχειν καὶ τὸν ἐν αὐταῖς λαὸν συνάγειν. οἱ δὲ ἅμα καὶ ἄλλοις ἐπισκόποις ἐν Παλαιστίνῃ συνελθόντες ἐπεψηφίσαντο τῇ Ἀρείου αἰτήσει, παρακελευσάμενοι συνάγειν μὲν αὐτοὺς ὡς πρότερον, ὑποτετάχθαι δὲ Ἀλεξάνδρῳ καὶ ἀντιβολεῖν ἀεὶ τῆς πρὸς αὐτὸν εἰρήνης καὶ κοινωνίας μετέχειν.

For it was the custom in Alexandria, as it still is in the present day, that all the churches should be under one bishop, but that each presbyter should have his own church, in which to assemble the people. These three bishops, in concurrence with others who were assembled in Palestine, granted the petition of Arius, and permitted him to assemble the people as before; but enjoined submission to Alexander, and commanded Arius to strive incessantly to be restored to peace and communion with him.[61]

It appears therefore that, despite his aforementioned travelling, Arius had been present at Alexandria, for only in that case it would have made sense to advise him on remaining in communion with the bishop. Furthermore, Sozomen notes that Eusebius of Nikomedia had presided over a synod convened at that city, with some followers of Arius among the participants, and it was decided that an appeal would be made to all the bishops, calling on them to give their support to Arius.

---

[61] Sozomen, *h.e.* I, 15 (NPNF 2,2).

II

EPISTOLAR WAR

Let us now focus on the most significant texts related to the unfolding controversy. After the condemnation of Arius and his loyal followers, Alexander wished to communicate the fact to the bishops, at least those with the greatest authority and influence. On his part, Arius also sought support for his cause by sending out letters (and he was not the only one to have done so). In my opinion, the first two epistles of relevance were: Alexander's letters addressed to all the bishops, written shortly after the synod, and Arius' letter to Eusebius of Nicomedia, in which the former complains of his condemnation and clarifies his position. Although it is possible that Arius' letter may have been the earlier of the two, let us first have a look at Alexander's letter, and his position as stated therein. We have already seen Arius' view on the issue in his letter to Alexander (see Ch. 1). Stead argued that Alexander had certainly formulated his position under Athanasius' influence and it had taken place as early as 318.[1] A similar opinion has been expressed by Timothy Barnes.[2] At that time, Athanasius would have been about 22-23 years old and, his intellectual acuity notwithstanding, such influence is hardly plausible, just as it is rather difficult to believe in some textbook opinions on Athanasius' considerable role at the Council of Nicaea, where he was present as a secretary or a *socius* of Alexander, which Charles Kannengiesser rightly calls highly fantastic.[3]

Alexander of Alexandria, *Letter to All the Bishops:*[4]

1. Τοῖς ἀγαπητοῖς καὶ τιμωτάτοις συλλειτουργοῖς τοῖς ἁπανταχοῦ τῆς καθολικῆς ἐκκλησίας, Ἀλέξανδρος ἐν Κυρίῳ χαίρειν.

1. To our beloved and most honored fellow-Ministers of the Catholic Church everywhere, Alexander sends greeting in the Lord.

[1] C. Stead, *Athanasius Earliest Written Works*, in JThS 39 (1988), 76-91; D. De Decker, *Eusèbe de Nicomédie*, 149.

[2] T.D. Barnes, *Athanasius and Constantius. Theology and Politics in the Constantinian Empire*, Harvard University Press, Cambridge (Mass.) – London (England) 1994 (2 ed.).

[3] CH. Kannengiesser, *Athanasius of Alexandria vs. Arius: the Alexandrian Crisis*, *The Roots of Egyptian Christianity, Studies in Antiquity & Christianity*, Fortress Press, Philadelphia 1986, 204-215; *Arius and Athanasius: two Alexandrian Theologians*, Variorum, London 1991, art. XII, 207.

[4] Socrates, *h.e.* I, 6 (NPNF 2,2); SCL 1, 78-82.

2. Ἑνὸς σώματος ὄντος τῆς καθολικῆς ἐκκλησίας, ἐντολῆς τε οὔσης ἐν ταῖς θείαις γραφαῖς, "τηρεῖν τὸν σύνδεσμον τῆς ὁμονοίας καὶ εἰρήνης", ἀκόλουθόν ἐστι γράφειν ἡμᾶς, καὶ σημαίνειν ἀλλήλοις τὰ παρ' ἑκάστοις γιγνόμενα, ἵνα "εἴτε πάσχει, ει χαίρει ἓν μέλος, ἢ συμπάσχωμεν, ἢ συγχαίρωμεν ἀλλήλοις".

2. Inasmuch as the Catholic Church is one body, and we are commanded in the holy Scriptures to maintain 'the bond of unity and peace,' it becomes us to write, and mutually acquaint one another with the condition of things among each of us, in order that 'if one member suffers or rejoices, we may either sympathize with each other, or rejoice together.'

3. Ἐν τῇ ἡμετέρᾳ τοίνυν παροικίᾳ,

3. Know therefore that in our diocese

Alexander emphasizes the local character of the controversy at the beginning. The term "diocese" is used to refer to a local church. Exchange of correspondence and transmission of information concerning various local matters had already become a tradition. Cyprian's letters are among the well-known examples.[5] As for Alexandria, we also know of Bishop Demetrius' letters to various sees, including Rome, following the condemnation of Origen *ca.* 230. It is mentioned by Jerome.[6] Such a practice was necessary, considering the existence of the prohibition, reaffirmed at a number of synods, against allowing the excommunicated person to be accepted at another diocese. The earliest synodal injunction of this kind is known from Elvira,[7] later reaffirmed at the Council of Nicaea (canon 5).[8]

ἐξῆλθον νῦν ἄνδρες παράνομοι καὶ Χριστομάχοι, διδάσκοντες ἀποστασίαν, ἣν εἰκότως ἄν τις πρόδρομον τοῦ Ἀντιχρίστου νομίσειε καὶ καλέσειε.
4. Καὶ ἐβουλόμην μὲν σιωπῇ παραδοῦναι τὸ τοιοῦτον, ἵν' ἴσως ἐν τοῖς ἀποστάταις μόνοις ἀναλωθῇ τὸ κακὸν, καὶ μὴ εἰς ἑτέρους τόπους διαβὰν, ῥυπώσῃ τινῶν ἀκεραίων τὰς ἀκοάς·

there have recently arisen lawless and anti-christian men, teaching apostasy such as one may justly consider and denominate the forerunner of Antichrist.
4. I wished indeed to consign this disorder to silence, that if possible the evil might be confined to the apostates alone, and not go forth into other districts and contaminate the ears of some of the simple.

[5] E.g., Cyprian, *epist.* 72, 1.
[6] Jerome, *vir. ill.* 54.
[7] Council of Elvira (306), c. 53; SCL 1, 57-58.
[8] See Ch. 5.

ἐπειδὴ δὲ Εὐσέβιος, ὁ νῦν ἐν τῇ Νικομηδείᾳ, νομίσας ἐπ' αὐτῷ κεῖσθαι τὰ τῆς ἐκκλησίας, ὅτι καταλείψας τὴν Βηρυτόν, καὶ ἐποφθαλμίσας τῇ ἐκκλησίᾳ Νικομηδέων, οὐκ ἐκδεδίκηται κατ' αὐτοῦ,

But since Eusebius, now in Nicomedia, thinks that the affairs of the Church are under his control because, forsooth, he deserted his charge at Berytus and assumed authority over the Church at Nicomedia with impunity,

Berytus is the present-day Beirut. It is therefore evident that there had existed a custom, if not a law, in the Church forbidding bishops to relocate from one see to another. It was to be formally prohibited by the Council of Nicaea,[9] though the decree would be never actually observed. In spite of Beirut's importance, Eusebius had clearly preferred to serve as a metropolitan, and Nicomedia, the Emperor's seat at the time, had fulfilled the role of the Imperial capital. Incidentally, Eusebius would relocate later on to the newly built city of Constantinople.

προΐσταται καὶ τούτων τῶν ἀποστατῶν, καὶ γράφειν ἐπεχείρησε πανταχοῦ, συνιστῶν αὐτοὺς, εἴπως ὑποσύρῃ τινὰς ἀγνοοῦντας εἰς τὴν ἐσχάτην καὶ Χριστομάχον αἵρεσιν, ἀνάγκην ἔσχον, εἰδὼς τὸ ἐν τῷ νόμῳ γεγραμμένον, μηκέτι μὲν σιωπῆσαι, ἀναγγεῖλαι δὲ πᾶσιν ὑμῖν, ἵνα γινώσκητε τούς τε ἀποστάτας γενομένους, καὶ τὰ τῆς αἱρέσεως αὐτῶν δύστηνα ῥημάτια, καὶ ἐὰν γράφῃ Εὐσέβιος, μὴ προσέχητε.

and has put himself at the head of these apostates, daring even to send commendatory letters in all directions concerning them, if by any means he might inveigle some of the ignorant into this most impious and anti-christian heresy, I felt imperatively called on to be silent no longer, knowing what is written in the law, but to inform you of all of these things, that ye might understand both who the apostates are, and also the contemptible character of their heresy, and pay no attention to anything that Eusebius should write to you.

It may be assumed that Eusebius had only started writing letters concerning Arius, as Alexander had hoped his own letter would pre-empt that of Eusebius. We may also conjecture that it is the first letter in which Alexander deals with the issue. We shall have a look at Eusebius' letter to Paulinus of Tyre further on:

---

[9] Council of Nicaea (325), c. 15, see commentary on the canons in Ch. 5.

5. Τὴν πάλαι γὰρ αὐτοῦ κακόνοιαν τὴν χρόνῳ σιωπηθεῖσαν, νῦν διὰ τούτων ἀνανεῶσαι βουλόμενος, σχηματίζεται μὲν ὡς ὑπὲρ τούτων γράφων· ἔργῳ δὲ δείκνυσιν, ὡς ὅτι ὑπὲρ ἑαυτοῦ σπουδάζων, τοῦτο ποιεῖ.

5. For now wishing to renew his former malevolence, which seemed to have been buried in oblivion by time, he affects to write in their behalf; while the fact itself plainly shows that he does this for the promotion of his own purposes.

The "purposes" in question may have referred to his wish to raise the stature of his new episcopal see. Until then, the precedence in the Church had belonged to the cities whose churches were of Apostolic provenance: Antioch, Alexandria, Caesarea, Jerusalem, and Rome. At that time, Jerusalem had been an almost entirely pagan city (called Aelia Capitolina), and without much significance, Rome was far away, Antioch was situated in central Syria, while Caesarea – a fairly modest city. In consequence, the Bishop of Alexandria had considered himself to be the most important among all the bishops in the East. If the bishop of the capital city were to acquire a greater significance, despite the lack of any Apostolic origin of his see, it would pose a certain threat to the important position of Alexandria. It was to be the case of Constantinople later on, as the new capital would indeed come to surpass Alexandria, the situation that the bishops of the latter city would be very reluctant to accept for a long time to come.[10]

6. Οἱ μὲν οὖν ἀποστάται γενόμενοι εἰσὶν, Ἄρειος, Ἀχιλλὰς, Ἀειθαλὴς καὶ Καρπώνης, καὶ ἕτερος Ἄρειος, καὶ Σαρμάτης, καὶ Εὐζώϊος, καὶ Λούκιος, καὶ Ἰουλιανὸς, καὶ Μηνᾶς, καὶ Ἑλλάδιος, καὶ Γάϊος, καὶ σὺν αὐτοῖς Σεκοῦνδος καὶ Θεωνᾶς, οἱ ποτὲ λεχθέντες ἐπίσκοποι.

6. These then are those who have become apostates: Arius, Achillas, Aithales, and Carpones, another Arius, Sarmates, Euzoïus, Lucius, Julian, Menas, Helladis, and Gaius; with these also must be reckoned Secundus and Theonas, who once were called bishops.

As we can see, all of those who were found guilty of apostasy were divested of ecclesiastical offices and removed from the clergy. Let us notice that Alexander enumerates the names of the excommunicated in the same order in which their names are stated as signatories of Arius' epistle to Alexander, with just one exception at the beginning: in this letter – Achillas comes before Aithales, whereas in Arius' letter – just the opposite. Hence, I would assume that Alexander's epistle is later than that of Arius. Alexander

---

[10] Cf. Council of Constantinople I (381) c. 3, DSP 1, 73.

condemned those who had signed Arius' letter and copied their names (with just one minor error), not the other way round. Consequently, it is rather unlikely that Arius had sent his letter to Alexander from his exile at Nicomedia, as it is argued by Manlio Simonetti and Domenico Spada.[11]

7. Ποῖα δὲ παρὰ τὰς γραφὰς ἐφευρόντες λαλοῦσιν, ἐστὶ ταῦτα. "Οὐκ ἀεὶ ὁ Θεὸς Πατὴρ ἦν, ἀλλ᾽ ἦν ὅτε ὁ Θεὸς Πατὴρ οὐκ ἦν· οὐκ ἀεὶ ἦν ὁ τοῦ Θεοῦ Λόγος, ἀλλ᾽ ἐξ οὐκ ὄντων γέγονεν. Ὁ γὰρ ὢν Θεὸς τὸν μὴ ὄντα ἐκ τοῦ μὴ ὄντος πεποίηκε· διὸ καὶ ἦν ποτὲ ὅτε οὐκ ἦν.

7. The dogmas they have invented and assert, contrary to the Scriptures, are these: That God was not always the Father, but that there was a period when he was not the Father; that the Word of God was not from eternity, but was made out of nothing; for that the ever-existing God ('the I AM'—the eternal One) made him who did not previously exist, out of nothing; wherefore there was a time when he did not exist,

This is ostensibly the traditional apologetic theory. Justin, Tertullian, and others, held that the Son of God had genuinely come into being at the beginning of the creation, because, as the Intermediary of the creation, he was "needed" precisely then. His everlasting existence did not seem necessary. Although it was emphasized that He was "from God," it was definitely an ambiguous statement. Origen demonstrated, in scriptural and philosophical terms, that the Son must be co-eternal with the Father and this thesis managed to find acceptance at Alexandria, despite the constant and interchangeable usage of the terms "creation" and "begetting."[12] Nonetheless, Arius was not able to free himself from the traditional and chronological mode of thinking about the Son's descent from the Father.

I have noted that this is only ostensibly the apologetic teaching, as they had never asserted that the Son was created out of nothing, i.e., from nothingness. Tertullian stressed that even though "at the beginning, God was alone," He had His *sensus* in Himself. In his view, therefore, the creation of the Son consisted in bringing out the Logos existing in the Father, not bringing Him into existence out of nothing.[13] Likewise, Justin, having assumed the chronological inception of the Son's existence, added that

[11] M. Simonetti, *La crisi ariana*, 33 and D. Spada, *Le formule trinitarie da Nicea a Costantinopoli*, (Subsidia Urbaniana 32), Pont. Univ. Urbaniana, Roma 1988, 35ff, citing Epiphanius, *Panarion* 69, 7.

[12] Cf. H. Pietras, *L'unità di Dio in Dionigi di Alessandria*, in *Gregorianum* 72 (1991), 459-490.

[13] Cf. Tertullian, *Against Praxeas* 5, 2-3.

"at the beginning, before all the created beings, God had created out of Himself an intelligent power."[14] And "out of Himself" does not mean "out of nothing" in any way.

Κτίσμα γάρ ἐστι καὶ ποίημα ὁ Υἱός. Οὔτε δὲ ὅμοιος κατ' οὐσίαν τῷ Πατρί ἐστιν, οὔτε ἀληθινὸς καὶ φύσει τοῦ Πατρὸς Λόγος ἐστὶν, οὔτε ἀληθινὴ Σοφία αὐτοῦ ἐστί·ἀλλ' εἷς μὲν τῶν ποιημάτων καὶ γενητῶν ἐστί· καταχρηστικῶς δὲ λόγος καὶ σοφία,	inasmuch as the Son is a creature and a work. That he is neither like the Father as it regards his essence, nor is by nature either the Father's true Word, or true Wisdom, but indeed one of his works and creatures, being erroneously called Word and Wisdom,

As can be seen, the later statement formulated by Basil of Ancyra, who had coined the new term *homoiousios*, i.e., similar as to the essence, is very much different from the expression which Alexander attributes to Arius. But did Arius really say that the Son is dissimilar to the Father as to the essence? In the excerpt of the *Thalia* cited by Athanasius, it is said that nothing is similar to God, that the hypostases in the Trinity are separate and their glories dissimilar to one another.[15]

γενόμενος καὶ αὐτὸς δὲ τῷ ἰδίῳ τοῦ Θεοῦ Λόγῳ, καὶ τῇ ἐν τῷ Θεῷ Σοφίᾳ, ἐν ᾗ καὶ τὰ πάντα καὶ αὐτὸν πεποίηκεν ὁ Θεός·	since he was himself made of God's own Word and the Wisdom which is in God, whereby God both made all things and him also.

According to Arius' view, God owns the true Wisdom as His inalienable and inherent feature. As he asserted, if that Wisdom came out of God, an inadmissible change would occur in God and the Father would cease to possess His Wisdom, which, as Arius believed (and perfectly rightly so), would be absurd. Attached to the conception of the indivisible Monad, he could not see beyond his assumption that the Son must have been created out of nothing.

8. διὸ καὶ τρεπτός ἐστι καὶ ἀλλοιωτὸς τὴν φύσιν, ὡς καὶ πάντα τὰ λογικά· ξένος τε καὶ ἀλλότριος, καὶ ἀπεσχοινισμένος ἐστὶν ὁ Λόγος τῆς τοῦ Θεοῦ οὐσίας.	8. Wherefore he is as to his nature mutable and susceptible of change, as all other rational creatures are: hence the Word is alien to and other than the essence of God;

[14] Justin, *A Dialogue with Trifon* 61 (ANF 1, revised).

[15] Athanasius, *De synodis* 15, see Ch. 1.

Καὶ ἄρρητός ἐστιν ὁ Πατὴρ τῷ Υἱῷ· οὔτε γὰρ τελείως καὶ ἀκριβῶς γινώσκει ὁ Λόγος τὸν Πατέρα, οὔτε τελείως ὁρᾶν αὐτὸν δύναται. Καὶ γὰρ ἑαυτοῦ τὴν οὐσίαν οὐκ οἶδεν ὁ Υἱὸς ὡς ἔστι·

9. δι' ἡμᾶς γὰρ πεποίηται, ἵνα ἡμᾶς δι' αὐτοῦ ὡς δι' ὀργάνου κτίσῃ ὁ Θεός· καὶ οὐκ ἂν ὑπέστη, εἰ μὴ ἡμᾶς ὁ Θεὸς ἤθελεν ποιῆσαι.

10. Ἠρώτησε γοῦν τις αὐτούς, εἰ δύναται ὁ τοῦ Θεοῦ Λόγος τραπῆναι ὡς ὁ διάβολος ἐτράπη· καὶ οὐκ ἐφοβήθησαν εἰπεῖν, "Ναὶ δύναται· τρεπτῆς γὰρ φύσεως ἐστὶ, γενητὸς καὶ τρεπτὸς ὑπάρχων".

and the Father is inexplicable by the Son, and invisible to him, for neither does the Word perfectly and accurately know the Father, neither can he distinctly see him. The Son knows not the nature of his own essence:

9. for he was made on our account, in order that God might create us by him, as by an instrument; nor would he ever have existed, unless God had wished to create us.

10. Some one accordingly asked them whether the Word of God could be changed, as the devil has been? and they feared not to say, 'Yes, he could; for being begotten, he is susceptible of change.'

Alexander suggests that Arius' assertion of the Logos' natural mutability is the outcome of his deliberation on the Logos' being created out of nothing. But, perhaps, it is just the opposite and the conviction of the susceptibility of change in Christ led him to speak of the distinction between the nature of the Logos and the nature of God? Both of the claims can go hand in hand. In my comments on Arius' letter, I have referred to the sentence from his *Thalia*, as cited by Athanasius. The Son is mutable and alterable by nature, but immutable *de facto*, as He did not wish to change.

Arius clearly referred to the Logos' immutability, but he had always meant the immutability *de facto*, not the impossibility of mutability, which is proper to the Divine nature. In his edition, Opitz substitutes "susceptible of change," at the end of the sentence, for "created." It seems, nonetheless, as much arbitrary as simply unnecessary. To Arius, the mutability of the Logos' nature stems from the fact of His being begotten, as everything which is begotten is susceptible of change. Of course, Arius could have used the term suggested by Opitz, but it does not result from the text and nothing calls for such an emendation.

The treatment of knowing and observing God as synonymous had already posed some difficulty to Origen. Thus, he would undertake to make a distinction between the two terms. The process of seeing pertains to the corporal reality, while the process of knowing may be purely intellectual. In Origen's view, therefore, the Son "knows the Father" (he does not "see the Father").[16] The failure to understand that distinction, or the rejection of

---

[16] Cf. Origenes, *De Principiis* I, 1, 8; John 6:32.

the understanding thereof, constituted one of Jerome's arguments for the alleged heretical tendencies of Origen.[17]

11. Ταῦτα λέγοντας τοὺς περὶ Ἄρειον, καὶ ἐπὶ τούτοις ἀναισχυντοῦντας, αὐτούς τε καὶ τοὺς συνακολουθήσαντας αὐτοῖς, ἡμεῖς μὲν μετὰ τῶν κατ' Αἴγυπτον ἐπισκόπων καὶ τὰς Λιβύας, ἐγγὺς ἑκατὸν ὄντων, συνελθόντες ἀνεθεματίσαμεν. Οἱ δὲ περὶ Εὐσέβιον προσεδέξαντο, σπουδάζοντες συγκαταμίξαι τὸ ψεῦδος τῇ ἀληθείᾳ, καὶ τῇ εὐσεβείᾳ τὴν ἀσέβειαν.

11. We then, with the bishops of Egypt and Libya, being assembled together to the number of nearly a hundred, have anathematized Arius for his shameless avowal of these heresies, together with all such as have countenanced them. Yet the partisans of Eusebius have received them; endeavoring to blend falsehood with truth, and that which is impious with what is sacred.

It does not have to signify that Arius and his followers among the clergy had migrated to Nicomedia. In his letter to Eusebius, Arius notes[18] that he entrusts it to "father Ammonius" and does not make a mention of any intention to go there. Arius' departure from Alexandria will be discussed in more detail further on.

Ἀλλ' οὐκ ἰσχύσουσι, νικᾷ γὰρ ἡ ἀλήθεια·καὶ οὐδεμία ἐστὶ κοινωνία φωτὶ πρὸς σκότος, οὐδὲ συμφώνησις Χριστῷ πρὸς Βελίαρ. (12.) Τίς γὰρ ἤκουσε πώποτε τοιαῦτα; ἢ τίς νῦν ἀκούων οὐ ξενίζεται, καὶ τὰς ἀκοὰς βύει, ὑπὲρ τοῦ μὴ τὸν ῥύπον τούτων τῶν ῥημάτων ψαῦσαι τῆς ἀκοῆς; Τίς ἀκούων Ἰωάννου λέγοντος, "Ἐν ἀρχῇ ἦν ὁ Λόγος, οὐ καταγινώσκει τούτων λεγόντων", "Ἦν ποτὲ ὅτε οὐκ ἦν";

But they shall not prevail, for the truth must triumph; and 'light has no fellowship with darkness, nor has Christ any concord with Belial.' (12.) Who ever heard such blasphemies? or what man of any piety is there now hearing them that is not horror-struck, and stops his ears, lest the filth of these expressions should pollute his sense of hearing? Who that hears John saying, 'In the beginning was the Word,'[19] does not condemn those that say, 'There was a period when the Word was not'?

None of Arius' many references to the creation of the Son records any sentence containing such a poignant expression. In his letter to Eusebius (see below), he writes that the Son "had not existed before being begotten or created, established, or set up," citing the expressions from Proverbs

[17] Cf. Jerome, *Letter* 51, 4.

[18] Cf. Epiphanius, *Panarion* 69, 6.

[19] *Jo* 1:1.

8:22-25, as He then would have been unbegotten, and it is the prerogative of God Himself. The expression as it is cited by Alexander must have been rather alien to Arius, as it would have implied the existence of time before the generation (the creation) of the Logos, and he certainly would not have subscribed to that view, considering his belief that everything, including time, is created through the Son. It is too similar to the teachings of Paul of Samosata, to whose views Arius had been particularly sensitive (Paul claimed that the Son had come into existence only when Jesus was born of Mary.[20] I think it is important to mention it as the condemnation of this statement at the Council of Nicaea was not necessarily an anti-Arian act.

ἢ τίς ἀκούων ἐν τῷ εὐαγγελίῳ, "μονογενὴς Υἰὸς," καὶ, "Δι᾽ αὐτοῦ ἐγένετο τὰ πάντα", οὐ μισήσει τούτους φθεγγομένους, ὅτι εἷς ἐστὶ τῶν ποιημάτων ὁ Υἰός; Πῶς δὲ δύναται εἷς εἶναι τῶν δι᾽ αὐτοῦ γενομένων; ἢ πῶς μονογενὴς, ὁ τοῖς πᾶσι κατ᾽ ἐκείνους συναριθμούμενος;	Or who, hearing in the Gospel of 'the only-begotten Son,'[21] and that 'all things were made by him,'[22] will not abhor those that pronounce the Son to be one of the things made? How can he be one of the things which were made by himself? Or how can he be the only-begotten, if he is reckoned among created things?

Alexander's account appears to be unfair. In Arius' letter to Alexander (cf. above), it is clearly stated that the Son is "a perfect creation, but unlike other creations." This distinction is due, for instance, to the fact that His generation/creation would have occurred "before all ages."

πῶς δὲ ἐξ οὐκ ὄντων ἂν εἴη, τοῦ Πατρὸς λέγοντος, "Ἐξηρεύξατο ἡ καρδία μου λόγον ἀγαθόν" καὶ, "Ἐκ γαστρὸς πρὸ ἑωσφόρου ἐγέννησα σέ";	And how could he have had his existence from nonentities, since the Father has said, 'My heart has indited a good matter';[23] and 'I begat thee out of my bosom[24] before the dawn?

[20] See the fragments published in: P. De Navascués, *Pablo de Samosata y sus adversarios. Estudio histórico-teológico del cristianismo antioqueno en el s. III*, SEA 87, Augustinianum, Roma 2004.

[21] *Jo.* 3:16.

[22] *Jo.* 1:3.

[23] *Ps.* 44:2.

[24] Ps. 109:3.

13. ἢ πῶς ἀνόμοιος τῇ οὐσίᾳ τοῦ Πατρὸς, ὁ ὢν εἰκὼν τελεία καὶ "ἀπαύγασμα" τοῦ Πατρὸς, καὶ λέγων, "Ὁ ἐμὲ ἑωρακὼς, ἑώρακε τὸν Πατέρα"; Πῶς δὲ εἰ Λόγος καὶ Σοφία ἐστὶ τοῦ Θεοῦ ὁ Υἱὸς, ἦν ποτὲ ὅτε οὐκ ἦν; ἴσον γὰρ ἐστιν αὐτοὺς λέγειν, ἄλογον καὶ ἄσοφον ποτὲ τὸν Θεόν.

13. Or how is he unlike the Father's essence, who is 'his perfect image,' and 'the brightness of his glory' and says: 'He that hath seen me, hath seen the Father'?[25] Again how if the Son is the Word and Wisdom of God, was there a period when he did not exist? for that is equivalent to their saying that God was once destitute both of Word and Wisdom.

Many commentators construed the verse of Ps 44 as spoken by the Father in reference to His Son, as it is affirmed by Origen,[26] but also noting that it does not have to be necessarily so, as it might as well be taken to refer to enunciations of the prophets. We have seen in Arius' letter to Alexander that Arius objected to speaking of any stages of the Logos' existence, as if He had been initially inherent in God, but thereafter externalized Himself (e.g., according to Tertullian). He also maintained, however, that the Logos could not be called, strictly speaking, "the Reason" and "the Wisdom of God," as it would then lead us on to the absurd thinking that there had been a time when God was without wisdom, i.e., to put it plainly, unwise.

14. Πῶς δὲ τρεπτὸς ἢ ἀλλοιωτὸς, ὁ λέγων δι' ἑαυτοῦ, "Ἐγὼ ἐν τῷ Πατρὶ, καὶ ὁ Πατὴρ ἐν ἐμοί" καὶ, "Ἐγὼ καὶ ὁ Πατὴρ ἕν ἐσμεν" διὰ δὲ τοῦ προφήτου, "Ἴδετέ με ὅτι ἐγὼ εἰμὶ, καὶ οὐκ ἠλλοίωμαι"; Εἰ δὲ καὶ ἐπ' αὐτόν τις τὸν Πατέρα τὸ ῥητὸν δύναται ἀναφέρειν, ἀλλὰ ἀρμοδιώτερον ἂν εἴη περὶ τοῦ Λόγου νῦν λεγόμενον, ὅτι καὶ γενομένος ἄνθρωπος οὐκ ἠλλοίωται, ἀλλ' ὡς ὁ Ἀπόστολος, "Ἰησοῦς Χριστὸς χθὲς καὶ σήμερον ὁ αὐτὸς, καὶ εἰς τοὺς αἰῶνας.

14. How can he be mutable and susceptible of change, who says of himself, 'I am in the Father, and the Father in me';[27] and 'I and the Father are one';[28] and again by the Prophet, 'Behold me because I am, and have not changed'?[29] But if any one may also apply the expression to the Father himself, yet would it now be even more fitly said of the Word; because he was not changed by having become man, but as the Apostle says, 'Jesus Christ, the same yesterday, today, and forever.'[30]

[25] Jo. 14:9.

[26] Origenes, CIo I, 38, 277 – 39, 292.

[27] Jo. 10:38.

[28] Jo. 10:30.

[29] Ml. 3:6.

[30] Hebr. 13:8.

Τί δὲ ἄρα εἰπεῖν αὐτοὺς ἔπεισεν, ὅτι δι' ἡμᾶς γέγονε, καίτοι τοῦ Παύλου γράφοντος, "Δι' ὃν τὰ πάντα", καὶ "δι' οὗ τὰ πάντα";

But what could persuade them to say that he was made on our account, when Paul has expressly declared that 'all things are for him, and by him'?[31]

In Arius' view, He can be immutable in accordance with His own will, and it is not due to His nature (see the commentary on Arius' letter above).

15. Περὶ μὲν οὖν τοῦ βλασφημεῖν αὐτοὺς, ὅτι οὐκ οἶδε τελείως ὁ Υἱὸς τὸν Πατέρα, οὐ δεῖ θαυμάζειν. Ἅπαξ γὰρ προθέμενοι Χριστομαχεῖν, παρακρούονται καὶ τὰς φωνὰς αὐτοῦ Κυρίου λέγοντος, "Καθὼς γινώσκει με ὁ Πατὴρ, κἀγὼ γινώσκω τὸν Πατέρα". Εἰ μὲν οὖν ἐκ μέρους γινώσκει ὁ Πατὴρ τὸν Υἱὸν, δῆλον ὅτι καὶ ὁ Υἱὸς ἐκ μέρους γινώσκει τὸν Πατέρα. Εἰ δὲ τοῦτο λέγειν οὐ θέμις, οἶδε δὲ τελείως ὁ Πατὴρ τὸν Υἱὸν, δῆλον ὅτι καθὼς γινώσκει ὁ Πατὴρ τὸν ἑαυτοῦ Λόγον, οὕτω καὶ ὁ Λόγος γινώσκει τὸν ἑαυτοῦ Πατέρα, οὗ καὶ ἔστι Λόγος.

15. One need not wonder indeed at their blasphemous assertion that the Son does not perfectly know the Father; for having once determined to fight against Christ, they reject even the words of the Lord himself, when he says, 'As the Father knows me, even so know I the Father.'[32] If therefore the Father but partially knows the Son, it is manifest that the Son also knows the Father but in part. But if it would be improper to affirm this, and it be admitted that the Father perfectly knows the Son, it is evident that as the Father knows his own Word, so also does the Word know his own Father, whose Word he is.

16. Καὶ ταῦτα λέγοντες, καὶ ἀναπτύσσοντες τὰς θείας γραφὰς, πολλάκις ἀνετρέψαμεν αὐτούς. Καὶ πάλιν ὡς χαμαιλέοντες μετεβάλλοντο, φιλονεικοῦντες εἰς ἑαυτοὺς ἐφελκύσαι τὸ γεγραμμένον, "Ὅτ' ἂν ἔλθῃ ὁ ἀσεβὴς εἰς βάθη κακῶν, καταφρονεῖ". Πολλαὶ γοῦν αἱρέσεις πρὸ αὐτῶν γεγόνασιν, αἵτινες πλέον τοῦ δέοντος τολμήσασαι, πεπτώκασιν εἰς ἀφροσύνην· οὗτοι δὲ διὰ πάντων αὐτῶν τῶν ῥημάτων, ἐπιχειρήσαντες ταῖς ἀναιρέσεσι τῆς τοῦ Λόγου θεότητος,

16. And we, by stating these things, and unfolding the divine Scriptures, have often confuted them: but again as chameleons they were changed, striving to apply to themselves that which is written, 'When the ungodly has reached the depths of iniquity, he becomes contemptuous.'[33] Many heresies have arisen before these, which exceeding all bounds in daring, have lapsed into complete infatuation: but these persons, by attempting in all their discourses to subvert the Divinity of the Word,

---

[31] *Hebr.* 2:10.

[32] *Jo.* 10:15.

[33] *Prov.* 18:3.

ἐδικαίωσαν ἐξ ἑαυτῶν ἐκείνας, ὡς
ἐγγύτεροι τοῦ Ἀντιχρίστου γενόμενοι.
Διὸ καὶ ἀπεκηρύχθησαν ἀπὸ τῆς
ἐκκλησίας, καὶ ἀνεθεματίσθησαν.

as having made a nearer approach
to Antichrist, have comparatively
lessened the odium of former ones.
Wherefore they have been publicly
repudiated by the Church, and
anathematized.

The scriptural argumentation had proved unreliable, nonetheless, as
Arius himself was able to cite a multitude of relevant passages. For each "I
and the Father are one,"[34] there is some quote such as "The Father is greater
than me"[35] and so forth.

17. Λυπούμεθα μὲν οὖν ἐπὶ τῇ ἀπωλείᾳ
τούτων, καὶ μάλιστα ὅτι μαθόντες
ποτὲ καὶ αὐτοὶ τὰ τῆς ἐκκλησίας,
νῦν ἀπεπήδησαν. Οὐ ξενιζόμεθα δέ·
τοῦτο γὰρ καὶ Ὑμέναιος καὶ Φίλητος
πεπόνθασι· καὶ πρὸ αὐτῶν Ἰούδας.
ἀκολουθήσας τῷ Σωτῆρι, ὕστερον δὲ
προδότης καὶ ἀποστάτης γενόμενος.

17. We are indeed grieved on
account of the perdition of these
persons, and especially so because,
after having been previously
instructed in the doctrines of the
Church, they have now apostatized
from them. Nevertheless we are
not greatly surprised at this, for
Hymenæus and Philetus fell in like
manner;[36] and before them Judas,
who had been a follower of the
Saviour, but afterwards deserted
him and became his betrayer.

18. Καὶ περὶ τούτων δὲ αὐτῶν, οὐκ
ἀδίδακτοι μεμενήκαμεν· ἀλλ' ὁ μὲν
Κύριος προείρηκε, "Βλέπετε μή τις
ὑμᾶς πλανήσῃ· πολλοὶ γὰρ ἐλεύσονται
ἐπὶ τῷ ὀνόματί μου λέγοντες, Ἐγὼ
εἰμί, καὶ ὁ καιρὸς ἤγγικε· καὶ πολλοὺς
πλανήσουσι· μὴ πορευθῆτε ὀπίσω
αὐτῶν". Ὁ δὲ Παῦλος μαθὼν ταῦτα
παρὰ τοῦ Σωτῆρος, ἔγραψεν, "Ὅτι
ἐν ὑστέροις καιροῖς ἀποστήσονταί
τινες τῆς πίστεως τῆς ὑγιαινούσης,
προσέχοντες πνεύμασι πλάνοις,
καὶ διδασκα-λίαις δαιμονίων,
ἀποστρεφομένων τὴν ἀλήθειαν".

18. Nor were we without forewarning
respecting these very persons: for
the Lord himself said: 'Take heed
that no man deceive you: for many
shall come in my name, saying, I
am Christ: and shall many deceive
many'; and 'the time is at hand;
Go you not therefore after them.'[37]
And Paul, having learned these
things from the Saviour, wrote,
'That in the latter times some
should apostatize from the faith,
giving heed to deceiving spirits, and
doctrines of devils,' who pervert the
truth.[38]

[34] Jo. 10:30.
[35] Jo. 14:28.
[36] 2 Tim. 2:17.
[37] Lc. 21:8.
[38] 1 Tim. 4:1.

19. Τοῦ τοίνυν Κυρίου καὶ Σωτῆρος ἡμῶν Ἰησοῦ Χριστοῦ, διά τε αὐτοῦ παραγγέλλοντος, καὶ διὰ τοῦἈποστόλου σημαίνοντος περὶ τῶν τοιούτων, ἀκολούθως ἡμεῖς αὐτήκοοι τῆς ἀσεβείας αὐτῶν γενόμενοι, ἀνεθεματίσαμεν, καθὰ προείπομεν, τοὺς τοιούτους, ἀποδείξαντες αὐτοὺς ἀλλοτρίους τῆς καθολικῆς ἐκκλησίας τε καὶ πίστεως. (20.) Ἐδηλώσαμεν δὲ καὶ τῇ ὑμετέρᾳ θεοσεβείᾳ, ἀγαπητοὶ καὶ τιμώτατοι συλλειτουργοὶ, ἵνα μήτε τινας ἐξ αὐτῶν, εἰ προπετεύσαιντο καὶ πρὸς ὑμᾶς ἐλθεῖν, μὴ προσδέξησθε, μήτε Εὐσεβίῳ, ἢ ἑτέρῳ τινὶ γράφοντι περὶ αὐτῶν πεισθῆτε. Πρέπει γὰρ ὑμᾶς ὡς Χριστιανοὺς ὄντας, πάντας τοὺς κατὰ Χριστοῦ λέγοντάς τε καὶ φρονοῦντας, ὡς Θεομάχους καὶ φθορέας τῶν ψυχῶν ἀποστρέφεσθαι, καὶ μηδὲ κἂν χαίρειν τοῖς τοιούτοις λέγειν, ἵνα μή ποτε καὶ ταῖς ἁμαρτίαις αὐτῶν κοινωνοὶ γενώμεθα, ὡς παρήγγειλεν ὁ μακάριος Ἰωάννης. Προσείπατε τοὺς παρ᾽ ὑμῖν ἀδελφούς. Ὑμᾶς οἱ σὺν ἐμοὶ προσαγορεύυυι.

19. Seeing then that our Lord and Saviour Jesus Christ has himself enjoined this, and has also by the apostle given us intimation respecting such men, we having ourselves heard their impiety have in consequence anathematized them, as we before said, and declared them to be alienated from the Catholic Church and faith. (20.) Moreover we have intimated this to your piety, beloved and most honored fellow-ministers, in order that ye might neither receive any of them, if they should presume to come to you, nor be induced to put confidence in Eusebius, or any other who may write to you about them. For it is incumbent on us who are Christians, to turn away from all those who speak or entertain a thought against Christ, as from those who are resisting God, and are destroyers of the souls of men: neither does it become us even 'to salute such men,' as the blessed John has prohibited, 'lest we should at any time be made partakers of their sins.'[39] Greet the brethren which are with you; those who are with me salute you.

Alexander publicly anathematized Arius and his followers. He also recalled the old decrees forbidding any communication with those excluded from the Church as well as accepting them in another Church.[40] Such incidents must have indeed taken place, as the Council of Nicaea would reaffirm this particular injunction in canon 5.[41]

Let us now turn our attention to the aforementioned Arius' letter to Eusebius of Nicomedia. I have already noted that it is often regarded as the first document relevant to the controversy. But let us also notice that Arius represents himself therein as "persecuted by Alexander the Pope" (1), not just at odds with him. Therefore, it must have been written rather after the synod at which Arius and his followers had been excluded from the Church.

[39] 2 Jo. 10:11.

[40] E.g., Council of Elvira (306), c. 53, SCL 1, 58.

[41] See commentary on this canon in Ch. 5.

Arius, *Letter to Eusebius of Nicomedia*[42]

To begin with, the addressee of the epistle also deserves our attention. He was an outstanding and renowned figure, mostly for political, rather than theological, reasons, but his influential role in the administration of the contemporary Church cannot be underestimated. Since, historically speaking, the interpretation of the events as represented by Athanasius, and later depicted by the most significant historians, i.e., Socrates, Sozomen, and Theodoret, Eusebius would be considered, for centuries to come, as one of the "villains" of the Arian controversy. It was probably only in Hanson's thorough study[43] where the positive activity of that bishop was first noticed. In turn, Daniel De Decker's work is truly apologetic. It is a very profound study, yet with certain fantastic elements therein.[44]

It is commonly accepted in encyclopaedic entries that Eusebius relocated to Nicomedia in 318, although it is not attested in any known source. For instance, it is stated by Charles Kannengiesser under the relevant entry in *Dizionario Patristico e di Antichità Christiana* and the new edition of this dictionary.[45] He also assumes as certain that Eusebius had been a disciple of Lucian of Antioch beforehand, which is plausible and attested by Philostorgius.[46] As regards the last sentence of Arius' letter, there is only a certain over-interpretation in the conclusion that Eusebius and Arius had been disciples at that school. An extremely late dating is suggested by Bardy, namely shortly before 324.[47] It means that the Arian controversy, in his opinion, would have started in 323, at the earliest. I agree with this view. Earlier, Eusebius had been a bishop of Beirut, but we do not know for how long. It also remains a mystery when, or where, he was born. De Decker argues for Syro-Palestine as the place of his origin and intellectual formation; in his view, the same school they had attended at Antioch also accounts for the fact that Arius would have reputedly headed to Palestine after he

---

[42] In: Theodoret of Cyrrhus, *h.e.* I, 4 (NPNF 2,3); Epiphanius, *Panarion* 69, 6; Opitz, 1; M. Simonetti, *Il Cristo* II, 68ff. Cf. W. Löhr, *Arius Reconsidered* (part 2), in ZAC 10 (2006), 129-130.

[43] R.P.C. Hanson, *The Search for the Christian Doctrine of God (The Arian Controversy 318-381)*, Edinburgh 1988.

[44] Cf. D. De Decker, *Eusèbe de Nicomédie...*, 95-170.

[45] Cf. NDPAC, Marietti 2006, I, 1858.

[46] Philostorgius, h.e.II, 14; PG 65, 477. He notes that the most outstanding disciples of Lucian of Antioch were: Eusebius of Nikomedia, Maridos of Chalcedon, Theognis of Nicaea, and Anthony of Tarsus.

[47] *Catholicisme* 4, 709-710.

had been condemned at Alexandria.[48] He also presumes that Eusebius may have been somehow related to Constantine's family.[49] De Decker's problem here is that he considers Constance, Constantine's half-sister, the offspring of Theodora, the second wife of Constantius Chlorus, as Helene's "true daughter,"[50] and Eusebius had been affiliated with the court of Constance and Licinius through some family ties and the common attachment to their Syro-Palestinian roots. The thing is that Constance had been indeed of Syrian descent (her grandmother Eutropia, Theodora's mother, had come from there), but it has nothing to do with Helene and her temperament. The scholar also favours the view that the same Eusebius would have been supposedly the author of a brief composition critical of image worshipping and usually attributed to Eusebius of Caesarea.[51] After his several-year-long exile in Gaul (it is not known what had caused it), the Emperor brought him back in grace. He also baptized Constantine on his death-bed, "probably in the Arian creed,"[52] in De Decker's view, which, it seems to me, is completely implausible, as at that time, in 337, Arianism was a much-criticized doctrine, not a parallel Church, precluding the possibility of a separate baptismal rite, or even a certain separate formula. If anything like that had taken place, some Catholic synod would have likely condemned and invalidated it; strangely enough, this is not the case, as even the so-called canon 7 of the First Council of Constantinople, known from Patriarch Gennadius' letter (the second half of the fifth century), recognizes that baptisms performed by Arians are valid.[53] Eusebius went on to become Bishop of Constantinople until his death in *ca.* 431.

1. Κυρίῳ ποθεινοτάτῳ, ἀνθρώπῳ θεοῦ, πιστῷ, ὀρθοδόξῳ Εὐσεβίῳ Ἄρειος ὁ διωκόμενος ὑπὸ Ἀλεξάνδρου τοῦ πάπα	1. To his very dear lord, the man of God, the faithful and orthodox Eusebius, Arius, unjustly persecuted by Alexander the Pope,

[48] Cf. D. De Decker, *Eusèbe de Nicomédie*, 116.

[49] D. De Decker, *Eusèbe de Nicomédie*, 124.

[50] D. De Decker, *Eusèbe de Nicomédie*, 125: "digne fille d'Hélène."

[51] The Acts of the Council of Nicaea II, J.D. Mansi, *Sacrorum Conciliorum Nova et Amplissima Collectio*, Florentiae 1759ff; reprint: Paris 1901, 13, 313-317; cf. G. Florovsky, Origenes, *Eusebius and the Iconoclastic Controversy*, in *Church History* 19 (1950), 3-22; R.P.C. Hanson, *The Search for the Christian Doctrine*, 72, D. De Decker, *Eusèbe de Nicomédie*, 127.

[52] D. De Decker, *Eusèbe de Nicomédie*, 164.

[53] Cf. P.-P. Joannou, *Les canons des conciles oecuméniques*, Pontificia commissione per la redazione del codice di diritto canonico orientale. Fonti, Fasc. IX, t. I/1, Grottaferrata – Roma 1962, 43-44; DSP 1, 92.

ἀδίκως διὰ τὴν πάντα νικῶσαν
ἀλήθειαν, ἧς καὶ σὺ ὑπερασπίζεις, ἐν
κυρίῳ χαίρειν.

on account of that all-conquering
truth of which you also are a
champion, sendeth greeting in the
Lord.

2. Τοῦ πατρός μου Ἀμμωνίου ἐρχο-
μένου εἰς τὴν Νικομήδειαν,

2. Ammonius, my father, being
about to depart for Nicomedia,

Representing himself to Eusebius as a person "persecuted by Alexander"
looks like an attempt at *captatio benevolentiae*; Arius knew that Alexander had
been very critical of Eusebius for his relocation from Beirut to Nicomedia,
and he may have thus counted on Eusebius' feelings of solidarity.
Nonetheless, the epistle is primarily of informative character and it probably
predates the above-mentioned Alexander's encyclical. It was a foregone
conclusion that such an encyclical would be produced after the synod, as
writing post-synodal letters informing of any possible cases of exclusions
from the Church was an ordinary practice, and Arius wanted to be the
first one to communicate the news of the beginning of the controversy to
Eusebius. Ammonius is most likely a senior monk or clergyman, held in
much regard by Arius. De Decker speculates that he may have been one
of the former disciples of Lucian of Antioch and Arius' spiritual father;
he also quotes Boularand's opinion that Ammonius was Arius' morganatic
father,[54] whatever it might have meant. Although Arius simply writes that a
certain man named Ammonius, respectfully called "father," is bound for
Nicomedia and politely agrees to take and deliver the said letter, De Decker
concludes that he had honoured Eusebius in the manner later reserved for
Bishops of Rome, namely by paying him an *ad limina* visit.[55] This is one of
those aspects of his study which I have already called fantastic; as we know,
bishops do not go to Rome *ad limina episcopi*, but *ad limina apostolorum*, and
the reference is to Peter and Paul, not the Bishop of Rome.

εὔλογον ὀφειλόμενον ἐφάνη προσ-
αγορεῦσαί σε δι' αὐτοῦ ὁμοῦ τε
καὶ ὑπομνῆσαι τὴν ἔμφυτόν σου
ἀγάπην καὶ διάθεσιν, ἣν ἔχεις εἰς
τοὺς ἀδελφοὺς διὰ τὸν θεὸν καὶ τὸν
Χριστὸν αὐτοῦ, ὅτι μεγάλως ἡμᾶς
ἐκπορθεῖ καὶ ἐκδιώκει καὶ πάντα
κάλων κινεῖ καθ' ἡμῶν ὁ ἐπίσκοπος,
ὥστε καὶ ἐκδιῶξαι ἡμᾶς ἐκ τῆς
πόλεως ὡς ἀνθρώπους ἀθέους,

I considered myself bound to salute
you by him, and withal to inform
that natural affection which you
bear towards the brethren for
the sake of God and His Christ,
that the bishop greatly wastes and
persecutes us, and leaves no stone
unturned against us. He has driven
us out of the city as atheists,

[54] E. Boularand, *L'hérésie d'Arius et la foi de Nicée*, Letouzey et Anè, Paris 1972, 12.

[55] D. De Decker, *Eusèbe de Nicomédie*, 131.

Literally, Arius writes of being driven "out of the city," as it is often rendered. In all probability, "the city" in question refers to the Church (notably, it is well attested in this particular sense). For instance, Origen states that "the city of God is the Church."[56] Πόλις refers to a city in the sense of a community rather than the space enclosed within the city walls, and it may be also used to denote a community of the Church. Moreover, it must be noted that neither bishops nor synods at that time had the authority to have anyone banished. Of course, a person excommunicated in a given city could feel alienated and, in consequence, move to another locality, as Origen did in 230 or 231,[57] but they were not compelled to do so by any formally issued order. We cannot really say anything certain about the harassing and persecuting mentioned in the letter, if it had indeed preceded the removal from the Church. As we have noted above, in Sozomen's account dealing with the beginnings of the controversy that Alexander had been reportedly rather cautious in passing judgements and, at least initially, he had not been a party to the dispute, attempting to act as an arbitrator. Nevertheless, it is difficult to resolve this question, as Constantine's letter to Alexander and Arius indicates that, according to the Emperor's knowledge, the whole controversy had started with a contention between them both.

ἐπειδὴ οὐ συμφωνοῦμεν αὐτῷ δημοσίᾳ λέγοντι· "ἀεὶ θεός, ἀεὶ υἱός· ἅμα πατήρ, ἅμα υἱός· συνυπάρχει ἀγεννήτως ὁ υἱὸς τῷ θεῷ, ἀειγενής ἐστιν, ἀγεννητογενής ἐστιν· οὔιε ἐπινοίᾳ οὔτε ἀτόμῳ τινὶ προάγει ὁ θεὸς τοῦ υἱοῦ· ἀεὶ θεός, ἀεὶ υἱός· ἐξ αὐτοῦ ἐστι τοῦ θεοῦ ὁ υἱός".	because we do not concur in what he publicly preaches, namely, God always, the Son always; as the Father so the Son; the Son co-exists unbegotten with God; He is everlasting; neither by thought nor by any interval does God precede the Son; always God, always Son; he is begotten of the unbegotten; the Son is of God Himself.

It would be difficult to judge whether these are exactly Alexander's words or Arius' summary of the bishop's teachings (let us add, a biased one). There is no doubt that Alexander had spoken of the everlasting Son, yet it is certainly hard to believe that he referred to the Son as "begotten of the unbegotten," which seems to be a term invented by Arius himself or derived from the Sabellian teachings. Alexander is more likely to have referred to the everlasting begetting of the Son by the Father. According to Origen's justification, the immutability of God demands that the begetting of the Son

---

[56] Origenes, HIer 9, 2 (in: The Fathers of the Church, The Catholic University of America, Washington 1998, vol. 97); for many other instances, see G.W.H. Lampe, A Patristic Greek Lexicon, 1112f.

[57] Cf. Eusebius of Caesarea, h.e. VI, 23, 4; VI, 26.

be an everlasting and unalterable process, not a single individual act. The
Father remains eternally antecedent in relation to the Son as the cause of
His existence, but this antecedence is everlasting, not chronological. As he
says in his *De principiis*:

> this expression which we employ – "that there never was a time when He did
> not exist" – is to be understood with an allowance. For these very words "when"
> or "never" have a meaning that relates to time, whereas the statements made
> regarding Father, Son, and Holy Spirit are to be understood as transcending
> all time, all ages, and all eternity. For it is the Trinity alone which exceeds
> the comprehension not only of temporal but even of eternal intelligence;
> while other things which are not included in it are to be measured by times
> and ages.[58]

Arius appears to think that each causality must be connected with
temporal antecedence, which is impossible in God. However, instead of
modifying his own assumption, he prefers to modify the Trinity. One may
have an impression that Arius endeavours to present the bishop's teachings
in such a way as to make it seem like it identifies the Father and the Son in
the Monarchian manner. The expression that the Son would have subsisted
"from God Himself," may have brought to mind the views of Paul of Samosata,
according to whom the Father and the Son are one and the same, and they
are not different from each other prior to [the Son's] being born of Mary.
Hilarius of Poitiers, Athanasius, and Basil[59] relate that Paul was to have used
the term *homoousios* to denote that union and it was precisely one of the
reasons for his condemnation.[60] He refused to recognize the Logos' own
hypostasis, as the conception of Jesus, the son of Mary, as a human being
would have signified the existence of two persons (hypostases) in Christ,
that is, there would have been two "Sons," and such a thought filled him
with horror.[61] Besides, Arius was not the only one who had an aversion to
speaking of the Son's descent "from God," ἐκ τοῦ θεου, as it was feared that
in this way the Son's spiritual descent from the Father would be represented
as the resulting of one matter from another. We shall be concerned with this
question as part of the commentary on the Nicene Creed.

---

[58] Origenes, *De principiis* IV, I, 28 (ANF 4). Cf. H. Pietras, *Argumentacja filozoficzna
za wiecznością Syna*, 89-97.

[59] Cf. Hilarius of Poitiers, *De synodis* 86, Athanasius, *De synodis* 45, Basil, *Letter* 52.

[60] Cf. C.I. Gonzalez, *Antecedentes de la cristologia ariana el el siglo III*, in *Medellin* 16
(1990), booklet 63, 358ff; L. Ayres, *Nicaea and Its Legacy*, 94.

[61] Cf. fr. 21 and 32; H. De Riedmatten, *Les actes du procès de Paul de Samosate.
Etude sur la cristologie du IIIe au IVe siecle*, Friburg en Suisse 1952, 147. 155. Also, see
commentary on canon 19 below.

3. καὶ ἐπειδὴ Εὐσέβιος ὁ ἀδελφός σου ὁ ἐν Καισαρείᾳ καὶ Θεόδοτος καὶ Παυλῖνος καὶ Ἀθανάσιος καὶ Γρηγόριος καὶ Ἀέτιος καὶ πάντες οἱ κατὰ τὴν Ἀνατολὴν λέγουσιν ὅτι προϋπάρχει ὁ θεὸς τοῦ υἱοῦ ἀνάρχως, ἀνάθεμα ἐγένοντο, δίχα μόνου Φιλογονίου καὶ Ἑλλανικοῦ καὶ Μακαρίου, ἀνθρώπων αἱρετικῶν ἀκατηχήτων, τὸν υἱὸν λεγόντων οἱ μὲν ἐρυγήν, οἱ δὲ προβολήν, οἱ δὲ συναγέννητον.

3. Eusebius, your brother bishop of Cæsarea, Theodotus, Paulinus, Athanasius, Gregorius, Aetius, and all the bishops of the East, have been condemned because they say that God had an existence prior to that of His Son; except Philogonius, Hellanicus, and Macarius, who are unlearned men, and who have embraced heretical opinions. Some of them say that the Son is an eructation, others that He is a production, others that He is also unbegotten.

These terms used in reference to the Son were disapproved of by theologians (hence the charge of ignorance). Being "also unbegotten" suggests the identification of the Father and the Son, "eructation" (referring to Ps 44:2 – "The beautiful word flows out of my heart") was denounced by Origen as depriving the Son of His own hypostasis,[62] while "emanation" ("production") belonged to the Gnostic vocabulary and was likewise rejected by Origen.[63]

The condemnation of the bishops enumerated in the letter remains an unresolved question. Who, and when, condemned them? We do know that the synod at Antioch, which took place in the spring of 325, condemned, or rather, strictly speaking, admonished and obliged to appear at a larger synod[64] the following figures: Eusebius of Caesarea, Theodotus of Laodicea, and Narcissus of Neoniade. But who are the others? According to Theodoret of Cyrrhus' account,[65] the above-mentioned Theodotus was renowned as a healer of the body and soul, as well as a God-fearing theologian.[66] He did not attend the Council of Nicaea. Athanasius was the Bishop of Anazarbus in Cilicia. He did not take part in the Council, either. In turn, Paulinus of Tyre, the addressee of the letter by Eusebius of Nikomedia (to be discussed a little further on) attended at Nicaea and signed the creed, but rather without much conviction, just as Eusebius of Caesarea[67] and all the rest

[62] Origenes, CIo. I, 24, 151-155.

[63] Origenes, De principiis I, 2, 6; cf. M. Simonetti, Il Cristo II, 546.

[64] For an analysis of the synodal document, see below.

[65] Theodoret of Cyrrhus, h.e. I, 5, 5.

[66] Cf. Eusebius of Caesarea, h.e. VII, 32, 23.

[67] For a commentary on his letter addressed to his diocese, and sent after the Council, see below.

of the bishops. Let us also mention a somewhat obscure figure of Bishop Gregory of Berytus (Beirut) and Bishop Aetius of Lydda (the present-day Lod), renamed to Diospoli by the close of Antiquity, who would later desert the ranks of Arius' followers.

The following three figures were not condemned: Philogonius, Bishop of Antioch (d. winter of 324/325), Hellanicus of Tripolis in Syria, and Macarius of Jerusalem. There is no information on where they all might have assembled, with the result that some of them were condemned, and the others were not. If the occasion in question had been the synod at Antioch, Philogonius' possible condemnation, or the lack thereof, would have taken place *post mortem*, as sometimes happened.

4. καὶ τούτων τῶν ἀσεβειῶν οὐδὲ ἀκοῦσαι δυνάμεθα, ἐὰν μυρίους θανάτους ἡμῖν ἐπαπειλῶσιν οἱ αἱρετικοί. Ἡμεῖς δὲ τί λέγομεν καὶ φρονοῦμεν καὶ ἐδιδάξαμεν καὶ διδάσκομεν; ὅτι ὁ υἱὸς οὐκ ἔστιν ἀγέννητος οὐδὲ μέρος ἀγεννήτου κατ' οὐδένα τρόπον, οὔτε ἐξ ὑποκειμένου τινός,	4. These are impieties to which we cannot listen, even though the heretics threaten us with a thousand deaths. But we say and believe, and have taught, and do teach, that the Son is not unbegotten, nor in any way part of the unbegotten; and that He does not derive His subsistence from any matter;

This caveat of Arius, to avoid conceiving of the Son as a "part" of God, is linked to the risk of a materialistic conception of God or an idea of some divine "mass" composed of parts. Two material things, one descended or derived from the other, were referred to as consubstantial and this issue would also become a subject of debate at Nicaea, as we shall see. Of course, Alexander did not think, either, that "the Son is unbegotten, or is a part of God, or descends with Him from some antecedent original substance" (ἐξ ὑποκειμένου τινός). This particular view was not merely an abstract possibility, as it much suited the stoics who converted to Christianity. For instance, Tertullian, who was one of them, regarded the divine substance as corporal, and each body was able to decrease or expand itself. In effect, such an "expansion" of the Father's substance had given rise to the Son's person.[68] It was obviously unacceptable to the Platonizing Christians, as they would follow Plato's view that only an absolutely incorporeal substance could be the real substance. Origen referred to this question in precise terms in his commentary on the Lord's Prayer and the supplication "give us this day our supersubstantial bread: "*Ousia*, properly understood (κυρίως οὐσία), is regarded as incorporeal by the philosophers who insist that the pre-eminent reality is incorporeal. It has, then, for them an unchanging existence which admits neither increase nor decrease."

[68] Tertullian, *Apologist* 21, 12.

ἀλλ' ὅτι θελήματι καὶ βουλῇ ὑπέστη
πρὸ χρόνων καὶ πρὸ αἰώνων πλήρης
θεός, μονογενής,

but that by His own will and counsel
He has subsisted before time, and
before ages, as perfect God, only
begotten.[69]

The subsistence of the Son by the Father's own free will is not an invention proposed by Arius. It looks as though copied from Justin:

In the beginning, before all creatures, God begat from Himself a certain rational power, who is called by the Holy Spirit, now the Glory of the Lord,[70] now the Son,[71] again Wisdom,[72] again an Angel, then God, and then Lord and Logos;[73] and on another occasion He calls Himself Captain,[74] when He appeared in human form to Joshua the son of Nave. For He can be called by all those names, since He ministers to the Father's will, and since He was begotten of the Father by an act of will.[75]

Tertullian also wrote that God had been alone since always, but at a certain moment, or rather before any moment could have existed, He "externalized" His Word. This is not to suggest some Tertullian's influence upon Arius, but only to demonstrate it was commonly spoken that the Son had come into existence before all things, when God had willed it. It had already turned up in Philo's deliberations on the creation of the Logos on "day one," as it is written in Genesis, with the cardinal, not the ordinal, number (as customarily rendered in all the editions of the Bible).[76] As we have noted before, it was only Origen who had substantiated that the begetting of the Son must be everlasting, as it is required by the immutability of God's nature.

Assigning the origin of the Son's existence before time was thus in agreement with the theological tradition and the absence of a much-feared precarious equalization between the Son and the Father had aligned Him, nonetheless, with God, not the creatures of "this world," which was to come

---

[69] Origenes, *De oratione* 27, 8 (in: *Ancient Christian Writers*, Newmann Press, New York 1954, vol. 19). See H. Pietras, *Pojęcie Bożej substancji w początkach Kościoła*, in: R. Woźniak (ed.), *Metafizyki i teologia. Debata u podstaw*, MT 62, Wydawnictwo WAM, Kraków 2008, 122-140.

[70] *Ex.* 16:7.

[71] *Ps.* 2:7.

[72] *Prov.* 8.

[73] *Ps.* 32:6; 106:20.

[74] *Ios.* 5:13-14.

[75] Justin, *A Dialogue with Trifon* 61 (ANF 1, revised).

[76] *Gen.* 1:5. See Philo of Alexandria, *De opificio mundi* 24.

into being only along with time itself. Therefore, in his *Letter to Alexander* (2), Arius writes that "the Son is a creature, but not like other creatures:"

It is also of significance that these are almost exactly the words used by the Wisdom, with reference to Herself, in Syrah: πρὸ τοῦ αἰῶνος ἀπ᾽ ἀρχῆς ἔκτισέν με, – *before ages, at the beginning, he created me.*[77]

The expression "a full (πλήρης) Only Begotten God" ought to be, in my opinion, taken as a whole, with no comma inserted between "God" and "Only Begotten," as opposed to what the editors usually do, to the detriment of the coherence of Arius' position.[78] Arius had never denied the adequacy of referring to the Son as God, but he reserved the usage of the definite article to the Father only, in which he had followed the traditional practice.[79] The expression "full," however, does not refer to the "God" Himself, as that is the Father, but to the "Only Begotten God," which is the Son's own name. Opitz inserts the comma (as Simonetti does, too), but deals with the consequent problem by adding the Biblical phrase: "full <of grace and truth>, God, Only Begotten," which is nonetheless an arbitrary choice. The designation "Only Begotten God" can be found in a greater part of the manuscripts at J 1:18, as a variation of the expression "Only Begotten Son" and there is no reason to reject the assumption that this is what Arius had read in his code. This particular expression seems to have belonged to the theological parlance of the proponents of Arianism in the later period as well. During the synod of Aquilaea (381), Ambrose of Milan attempted to make Secundianus refrain from saying it. Let us have a look at their discourse:

> 68. Bishop Ambrose asked: Is the Son of God the true God?
> Secundianus replied: So am I a liar then?
> Bishop Ambrose said: You are mistaken in that you do not call him the true God, but the true Only Begotten God. So simply say: the Only Begotten Son of God is the true God.[80]

I think there is therefore no reason to suspect that the author of the letter had misquoted the phrase. Arius used the same one in his *Thalia*, as we can see in the fragment cited by Athanasius.[81]

ἀναλλοίωτος·   and unchangeable,

---

[77] *Sir.* 24:8.

[78] Cf. Opitz and M. Simonetti, in *Il Cristo* II, 72.

[79] Cf. Origenes, *CIo.* II, 13.

[80] Council of Aquilaea (381), 68, SCL 4, 22 (Ambrose and Secundianus at the synod). The dispute over that expression reappears, e.g., nos. 74, 75.

[81] Athanasius, *De synodis* 15; cf. Ch. 1.

The Son's immutability *de facto* is constantly emphasized by Arius, yet we have already seen the texts where he expressly refers to the mutability by nature, therein noticing the difference between the natures of the Father and the Son. In his *Letter to All the Bishops* (8), Alexander also makes it clear that Arius espouses the Son's mutability "by nature" and the possibility of His disobedience towards the Father (10).

5. καὶ πρὶν γεννηθῇ ἤτοι κτισθῇ ἢ ὁρισθῇ ἢ θεμελιωθῇ, οὐκ ἦν	5. and that before He was begotten, or created, or purposed, or established, He was not.

All the four expressions draw upon the Bible, in particular Proverbs 8:22-25, where the Wisdom speaks the following words:

(22) The Lord created me (ἔκτισέν) at the beginning of his work, the first of his acts of old. (23) Ages ago, I was set up (ἐθεμελίωσέν), at the first, before the beginning of the earth. (24) When there were no depths I was brought forth [made] (ποιῆσαι) when there were no springs abounding with water. (25) Before the mountains had been shaped, before the hills, I was brought forth (γεννᾷ).

Arius considers these terms as synonymous and construes them in the sense of the chronological origin of the Son's existence, unlike Alexander, who abides by Origen's tradition on this point and refers all these terms to the Son's eternal and unchangeable descent from the Father.

ἀγέννητος γὰρ οὐκ ἦν. διωκόμεθα ὅτι εἴπαμεν· "ἀρχὴν ἔχει ὁ υἱός, ὁ δὲ θεὸς ἄναρχός ἐστιν".	For He was not unbegotten. We are persecuted, because we say that the Son has a beginning, but that God is without beginning.

Arius understands being unbegotten as the indispensable condition for the Divine nature. In his view, God must not have any cause of the existence. It leads him to deny the deity of the Son, as he identifies the Divine nature with the person of the Father. Ἀρχὴ does not have to signify the temporal beginning, but also the cause or essence of the existence. However, Arius apparently construes this term as both the cause of the existence and the chronological origin.

διὰ τοῦτο διωκόμεθα, καὶ ὅτι εἴπαμεν ὅτι ἐξ οὐκ ὄντων ἐστίν· οὕτως δὲ εἴπαμεν, καθότι οὐδὲ μέρος θεοῦ ἐστιν οὐδὲ ἐξ ὑποκειμένου τινός.	This is the cause of our persecution, and likewise, because we say that He is of the non-existent. And this we say, because He is neither part of God, nor of any essential being.

(cf. commentary on no. 4 above).

διὰ τοῦτο διωκόμεθα· λοιπὸν σὺ οἶδας. ἐρρῶσθαί σε ἐν κυρίῳ εὔχομαι, μεμνημένον τῶν θλίψεων ἡμῶν, συλλουκιανιστὰ ἀληθῶς Εὐσέβιε.

For this are we persecuted; the rest you know. I bid thee farewell in the Lord, remembering our afflictions, my fellow-Lucianist, and true Eusebius.

It is understood from this passage that both Arius and Eusebius were disciples of Lucian of Antioch. Nonetheless, it is difficult to resolve this question with any certainty, because Arius may have only kindly compared Eusebius to the eminent teacher Lucian of Antioch, by way of a compliment, with no reference to himself.[82] Winrich Löhr surmises that Arius may have referred in this way to the unjust persecution he had been suffering, and which would also come to afflict Eusebius for supporting him.[83] It is difficult to say what Lucian's teachings were; supposedly, Eusebius' support for Arius may have been based somehow on them.[84] A certain scholar argues that Lucian had radicalized Origen's views towards an extreme form of subordinationism,[85] but he cites no evidence to substantiate his assertion (unless he infers what Lucian's views were from Arius' own views, although we do not know anything about their mutual relations.

Assuming that Eusebius was indeed one of Lucian's disciples, this expression could be understood as "worthy disciple of your master." I have already noted, before my comments on the letter, that it is confirmed by Philostorgius, yet his words do not intimate at all that Arius had belonged to the same school. Kannengiesser has long questioned it (and I agree with him on this point), arguing that even though we do not know much about Lucian's teachings, it would have been difficult to trace Arius' views back to them.[86] It is perplexing indeed that we hear of no fellow-Origenists, fellow-Eusebianists, or other fellow-Parthenians, but there would have been fellow-Lucianists as Lucian's disciples.

I must admit that the letter strikes me as somewhat hastily written, which is obviously not very helpful as an academic argument. Arius reiterates the phrases "always Father, always Son" (2), perhaps because it seems too

[82] Likewise, R. Williams, *Arius, Heresy and Tradition*, Darton, Longman and Todd, London 1987, 31.

[83] Cf. W. Löhr, *Arius Reconsidered* (part 1), in *Zeitschrift für Antikes Christentum / Journal of Ancient Christianity* 9 (2006), 531-533.

[84] Cf. M. Simonetti, *Le origini dell'arianesimo*, in *Rivista di Storia e Letteratura Religiosa* 7 (1971), 330. For more on Lucian, see the section on the letter of Alexander of Alexandria to Alexander of Byzantium, at the close of this chapter.

[85] Ch. M. Odahl, *Constantine and the Christian Empire*, Routledge, Taylor & Francis Group, London – New York 2004, 167.

[86] CH. Kannengiesser, *Athanasius of Alexandria vs. Arius*, 210.

outrageous to him. He also writes that Eusebius of Caesarea and "all" the bishops of the East were condemned, except for several bishops whose views were described as Monarchian. It is hard to know exactly what he refers to. We do not know of any official synodal decision condemning the aforementioned figures prior to 324. Arius' words referring to an anathema should be therefore understood in a broader sense, not as pertaining to a formal excommunication. Arius also writes that he had been removed from the Church by the bishop (2). If it had involved the necessity of Arius' departure from the city, it may be merely speculated when it would have happened. Epiphanius notes[87] that Arius had visited Caesarea in Palestine, where he stayed with Eusebius and, presumably, wrote his letter to Nicomedia,[88] although he might as well have written it at Alexandria. We have noted that in his letter Alexander informs the bishops of the condemnation of Arius and his sympathizers, enumerating their names in the same order in which they are mentioned in Arius' letter to Alexander, which points out that Alexander would have simply copied them into his own letter one by one. Therefore, since Arius addressed his letter to Eusebius of Nicomedia after his condemnation, and complaining about it therein, the letter in question may be safely dated to after the synod of Alexandria. Likewise, the Arian historian Philostorgius makes a note of Arius' journey to the East, though not at that time.[89] He states that Hosius returned to Nicomedia, after his visit to Alexandria, and was followed by Arius and Alexander (the former set out by land, the latter – by sea).

I will discuss this point a little bit further on, but let us now turn our attention briefly to Constantine's letter to Alexander and Arius. The Emperor regards the subject of their dispute as a trifle one, an inside problem of the Church of Alexandria, and is only aware of the fact that it had caused a serious turmoil there. If Arius had indeed managed to travel around Palestine, and even Bithynia, as some scholars are inclined to think,[90] in hopes of mustering as much support as he could; if a synod had been convoked at Nicomedia in the matter of the controversy over Arius, after which letters would be dispatched to all of the bishops; if Alexander had already sent his letters around to let everybody know, would not the Emperor have known about it? Would not he have been informed by Hosius and the other high-ranking clergymen at the court? The accounts cited above appear to point out that the virtual scale of the controversy would have already reached and affected the entire Church by then, and

[87] Epiphanius, *Panarion* 69, 4.

[88] Cf. M. Simonetti, *La crisi ariana*, 31.

[89] Philostorgius, *h.e.* I, 7.

[90] M. Simonetti, *La crisi ariana* 33.

the epistle should have been addressed rather to Alexander and Eusebius (also, the Emperor would very likely have been angry at Eusebius). But we have no indication of anything like that.

Then, it is evident that the things must have been different.

In order to make the whole picture of the dispute more complete, we should also have a look at one of the letters (reputedly, there had been many) written by Eusebius in connection with the controversy over Arius. The only extant one is the aforementioned letter to Paulinus of Nola. It can be found as cited by Theodoret of Cyrrhus, who expressed his disgust by saying that Eusebius had "vomited forth his impiety."[91]

Eusebius of Nicomedia, *Letter to Paulinus of Tyre:*[92]

1. Τῷ δεσπότῃ μου Παυλίνῳ Εὐσέβιος ἐν κυρίῳ χαίρειν. Οὔτε ἡ τοῦ δεσπότου μου Εὐσεβίου σπουδή, ἡ ὑπὲρ τοῦ ἀληθοῦς λόγου, παρεσιωπήθη ἀλλ' ἔφθασεν ἕως καὶ ἡμῶν, οὔτε ἡ σοῦ ἐπὶ τούτῳ σιωπή, δέσποτα. καὶ ὡς ἦν ἀκόλουθον, ἐπὶ μὲν τῷ δεσπότῃ μου Εὐσεβίῳ ηὐφράνθημεν, ἐπὶ δὲ σοὶ λυπούμεθα, στοχαζόμενοι καὶ τὴν σιωπὴν ἀνδρὸς τοιούτου ἧτταν ἡμῶν εἶναι.

1. To my lord Paulinus, Eusebius sendeth greeting in the Lord. The zeal of my lord Eusebius in the cause of the truth, and likewise your silence concerning it, have not failed to reach our ears. Accordingly, if, on the one hand, we rejoiced on account of the zeal of my lord Eusebius; on the other we are grieved at you, because even the silence of such a man appears like a defeat of our cause.

2. διὸ παρακαλῶ εἰδότα σε ὡς ἀπρεπὲς ἀνδρὶ φρονίμῳ ἀλλοῖα φρονεῖν καὶ σιωπᾶν τἀληθῆ, ἀνασκαλεύσαντι τῷ πνεύματι τὸν λογισμὸν περὶ τὸ γράφειν περὶ τούτου ἄρχου, λυσιτελοῦντος καὶ σοὶ καὶ τοῖς ἀκούουσί σου, μάλισθ' ὅταν κατὰ ἀκολουθίαν τῆς γραφῆς καὶ τοῖς ἴχνεσι τῶν λόγων αὐτῆς καὶ τῶν βουλημάτων ἐθέλοις γράφειν.

2. Hence, as it behoves not a wise man to be of a different opinion from others, and to be silent concerning the truth, stir up, I exhort you, within yourself the spirit of wisdom to write, and at length begin what may be profitable to yourself and to others, specially if you consent to write in accordance with Scripture, and tread in the tracks of its words and will.

Reportedly, Arius had already written to Paulinus (as well as to Eusebius of Caesarea).[93] As the letter tells us, Eusebius replied, Paulinus did not. We do not know if the reason was his unfavourable attitude to Arius, or anything else. However, since Arius had addressed the letter to him at all,

---

[91] Theodoret of Cyrrhus, *h.e.* I, 4 (NPNF 2,3).

[92] In: Theodoret of Cyrrhus, *h.e.* I, 5 (NPNF 2,3).

[93] Cf. Sozomen, *h.e.* I, 15.

there would have been most probably no major disagreement between them and Arius had counted on his support. In all likelihood, Eusebius of Nicomedia felt obliged to provide him with a more accurate statement of the contested issue.

3. ὅτι γὰρ οὔτε δύο ἀγέννητα ἀκηκόαμεν οὔτε ἓν εἰς δύο διῃρημένον οὐδὲ σωματικόν τι πεπονθὸς μεμαθήκαμεν ἢ πεπιστεύκαμεν, δέσποτα, ἀλλ᾽ ἓν μὲν τὸ ἀγέννητον, ἓν δὲ τὸ ὑπ᾽ αὐτοῦ ἀληθῶς καὶ οὐκ ἐκ τῆς οὐσίας αὐτοῦ γεγονός, καθόλου τῆς φύσεως τῆς ἀγεννήτου μὴ μετέχον ἢ ὂν ἐκ τῆς οὐσίας αὐτοῦ, ἀλλὰ γεγονὸς ὁλοσχερῶς ἕτερον τῇ φύσει καὶ τῇ δυνάμει, πρὸς τελείαν ὁμοιότητα διαθέσεώς τε καὶ δυνάμεως τοῦ πεποιηκότος γενόμενον· οὗ τὴν ἀρχὴν οὐ λόγῳ μόνον ἀδιήγητον, ἀλλὰ καὶ ἐννοίᾳ οὐκ ἀνθρώπων μόνον ἀλλὰ καὶ τῶν ὑπὲρ ἀνθρώπους πάντων εἶναι ἀκατάληπτον πεπιστεύκαμεν.

3. We have never heard that there are two unbegotten beings, nor that one has been divided into two, nor have we learned or believed that it has ever undergone any change of a corporeal nature; but we affirm that the unbegotten is one and one also that which exists in truth by Him, yet was not made out of His substance, and does not at all participate in the nature or substance of the unbegotten, entirely distinct in nature and in power, and made after perfect likeness both of character and power to the maker. We believe that the mode of His beginning not only cannot be expressed by words but even in thought, and is incomprehensible not only to man, but also to all beings superior to man.

Apparently, this utterance aims to make more specific the words of Arius' letter to Alexander, whose contents may have been publicly known at that time. Once again, we can see the already encountered expressions referring to the one Unbegotten and the impossibility of dividing God's substance into two. Hence, Arius and Eusebius conclude that the other one, i.e., the Son, cannot be of the same nature as the Father. There is, however, an emphasis on the fundamental difference between the origin or creation of the Son and the other created beings, as the former is incomprehensible.

4. Καὶ ταῦτα οὐχὶ λογισμοὺς ἑαυτῶν ὑποθέμενοι, ἀλλ᾽ ἀπὸ τῆς ἁγίας γραφῆς μεμαθηκότες λέγομεν·

4. These opinions we advance not as having derived them from our own imagination, but as having deduced them from Scripture,

κτιστὸν εἶναι καὶ θεμελιωτὸν καὶ γεννητὸν τῇ οὐσίᾳ καὶ τῇ ἀναλλοιώτῳ καὶ ἀρρήτῳ φύσει καὶ τῇ ὁμοιότητι τῇ πρὸς τὸν πεποιηκότα μεμαθήκαμεν, ὡς αὐτὸς ὁ κύριός φησιν· "ὁ θεὸς ἔκτισέ με ἀρχὴν ὁδῶν αὐτοῦ, καὶ πρὸ τοῦ αἰῶνος ἐθεμελίωσέ με· πρὸ δὲ πάντων βουνῶν γεννᾷ με".

whence we learn that the Son was created, established, and begotten in the same substance and in the same immutable and inexpressible nature as the Maker; and so the Lord says, 'God created me in the beginning of His way; I was set up from everlasting; before the hills was I brought forth.'[94]

A citation of Proverbs 8:22-25 can be also found in Arius' letter to Eusebius of Nicomedia, and, as it appears, nowhere else (of course, as far as the extant writings are concerned).

5. εἰ δὲ ἐξ αὐτοῦ, τουτέστιν ἀπ' αὐτοῦ ἦν, ὡς ἂν μέρος αὐτοῦ ἢ ἐξ ἀπορροίας τῆς οὐσίας, οὐκ ἂν ἔτι κτιστὸν οὐδὲ θεμελιωτὸν εἶναι ἐλέγετο· οὐδὲ αὐτὸς ἀγνοεῖς, κύριε, ἀληθῶς. τὸ γὰρ ἐκ τοῦ ἀγεννήτου ὑπάρχον κτιστὸν ἔτι ὑφ' ἑτέρου ἢ ὑπ' αὐτοῦ ἢ θεμελιω-τὸν οὐκ ἂν εἴη, ἐξ ἀρχῆς ἀγέννητον ὑπάρχον.

5. If He had been from Him or of Him, as a portion of Him, or by an emanation of His substance, it could not be said that He was created or established; and of this you, my lord, are certainly not ignorant. For that which is of the unbegotten could not be said to have been created or founded, either by Him or by another, since it is unbegotten from the beginning.

There is apparently a misunderstanding in that both Arius and Eusebius seem to expect to find the "academic" precision in the Proverbs, even though it is not there at all. They may have been the first "victims" of the trend to construe the Scripture literally. According to Eusebius, that which would be of the Unbegotten "could not be said to have been created." At this point, the allegorist would rather ponder the question in what sense that would be possible. Unfortunately, Eusebius puts his method to use only selectively; as we shall see, he does not apply such consistency with regard to the notion of begetting.

6. εἰ δὲ τὸ γεννητὸν αὐτὸν λέγεσθαι ὑπόφασίν τινα παρέχει, ὡς ἂν ἐκ τῆς οὐσίας τῆς πατρικῆς αὐτὸν γεγονότα καὶ ἔχειν ἐκ τούτου τὴν ταυτότητα τῆς φύσεως, γιγνώσκομεν ὡς οὐ περὶ αὐτοῦ μόνου τὸ γεννητὸν εἶναί φησιν ἡ γραφή, ἀλλὰ καὶ ἐπὶ τῶν ἀνομοίων αὐτῷ κατὰ πάντα τῇ φύσει.

6. But if the fact of His being called the begotten gives any ground for the belief that, having come into being of the Father's substance, He also has from the Father likeness of nature, we reply that it is not of Him alone that the Scriptures have spoken as begotten, but that they also thus speak of those who are entirely dissimilar to Him by nature.

---

[94] *Prov.* 8:25.

Consistently, if one is to treat the creation in literal terms, there must exist a difference in the natures between the created Son and the unbegotten Father. The author realizes that the very concept of begetting would imply the oneness of the substance, but to speak of the creation would preclude such an interpretation.

7. καὶ γὰρ καὶ ἐπ᾽ ἀνθρώπων φησίν· "υἱοὺς ἐγέννησα καὶ ὕψωσα, αὐτοὶ δέ με ἠθέτησαν", καὶ "θεὸν τὸν γεννήσαντά σε ἐγκατέλιπες", καὶ ἐν ἑτέροις· "τίς", φησί, "ὁ τετοκὼς βώλους δρόσου"; οὐ τὴν φύσιν ἐκ τῆς φύσεως διηγούμενος, ἀλλὰ τὴν ἐφ᾽ ἑκάστῳ τῶν γενομένων ἐκ τοῦ βουλήματος αὐτοῦ γένεσιν. οὐδὲν γάρ ἐστιν ἐκ τῆς οὐσίας αὐτοῦ, πάντα δὲ βουλήματι αὐτοῦ γενόμενα ἕκαστον, ὡς καὶ ἐγένετο, ἐστίν.

7. For of men it is said, 'I have begotten and brought up sons, and they have rebelled against me;'[95] and in another place, 'Thou hast forsaken God who begat thee;'[96] and again it is said, 'Who begat the drops of dew?'[97] This expression does not imply that the dew partakes of the nature of God, but simply that all things were formed according to His will. There is, indeed, nothing which is of His substance, yet every thing which exists has been called into being by His will.

Eusebius admits the analogical usage of the notion of begetting in the Scriptures, yet he contradicts the identical comprehension of the notion of creation. It is a fairly obvious hermeneutical manipulation.

8. ὁ μὲν γὰρ θεός, τὰ δὲ πρὸς ὁμοιότητα αὐτοῦ λόγῳ ὅμοια ἐσόμενα, τὰ δὲ καθ᾽ ἑκουσιασμὸν γενόμενα· τὰ δὲ πάντα δι᾽ αὐτοῦ ὑπὸ τοῦ θεοῦ γενόμενα, πάντα δὲ ἐκ τοῦ θεοῦ. ἅπερ λαβὼν καὶ ἐξεργασάμενος κατὰ τὴν προσοῦσάν σοι θεόθεν χάριν, γράψαι τῷ δεσπότῃ μου Ἀλεξάνδρῳ σπούδασον· πεπίστευκα γὰρ ὡς εἰ γράψειας αὐτῷ, ἐντρέψειας αὐτόν. πρόσειπε πάντας τοὺς ἐν κυρίῳ. ἐρρωμένον σε καὶ ὑπὲρ ἡμῶν εὐχόμενον ἡ θεία χάρις διαφυλάττοι, δέσποτα".

8. He is God; and all things were made in His likeness, and in the future likeness of His Word, being created of His free will. All things were made by His means by God. All things are of God. When you have received my letter, and have revised it according to the knowledge and grace given you by God, I beg you will write as soon as possible to my lord Alexander. I feel confident that if you would write to him, you would succeed in bringing him over to your opinion. Salute all the brethren in the Lord. May you, my lord, be preserved by the grace of God, and be led to pray for us.

[95] *Is.* 1:2.

[96] *Dt.* 32:18.

[97] *Job* 38:28.

This expression of the belief in the possibility of any change in the position held by Alexander, whom Eusebius mentions in his letter, makes me venture a supposition that the reference is not to Alexander of Alexandria, unless he regarded Paulinus as a great authority, which we do not really know. It seems to me it is more likely that the reference is made to Alexander of Byzantium. Let us now focus on a letter addressed to Alexander of Byzantium (Constantinople) by Alexander of Alexandria, indicating that the former had been involved, or at least embroiled, in the controversy.

Alexander of Alexandria, *Letter to Alexander of Constantinople*[98]

It is speculated that the letter is in fact addressed to Bishop Alexander of Thessalonika,[99] as it is not certain if Alexander of Byzantium had become bishop before the year 325. He was known to posterity thanks to Gregory of Nazianzus, who, in his oration delivered at the turn of 380-381 at Constantinople,[100] recalled him as a renowned defender of the faith in the Holy Trinity and the one whose prayers for Arius' death were answered. Following the Emperor Constantine's rehabilitation of Arius, he was to spend a number of nights at the Church of the Holy Peace, praying for his own death if Arius was right or else for the Divine intervention preventing his restoration in the Church. As a result, Arius died on the eve of the solemnity. Those events are described by Athanasius, who was present at Constantinople at the time, in his letter to Apion (as cited by Theodoret of Cyrrhus).[101]

The relevant accounts by Socrates and Sozomen are similar, although each of them presents a different sequence of the events. At any rate, it appears that Alexander of Byzantium (the city later renamed to Constantinople) died at approximately the same time as Constantine, i.e., *ca.* 337, after 23 years of his episcopate, at the age of 98.[102] We know that the actual turn of the events may have been somewhat different than that represented by Socrates and Sozomen, but there is rather no significant reason to doubt that Alexander had served as bishop since as early as *ca.* 314. It is also evident from the narration of Theodoret's account, as he makes a note of Macarius' accession to the See of Jerusalem in 314 and then goes on to mention Alexander, stating (in fairly general terms only) that he became bishop "at the same time."[103]

---

[98] In: Theodoret of Cyrrhus, *h.e.* I, 3 (NPNF 2,3).

[99] Cf. M. Simonetti, *La crisi ariana* 34, n. 15.

[100] Gregory of Nazianzus, *Oration* 36, 1.

[101] Theodoret of Cyrrhus, *h.e.*, I, 14.

[102] Socrates, *h.e.* II, 6; Sozomen, *h.e.* III, 3.

[103] Theodoret of Cyrrhus, h.e., I, 3, 2-3.

At the close of the above letter by Eusebius of Nicomedia addressed to Paulinus of Tyre, the author asks the addressee to write to "my lord Alexander," in order to "persuade" him. It is not exactly specified which Alexander he refers to, but, in all probability, it is Alexander of Byzantium; as the addressee of the letter by Alexander of Alexandria, he may have been, for the time being, persuaded to agree with the author's views, rather than those of Eusebius. Apparently, however, it would not bring any desired result.

According to Theodoret, the epistle (to be cited and discussed below) is one of the letters addressed to the heads of the Churches. Therefore, most probably, this is Alexander's second circular letter, with a personalized address. It is also indicated by the final sentence of the letter: "Salute one another, with the brotherhood that is with you. I pray that you may be strong in the Lord, my beloved, ..." The order of Alexander's letters, the one addressed to all the bishops and the one to Alexander,[104] remains a somewhat contested issue, which would be of significance if we extended the duration of the controversy before the year 325 to a number of years, as many scholars tend to assume. Notably, Opitz considers Arius' letter to Eusebius as the first document of the dispute and dates it back to 318.[105] As I have noted before, the whole controversy arose rather suddenly, around 323, and the two documents are contemporaneous. The time interval between the letters in question is therefore very brief.

1. Τῷ τιμιωτάτῳ ἀδελφῷ καὶ ὁμοψύχῳ Ἀλεξάνδρῳ Ἀλέξανδρος ἐν κυρίῳ χαίρειν. Ἡ φίλαρχος τῶν μοχθηρῶν ἀνθρώπων καὶ φιλάργυρος πρόθεσις ταῖς δοκούσαις ἀεὶ μείζοσι παροικίαις πέφυκεν ἐπιβουλεύειν, διὰ ποικίλων προφάσεων τῶν τοιούτων ἐπιτιθεμένων τῇ ἐκκλησιαστικῇ εὐσεβείᾳ. οἰστρηλατούμενοι γὰρ ὑπὸ τοῦ ἐνεργοῦντος ἐν αὐτοῖς διαβόλου, εἰς τὴν προκειμένην αὐτοῖς ἡδονὴν πάσης εὐλαβείας ἀποσκιρτήσαντες, πατοῦσι τὸν τῆς κρίσεως τοῦ θεοῦ φόβον.

1. To his most revered and likeminded brother Alexander, Alexander sends greeting in the Lord. Impelled by avarice and ambition, evil-minded persons have ever plotted against the well being of the most important dioceses. Under various pretexts, they attack the religion of the Church; and, being maddened by the devil, who works in them, they start aside from all piety according to their own pleasure, and trample under foot the fear of the judgment of God.

It appears that the document depicts the conflict with Arius at its inception, following the first synodal verdict against him and his adherents,

[104] Cf. W. Löhr, *Arius Reconsidered* (part 1), 544-553.

[105] H.G. Opitz, *Athanasius Werke*, Bd. III/1, 1. Cf. Uta Loose, *Zur Chronologie des arianischen Streites*, in ZKG 101 (1990), 88-92.

most likely already after the initial response to that condemnation. The allusive mention of ambition and avarice does not seem to refer to Arius, against whom Alexander would bring different charges, but rather to his prominent protectors such as, notably, Eusebius of Nicomedia, mentioned in his *Letter to All the Bishops* (4), reproaching him for his relocation from Beirut to Nicomedia to pursue his own ambition.

The passage "plotted against the well-being of the most important dioceses" may be understood in terms of as a certain warning. Alexander considers Eusebius' letters as an attack on the great See of Alexandria and appears to suggest that it may be just the beginning of what his harmful ambitions can lead to.

2. Περὶ ὧν ἀναγκαῖον ἦν μοι τῷ πάσχοντι δηλῶσαι τῇ ὑμετέρᾳ εὐλαβείᾳ, ἵνα φυλάττησθε τοὺς τοιούτους μή τις αὐτῶν τολμήσῃ καὶ ταῖς ὑμετέραις παροικίαις ἐπιβῆναι, ἤτοι δι' ἑαυτῶν (ἱκανοὶ γὰρ ὑποκρίνασθαι πρὸς ἀπάτην οἱ γόητες), ἢ διὰ γραμμάτων ψευδῶς κεκομψευμένων, δυναμένων ὑφαρπάσαι τὸν ἁπλῇ πίστει καὶ ἀκεραίῳ προσεσχηκότα.

2. Suffering as I do from them myself, I deem it necessary to inform your piety, that you may be on your guard against them, lest they or any of their party should presume to enter your diocese (for these cheats are skilful in deception), or should circulate false and specious letters, calculated to delude one who has devoted himself to the simple and undefiled faith.

The letters of Arius and, in particular, those of Eusebius of Nicomedia are mentioned in Alexander's *Letter to All the Bishops*.[106] There is practically no mention, however, of any emissaries wandering from one church to another. Epiphanius recounts that Arius went to Caesarea, to Bishop Eusebius,[107] following his condemnation, but it is more likely that he had gone there with the purpose of seeking refuge rather than disseminating his doctrine.

3. Ἄρειος γοῦν καὶ Ἀχιλλᾶς, συνωμοσίαν ἔναγχος ποιησάμενοι, τὴν Κολλούθου φιλαρχίαν πολὺ χεῖρον ἢ ἐκεῖνος ἐζήλωσαν. ὁ μὲν γὰρ αὐτοῖς τούτοις ἐγκαλῶν τῆς ἑαυτοῦ μοχθηρᾶς προαιρέσεως εὗρε πρόφασιν·

3. Arius and Achillas have lately formed a conspiracy, and, emulating the ambition of Colluthus, have gone far beyond him. He indeed sought to find a pretext for his own pernicious line of action in the charges he brought against them.

[106] Alexander of Alexandria, *Letter to All the Bishops* 4.
[107] Epiphanius, *Panarion* 69, 4.

οἱ δὲ τὴν ἐκείνου χριστεμπορίαν θεωροῦντες οὐκ ἔτι τῆς ἐκκλησίας ὑποχείριοι μένειν ἐκαρτέρησαν, ἀλλ᾽ ἑαυτοῖς σπήλαια λῃστῶν οἰκοδομήσαντες ἀδιαλείπτους ἐν αὐτοῖς ποιοῦνται συνόδους, νύκτωρ τε καὶ μεθ᾽ ἡμέραν ἐν ταῖς κατὰ Χριστοῦ καὶ ἡμῶν διαβολαῖς ἀσκούμενοι.

But they, beholding his making a trade of Christ for lucre, refused to remain any longer in subjection to the Church; but built for themselves caves, like robbers,[108] and now constantly assemble in them, and day and night ply slanders there against Christ and against us.

Alexander mentions Achillas as Arius' chief associate. He also cites his name as the second one among those condemned at the synod of Alexandria, which, in my opinion, may be presumably dated to approximately 323, not to 318 or 320, as asserted by the proponents of the hypothesis that Arianism had already attained the status of the most serious problem in the Church prior to the year 325, which is not substantiated in the contemporary sources at all. We have no information on his later activity.

As for Colluthus, it is known that he had ordained presbyters and deacons in Egypt, even though he was himself only a presbyter. All those appointed were declared as laymen. It is mentioned in Athanasius' post-synodal epistle of 338.[109] There is a mention that the synod convened at Alexandria at the close of 324 or the beginning of 325, in order to deal with the Felician controversy, had been concerned with Colluthus' usurpation as well.[110] Athanasius refers to this figure only in passing, as he questions the validity of the presbyter Ischirus' ordination. It is evident from the text of the letter that Colluthus had commenced his activity at roughly the same time as the controversy over Arius. Nonetheless, the letter does not make it clear why the accusations against Arians would have justified his schismatic actions. Possibly, this is just a rhetorical juxtaposition of two heretics, where one follows the bad example of the other. Athanasius also notes that later on Colluthus and Meletians joined efforts to harm him.[111]

4. Οἳ πάσης τῆς εὐσεβοῦς ἀποστολικῆς δόξης κατηγοροῦντες Ἰουδαϊκῷ προσχήματι χριστομάχον συνεκρότησαν ἐργαστήριον, τὴν θεότητα τοῦ σωτῆρος ἡμῶν ἀρνούμενοι καὶ τοῖς πᾶσιν ἴσον εἶναι κηρύττοντες,

4. They revile every godly apostolical doctrine, and in Jewish fashion have organized a gang to fight against Christ, denying His divinity, and declaring Him to be on a level with other men.

[108] Mt. 21:13.

[109] Council of Alexandria (338/339), 12, 1; SCL 1, 103; Athanasius, Apol. c. ar. 12; Opitz, Athanasius Werke II/1, 97.

[110] Athanasius, Apol. c. ar. 76.

[111] Athanasius, Apol. c. ar. 78. 80.

πᾶσάν τε αὐτοῦ τῆς σωτηρίου οἰκονομίας καὶ δι' ἡμᾶς ταπεινώσεως φωνὴν ἐκλεξάμενοι ἐξ αὐτῶν συναγείρειν πειρῶνται τῆς ἀσεβείας ἑαυτῶν τὸ κήρυγμα, τῆς ἀρχῆθεν θεότητος αὐτοῦ καὶ παρὰ τῷ πατρὶ δόξης ἀλέκτου τοὺς λόγους ἀποστρεφόμενοι.

They pick out every passage which refers to the dispensation of salvation, and to His humiliation for our sake; they endeavour to collect from them their own impious assertion, while they evade all those which declare His eternal divinity, and the unceasing glory which He possesses with the Father.

Apparently, the passage intimates that the fundamental scriptural texts employed by Arius and his followers referred to the humiliation of the Son of God, to the effect of Philippians 2:6-10: He humbled Himself, became a man obedient to death, etc. It also concurs with the words of the *Thalia*, as cited by Athanasius, where Arius speaks of the mutability by nature, and the immutability *de facto*, of Christ.[112] He had humbled himself because He wanted to, not because He had to. However, it does not tally with the reconstruction of the events according to which the debate on Proverbs 8:22-25 is seen at the inception of the controversy.[113]

5. Τὴν γοῦν Ἑλλήνων τε καὶ Ἰουδαίων ἀσεβῆ περὶ Χριστοῦ δόξαν κρατύνοντες, τὸν παρ' αὐτοῖς ἔπαινον ὡς ἔνι μάλιστα θηρῶνται, πάντα μὲν ὅσα καθ' ἡμῶν παρ' αὐτοῖς γελᾶται πραγματευόμενοι, στάσεις δὲ ἡμῖν καθ' ἡμέραν καὶ διωγμοὺς ἐπεγείροντες· καὶ τοῦτο μὲν δικαστήρια συγκροτοῦντες δι' ἐντυχίας γυναικαρίων ἀτάκτων ἃ ἠπάτησαν, τοῦτο δὲ τὸν χριστιανισμὸν διασύροντες ἐκ τοῦ περιτροχάζειν πᾶσαν ἀγυιὰν ἀσέμνως τὰς παρ' αὐτοῖς νεωτέρας. ἀλλὰ καὶ τὸν ἄρρηκτον τοῦ Χριστοῦ χιτῶνα, ὃν οἱ δήμιοι διελεῖν οὐκ ἐβουλεύσαντο, αὐτοὶ σχίσαι ἐτόλμησαν.

5. They maintain the ungodly doctrine entertained by the Greeks and the Jews concerning Jesus Christ; and thus, by every means in their power, hunt for their applause. Everything which outsiders ridicule in us they officiously practise. They daily excite persecutions and seditions against us.[114] On the one hand they bring accusations against us before the courts, suborning as witnesses certain unprincipled women whom they have seduced into error. On the other they dishonour Christianity by permitting their young women to ramble about the streets. Nay, they have had the audacity to rend the seamless garment of Christ, which the soldiers dared not divide.[115]

[112] Athanasius, *Letter to the Bishops of Egypt and Libya* 12; PG 25, 564B-565C.

[113] Cf., e.g., M. Simonetti, *La crisi ariana*, 35.

[114] Cf. *Act.* 13:50.

[115] Cf. *Io.* 19:23-24.

It is difficult to say what the author alludes to. I have not come across any reference to processions of women used to propagate Arianism. May it have some sort of connection with the "entertaining" aspect of Arius' writings? Athanasius refers to his *Thalia* as "feminine in style and melody,"[116] and compares his style with that of the Egyptian author Sosates, who was, most likely, the 2nd-1st century BC poet from Alexandria, also called the "Jewish Homer." Clearly not a paragon of refined style to Athanasius, he is mentioned in the *Excerpta Latina Barbari* 36B.[117] "The seamless garment of Christ" serves as a figure of the entire Church: it ought to remain intact, but the heresies rend it apart. Painting the Greeks and the Jews with the same brush is probably intended to highlight the unique character of Christianity in relation to all of the earlier manifestations of religiousness.

6. Ἡμεῖς μὲν οὖν ἃ καὶ τῷ βίῳ αὐτῶν καὶ τῇ ἀνοσίῳ ἐπιχειρήσει πρέπει διὰ τὸ λανθάνειν βραδέως ἐπιστήσαντες, παμψηφὶ τῆς προσκυνούσης Χριστοῦ τὴν θεότητα ἐκκλησίας ἐξηλάσαμεν.

6. When these actions, in keeping with their course of life, and the impious enterprise which had been long concealed, became tardily known to us, we unanimously ejected them from the Church which worships the divinity of Christ.

Most probably, Alexander suggests that Arius had propagated his views long before the public dispute during which a confrontation with the bishop, and the revealing of Arius' teachings, took place. This would explain the appearance of his dedicated followers who had signed his letter to Alexander. The whole issue had been evidently well discussed beforehand, as they decided to risk being anathematized. Unfortunately, we have no more information about it.

7. Ἐπεχείρησαν δὲ περιδρομαῖς χρώμενοι καθ' ἡμῶν παρεκβαίνειν πρὸς τοὺς ὁμόφρονας συλλειτουργούς, σχήματι μὲν εἰρήνης καὶ ἐνώσεως ἀξίωσιν ὑποκρινόμενοι, τὸ δ' ἀληθὲς συναρπάσαι τινὰς αὐτῶν εἰς τὴν ἰδίαν νόσον διὰ χρηστολογίας σπουδάζοντες καὶ στωμυλώτερα γράμματα παρ' αὐτῶν αἰτοῦντες,

7. They then ran hither and thither to form cabals against us, even addressing themselves to our fellow-ministers who were of one mind with us, under the pretence of seeking peace and unity with them, but in truth endeavouring by means of fair words, to sweep some among them away into their own disease.

[116] Athanasius, *Contra Arianos* I, 5 (NPNF 2,4). For the extant fragments, see Ch. 1 – The Beginning of the Arian Controversy."

[117] *Excerpta Latina Barbari*, A. Schoene (ed.), *Eusebi Chronicorum libri duo*, Appendix VI, Berlin 1877, 177-239.

ἵνα παραναγιγνώσκοντες αὐτὰ τοῖς ὑπ' αὐτῶν ἠπατημένοις ἀμετανοήτους ἐφ' οἷς ἐσφάλησαν κατασκευάσωσιν, ἐπιτριβομένους εἰς ἀσέβειαν, ὡς ἂν συμψήφους αὐτοῖς καὶ ὁμόφρονας ἔχοντες ἐπισκόπους.

They ask them to write a wordy letter, and then read the contents to those whom they have deceived, in order that they may not retract, but be confirmed in their impiety, by finding that bishops agree with and support their views.

As it appears, the Arians' epistolar offensive was not limited to disseminating the information about "unfair treatment" and complaining of the bishop's attitude; in their letters, they would also formulate questions and offer very specific answers thereto. If, as I suppose, it is true[118] that Arius' principal problem was the mutability of Christ, that is, the theoretical possibility of His disobedience, it is not hard to imagine he would have communicated that problem to others. And it must be admitted that it was extremely difficult to answer the question of Jesus' obedience, as no one had as yet come up with the idea of postulating the Divine will and the human will in Christ, which would only come to pass formally at the Third Council of Constantinople (680). If, then, a certain bishop had happened to become embroiled in an epistolar debate, it would have been very likely he was not able to resolve the question in hand. Unfortunately, we do not know of any such letters, which is not surprising at all. There was simply no reason to have them copied.

8. οὐχ ἅπερ γοῦν παρ' ἡμῖν πονηρῶς ἐδίδαξάν τε καὶ διεπράξαντο ὁμολογοῦσιν αὐτοῖς, δι' ἃ καὶ ἐξώσθησαν· ἀλλ' ἢ σιωπῇ ταῦτα παραδιδόασιν, ἢ πεπλασμένοις λόγοις καὶ ἐγγράφοις ἐπισκιάζοντες ἀπατῶσιν.

8. They make no acknowledgment of the evil doctrines and practices for which they have been expelled by us, but they either impart them without comment, or carry on the deception by fallacies and forgeries.

It appears that after a certain period of the "latent" activity, when there had been no overt controversy yet (but, quite possibly, much debating and discussing), the Arian views eventually came into light at one of the meetings in the bishop's presence, which would result in the exclusion from the Church of the entire dissident group. Supposedly, it took place in 323. Considering the Emperor Constantine's knowledge of the issue, as evident in his letter, it may be assumed that his counsels, including Bishop Hosius,

---

[118] See the extant passage of the *Thalia* in: Athanasius, *Letter to the Bishops of Egypt and Libya* 12; PG 25, 564B-565C, as cited above in the commentary on Arius' *Letter to Alexander*.

did not have a very clear idea of the gist of the controversy.[119] Alexander's previous letter had unleashed a spate of correspondence, with Arius' supporters possibly gaining the upper hand, and herewith Alexander makes another attempt at defending his position.

9. Πιθανωτέραις γοῦν καὶ βωμολόχοις ὁμιλίαις τὴν φθοροποιὸν ἑαυτῶν διδασκαλίαν ἐπικρύπτοντες συναρπάζουσι τὸν εἰς ἀπάτην ἐγκείμενον, οὐκ ἀπεχόμενοι καὶ τοῦ παρὰ πᾶσι συκοφαντεῖν τὴν ἡμετέραν εὐσέβειαν· ὅθεν καὶ συμβαίνει τινὰς τοῖς γράμμασιν αὐτῶν ὑπογράφοντας εἰς ἐκκλησίαν εἰσδέχεσθαι, μεγίστης ὡς οἶμαι διαβολῆς ἐπικειμένης τοῖς τοῦτο τολμῶσι συλλειτουργοῖς τῷ μήτε τὸν ἀποστολικὸν κανόνα τοῦτο συγχωρεῖν ἀλλὰ καὶ ὑπεκκαίειν τὴν ἐπ' αὐτοῖς διαβολικὴν κατὰ Χριστοῦ ἐνέργειαν.

9. Thus concealing their destructive doctrine by persuasive and meanly truckling language, they catch the unwary, and lose no opportunity of calumniating our religion. Hence it arises that several have been led to sign their letter, and to receive them into communion, a proceeding on the part of our fellow-ministers which I consider highly reprehensible; for they thus not only disobey the apostolical rule, but even help to inflame their diabolical action against Christ.

"Meanly truckling language" is most probably the same what the letter makes reference to at item 5 above. It is difficult to say with certainty which apostolic canon Alexander refers to, but it is possible that he alludes to the prohibition on readmitting into communion those who had been excluded elsewhere. The earliest record of such an injunction dates back to the synod of Elvira,[120] and it is also present in one of the so-called Apostolic Canons.[121]

10. Δι' ἃ δὴ καὶ οὐδὲν μελλήσας, ἀγαπητοί, δηλῶσαι ὑμῖν τὴν τῶν τοιούτων ἀπιστίαν ἐμαυτὸν διανέστησα, λεγόντων ὅτι ἦν ποτε ὅτε οὐκ ἦν ὁ υἱὸς τοῦ θεοῦ, καὶ γέγονεν ὕστερον ὁ πρότερον μὴ ὑπάρχων, τοιοῦτος γενόμενος ὅτε καί ποτε γέγονεν, οἷος καὶ πᾶς πέφυκεν ἄνθρωπος.

10. It is on this account, beloved brethren, that without delay I have stirred myself up to inform you of the unbelief of certain persons who say that "There was a time when the Son of God was not;" and "He who previously had no existence subsequently came into existence; and when at some time He came into existence He became such as every other man is."

---

[119] See Ch. 3.

[120] Council of Elvira (306), c. 53, SCL 1, 57.

[121] Can. App. 32, SCL 2, 279.

The Arian tenets had been expressed in these, and other similar, words since the beginning of the controversy (cf. Arius' letter to Alexander, Alexander's letter to all the bishops, and the later anathematism accompanying the Nicene creed). Alexander represents Arius' teachings in a tendentious way, as it is explicitly said in his letter that the Son is a created being, but not like other created beings.[122] Arius had never taught that Christ was a man such as "every other." Considering that an assertion like this may be ascribed to Paul of Samosata,[123] Alexander may possibly have aimed to put them both on the same level in public eye.

11. "πάντα γάρ", φασίν, "ὁ θεὸς ἐξ οὐκ ὄντων ἐποίησε", συναναλαμβάνοντες τῇ τῶν ἀπάντων λογικῶν τε καὶ ἀλόγων κτίσει καὶ τὸν υἱὸν τοῦ θεοῦ. οἷς ἀκολούθως καί φασιν αὐτὸν τρεπτῆς εἶναι φύσεως, ἀρετῆς τε καὶ κακίας ἐπιδεκτικόν, καὶ τῇ ἐξ οὐκ ὄντων ὑποθέσει καὶ τὰς θείας τοῦ εἶναι αὐτὸν ἀεὶ συναναιροῦντες γραφάς, αἳ τὸ ἄτρεπτον τοῦ λόγου καὶ τὴν θεότητα τῆς σοφίας τοῦ λόγου σημαίνουσιν, ἅ ἐστιν ὁ Χριστός. "δυνάμεθα γοῦν καὶ ἡμεῖς", φασὶν οἱ ἀλάστορες, "υἱοὶ γενέσθαι θεοῦ, ὥσπερ κἀκεῖνος".

12. Γέγραπται γάρ· "υἱοὺς ἐγέννησα καὶ ὕψωσα". Ἐπιφερομένου δὲ αὐτοῖς τοῦ λέγοντος ἐξῆς ῥητοῦ "αὐτοὶ δέ με ἠθέτησαν",

11. God, they say, created all things out of that which was non-existent, and they include in the number of creatures, both rational and irrational, even the Son of God. Consistently with this doctrine they, as a necessary consequence, affirm that He is by nature liable to change, and capable both of virtue and of vice, and thus, by their hypothesis of his having been created out of that which was non-existent, they overthrow the testimony of the Divine Scriptures, which declare the immutability of the Word and the Divinity of the Wisdom of the Word, which Word and Wisdom is Christ. 'We are also able,' say these accursed wretches, 'to become like Him, the sons of God; 12. for it is written,—I have nourished and brought up children.' When the continuation of this text is brought before them, which is, 'and they have rebelled against Me,'[124]

---

[122] See Arius, *Letter to Alexander* 2.

[123] Cf. Eusebius of Caesarea, *h.e.* VII, 30, 11, Council of Antioch (268/269), SCL 1, 45; fragments in: P. De Navascués, *Pablo de Samosata y sus adversarios. Estudio histórico-teológico del cristianismo antioqueno en el s. III*, SEA 87, Augustinianum, Roma 2004.

[124] *Is.* 1:2.

ὅπερ οὐ φυσικόν ἐστι τῷ σωτῆρι ὄντι φύσεως ἀτρέπτου, πάσης εὐλαβείας ἑαυτοὺς ἐρημώσαντες, τοῦτό φασι προγνώσει καὶ προθεωρίᾳ περὶ αὐτοῦ εἰδότα τὸν θεὸν ὅτι οὐκ ἀθετήσει ἐξειλέχθαι αὐτὸν ἀπὸ πάντων.

and it is objected that these words are inconsistent with the Saviour's nature, which is immutable, they throw aside all reverence, and affirm that God foreknew and foresaw that His Son would not rebel against Him, and that He therefore chose Him in preference to all others.

13. οὐ γὰρ φύσει καὶ κατ' ἐξαίρετον τῶν ἄλλων υἱῶν ἔχοντά τι οὔτε γὰρ φύσει υἱός τίς ἐστι τοῦ θεοῦ, φασίν, οὔτε τινὰ ἔχων ἰδιότητα πρὸς αὐτόν, ἀλλὰ καὶ αὐτὸν τρεπτῆς τυγχάνοντα φύσεως, διὰ τρόπων ἐπιμέλειαν καὶ ἄσκησιν μὴ τρεπόμενον ἐπὶ τὸ χεῖρον, ἐξελέξατο·

13. They likewise assert that He was not chosen because He had by nature any thing superior to the other sons of God; for no man, say they, is son of God by nature, nor has any peculiar relation to Him. He was chosen, they allege, because, though mutable by nature, His painstaking character suffered no deterioration.

14. ὡς εἰ καὶ Παῦλος τοῦτο βιάσαιτο καὶ Πέτρος, μηδὲν διαφέρειν τούτων τὴν ἐκείνου υἱότητα· εἰς παράστασιν δὲ τῆς φρενοβλαβοῦς ταύτης διδασκαλίας καὶ ταῖς γραφαῖς ἐμπαροινοῦντες καὶ παρατιθέμενοι τὸ ἐν Ψαλμοῖς περὶ Χριστοῦ ῥητόν, τὸ οὕτως ἔχον· "ἠγάπησας δικαιοσύνην καὶ ἐμίσησας ἀδικίαν· διὰ τοῦτο ἔχρισέ σε ὁ θεός, ὁ θεός σου, ἔλαιον ἀγαλλιάσεως παρὰ τοὺς μετόχους σου".

14. As though, forsooth, even if a Paul and a Peter made like endeavours, their sonship would in no respects differ from His. To establish this insane doctrine they insult the Scriptures, and bring forward what is said in the Psalms of Christ, 'Thou hast loved righteousness and hated iniquity, therefore thy God hath anointed thee with the oil of gladness above thy fellows.'[125]

(For the mutability and immutability of Christ's nature, see the commentary on item 4 above and the commentary on Arius' letter to Alexander).

The above excerpt is of particular significance, as it identifies the Biblical passages used by Arius to support his argumentation. A listing of such excerpts, several pages long, can be found in Prof. Simonetti's book.[126] Interestingly, the scholar regards Proverbs 8:22-24 as the most important,

---

[125] *Ps.* 45 (44):8; *Hbr.* 1:9.

[126] M. Simonetti, *La crisi ariana*, 52ff.

even fundamental, to Arius, while in the extant writings of Arius there is only one reference to this passage, namely in his letter to Eusebius.[127]

15. Περὶ μὲν οὖν ὅτι ὁ υἱὸς τοῦ θεοῦ οὔτε ἐξ οὐκ ὄντων γεγένηται, οὔτε ἦν ποτε ὅτε οὐκ ἦν, αὐτάρκης παιδεῦσαι Ἰωάννης ὁ εὐαγγελιστὴς γράφων οὕτως περὶ αὐτοῦ· "ὁ μονογενὴς υἱός, ὁ ὢν εἰς τὸν κόλπον τοῦ πατρός". προνοούμενος γὰρ ὁ θεῖος δεικνύναι διδάσκαλος ἀλλήλων ἀχώριστα πράγματα δύο, τὸν πατέρα καὶ τὸν υἱόν, ὄντα αὐτὸν ἐν τοῖς κόλποις τοῦ πατρὸς ὠνόμασεν.

16. ἀλλὰ γὰρ καὶ ὅτι τοῖς ἐξ οὐκ ὄντων γενομένοις ὁ λόγος τοῦ θεοῦ οὐ συναριθμεῖται, πάντα δι' αὐτοῦ γεγονέναι φησὶν ὁ αὐτὸς Ἰωάννης. τὴν γὰρ ἰδιότροπον αὐτοῦ ὑπόστασιν ἐδήλωσεν εἰπών "ἐν ἀρχῇ ἦν ὁ λόγος καὶ ὁ λόγος ἦν πρὸς τὸν θεὸν καὶ θεὸς ἦν ὁ λόγος. πάντα δι' αὐτοῦ ἐγένετο, καὶ χωρὶς αὐτοῦ ἐγένετο οὐδὲ ἕν".

17. εἰ γὰρ πάντα δι' αὐτοῦ ἐγένετο, πῶς ὁ τοῖς γενομένοις τὸ εἶναι χαρισάμενος αὐτός ποτε οὐκ ἦν; οὐ γάρ πως ὁ λόγος, τὸ ποιοῦν, τοῖς γενομένοις τῆς αὐτῆς εἶναι φύσεως διορίζεται· εἴ γε αὐτὸς μὲν ἦν ἐν ἀρχῇ πάντα δὲ δι' αὐτοῦ ἐγένετο καὶ ἐξ οὐκ ὄντων ἐποίησεν.

15. Now that the Son of God was not created out of the non-existent, and that there never was a time in which He was not, is expressly taught by John the Evangelist, who speaks of Him as 'the only begotten Son which is in the bosom of the Father.'[128] This divine teacher desired to show that the Father and the Son are inseparable; and, therefore, he said, 'that the Son is in the bosom of the Father.'

16. Moreover, the same John affirms that the Word of God is not classed among things created out of the non-existent, for, he says that 'all things were made by Him,' and he also declares His individual personality in the following words: 'In the beginning was the Word, and the Word was with God, and the Word was God. All things were made by Him, and without Him was not any thing made that was made.'[129]

17. If, then, all things were made by Him, how is it that He who thus bestowed existence on all, could at any period have had no existence himself? The Word, the creating power, can in no way be defined as of the same nature as the things created, if indeed He was in the beginning, and all things were made by Him, and were called by Him out of the non-existent into being.

---

[127] Arius, *Letter to Eusebius of Nicomedia* 5.

[128] *Io.* 1:18.

[129] *Io.* 1:1-3.

18. ἐναντίον γὰρ δοκεῖ τοῖς ἐξ οὐκ ὄντων γενομένοις τὸ ὂν καὶ ἀφεστηκὸς σφόδρα. τὸ μὲν γὰρ μεταξὺ πατρὸς καὶ υἱοῦ οὐδὲν δείκνυσιν εἶναι διάστημα, οὐδ' ἄχρι τινὸς ἐννοίας τοῦτο φαντασιῶσαι τῆς ψυχῆς δυναμένης· τὸ δὲ ἐξ οὐκ ὄντων δημιουργεῖσθαι τὸν κόσμον νεωτέραν ἔχει τῆς ὑποστάσεως καὶ πρόσφατον τὴν γένεσιν, ὑπὸ τοῦ πατρὸς διὰ τοῦ υἱοῦ πάντων εἰληφότων τὴν τοιαύτην οὐσίωσιν.

18. 'That which is' must be of an opposite nature to, and essentially different from, things created out of the non-existent. This shows, likewise, that there is no separation between the Father and the Son, and that the idea of separation cannot even be conceived by the mind; while the fact that the world was created out of the non-existent involves a later and fresh genesis of its essential nature, all things having been endowed with such an origin of existence by the Father through the Son.

It is hypothetically conceivable that this is a reflection of the debate marking the beginning of the feud between Alexander and Arius. We read herein of a peculiar, or particular, hypostasis of the Son. It is perhaps not necessary to seek an explanation of the term in the vast body of Greek philosophy. It is sufficient to rely on the conventional sense alone, according to which the term "hypostasis" is identical with *ousia* and denotes the Son's own nature. Likewise, the word would come to be used later in the anathematism following the Nicene creed.

Alexander aims to demonstrate that the hypostasis of the entire creation is fundamentally different from that of the Son, as the latter one has been always with God, whereas the hypostasis of the world is "later," only created out of the non-existent and connected with time. There would have existed a certain "distance," διάστημα, between the Father and the Son, had the Son been a created being. It would have been, so to speak, a temporal distance. However, there is no distance at all, because of the Son's eternal presence with the Father.

19. Μακρὸν γοῦν θεωρήσας τοῦ θεοῦ λόγου τὸ ἦν καὶ ὑπεραῖρον τῆς τῶν γενητῶν διανοίας ὁ εὐλαβέστατος Ἰωάννης γένεσιν αὐτοῦ καὶ ποίησιν ἀπηξίωσεν εἰπεῖν, οὐδὲ ταῖς ὁμοστοίχοις συλλαβαῖς τὸ ποιοῦν τοῖς γιγνομένοις ὀνομάσαι τολμήσας,

19. John, the most pious apostle, perceiving that the word 'was' applied to the Word of God was far beyond and above the intelligence of created beings, did not presume to speak of His generation or creation, nor yet dared to name the Maker and the creature in equivalent syllables.

οὐχ ὅτι ἀγέννητος ἦν ἓν γὰρ ἀγέννητον ὁ πατήρ, ἀλλ' ὅτι τῆς ἐξεσμένης τῶν εὐαγγελιστῶν, τάχα δὲ καὶ ἀγγέλων καταλήψεως ὑπερέκεινά ἐστιν ἡ τοῦ μονογενοῦς θεοῦ ἀνεκδιήγητος ὑπόστασις. εἰς εὐσεβεῖς οὐκ οἶμαι λογιζομένους τοὺς μέχρι τούτων ἐπερωτᾶν τι τολμῶντας, διὰ τὸ ἀνήκοον τοῦ "χαλεπώτερά σου μὴ ζήτει, καὶ ὑψηλότερά σου μὴ ἐξέταζε".

Not that the Son of God is unbegotten, for the Father alone is unbegotten; but that the ineffable personality of the only-begotten God is beyond the keenest conception of the evangelists and perhaps even of angels. Therefore, I do not think men ought to be considered pious who presume to investigate this subject, in disobedience to the injunction, 'Seek not what is too difficult for thee, neither enquire into what is too high for thee.' [130]

Alexander is aware of the situation that the argumentation based on the beginning of the Gospel of John is not very obvious from the rational point of view and resorts to mystery as an excuse. The hypostasis of the Son, which is "ineffable," cannot be deduced from the knowledge of the hypostases of the created world. Thus, searching for insight at any cost is not a sign of godliness at all, as there exist mysteries that are unfathomable. Possibly, the origin of the controversy had been related to the Emperor Constantine as a debate over certain passages from the Scriptures, a debate that had grown so intense as to lead to some far-reaching, and indeed far-fetched, conclusions. As Constantine writes in his *Letter to Alexander and Arius*:

I understand, then, that the origin of the present controversy is this. When you, Alexander, demanded of the presbyters what opinion they severally maintained respecting a certain passage in the Divine law, or rather, I should say, that you asked them something connected with an unprofitable question, then you, Arius, inconsiderately insisted on what ought never to have been conceived at all, or if conceived, should have been buried in profound silence. Hence it was that a dissension arose between you, fellowship was withdrawn, and the holy people, rent into diverse parties, no longer preserved the unity of the one body. Now, therefore, do ye both exhibit an equal degree of forbearance, and receive the advice which your fellow-servant righteously gives.[131]

According to the Emperor, who had only a limited understanding of the Christians' peculiar attitude towards striving for orthodoxy, and viewed Christianity in analogy to the religions he was familiar with, it was purposeless and detrimental. On the other hand, Alexander reckoned it was a godless and presumptuous matter, not something trifling or insignificant.

---

[130] *Sir.* 3:21.

[131] Eusebius of Caesarea, VC II 69 (NPNF 1).

In Alexandria, referring to the Logos as begotten and made (ποίησις) was by all means orthodox and traditional. It was spoken and written by, e.g., Dionysius of Alexandria, who explained it was the Greek way of speaking and of how the spiritual or mental "fatherhood" was referred to, for instance, artistic creation or "makers" of the motions of the heart:

For as I do not hold that the Word is a creature, and call God not His maker but His Father, even if I in passing, while referring to the Son, call God a creator, yet even here I am able to defend myself. For the Greek philosophers call themselves makers (ποιηταί) of their own discourses (λόγοι), although they are their fathers; while the Divine Scripture describes us as makers (doers) even of the motions of our hearts, speaking of "doers" of the law and of judgment and justice.[132]

Therefore, speaking of the Logos as "the work of God" does not have to amount to reducing Him to the rank of created beings.

20. εἰ γὰρ ἑτέρων πολλῶν ἡ γνῶσις, καὶ τούτου ἀσυγκρίτως κολοβωτέρων, κέκρυπται τὴν ἀνθρωπίνην κατάληψιν (οἷά ἐστι παρὰ Παύλῳ· "ἃ ὀφθαλμὸς οὐκ εἶδε καὶ οὖς οὐκ ἤκουσε καὶ ἐπὶ καρδίαν ἀνθρώπου οὐκ ἀνέβη ἃ ἡτοίμασεν ὁ θεὸς τοῖς ἀγαπῶσιν αὐτόν", ἀλλὰ καὶ τὰ ἄστρα φησὶν ὁ θεὸς τῷ Ἀβραὰμ ἀριθμῆσαι μὴ δύνασθαι, καὶ ἔτι "ἄμμον θαλασσῶν καὶ σταγόνας ὑετοῦ", φησί, "τίς ἐξαριθμήσει"), (21.) πῶς ἂν περιεργάσαιτό τις τὴν τοῦ θεοῦ λόγου ὑπόστασιν, ἐκτὸς εἰ μὴ μελαγχολικῇ διαθέσει ληφθεὶς τυγχάνοι; περὶ ἧς τὸ προφητικὸν πνεῦμά φησι· "τὴν γενεὰν αὐτοῦ τίς διηγήσεται";

20. For if the knowledge of many other things incomparably inferior is beyond the capacity of the human mind, and cannot therefore be attained, as has been said by Paul, 'Eye hath not seen, nor ear heard, neither have entered into the heart of man, the things which God hath prepared for them that love Him,'[133] and as God also said to Abraham, that the stars could not be numbered by him;[134] and it is likewise said, 'Who shall number the grains of sand by the sea-shore, or the drops of rain?'[135] (21.) how then can any one but a madman presume to enquire into the nature of the Word of God? It is said by the Spirit of prophecy, 'Who shall declare His generation?'[136]

---

[132] Cf. Athanasius, *De sententia Dionysii* 21, 3 (NPNF 2,4).

[133] *1 Cor.* 2:9.

[134] Cf. *Gen.* 15:5.

[135] *Sir.* 1:2.

[136] *Is.* 53:8.

ἦν καὶ αὐτὸς ὁ σωτὴρ ἡμῶν, εὐεργετῶν τοὺς πάντων τῶν ἐν τῷ κόσμῳ κίονας, τὴν περὶ τούτου γνῶσιν αὐτῶν ἀποφορτίσασθαι ἐσπούδασεν, πᾶσι μὲν οὖν αὐτοῖς ἀφύσικον εἶναι λέγων εἰς κατάληψιν, μόνῳ δὲ τῷ πατρὶ ἀνακεῖσθαι τὴν τοῦ θειοτάτου τούτου μυστηρίου εἴδησιν·"οὐδεὶς γὰρ ἔγνω τίς ἐστιν ὁ υἱός" λέγων "εἰ μὴ ὁ πατήρ· καὶ τὸν πατέρα οὐδεὶς ἔγνωκεν εἰ μὴ ὁ υἱός". περὶ οὗ καὶ τὸν πατέρα οἶμαι λέγειν "τὸ μυστήριόν μου ἐμοί".

22. Ὅτι δὲ μανιῶδες τὸ ἐξ οὐκ ὄντων τὸν υἱὸν γεγονέναι φρονεῖν, χρονικὴν ἔχον τὴν πρόθεσιν αὐτόθεν δείκνυται τὸ ἐξ οὐκ ὄντων, κἂν ἀγνοῶσιν οἱ ἀνόητοι τὴν τῆς φωνῆς αὐτῶν μανίαν. ἢ γὰρ χρόνοις ἐμπολιτεύεσθαι δεῖ τὸ οὐκ ἦν, ἢ αἰῶνός τινι διαστήματι.

23. εἰ τοίνυν ἀληθὲς τὸ πάντα δι' αὐτοῦ γεγονέναι, δῆλον ὅτι καὶ πᾶς αἰὼν καὶ χρόνος καὶ διαστήματα καὶ τὸ ποτέ, ἐν οἷς τὸ οὐκ ἦν εὑρίσκεται, δι' αὐτοῦ ἐγένετο. καὶ πῶς οὐκ ἀπίθανον τὸν καὶ χρόνους καὶ αἰῶνας καὶ καιρούς, ἐν οἷς τὸ οὐκ ἦν συμπέφυρται, ποιήσαντα, αὐτόν ποτε μὴ εἶναι λέγειν; ἀδιανόητον γὰρ καὶ πάσης ἀμαθίας ἀνάπλεων τὸν αἴτιον γενόμενόν τινος αὐτὸν μεταγενέστερον λέγειν τῆς ἐκείνου γενέσεως.

And, therefore, our Saviour in His kindness to those men who were the pillars of the whole world,[137] desiring to relieve them of the burden of striving after this knowledge, told them that it was beyond their natural comprehension, and that the Father alone could discern this most divine mystery; 'No man,' said He, 'knoweth the Son but the Father, and no man knoweth the Father save the Son.'[138] It was, I think, concerning this same subject that the Father said, 'My secret is for Me and for Mine.'[139]

22. But the insane folly of imagining that the Son of God came into being out of that which had no being, and that His sending forth took place in time, is plain from the words 'which had no being,' although the foolish are incapable of perceiving the folly of their own utterances. For the phrase 'He was not' must either have reference to time, or to some interval in the ages.

23. If then it be true that all things were made by Him,[140] it is evident that every age, time, all intervals of time, and that 'when' in which 'was not' has its place, were made by Him. And is it not absurd to say that there was a time when He who created all time, and ages, and seasons, with which the 'was not' is confused, was not? For it would be the height of ignorance, and contrary indeed to all reason, to affirm that the cause of any created thing can be posterior to that caused by it.

---

[137] That is, the Apostles.

[138] *Mt.* 11:27.

[139] *Is.* 24:16 (LXX).

[140] *Io.* 1:3.

Alexander attempts to portray Arius' view as utterly absurd, even though it was not that absurd at all. Arius had never claimed that the Son came into being later than all things, including time. He wrote clearly of the Son as "being begotten apart from time before all things, alone was made to subsist by the Father."[141] Contrary to appearances, it did not have to be seen as heretical, though it might have been, depending on interpretation. Similar statements were formulated by such apologists as Justin, whose orthodoxy was never questioned. To illustrate this point, let us quote again the following passage:

In the beginning, before all creatures, God begat from Himself a certain rational power, who is called by the Holy Spirit, now the Glory of the Lord,[142] now the Son,[143] again Wisdom,[144] again an Angel, then God, and then Lord and Logos;[145] and on another occasion He calls Himself Captain,[146] when He appeared in human form to Joshua the son of Nave. For He can be called by all those names, since He ministers to the Father's will, and since He was begotten of the Father by an act of will.[147]

The difference between Justin and Arius does not consist in a differently defined origin of the Son's existence, but in the source of His existence: in Arius' view, it is the NON-EXISTENT, whereas Justin asserts that the Father begets the Son "from Himself."

24. προηγεῖται γὰρ κατ' αὐτοὺς τῆς τὰ ὅλα δημιουργούσης τοῦ θεοῦ σοφίας ἐκεῖνο τὸ διάστημα ἐν ᾧ φασι μὴ γεγενῆσθαι τὸν υἱὸν ὑπὸ τοῦ πατρός, ψευδομένης κατ' αὐτοὺς καὶ τῆς πρωτότοκον αὐτὸν εἶναι πάσης κτίσεως ἀναγορευούσης γραφῆς.

24. The interval during which they say the Son was still unbegotten of the Father was, according to their opinion, prior to the wisdom of God, by whom all things were created. They thus contradict the Scripture which declares Him to be 'the firstborn of every creature.'[148]

---

[141] Arius, *A Letter to Alexander* 3.

[142] *Ex.* 16:7.

[143] *Ps.* 2:7.

[144] *Prov.* 8.

[145] *Ps.* 32:6; 106:20.

[146] *Ios.* 5:13-14.

[147] Justin, *A Dialogue with Trifon* 61 (ANF 1, revised).

[148] Cf. *Col.* 1:15.

25. σύμφωνα γοῦν τούτοις βοᾷ καὶ ὁ μεγαλοφωνότατος Παῦλος φάσκων περὶ αὐτοῦ· "ὃν ἔθηκε κληρονόμον πάντων, δι' οὗ καὶ τοὺς αἰῶνας ἐποίησεν", ἀλλὰ καὶ "ἐν αὐτῷ ἐκτίσθη τὰ πάντα, τὰ ἐν τοῖς οὐρανοῖς καὶ τὰ ἐπὶ τῆς γῆς, τὰ ὁρατὰ καὶ τὰ ἀόρατα, εἴτε ἀρχαί, εἴτε ἐξουσίαι, εἴτε κυριότητες, εἴτε θρόνοι· πάντα δι' αὐτοῦ καὶ εἰς αὐτὸν ἔκτισται· καὶ αὐτός ἐστι πρὸ πάντων".

26. Ἀσεβεστάτης οὖν φανείσης τῆς ἐξ οὐκ ὄντων ὑποθέσεως, ἀνάγκη τὸν πατέρα ἀεὶ εἶναι πατέρα· ἔστι δὲ πατὴρ ἀεὶ παρόντος τοῦ υἱοῦ, δι' ὃν χρηματίζει πατήρ· ἀεὶ δὲ παρόντος αὐτῷ τοῦ υἱοῦ, ἀεί ἐστιν ὁ πατὴρ τέλειος, ἀνελλιπὴς τυγχάνων ἐν τῷ καλῷ, οὐ χρονικῶς οὐδὲ ἐκ διαστήματος οὐδὲ ἐξ οὐκ ὄντων γεννήσας τὸν μονογενῆ υἱόν.

25. In consonance with this doctrine, Paul with his usual mighty voice cries concerning Him; 'whom He hath appointed heir of all things, by whom also He made the worlds,'[149] 'For by Him were all things created that are in heaven, and that are in earth, visible and invisible, whether they be thrones, or dominions, or principalities, or powers: all things were created by Him and for Him: and He is before all things.'[150]

26. Since the hypothesis implied in the phrase 'out of the non-existent' is manifestly impious, it follows that the Father is always Father. And He is Father from the continual presence of the Son, on account of whom He is called Father. And the Son being ever present with Him, the Father is ever perfect, wanting in no good thing, for He did not beget His only Son in time, or in any interval of time, nor out of that which had no previous existence.

As noted before, the first one to have substantiated the everlasting existence of the Father as Father, and thus the everlasting existence of the Son as well, was Origen.[151]

27. τί δέ; οὐκ ἀνόσιον τὸ λέγειν μὴ εἶναί ποτε τὴν σοφίαν τοῦ θεοῦ, τὴν λέγουσαν· "ἐγὼ ἤμην παρ' αὐτῷ ἁρμόζουσα, ἐγὼ ἤμην ᾗ προσέχαιρεν", ἢ τὴν δύναμιν τοῦ θεοῦ ποτε μὴ ὑπάρχειν, ἢ τὸν λόγον αὐτοῦ ἠκρωτηριάσθαι ποτέ, ἢ τὰ ἄλλα ἐξ ὧν ὁ υἱὸς γνωρίζεται καὶ ὁ πατὴρ χαρακτηρίζεται;

27. Is it not then impious to say that there was a time when the wisdom of God was not? Who saith, 'I was by Him as one brought up with Him: I was daily His delight?'[152] Or that once the power of God was not, or His Word, or anything else by which the Son is known, or the Father designated, defective?

---

[149] *Hbr.* 1:2.

[150] *Col.* 1:16-17.

[151] Cf. commentary on Arius' *Letter to Alexander*.

[152] *Prov.* 8:30.

τὸ γὰρ ἀπαύγασμα τῆς δόξης μὴ εἶναι λέγειν συναναιρεῖ καὶ τὸ πρωτότυπον φῶς, οὗ ἐστιν ἀπαύγασμα. εἰ δὲ καὶ ἡ εἰκὼν τοῦ θεοῦ οὐκ ἦν ἀεί, δῆλον ὅτι οὐδὲ οὗ ἐστιν εἰκὼν ἔστιν ἀεί. 28. ἀλλὰ καὶ τῷ μὴ εἶναι τὸν τῆς ὑποστάσεως τοῦ θεοῦ χαρακτῆρα, συναναιρεῖται κἀκεῖνος ὁ πάντως ὑπ' αὐτοῦ χαρακτηριζόμενος. ἐξ ἧς ἐστιν ἰδεῖν τὴν υἱότητα τοῦ σωτῆρος ἡμῶν οὐδεμίαν ἔχουσαν κοινωνίαν πρὸς τὴν τῶν λοιπῶν υἱότητα.

To assert that the brightness of the Father's glory 'once did not exist,'[153] destroys also the original light of which it is the brightness; and if there ever was a time in which the image of God was not,[154] it is plain that He Whose image He is, is not always: 28. nay, by the non-existence of the express image of God's Person,[155] He also is taken away of whom this is ever the express image. Hence it may be seen, that the Sonship of our Saviour has not even anything in common with the sonship of men.

29. ὃν τρόπον γὰρ ἡ ἄρρητος αὐτοῦ ὑπόστασις ἀσυγκρίτῳ ὑπεροχῇ ἐδείχθη ὑπερκειμένη πάντων οἷς αὐτὸς τὸ εἶναι ἐχαρίσατο, οὕτως καὶ ἡ υἱότης αὐτοῦ, κατὰ φύσιν τυγχάνουσα τῆς πατρικῆς θεότητος, ἀλέκτῳ ὑπεροχῇ διαφέρει τῶν δι' αὐτοῦ θέσει υἱοθετηθέντων. ὁ μὲν γὰρ ἀτρέπτου φύσεως τυγχάνει, τέλειος ὢν καὶ διὰ πάντων ἀνενδεής· οἱ δὲ τῇ εἰς ἑκάτερα τροπῇ ὑποκείμενοι τῆς παρὰ τούτου βοηθείας δέονται.

29. For just as it has been shown that the nature of His existence cannot be expressed by language, and infinitely surpasses in excellence all things to which He has given being, so His Sonship, naturally partaking in His paternal Divinity, is unspeakably different from the sonship of those who, by His appointment, have been adopted as sons. He is by nature immutable, perfect, and all-sufficient, whereas men are liable to change, and need His help.

Let us recall that Arius speaks of the Son's immutability *de facto*, not the immutability by nature. Conversely, Alexander writes of the natural immutability.

30. τί γὰρ ἂν καὶ προκόψαι ἔχοι ἡ τοῦ θεοῦ σοφία, ἢ τί προσλαβεῖν ἡ αὐτοαλήθεια; ἢ ὁ θεὸς λόγος πῶς ἂν ἔχοι βελτιωθῆναι ἢ ἡ ζωὴ ἢ τὸ ἀληθινὸν φῶς;

30. What further advance can be made by the wisdom of God? What can the Very Truth, or God the Word, add to itself? How can the Life or the True Light in any way be bettered?

[153] Cf. *Hbr.* 1:3.

[154] Cf. *2 Cor.* 4:4; *Col.* 1:15.

[155] Cf. *Hbr.* 1:3.

εἰ δὲ τοῦτο, πόσῳ πλέον ἀφύσικον τυγχάνει μωρίας ποτὲ δεκτικὴν γενέσθαι τὴν σοφίαν ἢ τὴν τοῦ θεοῦ δύναμιν ἀσθενείᾳ προσπλακῆναι, ἢ ἀλογίᾳ τὸν λόγον ἀμαυρωθῆναι ἢ τῷ ἀληθινῷ φωτὶ ἐπιμιχθῆναι σκότος, τοῦ μὲν ἀποστόλου αὐτόθεν λέγοντος "τίς κοινωνία φωτὶ πρὸς σκότος, ἢ τίς συμφώνησις Χριστῷ πρὸς Βελίαρ", τοῦ δὲ Σολομῶντος ὅτι ἀδύνατον ἂν εἴη κἂν μέχρι πρὸς ἐννοίας εὑρεθῆναι ὁδοὺς ὄφεως ἐπὶ πέτρας, ἥτις κατὰ Παῦλόν ἐστιν ὁ Χριστός; οἱ δὲ κτίσματα αὐτοῦ τυγχάνοντες, ἄνθρωποί τε καὶ ἄγγελοι, καὶ εὐλογίας εἰλήφασι προκόπτειν ἀρεταῖς ἀσκούμενοι καὶ νομίμοις ἐντολαῖς πρὸς τὸ μὴ ἁμαρτάνειν.

31. διὸ δὴ ὁ κύριος ἡμῶν, φύσει τοῦ πατρὸς υἱὸς τυγχάνων, ὑπὸ πάντων προσκυνεῖται· οἱ δὲ ἀποθέμενοι τὸ πνεῦμα τῆς δουλείας, ἐξ ἀνδραγαθημάτων καὶ προκοπῆς τὸ τῆς υἱοθεσίας λαβόντες πνεῦμα, διὰ τοῦ φύσει υἱοῦ εὐεργετούμενοι γίγνονται αὐτοὶ θέσει υἱοί.

32. Τὴν μὲν οὖν γνησίαν αὐτοῦ καὶ ἰδιότροπον καὶ φυσικὴν καὶ κατ' ἐξαίρετον υἱότητα ὁ Παῦλος οὕτως ἀπεφήνατο, περὶ θεοῦ εἰπών· "ὅς γε τοῦ ἰδίου υἱοῦ οὐκ ἐφείσατο, ἀλλ' ὑπὲρ ἡμῶν δηλονότι τῶν μὴ φύσει υἱῶν παρέδωκεν αὐτόν".

And is it not still more contrary to nature to suppose that wisdom can be susceptible of folly? that the power of God can be united with weakness? that reason itself can be dimmed by unreasonableness, or that darkness can be mixed with the true light? Does not the Apostle say, 'What communion hath light with darkness? and what concord hath Christ with Belial?'[156] and Solomon, that 'the way of a serpent upon a rock' was 'too wonderful' for the human mind to comprehend,[157] which 'rock,' according to St. Paul is Christ.[158] Men and angels, however, who are His creatures, have received His blessing, enabling them to exercise themselves in virtue and in obedience to His commands, that thus they may avoid sin.

31. And it is on this account that our Lord being by nature the Son of the Father, is worshipped by all; and they who have put off the spirit of bondage, and by brave deeds and advance in virtue have received the spirit of adoption[159] through the kindness of Him Who is the Son of God by nature, by adoption also become sons.

32. His true, peculiar, natural, and special Sonship was declared by Paul, who, speaking of God, says, that 'He spared not His own Son, but delivered Him up for us,' who are not by nature His sons.[160]

---

[156] *2 Cor.* 6:14-15.

[157] Cf. *Prov.* 30:19.

[158] Cf. *1 Cor.* 10:4.

[159] Cf. *Rom.* 8:15.

[160] *Rom.* 8:32.

33. πρὸς γὰρ ἀντιδιαστολὴν τῶν οὐκ ἰδίων αὐτὸν ἴδιον υἱὸν ἔφησεν εἶναι. ἐν δὲ τῷ Εὐαγγελίῳ· "οὗτός ἐστιν ὁ υἱός μου ὁ ἀγαπητός, ἐν ᾧ εὐδόκησα". ἐν δὲ Ψαλμοῖς ὁ σωτὴρ φησιν· "κύριος εἶπε πρός με· υἱός μου εἶ σύ". γνησιότητα ἐμφανίζων σημαίνει μὴ εἶναι αὐτοῦ γνησίους υἱοὺς ἄλλους τινὰς παρ' αὐτόν.

34. τί δὲ καὶ τὸ "ἐκ γαστρὸς πρὸ ἑωσφόρου ἐγέννησά σε"; οὐχὶ ἄντικρυς τῆς πατρικῆς μαιώσεως φυσικὴν ἐνδείκνυται υἱότητα, οὐ τρόπων ἐπιμελείᾳ καὶ προκοπῆς ἀσκήσει, ἀλλὰ φύσεως ἰδιώματι ταύτην λαχόντος; ὅθεν καὶ ἀμετάπτωτον ἔχει τὴν υἱότητα ὁ μονογενὴς υἱὸς τοῦ πατρός. τὴν δὲ τῶν λογικῶν υἱοθεσίαν, οὐ κατὰ φύσιν αὐτοῖς ὑπάρχουσαν ἀλλὰ τρόπων ἐπιτηδειότητι καὶ δωρεᾷ θεοῦ, καὶ μεταπτωτὴν οἶδεν ὁ λόγος· "ἰδόντες γὰρ οἱ υἱοὶ τοῦ θεοῦ τὰς θυγατέρας τῶν ἀνθρώπων ἔλαβον ἑαυτοῖς γυναῖκας" καὶ τὰ ἑξῆς·

35. καὶ "υἱοὺς ἐγέννησα καὶ ὕψωσα, αὐτοὶ δέ με ἠθέτησαν" διὰ Ἡσαΐου εἰρηκέναι τὸν θεὸν ἐδιδάχθημεν. Πολλὰ λέγειν ἔχων, ἀγαπητοί, παρέρχομαι, φορτικὸν εἶναι νομίσας διὰ πλειόνων διδασκάλους ὁμόφρονας ὑπομιμνήσκειν.

33. It was to distinguish Him from those who are not 'His own,' that he called Him 'His own son.' It is also written in the Gospel, 'This is My beloved Son in whom I am well pleased;'[161] and in the Psalms the Saviour says, 'The Lord said unto Me, Thou art My Son.'[162] By proclaiming natural sonship He shows that there are no other natural sons besides Himself.

34. And do not these words, I begot thee 'from the womb before the morning,'[163] plainly show the natural sonship of the paternal birth of One whose lot it is, not from diligence of conduct, or exercise in moral progress, but by individuality of nature? Hence it ensues that the filiation of the only-begotten Son of the Father is incapable of fall; while the adoption of reasonable beings who are not His sons by nature, but merely on account of fitness of character, and by the bounty of God, may fall away, as it is written in the word, 'The sons of God saw the daughters of men, and took them as wives,'[164] and so forth.

35. And God, speaking by Isaiah, said, 'I have nourished and brought up children, and they have rebelled against Me.'[165] I have many things to say, beloved, but because I fear that I shall cause weariness by further admonishing teachers who are of one mind with myself, I pass them by.

[161] *Mt.* 3:17; 12:18; 17:5. Cf. Is 42:1.

[162] *Ps.* 2:7.

[163] *Ps.* 110 (109):3.

[164] *Gen.* 6:2.4.

[165] *Is.* 1:2.

αὐτοὶ γὰρ ὑμεῖς θεοδίδακτοί ἐστε, οὐκ ἀγνοοῦντες ὅτι ἡ ἔναγχος ἐπαναστᾶσα τῇ ἐκκλησιαστικῇ εὐσεβείᾳ διδασκαλία Ἐβίωνός ἐστι καὶ Ἀρτεμᾶ, καὶ ζῆλος τοῦ κατὰ Ἀντιόχειαν Παύλου τοῦ Σαμοσατέως, συνόδῳ καὶ κρίσει τῶν ἁπανταχοῦ ἐπισκόπων ἀποκηρυχθέντος τῆς ἐκκλησίας.

You, having been taught of God,[166] are not ignorant that the teaching at variance with the religion of the Church which has just arisen, is the same as that propagated by Ebion and Artemas, and rivals that of Paul of Samosata, bishop of Antioch, who was excommunicated by a council of all the bishops.

Alexander makes his address to the readers in plural, which also marks it as a circular letter. The juxtaposition of Arius' position and the views of the various proponents of heterodox teachings are only partly true. Ebion had never existed, unlike the Ebionites (the poor), a Judeo-Christian movement in whose views Christ was only a man. They endeavoured to live by the precepts of the Jewish law, simultaneously acknowledging the Gospel of Matthew.[167] Artemas is mentioned solely by Eusebius of Caesarea.[168] According to Eusebius, Artemas asserted that Christ was just a man; his views would be later developed further by Paul of Samosata. Eusebius also provides some information about Paul.[169] Several synods took place to discuss his activity and teachings, notably the emphasis on Christ's humanity and His adoption by the Father (on Paul of Samosata, see above: the commentary on Arius' *Letter to Eusebius of Nicomedia*, and esp. the commentary on canon 19 of the Council below).

36. ὃν διαδεξάμενος Λουκιανὸς ἀποσυνάγωγος ἔμεινε τριῶν ἐπισκόπων πολυετεῖς χρόνους. ὧν τῆς ἀσεβείας τὴν τρύγα ἐρροφηκότες νῦν ἡμῖν οἱ ἐξ οὐκ ὄντων ἐπεφύησαν, τὰ ἐκείνων κεκρυμμένα μοσχεύματα, Ἄρειός τε καὶ Ἀχιλλᾶς καὶ ἡ τῶν σὺν αὐτοῖς πονηρευομένων σύνοδος.

36. Lucianus, his successor, withdrew himself from communion with these bishops during a period of many years. And now amongst us there have sprung up, 'out of the non-existent' men who have greedily sucked down the dregs of this impiety, offsets of the same stock: I mean Arius and Achillas, and all their gang of rogues.

[166] Cf. *1 Thess.* 4:9.

[167] Cf. A.F.J. Klijn, the entry "Ebioniti" in: NDPAC; the following sources are indicated: Tertullian, *De carne Christi* 14, *De praescriptione haereticorum* 4, 8; Irenaeus, *Adversus haereses* I, 26, 2; Origenes, *De principiis* IV, 3, 5; 3, 8; *CIo.* II, 12; *CMtSer.* 79.

[168] Eusebius of Caesarea, *h.e.* V, 28, 1.

[169] Eusebius of Caesarea, *h.e.* VII, 29-30.

37. καὶ οὐκ οἶδ' ὅπως ἐν Συρίᾳ χειροτονηθέντες ἐπίσκοποι τρεῖς, διὰ τὸ συναινεῖν αὐτοῖς, ἐπὶ τὸ χεῖρον ὑπεκκαίουσι, περὶ ὧν ἡ κρίσις ἀνακείσθω τῇ ὑμετέρᾳ δοκιμασίᾳ· οἳ τὰς μὲν τοῦ σωτηρίου πάθους ταπεινώσεώς τε καὶ κενώσεως καὶ τῆς καλουμένης αὐτοῦ πτωχείας καὶ ὧν ἐπικτήτους ὁ σωτὴρ δι' ἡμᾶς ἀνεδέξατο φωνὰς διὰ μνήμης ἔχοντες, παρατίθενται ἐπὶ παραγραφῇ τῆς ἀνωτάτω καὶ ἀρχῆθεν αὐτοῦ θεότητος, τῶν δὲ τῆς φυσικῆς αὐτοῦ δόξης τε καὶ εὐγενείας καὶ παρὰ τῷ πατρὶ μονῆς σημαντικῶν λόγων ἐπιλήσμονες γεγόνασιν· οἷόν ἐστι τὸ "ἐγὼ καὶ ὁ πατὴρ ἕν ἐσμεν".

37. Three bishops of Syria, appointed no one knows how, by consenting to them, fire them to more fatal heat. I refer their sentence to your decision. Retaining in their memory all that they can collect concerning the suffering, humiliation, emptying of Himself, and so-called poverty, and everything of which the Saviour for our sake accepted the acquired name, they bring forward those passages to disprove His eternal existence and divinity, while they forget all those which declare His glory and nobility and abiding with the Father; as for instance, 'I and My father are one.'[170]

The information referring to Lucian is indeed very enigmatic. It is astonishing how many substantial biographical entries can be found in various encyclopaedias, in spite of the actual scarcity of the source-based evidence. Eusebius delivers a very nice testimony of Lucian:

"(2.) Among the martyrs at Antioch was Lucian, a presbyter of that parish, whose entire life was most excellent. At Nicomedia, in the presence of the emperor, he proclaimed the heavenly kingdom of Christ, first in an oral defense, and afterwards by deeds as well."[171]

And further on:

"And Lucian, a presbyter of the parish at Antioch, and a most excellent man in every respect, temperate in life and famed for his learning in sacred things, was brought to the city of Nicomedia, where at that time the emperor happened to be staying, and after delivering before the ruler an apology for the doctrine which he professed, was committed to prison and put to death."[172]

Eusebius reports that Maximinus Daia had been emperor (as part of the tetrarchy system) at that time. He was to rule over a steadily dwindling territory until as late as 313, when he was finally defeated by Licinius.

[170] Io. 10:30.

[171] Eusebius of Caesarea, h.e. VIII, 13, 2 (NPNF 2,1).

[172] Eusebius of Caesarea, h.e. IX, 6, 3 (NPNF 2,1).

More favourable information can be found in Jerome, who adds that Lucian studied the Scripture very thoroughly, amended the editions, and also wrote *On Faith* and various brief epistles.[173] Besides, we know from Arius' letter to Eusebius (cf. above) that the addressee is called "fellow-Lucianist," which is not clear, yet "everybody" knows that it is supposed to mean that both Arius and Eusebius were disciples of Lucian's school. It is said, in Alexander's letter, that he was Paul's successor and "withdrew himself from communion" with three bishops. However, it would be difficult to say anything certain about his succession. It is likewise difficult to see how he could have been an intermediate between Paul and Arius. The teachings of the two heresiarchs are very different, although there are certain similarities in how their views are formulated, for instance, as regards the Son, that "there was a time when He was not." Paul referred it to the moment of the Son's birth from the Virgin Mary, whereas Arius to His generation at the beginning of time. Lucian may have possibly over-emphasized speaking of Christ's humanity, to the detriment of His divinity, yet no further details are available.

Unfortunately, there is no information on the identity of the three bishops consecrated in Syria.

38. ὅπερ φησὶν ὁ κύριος, οὐ πατέρα ἑαυτὸν ἀναγορεύων οὐδὲ τὰς τῇ ὑποστάσει δύο φύσεις μίαν εἶναι σαφηνίζων, ἀλλ' ὅτι τὴν πατρικὴν ἐμφέρειαν ἀκριβῶς πέφυκε σώζειν ὁ υἱὸς τοῦ πατρός, τὴν κατὰ πάντα ὁμοιότητα αὐτοῦ ἐκ φύσεως ἀπομαξάμενος καὶ ἀπαράλλακτος εἰκὼν τοῦ πατρὸς τυγχάνων καὶ τοῦ πρωτοτύπου ἔκτυπος χαρακτήρ.

39. Ὅθεν καὶ τῷ τηνικαῦτα ποθοῦντι ἰδεῖν Φιλίππῳ ἀφθόνως ὁ κύριος ἐμφανίζει, πρὸς ὃν λέγοντα "δεῖξον ἡμῖν τὸν πατέρα" λέγει· "ὁ ἑωρακὼς ἐμὲ ἑώρακε τὸν πατέρα", ὥσπερ δι' ἐσόπτρου ἀκηλιδώτου καὶ ἐμψύχου θείας εἰκόνος αὐτοῦ θεωρουμένου τοῦ πατρός.

38. In these words the Lord does not proclaim Himself to be the Father, neither does He represent two natures as one; but that the essence of the Son of the Father preserves accurately the likeness of the Father, His nature taking off the impress of likeness to Him in all things, being the exact image of the Father and the express stamp of the prototype.

39. When, therefore, Philip, desirous of seeing the Father, said to Him, 'Lord, show us the Father,' the Lord with abundant plainness said to him, 'He that hath seen Me hath seen the Father,'[174] as though the Father were beheld in the spotless and living mirror of His image.

---

[173] Jerome, *vir. ill.* 77.

[174] *Io.* 14:8-9.

Let us note the phrase "neither does He represent two natures as one." In this context, it is therefore evident that Alexander refers to the two natures of the Father and the Son (cf. the commentary on item 45 below).

40. ὧν ὅμοιον ἐν Ψαλμοῖς οἱ ἁγιώτατοί φασιν· "ἐν τῷ φωτί σου ὀψόμεθα φῶς". διὸ δὴ καὶ ὁ τιμῶν τὸν υἱὸν τιμᾷ τὸν πατέρα, καὶ εἰκότως· πᾶσα γὰρ ἀσεβὴς φωνὴ εἰς τὸν υἱὸν λέγεσθαι τολμωμένη εἰς τὸν πατέρα τὴν ἀναφορὰν ἔχει. Καὶ τί λοιπὸν ἔτι θαυμαστὸν ὃ μέλλω γράφειν, ἀγαπητοί, εἰ τὰς κατ' ἐμοῦ ψευδεῖς διαβολὰς καὶ τοῦ εὐσεβεστάτου ἡμῶν λαοῦ ἐκθήσομαι;

40. The same idea is conveyed in the Psalms, where the saints say, 'In Thy light we shall see light.'[175] It is on this account that 'he who honoureth the Son, honoureth the Father.'[176] And rightly, for every impious word which men dare to utter against the Son is spoken also against the Father. After this no one can wonder at the false calumnies which I am about to detail, my beloved brethren, propagated by them against me, and against our most religious people.

41. οἱ γὰρ κατὰ τῆς θεότητος τοῦ υἱοῦ τοῦ θεοῦ παραταξάμενοι οὐδὲ τὰς καθ' ἡμῶν ἀχαρίστους παροινίας παραιτοῦνται λέγειν· οἵ γε οὐδὲ τῶν ἀρχαίων τινὰς συγκρίνειν ἑαυτοῖς ἀξιοῦσιν οὐδὲ οἷς ἡμεῖς ἐκ παίδων ὡμιλήσαμεν διδασκάλοις ἐξισοῦσθαι ἀνέχονται, ἀλλ' οὐδὲ τῶν νῦν πανταχοῦ συλλειτουργῶν τινα εἰς μέτρον σοφίας ἡγοῦνται, μόνοι σοφοὶ καὶ ἀκτήμονες καὶ δογμάτων εὑρεταὶ λέγοντες εἶναι, καὶ αὐτοῖς ἀποκεκαλύφθαι μόνοις ἅπερ οὐδενὶ τῶν ὑπὸ τὸν ἥλιον ἑτέρῳ πέφυκεν ἐλθεῖν εἰς ἔννοιαν.

41. They not only set their battle in array against the divinity of Christ, but ungratefully insult us. They think it beneath them to be compared with any of those of old time, nor do they endure to be put on a par with the teachers we have been conversant with from childhood. They will not admit that any of our fellow-ministers anywhere possess even mediocrity of intelligence. They say that they themselves alone are the wise and the poor, and discoverers of doctrines, and to them alone have been revealed those truths which, say they, have never entered the mind of any other individuals under the sun.

42. ὦ ἀνοσίου τύφου καὶ ἀμέτρου μανίας καὶ μελαγχολικῆς ἡρμοσμένης δόξης κενῆς καὶ σατανικοῦ φρονήματος εἰς τὰς ἀνοσίους αὐτῶν ψυχὰς ἀποσκιρώσαντος.

42. O what wicked arrogance! O what excessive folly! What false boasting, joined with madness and Satanic pride, has hardened their impious hearts!

[175] *Ps.* 36 (35):10.

[176] Cf. *Io.* 5:23.

43. οὐ κατήδεσεν αὐτοὺς ἡ τῶν ἀρχαίων γραφῶν φιλόθεος σαφήνεια, οὐδὲ ἡ τῶν συλλειτουργῶν σύμφωνος περὶ Χριστοῦ εὐλάβεια τὴν κατ᾽ αὐτοῦ θρασύτητα αὐτῶν ἡμαύρωσεν. ὧν οὐδὲ τὰ δαιμόνια τῆς ἀνοσιουργίας ἀνέξεται, φωνὴν βλάσφημον κατὰ τοῦ υἱοῦ τοῦ θεοῦ εἰπεῖν φυλαττόμενα. Ταῦτα μὲν οὖν ἡμῖν κατὰ τὴν παροῦσαν δύναμιν ἐπηπορήσθω πρὸς τοὺς ἀπαιδεύτῳ ὕλῃ κατὰ τοῦ Χριστοῦ κονισαμένους καὶ τὴν εἰς αὐτὸν εὐσέβειαν ἡμῶν συκοφαντεῖν προθεμένους.

43. They are not ashamed to oppose the godly clearness of the ancient scriptures, nor yet does the unanimous piety of all our fellow-ministers concerning Christ blunt their audacity. Even devils will not suffer impiety like this; for even they refrain from speaking blasphemy against the Son of God. These then are the questions I have to raise, according to the ability I possess, with those who from their rude resources throw dust on the Christ, and try to slander our reverence for Him.

Introducing novelties was an argument used in this type of rhetoric. Representing heresy as views contradicting the tradition of the old Church Fathers would go on to develop further in the course of the Christological disputes of the fifth century; it can be seen as early as in Tertullian's *Prescription Against Heretics*. Ancient writings most likely refer to the Holy Scripture. The ancient Church compiled and used the so-called *testimonia*, i.e., anthologies of citations relating to various important themes, for instance, excerpts from the Prophets concerned with the divinity of Christ. An extant example of such a collation is *Testimonium ad Quirinum* by Cyprian of Carthage, especially II, 6.

44. φασὶ γὰρ ἡμᾶς οἱ φληνάφων ἐφευρεταὶ μύθων, ἀποστρεφομένους τὴν ἐξ οὐκ ὄντων ἀσεβῆ καὶ ἄγραφον κατὰ Χριστοῦ βλασφημίαν, ἀγέννητα διδάσκειν δύο, δυοῖν θάτερον δεῖν εἶναι λέγοντες οἱ ἀπαίδευτοι, ἢ ἐξ οὐκ ὄντων αὐτὸν εἶναι φρονεῖν, ἢ πάντως ἀγέννητα λέγειν δύο· ἀγνοοῦντες οἱ ἀνάσκητοι ὡς μακρὸν ἂν εἴη μεταξὺ πατρὸς ἀγεννήτου καὶ τῶν κτισθέντων ὑπ᾽ αὐτοῦ ἐξ οὐκ ὄντων, λογικῶν τε καὶ ἀλόγων.

44. These inventors of silly tales assert that we, who reject their impious and unscriptural blasphemy concerning the creation of Christ from the non-existent, teach that there are two unbegotten Beings. For these ill-instructed men contend that one of these alternatives must hold; either He must be believed to have come out of the non-existent, or there are two unbegotten Beings. In their ignorance and want of practice in theology they do not realize how vast must be the distance between the Father who is uncreate, and the creatures, whether rational or irrational, which He created out of the non-existent;

45. ὧν μεσιτεύουσα φύσις μονογενής, δι' ἧς τὰ ὅλα ἐξ οὐκ ὄντων ἐποίησεν ὁ πατὴρ τοῦ θεοῦ λόγου, ἐξ αὐτοῦ τοῦ ὄντος πατρὸς γεγέννηται· ὡς καὶ αὐτός που διεμαρτύρατο λέγων ὁ κύριος· "ὁ ἀγαπῶν τὸν πατέρα ἀγαπᾷ καὶ τὸν υἱὸν τὸν ἐξ αὐτοῦ γεγεννημένον".

45. and that the only-begotten nature of Him Who is the Word of God, by Whom the Father created the universe out of the non-existent, standing, as it were, in the middle between the two, was begotten of the self-existent Father, as the Lord Himself testified when He said, 'Every one that loveth the Father, loveth also the Son that is begotten of Him.'[177]

Arius' conception of the Father's unbegotten existence and the Son's creation appeared in his letter to Alexander. In his view, begetting was synonymous with creating and therefore he was not able to conceive of anything but the unbegotten God and the created beings. Alexander speaks of the intermediate only-begotten nature and, on this occasion, also explains his idea of what nature means (item 36). It is clearly not what *ousia* comes to signify in the later sense, i.e., what is common to the Father, the Son, and the Holy Spirit. Previously, we were concerned with the two natures, of the Father and the Son, whereas we are now faced with three, characterized as follows: unbegotten/uncreated = Father (1), begotten/uncreated = Son (2), created = the universe (3). The Holy Spirit was not mentioned in the dispute.

46. Περὶ ὧν ἡμεῖς οὕτως πιστεύομεν, ὡς τῇ ἀποστολικῇ ἐκκλησίᾳ δοκεῖ· εἰς μόνον ἀγέννητον πατέρα, οὐδένα τοῦ εἶναι αὐτῷ τὸν αἴτιον ἔχοντα, ἄτρεπτόν τε καὶ ἀναλλοίωτον, ἀεὶ κατὰ τὰ αὐτὰ καὶ ὡσαύτως ἔχοντα, οὔτε προκοπὴν οὔτε μείωσιν ἐπιδεχόμενον, νόμου καὶ προφητῶν καὶ εὐαγγελίων δοτῆρα, πατριαρχῶν καὶ ἀποστόλων καὶ ἁπάντων ἁγίων κύριον· καὶ εἰς ἕνα κύριον Ἰησοῦν Χριστόν, τὸν υἱὸν τοῦ θεοῦ μονογενῆ, γεννηθέντα οὐκ ἐκ τοῦ μὴ ὄντος ἀλλ' ἐκ τοῦ ὄντος πατρός, οὐ κατὰ τὰς τῶν σωμάτων ὁμοιότητας ταῖς τομαῖς ἢ ταῖς ἐκ διαιρέσεων ἀπορροίαις, ὥσπερ Σαβελλίῳ καὶ Βαλεντίνῳ δοκεῖ,

46. We believe, as is taught by the apostolical Church, in an only unbegotten Father, Who of His being hath no cause, immutable and invariable, and Who subsists always in one state of being, admitting neither of progression nor of diminution; Who gave the law, and the prophets, and the gospel; of patriarchs and apostles, and of all saints, Lord. And in one Lord Jesus Christ, the only-begotten Son of God, begotten not out of that which is not, but of the Father, Who is; yet not after the manner of material bodies, by severance or emanation, as Sabellius and Valentinus taught;

[177] *1 Io.* 5:1.

ἀλλ' ἀρρήτως καὶ ἀνεκδιηγήτως, κατὰ τὸν εἰπόντα, ὡς ἀνωτέρω παρεθήκαμεν· "τὴν γενεὰν αὐτοῦ τίς διηγήσεται"; τῆς ὑποστάσεως αὐτοῦ πάσῃ τῇ γενητῇ φύσει ἀπεριεργάστου τυγχανούσης, καθὼς καὶ αὐτὸς ὁ πατὴρ ἀπεριέργαστός ἐστι, διὰ τὸ μὴ χωρεῖν τὴν τῶν λογικῶν φύσιν τῆς πατρικῆς θεογονίας τὴν εἴδησιν.

but in an inexpressible and inexplicable manner, according to the saying which we quoted above, 'Who shall declare His generation?'[178] since no mortal intellect can comprehend the nature of His Person, as the Father Himself cannot be comprehended, because the nature of reasonable beings is unable to grasp the manner in which He was begotten of the Father.

The features by which God the Father is described herein, or His nature, as it may be said in view of the above assertion, are those of the ideal unchanging substance derived from Plato's philosophy. This is how it is depicted by Origen, as neither decreasing nor increasing, and not subject to change. He described it while commenting on the "supersubstantial bread" from Lord's Prayer:

Ousia, properly understood (κυρίως οὐσία) is regarded as incorporeal by the philosophers who insist that the pre-eminent reality is incorporeal (τῶν ἀσωμάτων ὑπόστασιν εἶναι). It has, then, for them an unchanging existence which admits neither increase nor decrease. To admit either increase or decrease is the property of corporeal things which, because they are subject to change, need something to sustain and nourish them. If within a given time they acquire more than they lose, they increase; if less, they decrease. Again, it may happen that they receive nothing from outside, in which case they are, so to speak, in a state of pure decrease.[179]

In his letter to Alexander, Arius distanced himself from Sabellius and Valentinian.

47. ἅπερ οὐ παρ' ἐμοῦ δεῖ μαθεῖν ἄνδρας τῷ τῆς ἀληθείας πνεύματι κινουμένους, ὑπηχούσης ἡμᾶς καὶ τῆς φθασάσης Χριστοῦ περὶ τούτου φωνῆς καὶ διδασκούσης· "οὐδεὶς οἶδε τίς ἐστιν ὁ πατήρ, εἰ μὴ ὁ υἱός· καὶ οὐδεὶς οἶδε τίς ἐστιν ὁ υἱός, εἰ μὴ ὁ πατήρ".

47. But those who are led by the Spirit of truth have no need to learn these things of me, for the words long since spoken by the Saviour yet sound in our ears, 'No one knoweth who the Father is but the Son, and no one knoweth who the Son is but the Father.'[180]

---

[178] Is. 53:8.

[179] Origenes, De oratione 27, 8 (in: Ancient Christian Writers, Newmann Press, New York 1954, vol. 19) ; cf. H. Pietras, Pojęcie Bożej substancji absolutnej u Orygenesa – próba ujęcia, Zeszyty Naukowe UJ MCCXLVI, Studia Religiologica 33 (2000), 127-140.

[180] Mt. 11:27.

ἄτρεπτον τοῦτον καὶ ἀναλλοίωτον ὡς τὸν πατέρα, ἀπροσδεῆ καὶ τέλειον υἱόν, ἐμφερῆ τῷ πατρὶ μεμαθήκαμεν, μόνῳ τῷ ἀγεννήτῳ λειπόμενον ἐκείνου. 48. εἰκὼν γάρ ἐστιν ἀπηκριβωμένη καὶ ἀπαράλλακτος τοῦ πατρός. πάντων γὰρ εἶναι τὴν εἰκόνα πλήρη δι᾽ ὧν ἡ μείζων ἐμφέρεια, δῆλον, ὡς αὐτὸς ἐπαίδευσεν ὁ κύριος "ὁ πατήρ μου" λέγων "μείζων μού ἐστι". καὶ κατὰ τοῦτο καὶ τὸ ἀεὶ εἶναι τὸν υἱὸν ἐκ τοῦ πατρὸς πιστεύομεν· ἀπαύγασμα γάρ ἐστι τῆς δόξης καὶ χαρακτὴρ τῆς πατρικῆς ὑποστάσεως. ἀλλὰ μή τις τὸ ἀεὶ πρὸς ὑπόνοιαν ἀγεννήτου λαμβανέτω, ὡς οἴονται οἱ τὰ τῆς ψυχῆς αἰσθητήρια πεπωρωμένοι·

49. οὔτε γὰρ τὸ ἦν, οὔτε τὸ ἀεί, οὔτε τὸ πρὸ αἰώνων ταὐτόν ἐστι τῷ ἀγεννήτῳ. ἀλλ᾽ οὐδ᾽, ὁτιοῦν ἀνθρώπων ἔννοια ὀνοματοποιῆσαι σπουδάσει, δηλοῖ τὸ ἀγέννητον ὡς καὶ ὑμᾶς οὕτως ἐκδέχεσθαι πιστεύω καὶ τεθάρρηκα τῇ περὶ πάντων ὑμῶν ὀρθῇ προθέσει, κατὰ μηδένα τρόπον τούτων τῶν ὀνομάτων τὸ ἀγέννητον δηλούντων.

50. ἔοικε γὰρ οἱονεὶ χρόνων εἶναι παρέκτασις ταῦτα τὰ ὀνόματα, τὴν μέντοι κατ᾽ ἀξίαν τοῦ μονογενοῦς θεότητα καὶ οἷον ἀρχαιότητα σημαίνειν μὴ δυναμένων, τῶν δὲ ἁγίων ἀνδρῶν ὡς δύναμις ἑκάστῳ ἐμφανίσαι τὸ μυστήριον βιαζομένων καὶ συγγνώμην αἰτούντων παρὰ τῶν ἀκροατῶν δι᾽ εὐλόγου ἀπολογίας διὰ τοῦ λέγειν· εἰς ἃ ἐφθάσαμεν.

We have learnt that the Son is immutable and unchangeable, all-sufficient and perfect, like the Father, lacking only His "unbegotten."

48. He is the exact and precisely similar image of His Father. For it is clear that the image fully contains everything by which the greater likeness exists, as the Lord taught us when He said, 'My Father is greater than I.'[181] And in accordance with this we believe that the Son always existed of the Father; for he is the brightness of His glory, and the express image of His Father's Person."[182] But let no one be led by the word 'always' to imagine that the Son is unbegotten, as is thought by some who have their intellects blinded:

49. for to say that He was, that He has always been, and that before all ages, is not to say that He is unbegotten. The mind of man could not possibly invent a term expressive of what is meant by being unbegotten. I believe that you are of this opinion; and, indeed, I feel confident in your orthodox view that none of these terms in any way signify the unbegotten.

50. For all the terms appear to signify merely the extension of time, and are not adequate to express the divinity and, as it were, the primæval being of the only-begotten Son. They were used by the holy men who earnestly endeavoured to clear up the mystery, and who asked pardon from those who heard them, with a reasonable excuse for their failure, by saying 'as far as our comprehension has reached.'[183]

---

[181] *Io.* 14:28.

[182] Cf. *Hbr. 1:3.*

[183] *Phil.* 3:16.

Let us notice Alexander's caution here: he realizes that his opponents invariably tend to associate the word "always" with the Father's unbegotten eternity, while attributing the temporal origin to the Son. The author of the letter is right in saying that the terms routinely used to denote eternity do not really indicate eternity but the extension of time that is "not adequate to express the divinity."

51. εἰ δέ τι παρὰ τὸ ἀνθρώπινον διὰ χειλέων φθέγμα μεῖζόν τι προσδοκῶσιν οἱ ἄνδρες, τὰ ἐκ μέρους αὐτοῖς γνωσθέντα καταργεῖσθαι λέγοντες, δῆλον ὅτι πολὺ τοῦ ἐλπιζομένου λείπεται τὸ ἦν καὶ τὸ ἀεὶ καὶ τὸ πρὸ αἰώνων· ὅπερ δ' ἂν ᾖ, οὐκ ἔστι ταὐτὸν τῷ ἀγεννήτῳ.

52. οὐκοῦν τῷ μὲν ἀγεννήτῳ πατρὶ οἰκεῖον ἀξίωμα φυλακτέον, μηδένα τοῦ εἶναι αὐτῷ τὸν αἴτιον λέγοντας· τῷ δὲ υἱῷ τὴν ἁρμόζουσαν τιμὴν ἀπονεμητέον, τὴν ἄναρχον αὐτῷ παρὰ τοῦ πατρὸς γέννησιν ἀνατιθέντας· καὶ ὡς ἐφθάσαμεν αὐτῷ σέβας ἀπονέμοντες, μόνον εὐσεβῶς καὶ εὐφήμως τὸ ἦν καὶ τὸ ἀεὶ καὶ τὸ πρὸ αἰώνων λέγοντες ἐπ' αὐτοῦ, τὴν μέντοι θεότητα αὐτοῦ μὴ παραιτούμενοι, ἀλλὰ τῇ εἰκόνι καὶ τῷ χαρακτῆρι τοῦ πατρὸς ἀπηκριβωμένην ἐμφέρειαν κατὰ πάντα ἀνατιθέντες, τὸ δὲ ἀγέννητον τῷ πατρὶ μόνον ἰδίωμα παρεῖναι δοξάζοντες, ἅτε δὴ καὶ αὐτοῦ φάσκοντος τοῦ σωτῆρος· "ὁ πατήρ μου μείζων μού ἐστι".

53. Πρὸς δὲ τῇ εὐσεβεῖ ταύτῃ περὶ πατρὸς καὶ υἱοῦ δόξῃ, καθὼς ἡμᾶς αἱ θεῖαι γραφαὶ διδάσκουσιν, ἓν πνεῦμα ἅγιον ὁμολογοῦμεν, τὸ καινίσαν τούς τε τῆς παλαιᾶς διαθήκης ἁγίους ἀνθρώπους καὶ τοὺς τῆς χρηματιζούσης καινῆς παιδευτὰς θείους·

51. But if those who allege that what was 'known in part' has been 'done away' for them, expect from human lips anything beyond human powers, it is plain that the terms 'was,' and 'ever,' and 'before all ages,' fall far short of this expectation. But whatever they may mean, it is not the same as 'the unbegotten.'

52. Therefore His own individual dignity must be reserved to the Father as the Unbegotten One, no one being called the cause of His existence: to the Son likewise must be given the honour which befits Him, there being to Him a generation from the Father which has no beginning; we must render Him worship, as we have already said, only piously and religiously ascribing to Him the 'was' and the 'ever,' and the 'before all ages;' not however rejecting His divinity, but ascribing to Him a perfect likeness in all things to His Father, while at the same time we ascribe to the Father alone His own proper glory of 'the unbegotten,' even as the Saviour Himself says, 'My Father is greater than I.'[184]

53. And in addition to this pious belief respecting the Father and the Son, we confess as the Sacred Scriptures teach us, one Holy Ghost, who moved the saints of the Old Testament, and the divine teachers of that which is called the New.

---

[184] *Io.* 14:28.

μίαν καὶ μόνην καθολικὴν τὴν ἀποστολικὴν ἐκκλησίαν, ἀκαθαίρετον μὲν ἀεὶ κἂν πᾶς ὁ κόσμος αὐτῇ πολεμεῖν βουλεύηται, νικηφόρον δὲ πάσης τῆς τῶν ἑτεροδόξων ἀσεβεστάτης ἐπαναστάσεως, εὐθαρσεῖς ἡμᾶς κατασκευάζοντος τοῦ οἰκοδεσπότου αὐτῆς διὰ τοῦ βοᾶν· "θαρσεῖτε, ἐγὼ νενίκηκα τὸν κόσμον".

54. Μετὰ τοῦτον ἐκ νεκρῶν ἀνάστασιν οἴδαμεν, ἧς ἀπαρχὴ γέγονεν ὁ κύριος ἡμῶν Ἰησοῦς Χριστός, σῶμα φορέσας ἀληθῶς καὶ οὐ δοκήσει ἐκ τῆς θεοτόκου Μαρίας, ἐπὶ συντελείᾳ τῶν αἰώνων εἰς ἀθέτησιν ἁμαρτίας ἐπιδημήσας τῷ γένει τῶν ἀνθρώπων, σταυρωθεὶς καὶ ἀποθανών, ἀλλ' οὐ διὰ ταῦτα τῆς ἑαυτοῦ θεότητος ἥττων γεγενημένος, ἀναστὰς ἐκ νεκρῶν, ἀναληφθεὶς ἐν οὐρανοῖς, καθήμενος ἐν δεξιᾷ τῆς μεγαλωσύνης.

55. Ταῦτα ἐκ μέρους ἐνεχάραξα τῇ ἐπιστολῇ, τὸ καθ' ἕκαστον ἐπ' ἀκριβείας γράφειν φορτικόν, ὡς ἔφην, εἶναι νομίσας, διὰ τὸ μηδὲ τὴν ἱερὰν ὑμῶν ταῦτα λεληθέναι σπουδήν. ταῦτα διδάσκομεν, ταῦτα κηρύττομεν, ταῦτα τῆς ἐκκλησίας τὰ ἀποστολικὰ δόγματα, ὑπὲρ ὧν καὶ ἀποθνήσκομεν, τῶν ἐξόμνυσθαι αὐτὰ βιαζομένων ἧττον πεφροντικότες, εἰ καὶ διὰ βασάνων ἀναγκάζουσι, τὴν ἐν αὐτοῖς ἐλπίδα μὴ ἀποστρεφόμενοι.

56. ὧν ἐναντίοι γενόμενοι οἱ ἀμφὶ τὸν Ἄρειον καὶ Ἀχιλλᾶν καὶ οἱ τῆς ἀληθείας σὺν αὐτοῖς πολέμιοι ἀπεώσθησαν τῆς ἐκκλησίας, ἀλλότριοι γενόμενοι τῆς εὐσεβοῦς ἡμῶν διδασκαλίας,

We believe in one only Catholic Church, the apostolical, which cannot be destroyed even though all the world were to take counsel to fight against it, and which gains the victory over all the impious attacks of the heterodox; for we are emboldened by the words of its Master, 'Be of good cheer, I have overcome the world.'[185]

54. After this, we receive the doctrine of the resurrection from the dead, of which Jesus Christ our Lord became the first-fruits; Who bore a Body, in truth, not in semblance, derived from Mary the mother of God; in the fulness of time sojourning among the race, for the remission of sins:[186] who was crucified and died, yet for all this suffered no diminution of His Godhead. He rose from the dead, was taken into heaven, and sat down at the right hand of the Majesty on high.[187]

55. In this epistle I have only mentioned these things in part, deeming it, as I have said, wearisome to dwell minutely on each article, since they are well known to your pious diligence. These things we teach, these things we preach; these are the dogmas of the apostolic Church, for which we are ready to die, caring little for those who would force us to forswear them; for we will never relinquish our hope in them, though they should try to compel us by tortures.

56. Arius and Achillas, together with their fellow foes, have been expelled from the Church, because they have become aliens from our pious doctrine:

[185] *Io.* 16:33.

[186] Cf. *Hbr.* 9:26.

[187] Cf. *Hbr.* 1:3.

κατὰ τὸν μακάριον Παῦλον λέγοντα·
"εἴ τις ὑμᾶς εὐαγγελίζεται παρ'
ὃ παρελάβετε, ἀνάθεμα ἔστω"
κἂν ἄγγελος ἐξ οὐρανοῦ εἶναι
προσποιῆται,

57. ἀλλὰ καὶ "εἴ τις ἑτεροδιδασκαλεῖ
καὶ μὴ προσέρχεται τοῖς ὑγιαίνουσι
λόγοις τοῖς τοῦ κυρίου ἡμῶν Ἰησοῦ
Χριστοῦ καὶ τῇ κατ' εὐσέβειαν
διδασκαλίᾳ, τετύφωται, μηδὲν
ἐπιστάμενος" καὶ τὰ ἑξῆς. Τούτους
οὖν ἀναθεματισθέντας ἀπὸ τῆς
ἀδελφότητος μηδεὶς ὑμῶν δεχέσθω
μηδὲ ἀνεχέσθω τῶν λεγομένων ἢ
γραφομένων ὑπ' αὐτῶν· πάντα γὰρ
οἱ γόητες ψεύδονται, ἀλήθειαν οὐ μὴ
λαλήσουσιν.

58. περιέρχονται γὰρ τὰς πόλεις,
οὐδὲν ἕτερον σπουδάζοντες ἢ τῷ
τῆς φιλίας προσχήματι καὶ τῷ τῆς
εἰρήνης ὀνόματι δι' ὑποκρίσεως
καὶ κολακείας γράμματα διδόναι
καὶ λαμβάνειν, πρὸς τὸ πλανᾶν διὰ
τούτων τὰ ὑπ' αὐτῶν ἠπατημένα ὀλίγα
γυναικάρια σεσωρευμένα ἁμαρτίαις
καὶ τὰ ἑξῆς.
59. Τούτους οὖν τοὺς τὰ τοσαῦτα
κατὰ Χριστοῦ τολμήσαντας, τοὺς τὸν
χριστιανισμὸν τοῦτο μὲν δημοσίᾳ
διασύραντας, τοῦτο δὲ ἐπὶ δικαστηρίων
ἐπιδεικτιᾶν φιλοτιμουμένους,
τοὺς διωγμὸν ἡμῖν ἐν εἰρήνη τὸ
ὅσον ἐπ' αὐτοῖς ἐπεγείραντας,
τοὺς τὸ ἄρρητον μυστήριον τῆς
Χριστοῦ γεννήσεως ἐκνευρίσαντας,

according to the blessed Paul, who said, 'If any of you preach any other gospel than that which you have received, let him be accursed,[188] even though he should pretend to be an angel from heaven,'[189]

57. and 'But if any man teach otherwise, and consent not to wholesome words, even the words of our Lord Jesus Christ, and to the doctrine which is according to godliness, he is proud, knowing nothing,'[190] and so forth. Since, then, they have been condemned by the brotherhood, let none of you receive them, nor attend to what they say or write. They are deceivers, and propagate lies, and they never adhere to the truth.

58. They go about to different cities with no other intent than to deliver letters under the pretext of friendship and in the name of peace, and by hypocrisy and flattery to obtain other letters in return, in order to deceive a few 'silly women who are laden with sins.'[191]

59. I beseech you, beloved brethren, to avoid those who have thus dared to act against Christ, who have publicly held up the Christian religion to ridicule, and have eagerly sought to make a display before judicial tribunals, who have endeavoured to excite a persecution against us at a period of the most entire peace, and who have enervated the unspeakable mystery of the generation of Christ.

---

[188] *Gal.* 1:9.
[189] Cf. *Gal.* 1:8.
[190] *1 Tim.* 6:3-4.
[191] Cf. *2 Tim.* 3:6.

τούτους ἀποστρεφόμενοι, ἀγαπητοὶ καὶ ὁμόψυχοι ἀδελφοί, σύμψηφοι γένεσθε κατὰ τῆς μανιώδους αὐτῶν τόλμης, καθ' ὁμοιότητα τῶν ἀγανακτησάντων συλλειτουργῶν ἡμῶν καὶ ἐπιστειλάντων μοι κατ' αὐτῶν καὶ τῷ τόμῳ συνυπογραψάντων· ἃ καὶ διεπεμψάμην ὑμῖν διὰ τοῦ υἱοῦ μου Ἄπι τοῦ διακόνου, τοῦτο μὲν πάσης Αἰγύπτου καὶ Θηβαΐδος, τοῦτο δὲ Λιβύης τε καὶ Πενταπόλεως καὶ Συρίας καὶ ἔτι Λυκίας καὶ Παμφυλίας, Ἀσίας, Καππαδοκίας καὶ τῶν ἄλλων περιχώρων· ὧν καθ' ὁμοιότητα καὶ παρ' ὑμῶν δέξασθαι πέποιθα.

60. πολλῶν γάρ μοι βοηθημάτων πρὸς τοὺς βλαβέντας πεπορισμένων, καὶ τοῦτο εὕρηται λυσιφάρμακον τοῦ ὑπ' αὐτῶν ἀπατηθέντος λαοῦ, πειθομένων καὶ ταῖς τῶν συλλειτουργῶν ἡμῶν συγκαταθέσεσιν, εἰς μετάνοιαν διὰ τούτου ἔρχεσθαι σπουδαζόντων. ἀσπάσασθε ἀλλήλους σὺν τῇ παρ' ὑμῶν ἀδελφότητι. ἐρρῶσθαι ὑμᾶς ἐν κυρίῳ εὔχομαι, ἀγαπητοί· ὀναίμην ὑμῶν τῆς φιλοχρίστου ψυχῆς.

61. Εἰσὶ δὲ οἱ ἀναθεματισθέντες αἱρεσιῶται, ἀπὸ πρεσβυτέρων μὲν Ἄρειος, ἀπὸ διακόνων δὲ Ἀχιλλᾶς, Εὐζώϊος, Ἀειθαλής, Λούκιος, Σαρμάτης, Ἰούλιος, Μηνᾶς, Ἄρειος ἕτερος, Ἑλλάδιος".

Unite unanimously in opposition to them, as some of our fellow-ministers have already done, who, being filled with indignation, wrote to me against them, and signed our formulary. I have sent you these letters by my son Apion, the deacon; being those of (the ministers in) all Egypt and the Thebaid, also of those of Libya, and the Pentapolis, of Syria, Lycia, Pamphylia, Asia, Cappadocia, and in the other adjoining countries. Whose example you likewise, I trust, will follow.

60. Many kindly attempts have been made by me to gain back those who have been led astray, but no remedy has proved more efficacious in restoring the laity who have been deceived by them and leading them to repentance, than the manifestation of the union of our fellow-ministers. Salute one another, with the brotherhood that is with you. I pray that you may be strong in the Lord, my beloved, and that I may receive the fruit of your love to Christ.

61. The following are the names of those who have been anathematized as heretics: among the presbyters, Arius; among the deacons, Achillas, Euzoius, Aïthales, Lucius, Sarmates, Julius, Menas, another Arius, and Helladius.

Alexander's letter is most likely the most comprehensive exposition of the theology in defence of Christ's divinity against the teachings of Arius. The sheer volume and the scope of the epistle indicate that Alexander of Alexandria had been very much concerned with seeking supporters before a synodal debate which was likely to take place at Nicaea. His line of argumentation lacks the accuracy which would be attained only in the course of the years between the Council of Nicaea and the Emperor Theodosius' decree imposing the Nicene creed as obligatory. Still, the letter is a reflection of the contemporary state of the Trinitarian dispute.

III

CONSTANTINE'S LETTER TO ALEXANDER AND ARIUS

The only dated document from the early period of the Arian controversy is the Emperor Constantine's letter to Bishop Alexander of Alexandria and Arius.

It can be found in Eusebius of Caesarea's panegyrical biography of Constantine.[1] Excerpts of the letter were copied from there by Socrates Scholasticus and some other authors. It is important in understanding its contents and sense, since Eusebius, as it would later turn out, was inclined to adhere to Arius', rather than Alexander's, statements. In his account of Constantine's intervention, Socrates assumes his fifth-century perspective and gives almost full credence to Athanasius' late interpretation, which the latter set out to propagate about 25 years after the Council. Contrary to appearances, it is not entirely clear what the text aims to convey.

One can but speculate as to the circumstances connected with the composition of the letter. We know that Constantine had been involved in a civil war with Licinius, sometimes referred to as "crusade" owing to its religious dimension and implications: Constantine had given Christianity his support, while Licinius persecuted it.[2] The final and decisive battle took place at Chrysopolis on the Bosphorus on September 18, 324, after which Constantine captured the old Imperial palace at Nicomedia. Bishop Eusebius of Nicomedia, who was a friend of Constantia, the victorious emperor's half-sister and Licinius' wife, met with Constantine at the court. Supposedly, the whole thing was not to Eusebius' advantage, as he must have been distrustful of the friends of his enemies, even if they happened to be part of the family. Bishop Hosius of Cordoba, Constantine's friend and counsel in church matters, must have been somewhere not very far from there at that time or he may have accompanied Constantine on his arrival at Nicomedia. As the *Pontifex Maximus* responsible for all the religions of the Empire, the Emperor showed much interest in the affairs of the Church, e.g., summoning a number of synods to handle various church matters in

[1] In Eusebius of Caesarea, *v.C.* II, 64-72 (NPNF 2,1); (ed.) F. Winkelmann, GCS 7a, 74-79.

[2] Cf. CH. M. Odahl, *Constantine and the Christian Empire*, Ch. VII: "The Eastern Crusade and the Nicene Council."

the Western part of the Empire, formerly under Constantine's rule.[3] The controversy between Bishop Alexander and Arius, then a presbyter at Alexandria, was among the issues presented to the Emperor at Nicomedia.

Nonetheless, Constantine had to cope with some other problems concerning the Church. In 313, when he recognized Christianity as a legitimate religion in the Empire, he had no doubt that his official competence as *Pontifex Maximus* also extends to the Church. None of the bishops cast doubt on it, either. His jurisdiction over the Church remained unchallenged. At this point, let us recall that the Greek term *episkopos* ("bishop") denotes someone in supervision, in charge of something. This is the reason why Eusebius of Caesarea writes of Constantine as "general bishop."[4] His authority does not come from his being elected by bishops, either by vote or the laying of hands, as in the case of "ordinary" bishops, but from the very nature of things, the fact that he is the *imperator* and, as such, *Pontifex Maximus*. He is therefore in possession of the authority over worship, teaching, and governance.[5] Likewise, any decrees of individual bishops or synods can be valid for the Church throughout the Empire only when approved by the Emperor.[6] Eusebius commends Constantine for his conduct: despite his status as the actual superior of the bishops, he graciously regarded himself as one of them, even though he was in charge of summoning and presiding over their synodal proceedings.[7] Eusebius was not alone in expressing such favourable opinion. Several decades later in the Western Empire, Ambrosiaster wrote that the Emperor's authority over bishops resembled that of God the Father over Christ.[8] In consequence, the bishops ought to be obedient to the Emperor just as Christ had been to the Father.

Eusebius recounts the Emperor's Church-related concerns. In his *Vita Constantini* (II, 61f), he writes of the dispute between Alexander and Arius

[3] For instance, Council of Rome (313), SCL 1, 62; of Arles (314), SCL 1, 68ff. See S. Bralewski, *Imperatorzy późnego Cesarstwa Rzymskiego wobec zgromadzeń biskupów*, Byzantina Lodziensia 1, Wydawnictwo Uniwersytetu Łódzkiego 1997, 23-27.

[4] *v.C.* I, 44 (NPNF 2,1). Cf. M.R. Cataudella, *Costantino „episcopos" e l' „Oratio ad Sanctorum coetum"*, Omaggio a Rosario Soraci. *Politica, retorica e simbolismo del primato: Roma e Costantinopoli (IV-VII)*, Atti del Convegno Internazionale, 4-7 ott. 2001, a cura di F. Elia, Catania 2002, 263-280.

[5] Cf. R. Farina, *L'Impero e l'Imperatore cristiano in Eusebio di Cesarea. La prima teologia politica del cristianesimo*, Pas Verlag – Zürich 1966, 240ff.

[6] *v.C.* IV, 27.

[7] *v.C.* I, 44.

[8] *Questiones Veteris et Novi Testamenti* CXXVII, 35 and 110 (Pseudo-Augustinus), CSEL 50; cf. R. Farina, *L'Impero* 247.

as well as the Meletian schism. At III, 5, he also adds the unresolved issue of determining the date of Easter. The amount of attention and emphasis given to these matters is noteworthy. He spares just one verse to the controversy between the two clergymen, and one sentence to the schism, while devoting an entire chapter to the date of Easter and referring to the lack of one definite date as "the most serious illness." It is evident then how much significance he attached to the respective issues. Did the Emperor share this particular opinion?

The issue of the Meletian schism was definitely of great importance, as it concerned the unity of the entire Church. During the persecutions of 303 – 312, a man named Meletius of Likopolis came to lead the followers of the rigorous view that the people unworthy of holding any church offices are not only those who had denied their faith, but also those who fled persecutions. As a result, he appointed "his own" bishops and presbyters for the abandoned episcopal sees, including those which had remained vacant due to the continued imprisonment of their bishops. This practice led to the forming of a virtually parallel, and schismatic, Church in Egypt and Libya.

As we shall see, the letter in question appears to make a connection between the schism issue and a doctrinal dispute. A certain confirmation of this can be found in Sozomen's work.[9] Although he had usually tended to draw on the works of his older colleague Socrates, he seems to have relied here on his own, and more complete, sources. Namely, he states that Arius had supported bishop Meletius in his disputes with the legitimate bishop Peter, even prior to 311. Thereafter, Arius would be reconciled with and ordained deacon by Peter, and then he would again come into conflict with him over the question of supporting Meletius' followers. It appears to be doubtful, however, whether he had still harboured his pro-Meletian sympathies at the time of Alexander's episcopate, which would have been most probably used against him as yet another incriminating circumstance.

The direct reason for the letter was the Emperor's concern about the increasingly spreading controversy in Alexandria between the bishop and Arius. There was, nonetheless, another important reason: the Emperor wished to send Hosius on a mission to the East,[10] not just to Alexandria. And indeed, not only did he deliver the Emperor's epistle to Alexander and Arius, but he also took part in a synod,[11] and then he went on to preside over a synod at Antioch, in the spring of 325, where a new bishop of the city, Eustatius, was elected and something in the form of a creed was

[9] Sozomen, *h.e.* I, 15.

[10] Sozomen, *h.e.* I, 16.

[11] Cf. Council of Alexandria (324/325), SCL 1, 82.

formulated.[12] Stuart Hall cites Warmington's opinion that the Emperor's messenger was most likely someone else, notably a certain notary named Marianus, who would be also sent later on to Jerusalem.[13] It does not seem very convincing, though, as the information on Hosius' mission is also noted by Athanasius, alongside his mention of the said synod, in which Hosius had participated. The letter may have been written, as we already know, after September 20, 324. Hosius could not have afforded to delay his journey, as all the Mediterranean ports of the Roman Empire were ordinarily closed on November 12 (*mare clausum*). In winter, until March 10, there was no maritime navigation at all; even in springtime, until as late as May 25, it was still very limited, and undertaken only by those who were willing to take the risk. [14] A journey by land, from Nicomedia to Alexandria, cannot be taken into consideration as it would have drawn on for several months in harsh winter conditions.

The letter to Alexander was not the only document issued by the Emperor following his victory over Licinius. According to Eusebius' account,[15] Constantine issued a whole sequence of decrees dealing with the church property previously seized by Licinius, freedom of worship, release of those who were exiled for their Christian faith, graves and cemeteries, proscription of pagan sacrifices. Moreover, Eusebius cites the Emperor's epistle encouraging construction of churches, condemning idolatry, and calling for religious peace in the Empire. Following all these general directives, he goes on to relate the specific problem of the controversy in Alexandria.

Before quoting the contents of the letter, Eusebius notes that Constantine had received the news of the dispute between Alexander and Arius "with deep concern."[16] It is not said who had informed the Emperor. If that

---

[12] See commentary on this document below.

[13] Cf. Eusebius of Caesarea, *v.C.* 4, 44; S.G. Hall, *Some Constantinian Documents in the Vita Constantini*, in: *Constantine. History, Historiography and Legend*, ed. by S.N.C. Lieu and D. Montserrat, Routledge, London – New York 1998, 95.

[14] Cf. R. Chevallier, *Voyages et déplacements dans l'Empire Romain*, 119. Cf. A.L. Udovitch, *Time, the Sea and Society: duration of commercial voyages on the southern shores of the Mediterranean during the high Middle Ages*, Princeton University 1981, 503-546; D. Gorce, *Le voyages, l'hospitalité et le port des lettres dans le monde chrétien des IV et V siècles*, Librairie Auguste Picard, Paris 1925, 97-99. According to Mark Deacon's *Life of Porphyry, Bishop of Gaza*, fr. 33, 117, the bishop believed that it was already too late to set out on a sea voyage in August!

[15] Eusebius of Caesarea, *v.C.* II, 20-60.

[16] Eusebius of Caesarea, *v.C.* II, 61 (NPNF 2,1).

person had been Eusebius of Nicomedia, as it is asserted by De Decker,[17] the contention would have been likely represented as caused by Alexander, with Arius in the role of a victim. Since Eusebius had been familiar with the details of the dispute, he had already managed to voice his support for Arius. It is rather more conceivable that both Eusebius and Hosius had endeavoured to put forward their version of the dispute to the Emperor. As Constantine could not possibly comprehend the subtleties involved in the debate, he found it to have been an academic dispute with no practical significance, although still a festering and alarming one. As we shall see, this is exactly the spirit of the letter. According to De Decker, however, Eusebius was the Emperor's sole counsel, already an important figure at Licinius' court,[18] while Nicomedia had become the most significant city of the Empire and Church in the East on account of the Emperor's residence there.[19] He even describes him as *le premier prélat de l'hisoire de Eglise byzantine*.[20] I would like to note that even though Theodosius the Great had resided at Milan, the actual reason for the important role of the city in the Church was not the Imperial residence, but Bishop Ambrose. And, in my opinion, Eusebius' stature was no match to that of Ambrose.

Eusebius of Caesarea recounts that everything began from a barely noticeable problem, which would spread immensely, because of "the contentious spirit," over Egypt and Libya and would eventually engulf the other provinces of the Empire, so that not only the bishops but the whole of the faithful fought a war of words among themselves, and the unfaithful ridiculed it, unable to understand the meaning of such heated agitation. Apparently, however, this is a certain shortcut on Eusebius' part, as he speaks of the entire course of the controversy, until the time of the composition of the *Vita Constantini* after the Emperor's death, not the very beginning of the dispute. Yet he first appointed Hosius and "he also made him the bearer of a most needful and appropriate letter to the original movers of the strife."[21]

It is difficult to avoid the impression that the letter is actually concerned with much more than just the dispute between Alexander and Arius, and the author addresses his document to a wider audience than those two figures from Alexandria. I will return to this question in the commentary below the letter.

Let us now have a closer look at the content.

---

[17] D. De Decker, *Eusèbe de Nicomédie*, 158.

[18] D. De Decker, *Eusèbe de Nicomédie*, 164

[19] D. De Decker, *Eusèbe de Nicomédie*, 161.

[20] D. De Decker, *Eusèbe de Nicomédie*, 170.

[21] Eusebius of Caesarea, *v.C.* II, 63 (NPNF 2,1).

Constantine's Letter to Alexander the Bishop, and Arius the Presbyter[22]

64. Νικητὴς Κωνσταντῖνος Μέγιστος Σεβαστὸς Ἀλεξάνδρῳ καὶ Ἀρείῳ. Διπλῆν μοι γεγενῆσθαι πρόφασιν τούτων, ὧν ἔργῳ τὴν χρείαν ὑπέστην, αὐτονώς εἰκὸς τὸν τῶν ἐμῶν ἐγχειρημάτων βοηθὸν καὶ σωτῆρα τῶν ὅλων θεὸν ποιοῦμαι μάρτυρα.

65. Πρῶτον μὲν γὰρ τὴν ἁπάντων τῶν ἐθνῶν περὶ τὸ θεῖον πρόθεσιν εἰς μίαν ἕξεως σύστασιν ἐνῶσαι, δεύτερον δὲ τὸ τῆς κοινῆς οἰκουμένης σῶμα καθάπερ χαλεπῷ τινι τραύματι πεπονηκὸς ἀνακτήσασθαι καὶ συναρμόσαι προύθυμήθην.

64. Victor Constantinus, Maximus Augustus, to Alexander and Arius. I call that God to witness, as well I may, who is the helper of my endeavors, and the Preserver of all men, that I had a twofold reason for undertaking that duty which I have now performed.

65. My design then was, first, to bring the diverse judgments formed by all nations respecting the Deity to a condition, as it were, of settled uniformity; and, secondly, to restore to health the system of the world, then suffering under the malignant power of a grievous distemper.

It appears as if the Emperor showed his intention to effect some form of unification of the faith in God in all the religions of the Empire. It may have seemed to him that he would have been able to introduce religious peace, where all the religions would find their proper place and co-operate for the benefit of the common good. This is how the role of the Highest Pontiff and the entire College of Pontiffs was perceived: they were to watch over the harmony of religions within the state. The Emperor had embraced Christianity within his pontifical authority and it is now fitting that we take a closer look at his duties. They are best described in the accounts given by Cicero and Livy.

The office of the Highest Pontiff and his College of Pontiffs had existed at Rome since time immemorial. All we know is that by as early as 300 BC it had been reformed on the strength of the so-called *lex Ogulnia.* Livy, the ancient author of the history of Rome, writes of the reform enacted by king Numa:

Pontificem deinde Numam Marcium Marci filium ex patribus legit eique sacra omnia exscripta exsignataque attribuit, quibus hostiis quibus diebus, ad quae templa sacra fierent, atque unde in eos sumptus pecunia erogaretur.

He chose out of the number of the fathers Numa Marcius, son of Marcus, as pontiff, and consigned to him an entire system of religious rites written out and sealed, (showing) with what victims, upon what days, and in what temples the sacred rites were to be performed; and from what funds the money was to be taken for these expenses.

[22] Eusebius of Caesarea, *v.C.* II, 64-72.

Cetera quoque omnia publica privataque sacra pontificis scitis subiecit, ut esset quo consultum plebes veniret, ne quid divini iuris neglegendo patrios ritus peregrinosque adsciscendo turbaretur; nec caelestes modo caerimonias, sed iusta quoque funebria placandosque manes ut idem pontifex edoceret, quaeque prodigia fulminibus aliove quo visu misa susciperentur atque curarentur.

He placed all religious institutions, public and private, under the cognisance of the pontiff, to the end that there might be some place where the people should come to consult, lest any confusion in the divine worship might be occasioned by neglecting the ceremonies of their own country, and introducing foreign ones. (He ordained) that the same pontiff should instruct the people not only in the celestial ceremonies, but also in (the manner of performing) funeral solemnities, and of appeasing the manes of the dead; and what prodigies sent by lightning or any other phenomenon were to be attended to and expiated.[23]

According to Cicero, whose account reflects the reality of the Republican-era Rome, i.e., before the emperors claimed the pontifical office for themselves, the competence of the pontifical body, consisting of 19 members, comprised the matters defined as *de sacris*, *de votis*, *de feriis*, and *de sepulchris*.[24] *De sacris* referred to the enforcement of the accuracy due in the saying of all the prescribed prayers; no public spontaneity in this respect was allowed, even though it was permitted in private. Another question subject to strict regulation was the offering of sacrifices "in purity," which pertained primarily to sexual chastity, depending on the specific requirements imposed by the individual cults, but it also applied to the priest's general conduct. On the strength of the *de votis* competence, the pontiffs determined the proper oath formulas to be used on various occasions. They could also relieve a person of a previously taken oath. *De feriis* signified, as a matter of fact, the authority over the calendar. As Tadeusz Zieliński sums up: "The pontiffs were not so much priests of a specific deity as experts and advisors in religious matters in general."[25] Notably, the pontiff exercised the authority over the vestals, in whose house he had resided. The dwelling was known as *Domus publica*. Julius Caesar chose to abide by the long-standing tradition upon his election to the office of the *Pontifex Maximus*. It was only then that he could afford to undertake his reform of the calendar; no other

[23] Livy, *Ab urbe condita* I, 20 (Titus Livius, *History of Rome*, G. Bell, London 1892, vol. 1).

[24] Cicero, *De legibus* II, 47

[25] T. Zieliński, *Religia Rzeczypospolitej Rzymskiej*, II, 33.

office could have invested him with the authority to do so in the tradition-loving milieu of Rome. Augustus had been elected to the office (title?) only in 12 BC after Lepidus, who had managed to claim the title for himself following Caesar's death. Only then was he able to introduce amendments in the calendar of festivals and fill in the vacant priestly positions. He also remained true to the tradition of dwelling with the vestals, except for the fact that instead of taking up his residence with them, he had them moved into his new residence at the Palatine. Since then, each emperor had been appointed as the *Pontifex Maximus* until as late as 379, when the Western emperor Gratian relinquished the title, while the newly elected emperor in the East Theodosius did not assume it at all. Let us also note, for a more complete picture, that the Byzantine emperors' resignation of the pontifical title did not entail, in practical terms, the relinquishment of his competence.

The *Pontifex Maximus* kept the *Pontifical Books*, in which worship formulas of all the religions were recorded. As the Emperor Constantine had to fulfil those duties as well, he attempted to obtain some formulas of the Christian faith, obligatory to all the faithful, in order to have them entered in the books. The Christians did not have very much to offer in this regard, as their liturgy had not been subject to any measure of codification yet and there were no generally obligatory prayers, except for the Lord's Prayer from the Gospel.

This tyranny, herein compared to a grave illness, is most probably the rule of Maximinus Daia, who campaigned against Constantine and whose persecution of the Christians was contrary to Constantine's irenic designs.

ἃ δὴ προσκοπῶν ἕτερον μὲν ἀπορρήτῳ τῆς διανοίας ὀφθαλμῷ συνελογιζόμην, ἕτερον δὲ τῇ τῆς στρατιωτικῆς χειρὸς ἐξουσίᾳ κατορθοῦν ἐπειρώμην, εἰδὼς ὡς εἰ κοινὴν ἅπασι τοῖς τοῦ θεοῦ θεράπουσιν ἐπ' εὐχαῖς ταῖς ἐμαῖς ὁμόνοιαν καταστήσαιμι, καὶ ἡ τῶν δημοσίων πραγμάτων χρεία σύνδρομον ταῖς ἁπάντων εὐσεβέσι γνώμαις τὴν μεταβολὴν καρπώσεται.

Keeping these objects in view, I sought to accomplish the one by the secret eye of thought, while the other I tried to rectify by the power of military authority. For I was aware that, if I should succeed in establishing, according to my hopes, a common harmony of sentiment among all the servants of God, the general course of affairs would also experience a change correspondent to the pious desires of them all.

In the Roman world-view, religious matters were inseparable from those of the public and political nature. The civil and religious liturgy encompassed attending to official matters as well as making public offerings to the gods, especially as their good favour was understood as indispensable for the welfare and good organization of the state. As part of his efforts to establish general harmony, Constantine convoked synods and actively worked to counter the Donatist schism in Africa. He puts it very clearly in the following passage:

66. μανίας γὰρ δήπουθεν οὐκ ἀνεκτῆς ἅπασαν τὴν Ἀφρικὴν ἐπιλαβούσης [καὶ] διὰ τοὺς ἀβούλῳ κουφότητι τὴν τῶν δήμων θρησκείαν εἰς διαφόρους αἱρέσεις σχίσαι τετολμηκότας, ταύτην ἐγὼ τὴν νόσον καταστεῖλαι βουληθείς, οὐδεμίαν ἑτέραν ἀρκοῦσαν τῷ πράγματι θεραπείαν ηὕρισκον, ἢ εἰ τὸν κοινὸν τῆς οἰκουμένης ἐχθρὸν ἐξελών, ὃς ταῖς ἱεραῖς ὑμῶν συνόδοις τὴν ἀθέμιτον ἑαυτοῦ γνώμην ἀντέστησεν, ἐνίους ὑμῶν πρὸς τὴν τῶν πρὸς ἀλλήλους διχονοούντων ὁμόνοιαν βοηθοὺς ἀποστείλαιμι.

66. Finding, then, that the whole of Africa was pervaded by an intolerable spirit of mad folly, through the influence of those who with heedless frivolity had presumed to rend the religion of the people into diverse sects; I was anxious to check this disorder, and could discover no other remedy equal to the occasion, except in sending some of yourselves to aid in restoring mutual harmony among the disputants, after I had removed that common enemy of mankind who had interposed his lawless sentence for the prohibition of your holy synods.

The expression "common enemy of mankind," as mentioned in the passage, would be commonly attributed to Licinius.[26] Eusebius writes of his proscription against convoking synods.[27] As for the sects, the mention is most likely a reference to the problems caused by the Donatist schism in Africa,[28] which the Emperor had previously attempted to resolve by summoning the synods of Rome (313) and Arles (314). Chronologically speaking, it would be incongruous in view of the fact that the Donatist controversy had burgeoned following the year 312, and definitely not as late as Licinius' downfall in 324. As a matter of fact, Constantine wrote his letter immediately after his victory over Licinius; therefore, it was still too soon to speak of any significant result of his actions. In my opinion, he refers to the emperor Maximinus Daia, whom Eusebius describes as "a thorough hater of the good and an enemy of every virtuous person."[29] A major part of Book IX deals with Maximinus' cruel treatment of the Christians exactly in terms of tyranny. Eusebius goes on to say that Maximinus and Diocletian

[26] Cf., e.g., J.-L. Maier, *Le dossier du donatisme*, vol. I, Akademie Verlag, Berlin 1987, 244.

[27] Eusebius of Caesarea, *v.C.* I, 51.

[28] Cf. S.G. Hall, *Some Constantinian Documents in the Vita Constantini*, in: *Constantine. History, Historiography and Legend*.

[29] Eusebius of Caesarea, *h.e.* IX, 2, 1 (NPNF 2,1).

had proscribed Christian assemblies,[30] using the same term "synod," which, strictly speaking, does not have to designate solely assemblies of bishops. In all likelihood, the figure in question is not Maxentius, as he was not much of a concern to the Alexandrians. On the contrary, they had experienced the tyrannical rule of Maximinus. After his victory over Maxentius in 312 and the death of Maximinus in 313, Constantine did intervene in the African controversies for several times. Eusebius records a *dossier* of the documents issued with regard to this particular problem.[31] As in the case of Constantine's letter discussed in this chapter (delivered by Hosius), those documents had been very likely delivered by some clergymen. Constantine seems to use this reminder to stress that he writes his letter on the strength of the law and had previously done so as well, whenever necessary. It may be also in order to recall at this point that Egypt had not formed a part of Africa in the Empire's administrative system.

The mention of "some of yourselves" having been sent implies that there must have been actually more addressees of the letter than just Alexander and Arius. Stuart Hall supposes that it may have been rather a circular letter concerning the contentious doctrinal disputes in the Church and possibly in connection with the synod at Antioch (which took place in the spring of 325), to be discussed in more detail further on.[32]

67. Ἐπειδὴ γὰρ ἡ τοῦ φωτὸς δύναμις καὶ ὁ τῆς ἱερᾶς θρησκείας νόμος, ὑπὸ τῆς τοῦ κρείττονος εὐεργεσίας οἷον ἔκ τινων τῆς ἀνατολῆς κόλπων ἐκδοθείς, ἅπασαν ὁμοῦ τὴν οἰκουμένην ἱερῷ λαμπτῆρι κατήστραψεν, εἰκότως ὑμᾶς, ὥσπερ τινὰς ἀρχηγοὺς τῆς τῶν ἐθνῶν σωτηρίας ὑπάρξειν πιστεύων, ὁμοῦ καὶ ψυχῆς νεύματι καὶ ὀφθαλμῶν ἐνεργείᾳ ζητεῖν ἐπειρώμην. ἅμα γοῦν τῇ μεγάλῃ νίκῃ καὶ τῇ κατὰ τῶν ἐχθρῶν ἀληθεῖ θριαμβείᾳ τοῦτο πρῶτον εἱλόμην ἐρευνᾶν, ὃ δὴ πρῶτόν μοι καὶ τιμιώτατον ἁπάντων ὑπάρχειν ἡγούμην.

67. For since the power of Divine light, and the law of sacred worship, which, proceeding in the first instance, through the favor of God, from the bosom, as it were, of the East, have illumined the world, by their sacred radiance, I naturally believed that you would be the first to promote the salvation of other nations, and resolved with all energy of thought and diligence of enquiry to seek your aid. As soon, therefore, as I had secured my decisive victory and unquestionable triumph over my enemies, my first enquiry was concerning that object which I felt to be of paramount interest and importance.

[30] Eusebius of Caesarea, *h.e.* IX, 10, 8.

[31] Eusebius of Caesarea, *h.e.* X, 5-6.

[32] Cf. S.G. Hall, *Some Constantinian Documents in the* Vita Constantini, 87-88.

Constantine uses the word θρησκεία and adds νόμος, in the vein of a true Roman. From the perspective of the traditional Roman religion, those were the two most significant factors: worship and the pertinent regulations. According to the Roman view, this is what the true religion is all about. A person's individual relation to a given deity was definitely of less importance than taking part in the strictly regulated official celebrations. It was the *Pontifex Maximus'* duty to ensure that they were performed properly.

It would mean that Constantine cannot see any qualitative difference between Christianity and the other religions; nor does he evidently realize the actual significance of the doctrine in the Church. In his view, orthopraxis is clearly more important than orthodoxy. While the former can be *established*, one needs to be *persuaded* to accept the latter. The mention to the effect that he wished to see, with his own eyes, how the things were is probably a reference to his plan of a great journey from the East to the West, to be concluded in Rome and crowned with solemnities in celebration of the jubilee year marking the twentieth anniversary of his reign. It is further discussed below. I think this is a fairly sufficient assumption and there is no need to suspect that the letter was actually addressed to Antioch, as Stuart Hall asserts in his work. Nevertheless, it confirms his insightful assumption that the letter should not be treated as a completely private one; on the contrary, it was intended to be publicized and thus, indirectly, addressed the entire Church (primarily, as represented by the bishops) in the East.

68. Ἀλλ', ὦ καλλίστη καὶ θεία πρόνοια, οἷόν μου τῆς ἀκοῆς μᾶλλον δὲ τῆς καρδίας αὐτῆς τραῦμα καίριον ἥψατο, πολλῷ χαλεπωτέραν τῶν ἐκεῖ καταλειφθέντων τὴν ἐν ὑμῖν γιγνομένην διχοστασίαν σημαῖνον, ὡς πλείονος ἤδη τὰ καθ' ὑμᾶς μέρη θεραπείας δεῖσθαι, παρ' ὧν τοῖς ἄλλοις τὴν ἴασιν ὑπάρξειν ἤλπισα. διαλογιζομένῳ δή μοι τὴν ἀρχὴν καὶ τὴν ὑπόθεσιν τούτων ἄγαν εὐτελὴς καὶ οὐδαμῶς ἀξία τῆς τοσαύτης φιλονεικίας ἡ πρόφασις ἐφωράθη.

68. But, O glorious Providence of God! how deep a wound did not my ears only, but my very heart receive in the report that divisions existed among yourselves more grievous still than those which continued in that country! so that you, through whose aid I had hoped to procure a remedy for the errors of others, are in a state which needs healing even more than theirs. And yet, having made a careful enquiry into the origin and foundation of these differences, I find the cause to be of a truly insignificant character, and quite unworthy of such fierce contention.

Constantine is surprised that the theoretical deliberations may cause discord and contention. He states that these divisions, referred to as διχοστασία, are even more serious than those already mentioned, namely the Donatist controversy in Africa. Is this a rhetorical overstatement? Or is it simply his opinion? He goes on to add that the cause of the differences is insignificant. Socrates notes[33] that the intense epistolar commotion, with the letters addressed to all the bishops by both Alexander and Eusebius, the responses to those letters, and so forth, led to a great uproar, reflected even by some theatrical performances ridiculing the whole controversy. Apparently, Constantine was not the only one who had difficulty understanding the reason for quarrelling over some issues of orthodoxy.

διόπερ ἐπὶ τὴν τῆς ἐπιστολῆς ταύτης ἀνάγκην ἐπειχθείς, καὶ πρὸς τὴν ὁμόψυχον ὑμῶν ἀγχίνοιαν γράφων, τήν τε θείαν πρόνοιαν καλέσας ἀρωγὸν τῷ πράγματι, μέσον τῆς πρὸς ἀλλήλους ὑμῶν ἀμφισβητήσεως οἷον εἰρήνης πρύτανιν ἐμαυτὸν εἰκότως προσάγω. ὅπερ γὰρ δὴ συναιρομένου τοῦ κρείττονος, εἰ καὶ μείζων ἦν τις ἀφορμὴ διχονοίας, οὐ χαλεπῶς ἂν ἠδυνήθην, ὁσίαις τῶν ἀκουόντων γνώμαις ἐγχειρίζων τὸν λόγον, εἰς τὸ χρησιμώτερον ἕκαστον μεταστῆσαι, τοῦτο, μικρᾶς καὶ λίαν εὐτελοῦς ἀφορμῆς ὑπαρχούσης, ἢ πρὸς τὸ ὅλον ἐμποδὼν ἵσταται, πῶς οὐκ εὐχερεστέραν καὶ πολλῷ ῥᾳδιωτέραν μοι τοῦ πράγματος τὴν ἐπανόρθωσιν μνηστεύσει;

Feeling myself, therefore, compelled to address you in this letter, and to appeal at the same time to your unanimity and sagacity, I call on Divine Providence to assist me in the task, while I interrupt your dissension in the character of a minister of peace. And with reason: for if I might expect, with the help of a higher Power, to be able without difficulty, by a judicious appeal to the pious feelings of those who heard me, to recall them to a better spirit, even though the occasion of the disagreement were a greater one, how can I refrain from promising myself a far easier and more speedy adjustment of this difference, when the cause which hinders general harmony of sentiment is intrinsically trifling and of little moment?

The tone of the Emperor's words seems to point out that he had dealt with even more serious problems before and induced many people to change their ways, thus making it easier for him to bring the contention under control. The issue had grown to even larger proportions than the Donatist controversy in Africa, as he says, yet the real cause is trifling. Apparently, in the Emperor's view, the cause of the Donatist crisis was more serious than the subject of the dispute between Alexander and Arius. The reason why is plain to see: the actual problems in Africa involved, among other things, the disciplinary practice in the Church, admitting the penitents back into the Church, and recognizing the validity of the sacraments officiated by the clergymen guilty of sins. Those questions of foremost importance were followed by certain doctrinal issues, which Constantine did not have

[33] Socrates, *h.e.* I, 6, Alexander, *Letter to All the Bishops.*

to understand very thoroughly. In this case, however, no practical issue, nothing connected with worship-related matters, with the above-mentioned θρησκεία, (76), and the Emperor could not understand it. Let us see what he had known about the causes of the contention.

69. Μανθάνω τοίνυν ἐκεῖθεν ὑπῆρχθαι τοῦ παρόντος ζητήματος τὴν καταβολήν. ὅτε γὰρ σύ, ὦ Ἀλέξανδρε, παρὰ τῶν πρεσβυτέρων ἐζήτεις, τί δήποτε αὐτῶν ἕκαστος ὑπέρ τινος τόπου τῶν ἐν τῷ νόμῳ γεγραμμένων, μᾶλλον δ' ὑπὲρ ματαίου τινὸς ζητήσεως μέρους ἠσθάνετο, σύ {τε}, ὦ Ἄρειε, τοῦθ', ὅπερ ἢ μηδὲ τὴν ἀρχὴν ἐνθυμηθῆναι ἢ ἐνθυμηθέντα σιωπῇ παραδοῦναι προσῆκον ἦν, ἀπροόπτως ἀντέθηκας, ὅθεν τῆς ἐν ὑμῖν διχονοίας ἐγερθείσης ἡ μὲν σύνοδος ἠρνήθη, ὁ δὲ ἁγιώτατος λαὸς εἰς ἀμφοτέρους σχισθεὶς ἐκ τῆς τοῦ κοινοῦ σώματος ἁρμονίας ἐχωρίσθη. οὐκοῦν ἑκάτερος ὑμῶν, ἐξ ἴσου τὴν συγγνώμην παρασχών, ὅπερ ἂν ὑμῖν ὁ συνθεράπων ὑμῶν δικαίως παραινῇ δεξάσθω.

69. I understand, then, that the origin of the present controversy is this. When you, Alexander, demanded of the presbyters what opinion they severally maintained respecting a certain passage in the Divine law, or rather, I should say, that you asked them something connected with an unprofitable question, then you, Arius, inconsiderately insisted on what ought never to have been conceived at all, or if conceived, should have been buried in profound silence. Hence it was that a dissension arose between you, fellowship was withdrawn, and the holy people, rent into diverse parties, no longer preserved the unity of the one body. Now, therefore, do ye both exhibit an equal degree of forbearance, and receive the advice which your fellow-servant righteously gives.

From this point on, the letter is cited by Socrates Scholasticus (HE I, 7). According to his perspective, after more than a hundred years, the character of the Council of Nicaea had been predominantly anti-Arian. Consequently, he is not concerned with the initial part of the letter. The commentator of the Polish edition of Socrates' *History*, Adam Ziółkowski, is certain that the dispute arose from Proverbs 8:22-25, where the Wisdom says: "The Lord created me at the beginning of his work," "ages ago," and "before the hills, I was brought forth." Therefore, the real subject of the dispute would be the creation and generation of the Son of God. Similar views have been expressed by Manlio Simonetii in his extensive work on Arianism, and a number of various articles beginning from the early 1960s, Charles Pietri,[34] and many other scholars. I suppose that it was Prof. Simonetti who put forward this particular opinion for the first time in the 1960s and it has garnered much support among scholars since then. Nonetheless, the

[34] M. Simonetti, *La crisi ariana*, 35; Ch. Pietri, in: *Histoire du christianisme*, sous la direction de J.-M. Mayeur, Ch (†) et L. Pietri, A. Vauches, M. Venard, vol. 2, Desclée 1995, 263.

whole thing is not that obvious, as we do not really know the actual object of the dispute. I have already noted that one of the principal points of the accusation levelled at Arius was the question of the Logos' mutability. It may have been connected with the question of Jesus' obedience and some relevant text.

There is a widespread opinion that Arius was a disciple of Lucian of Antioch and a colleague of, among others, Eusebius of Nicomedia. It is based on just one single word referring to Eusebius of Nicomedia. As I have noted before, Arius used the vocative form (συλλουκιανιστὰ), meaning "fellow-Lucianist," in his letter. The expression would indicate that Arius and Eusebius had both attended Lucian's school. Yet it might have as well pointed to Arius' polite way of putting the addressee of his letter on par with the renowned teacher Lucian. The authors who assume that Arius had attended Lucian's school at Antioch also tend to attribute to him the "ascending" approach to Christology, peculiar to the Antiochene tradition, i.e., with its emphasis first on the humanity, and only then on the divinity of Christ, which was fundamentally different from the Alexandrian approach, with its primary focus on the view that Christ is God's Logos, and only then on Christ becoming a man. There is just a difference in the method applied, nonetheless it involves certain implications. I can hardly see any trace of such different Christology in Arius' teachings. According to his view, Christ is not a man who is God's Logos, but the Logos that has become a man, as any decent Alexandrian would assert with no hesitation. The difference between Arius and Alexander pertained to the mutability of this Logos and thus, necessarily, His being as a creation.

As we have seen, Constantine calls himself a "fellow-servant" of the bishop and the presbyter on the authority of his office of the *Pontifex Maximus*.

τί δὲ τοῦτό ἐστιν; οὔτε ἐρωτᾶν ὑπὲρ τῶν τοιούτων ἐξ ἀρχῆς προσῆκον ἦν, οὔτε ἐρωτώμενον ἀποκρίνασθαι. τὰς γὰρ τοιαύτας ζητήσεις, ὁπόσας μὴ νόμου τινὸς ἀνάγκη προστάττει ἀλλ' ἀνωφελοῦς ἀργίας ἐρεσχελία προτίθησιν, εἰ καὶ φυσικῆς τινος γυμνασίας ἕνεκα γίγνοιτο, ὅμως ὀφείλομεν εἴσω τῆς διανοίας ἐγκλείειν καὶ μὴ προχείρως εἰς δημοσίας συνόδους ἐκφέρειν, μηδὲ ταῖς τῶν δήμων ἀκοαῖς ἀπρονοήτως πιστεύειν.

What then is this advice? It was wrong in the first instance to propose such questions as these, or to reply to them when propounded. For those points of discussion which are enjoined by the authority of no law, but rather suggested by the contentious spirit which is fostered by misused leisure, even though they may be intended merely as an intellectual exercise, ought certainly to be confined to the region of our own thoughts, and not hastily produced in the popular assemblies, nor unadvisedly intrusted to the general ear.

The Emperor's Roman mindset is noteworthy: he pays particular attention to the things prescribed by law. Debates on doctrinal issues were not regulated by legal precepts, and therefore should not be of significance in terms of the state and society. In consequence, disseminating the information on such controversies among the common people is inappropriate as it disturbs the peace and public order. In addition, it may have been also of importance that Constantine had been reputedly conversant with some cults practising mystery rites, regardless of his own possible involvement in initiations, where degrees of initiation played a pivotal role. Participants were not allowed to violate them or share the strictly confidential matters with the uninitiated.

πόσος γάρ ἐστιν ἕκαστος, ὡς πραγμάτων οὕτω μεγάλων καὶ λίαν δυσχερῶν δύναμιν ἢ πρὸς τὸ ἀκριβὲς συνιδεῖν ἢ κατ' ἀξίαν ἑρμηνεῦσαι; εἰ δὲ καὶ τοῦτό τις εὐχερῶς ποιεῖν νομισθείη, πόσον δήπου μέρος τοῦ δήμου πείσει; ἢ τίς ταῖς τῶν τοιούτων ζητημάτων ἀκριβείαις ἔξω τῆς ἐπικινδύνου παρολισθήσεως ἀντισταίη;	For how very few are there able either accurately to comprehend, or adequately to explain subjects so sublime and abstruse in their nature? Or, granting that one were fully competent for this, how many people will he convince? Or, who, again, in dealing with questions of such subtle nicety as these, can secure himself against a dangerous declension from the truth?

The conviction that the knowledge of the divine matters surpasses the intellectual capabilities of wise men (and even if they managed to attain that knowledge, they should not communicate it to others, as they would not be properly understood anyway) was expressed by Plato as follows: "The chief good can by no means be described in words, but is produced by long habit, and bursts forth suddenly as a light in the soul, as from a fire which had leapt forth,"[35] and even more clearly so: "The father and maker of all this universe is past finding out, and even if we found him, to tell of him to all men would be impossible,"[36] as cited by Celsus in his *True Word,* a work written against Christians (it elicited Origen's response).[37] Constantine demonstrates his knowledge of classical authors and also seems to concur with Plato's view. Evidently, he does not think it is appropriate to turn theological subtleties into publicly discussed matters. It is noteworthy that the ancient Greek and Roman religions left no theological treatises at all. A multitude of myths may convey theological content, yet they do not presume to contain any religious

[35] Plato, *Letters* 7, 341, as in: Origenes, *Contra Celsum* VI, 3 (ANF 4).

[36] Plato, *Timaios* 28c (in: E. Hamilton, H. Cairns (eds.), *The Collected Dialogues of Plato,* Bollington, New York 1963, 2nd ed.).

[37] Origenes, *Contra Celsum* VII, 42.

interpretation to be held as obligatory by the believers. Myths may be even mutually contradictory, with no detriment to themselves or inconvenience to listeners and readers. Apparently, the first coherent theological writings were composed by Julian the Apostate. Brought up and educated in the Christian environment, he may have become convinced of the necessity of a cohesive doctrine. As a consequence, he made efforts to provide theoretical foundations for the restoration of the ancient cults.

οὐκοῦν ἐφεκτέον ἐστὶν ἐν τοῖς τοιούτοις τὴν πολυλογίαν, ἵνα μήπως, ἢ ἡμῶν ἀσθενείᾳ φύσεως τὸ προταθὲν ἑρμηνεῦσαι μὴ δυνηθέντων, ἢ τῶν ἀκροατῶν βραδυτέρᾳ συνέσει πρὸς ἀκριβῆ τοῦ ῥηθέντος κατάληψιν ἐλθεῖν μὴ χωρησάντων, ἐξ ὁποτέρου τούτων ἢ βλασφημίας ἢ σχίσματος εἰς ἀνάγκην ὁ δῆμος περισταίη.

It is incumbent therefore on us in these cases to be sparing of our words, lest, in case we ourselves are unable, through the feebleness of our natural faculties, to give a clear explanation of the subject before us, or, on the other hand, in case the slowness of our hearers' understandings disables them from arriving at an accurate apprehension of what we say, from one or other of these causes the people be reduced to the alternative either of blasphemy or schism.

The author's practical approach is very striking in this passage. Imperial letters were basically the work of the chancery, yet in this case it is not easy (at least, to me) to imagine the competence of the secretary responsible for this one. It is plain to see that the author is adept at, to use a modern phrase, the human resources management: do not speak if you cannot explain clearly what you mean to say; there is no use speaking at all if the listeners are too dumb to understand. Something to that effect must have occurred, considering that the confused people had been left with "the alternative either of blasphemy or schism." The fact that the Emperor cannot see any other option means that he does not think any of the adversaries is right.

70. Διόπερ καὶ ἐρώτησις ἀπροφύλακτος καὶ ἀπόκρισις ἀπρονόητος ἴσην ἀλλήλαις ἀντιδότωσαν ἐφ᾽ ἑκάτερα συγγνώμην. οὐδὲ γὰρ ὑπὲρ τοῦ κορυφαίου τῶν ἐν τῷ νόμῳ παραγγελμάτων ὑμῖν ἡ τῆς φιλονεικίας ἐξήφθη πρόφασις, οὐδὲ καινή τις ὑμῖν ὑπὲρ τῆς τοῦ θεοῦ θρησκείας αἵρεσις ἀντεισήχθη, ἀλλ᾽ ἕνα καὶ τὸν αὐτὸν ἔχετε λογισμόν, ὡς πρὸς τὸ τῆς κοινωνίας σύνθημα δύνασθαι συνελθεῖν.

70. Let therefore both the unguarded question and the inconsiderate answer receive your mutual forgiveness. For the cause of your difference has not been any of the leading doctrines or precepts of the Divine law, nor has any new heresy respecting the worship of God arisen among you. You are in truth of one and the same judgment: you may therefore well join in communion and fellowship.

71. ὑμῶν γὰϱ ἐν ἀλλήλοις ὑπὲϱ μιϰϱῶν καὶ λίαν ἐλαχίστων φιλονεικούντων, τοσοῦτον τοῦ θεοῦ λαόν, ὃν ὑπὸ ταῖς ὑμετέϱαις φϱεσὶν εὐθύνεσθαι πϱοσήϰει, διχονοεῖν οὔτε πϱέπον οὔθ' ὅλως θεμιτὸν εἶναι πιστεύεται.

71. For as long as you continue to contend about these small and very insignificant questions, it is not fitting that so large a portion of God's people should be under the direction of your judgment, since you are thus divided between yourselves. I believe it indeed to be not merely unbecoming, but positively evil, that such should be the case.

In the Emperor's opinion, the cause of the dispute is of no significance to the unity of the Church, as it does not affect any precept of the law and the veneration due to God, nor does it create any new heresy. As far as I can tell, all the commentators of the text ascribe such a perception of this controversy to Constantine's unfamiliarity with the issues relating to Christianity. He did not realize that Christianity, unlike the traditional ancient religions, attached enormous importance not only to the questions of worship and the related regulations, but also, and above all, the doctrine (orthodoxy) as revealed by God and requiring the proper interpretation. It is evident that Constantine considers this dispute as insignificant. Another important circumstance is the Emperor's indirect knowledge of the issue. At Nicomedia, he was most likely notified of the dispute by Eusebius of Nicomedia, undoubtedly a well-educated theologian, and Bishop Hosius, whom the Emperor had trusted so much as to send him on a mission in the East, during which he was to meet with Alexander and Arius. Therefore, the Emperor had no choice but to formulate his opinion as based on their own, at least until he could find any evidence to the contrary. It would be thus reasonable to assume that it was exactly the opinion held as valid at the Imperial court, taking into account the views of the both bishops then present at the capital, and not just Constantine's personal opinion. But how can one possibly agree with the view that either Eusebius or Hosius had attempted to persuade the Emperor to consider the subject of the dispute as fairly insignificant? None of them should have remained indifferent to the problem. Who told the Emperor that Alexander and Arius were of the same opinion? Obviously, they were not. In any case, Constantine is convinced that the discord between them can be easily rectified with the good will of the both parties, as there is no serious matter involved in the whole controversy.

Let us also note the absence of any information on the relation between Eusebius and Hosius. Was it friendly, or not? Were they involved in any rivalry for the Emperor's favour? Or did they co-operate?

ἵνα δὲ μικρῷ παραδείγματι τὴν ὑμετέραν σύνεσιν ὑπομνήσαιμι, ἴστε δήπου καὶ τοὺς φιλοσόφους αὐτοὺς ὡς ἑνὶ μὲν ἅπαντες δόγματι συντίθενται, πολλάκις δὲ ἐπειδὰν ἔν τινι τῶν ἀποφάσεων μέρει διαφωνῶσιν, εἰ καὶ τῇ τῆς ἐπιστήμης ἀρετῇ χωρίζονται, τῇ μέντοι τοῦ δόγματος ἑνώσει πάλιν εἰς ἀλλήλους συμπνέουσιν. εἰ δὴ τοῦτό ἐστι, πῶς οὐ πολλῷ δικαιότερον ἡμᾶς τοὺς τοῦ μεγάλου θεοῦ θεράποντας καθεστῶτας ἐν τοιαύτῃ προαιρέσει θρησκείας ὁμοψύχους ἀλλήλοις εἶναι;

But I will refresh your minds by a little illustration, as follows. You know that philosophers, though they all adhere to one system, are yet frequently at issue on certain points, and differ, perhaps, in their degree of knowledge: yet they are recalled to harmony of sentiment by the uniting power of their common doctrines. If this be true, is it not far more reasonable that you, who are the ministers of the Supreme God, should be of one mind respecting the profession of the same religion?

In the Emperor's view, which may have been also shared by Eusebius and Hosius, his advisors, the difference of opinion should not disrupt the unity of the Church, just as debates within one school of philosophy do not have to divide it; on the contrary, they attest to its vibrant character, provided that they serve to strive for the truth, not a mere reflection of vainglorious ambitions. Constantine regards the Christian doctrine as a philosophy of just one school, where any difference of opinion is treated as an inside matter. Debates between the individual schools were something completely different, as Gregory Thaumaturgos described in his *Oration Panegyrical* (in honour of Origen) several decades before: "(158) Was it not these mutual conflicts and oppositions in doctrines among philosophers that led to the quarrels where they opposed each other's teachings, some prevailing over others and others yielding to yet others? (159) … they refuse to pay attention to any of the arguments of those who think differently."[38] In this particular case, it is clear that we are concerned with only one system, greater and more important than a variety of minor disputes. The Emperor makes yet another reference to unity (θρησκεία), just as we could see above (67). I would render the term as "religion," which is just one of the possibilities, as the Roman concept of religion did not embrace doctrine, or even morality, but a definite set of cult-related practices. According to Constantine's idea, Christianity follows the same pattern and, as a result, the specific conduct can be ensured by way of appropriate regulations.

Once again, we come across the same unresolved question: what did Hosius and Eusebius really think? As we know, the former delivered the letter and was supposed to make sure that the opponents' positive response could be obtained. Is it possible he had not known the contents? Could it

---

[38] Gregory Thaumaturgos, *Oration Panegyrical* 158-159 (in: *The Fathers of the Church*, The Catholic University of America, Washington 1998, vol. 98).

be that the Emperor had not informed Hosius about the contents of the letter and what the bishop was expected to do? On the other hand, if he had known, how could he have possibly agreed with it? It is noteworthy that Eusebius of Nicomedia is very similar in this regard. There is nothing in his letter to Paulinus of Tyre that would suggest Eusebius had thought of the dispute between Alexander and Arius as an insignificant dialectic question.

ἐπισκεψώμεθα δὴ λογισμῷ μείζονι καὶ πλείονι συνέσει τὸ ῥηθέν, εἴπερ ὀρθῶς ἔχει δι᾿ ὀλίγας καὶ ματαίας ῥημάτων ἐν ὑμῖν φιλονεικίας ἀδελφοὺς ἀδελφοῖς ἀντικεῖσθαι καὶ τὸ τῆς συνόδου τίμιον ἀσεβεῖ διχονοίᾳ χωρίζεσθαι δι᾿ ἡμῶν, οἳ πρὸς ἀλλήλους ὑπὲρ μικρῶν οὕτω καὶ μηδαμῶς ἀναγκαίων φιλονεικοῦμεν. δημώδη ταῦτά ἐστι καὶ παιδικαῖς ἀνοίαις ἁρμόττοντα μᾶλλον ἢ τῇ τῶν ἱερέων καὶ φρονίμων ἀνδρῶν συνέσει προσήκοντα. ἀποστῶμεν ἑκόντες τῶν διαβολικῶν πειρασμῶν. ὁ μέγας ἡμῶν θεός, ὁ σωτὴρ ἁπάντων, κοινὸν ἅπασι τὸ φῶς ἐξέτεινεν·

But let us still more thoughtfully and with closer attention examine what I have said, and see whether it be right that, on the ground of some trifling and foolish verbal difference between ourselves, brethren should assume towards each other the attitude of enemies, and the august meeting of the Synod be rent by profane disunion, because of you who wrangle together on points so trivial and altogether unessential? This is vulgar, and rather characteristic of childish ignorance, than consistent with the wisdom of priests and men of sense. Let us withdraw ourselves with a good will from these temptations of the devil. Our great God and common Saviour of all has granted the same light to us all.

The word "synod," as used in the letter, refers to the Church as a community that ought to live in harmony rather than to any specific assembly of bishops. Constantine used the term in a similar sense in one of the previous passages, where it is mentioned that a certain ruler (Maximinus, as I suppose) had once forbidden the Christians to assemble. The Emperor describes the subject of the controversy as a thing of minor importance, and the dispute itself as unworthy of respectable people. Since that was exactly his view of the problem, it seems implausible that he had ever intended to convoke a general assembly of the bishops in order to resolve it.

ὑφ᾿ οὗ τῇ προνοίᾳ ταύτην ἐμοὶ τῷ θεραπευτῇ τοῦ κρείττονος τὴν σπουδὴν εἰς τέλος ἐνεγκεῖν συγχωρήσατε, ὅπως αὐτοὺς τοὺς ἐκείνου δήμους ἐμῇ προσφωνήσει καὶ ὑπηρεσίᾳ καὶ νουθεσίας ἐνστάσει πρὸς τὴν τῆς συνόδου κοινωνίαν ἐπαναγάγοιμι.

Permit me, who am his servant, to bring my task to a successful issue, under the direction of his Providence, that I may be enabled, through my exhortations, and diligence, and earnest admonition, to recall his people to communion and fellowship.

ἐπειδὴ γάρ, ὡς ἔφην, μία τίς ἐστιν ἐν ἡμῖν πίστις καὶ μία τῆς καθ' ἡμᾶς αἱρέσεως σύνεσις, τό τε τοῦ νόμου παράγγελμα τοῖς δι' ἑαυτοῦ μέρεσιν εἰς μίαν ψυχῆς πρόθεσιν τὸ ὅλον συγκλείει, τοῦτο ὅπερ ὀλίγην ἐν ὑμῖν ἀλλήλοις φιλονεικίαν ἤγειρεν, ἐπειδὴ μὴ πρὸς τὴν τοῦ παντὸς νόμου δύναμιν ἀνήκει, χωρισμόν τινα καὶ στάσιν ὑμῖν μηδαμῶς ἐμποιείτω.

καὶ λέγω ταῦτα, οὐχ ὡς ἀναγκάζων ὑμᾶς ἐξ ἅπαντος τῇ λίαν εὐήθει, καὶ οἵα δήποτέ ἐστιν ἐκείνη, ζητήσει συντίθεσθαι. δύναται γὰρ καὶ τὸ τῆς συνόδου τίμιον ὑμῖν ἀκεραίως σῴζεσθαι καὶ μία καὶ ἡ αὐτὴ κατὰ πάντων κοινωνία τηρεῖσθαι, κἂν τὰ μάλιστά τις ἐν μέρει πρὸς ἀλλήλους ὑμῖν ὑπὲρ ἐλαχίστου διαφωνία γένηται, ἐπειδὴ μηδὲ πάντες ἐν ἅπασι ταὐτὸν βουλόμεθα, μηδὲ μία τις ἐν ἡμῖν φύσις ἢ γνώμη πολιτεύεται. περὶ μὲν οὖν τῆς θείας προνοίας μία τις ἐν ὑμῖν ἔστω πίστις μία σύνεσις μία συνθήκη τοῦ κρείττονος,

For since you have, as I said, but one faith, and one sentiment respecting our religion, and since the Divine commandment in all its parts enjoins on us all the duty of maintaining a spirit of concord, let not the circumstance which has led to a slight difference between you, since it does not affect the validity of the whole, cause any division or schism among you.

And this I say without in any way desiring to force you to entire unity of judgment in regard to this truly idle question, whatever its real nature may be. For the dignity of your synod may be preserved, and the communion of your whole body maintained unbroken, however wide a difference may exist among you as to unimportant matters. For we are not all of us like-minded on every subject, nor is there such a thing as one disposition and judgment common to all alike. As far, then, as regards the Divine Providence, let there be one faith, and one understanding among you, one united judgment in reference to God.

As the *Pontifex Maximus*, the emperor had neither authority nor duty to unify the religions at Rome, but he was obliged to have regard for all of them and respect the existing differences. It appears that Constantine applies the same measure to Christianity and requires that the distinct way of thinking of either party be respected. He only demands complete unanimity and harmony as far as the Divine Providence is concerned.

It is also worth having a closer look at the terms and notions used by Constantine. First and foremost, let us note the term πρόνοια, i.e., providence. It is hard to decide whether his idea of "providence" was the same as that of his advisors, the aforementioned bishops. The concept of πρόνοια was well known at Rome and of great significance to the Roman religions as well as the exercise of authority. It is attested, for instance, by an impressive catalogue of as many as 127 coins from Tiberius to Alexander

Severus with the depiction of the Providence (*Providentia*).[39] The Providence also constituted the basis of the Stoic philosophical system, encompassing all the beings, i.e., the whole of the existence.[40] In the Roman world, Cicero made it the foundation of his theology, by stating, among other things, that "the gods exist, by their foresight the world is governed."[41] In the third and fourth centuries, the *providentia* became associated with dynastic success and military victories.[42] The context of the letter in question is military, in a way, as the Emperor sent it following his victory over Licinius, at the time when he had been faced with the necessity to consolidate his sole rule over the Empire. Aware of the weight of the Providence, he just could not have afforded to risk playing with it. All the other religious issues are of much less importance in comparison.

Another expression is συνόδου κοινωνία, rendered as "the dignity of your synod," but there are also some other possibilities such as "unity," "communion," "concord of assembly," with the meaning of "synod" remaining the same as in the above-mentioned two instances.

Let us now turn to this interesting, and somewhat more intriguing, phrase: μία πίστις καὶ μία τῆς καθ' ἡμᾶς αἱρέσεως σύνεσις. The author no longer speaks of Christianity in terms of a state religion, where the most important thing is the worship as determined by the *Pontifex Maximus* and its conformity with the law. Instead, he appears to speak as if in reference to the idea and the doctrine. Πίστις denotes a faith manifesting itself in the intellectual recognition of a given belief as well as in putting trust or confiding in somebody or something; in turn, αἵρεσις refers to a chosen view or opinion which one is determined to follow, whereas σύνεσις denotes an intellectual reality again, an agreement to accept a certain view, or an understanding, an awareness of something. No similar expression had been used in the letter before. So what is the reason for their appearance in this passage?

And what is the sense of μηδὲ μία τις ἐν ἡμῖν φύσις ἢ γνώμη πολιτεύεται? What does it mean that we do not have one "disposition" or one "judgment"? Perhaps, we are all different in our birth (descent) and education (culture)? It may possibly hint at the author's view that the two opponents are dependent on different schools, although this interpretation may be a bit too far-reaching.

---

[39] Cf. J.-P. Martin, *Providentia deorum. Aspects religieux du pouvoir romain*, Ecole française de Roma 1982, 431-433.

[40] Cf. Diogenes Laertios, *The Lives and Views of Famous Philosophers* VII, 1; Anonymous, *Philosophoumena* 21, 1.

[41] Cicero, *De divinatione* I, 117 (in: *Cicero on Divination*, D. Wardle (trans.), Clarendon Press, Oxford 2006).

[42] Cf. J.-P. Martin, *Providentia deorum*, 428.

Once again, at the close of the excerpt, the author reverts to one faith and one understanding, also adding one "united judgment" concerning the most important issue. Notably, the author speaks of the Providence throughout the passage. However, he apparently allows of some differences in this regard as well, since he only demands unity on the most fundamental question.

ἃ δ'ὑπὲρ τῶν ἐλαχίστων τούτων ζητήσεων ἐν ἀλλήλοις ἀκριβολογεῖσθε, κἂν μὴ πρὸς μίαν γνώμην συμφέρησθε, μένειν εἴσω λογισμοῦ προσήκει, τῷ τῆς διανοίας ἀπορρήτῳ τηρούμενα. τὸ μέντοι τῆς κοινῆς φιλίας ἐξαίρετον καὶ ἡ τῆς ἀληθείας πίστις ἥ τε περὶ τὸν θεὸν καὶ τὴν τοῦ νόμου θρησκείαν τιμὴ μενέτω παρ' ὑμῖν ἀσάλευτος· ἐπανέλθετε δὴ πρὸς τὴν ἀλλήλων φιλίαν τε καὶ χάριν, ἀπόδοτε τῷ λαῷ ξύμπαντι τὰς οἰκείας περιπλοκάς, ὑμεῖς τε αὐτοὶ καθάπερ τὰς ἑαυτῶν ψυχὰς ἐκκαθήραντες αὖθις ἀλλήλους ἐπίγνωτε. ἡδίων γὰρ πολλάκις φιλία γίνεται μετὰ τὴν τῆς ἔχθρας ἀπόθεσιν αὖθις εἰς καταλλαγὴν ἐπανελθοῦσα.

But as to your subtle disputations on questions of little or no significance, though you may be unable to harmonize in sentiment, such differences should be consigned to the secret custody of your own minds and thoughts. And now, let the preciousness of common affection, let faith in the truth, let the honor due to God and to the observance of his law continue immovably among you. Resume, then, your mutual feelings of friendship, love, and regard: restore to the people their wonted embracings; and do ye yourselves, having purified your souls, as it were, once more acknowledge one another. For it often happens that when a reconciliation is effected by the removal of the causes of enmity, friendship becomes even sweeter than it was before.

It is noteworthy that the Emperor counts on a reconciliation between Alexander and Arius, and sees the whole controversy in terms of an acrimonious dispute between them, without a sufficiently justified cause. He assumes that they may fail to reach one understanding and comprehension in the matters of lesser importance, yet he encourages them to abstain from showing enmity to one another. Once again, the belief in the superiority of the external conduct over convictions gains the upper hand. Unless the Emperor is indeed of the opinion that the different views are of no significance here.

72. Ἀπόδοτε οὖν μοι γαληνὰς μὲν ἡμέρας νύκτας δ' ἀμερίμνους, ἵνα κἀμοί τις ἡδονὴ καθαροῦ φωτὸς καὶ βίου λοιπὸν ἡσύχου εὐφροσύνη σῴζηται·

72. Restore me then my quiet days, and untroubled nights, that the joy of undimmed light, the delight of a tranquil life, may henceforth be my portion.

εἰ δὲ μή, στένειν ἀνάγκη καὶ δακρύοις δι' ὅλου συγχεῖσθαι καὶ μηδὲ τὸν τοῦ ζῆν αἰῶνα πράως ὑφίστασθαι. τῶν γάρ τοι τοῦ θεοῦ λαῶν, τῶν συνθεραπόντων λέγω τῶν ἐμῶν, οὕτως ἀδίκῳ καὶ βλαβερᾷ πρὸς ἀλλήλους φιλονεικίᾳ κεχωρισμένων, ἐμὲ πῶς ἐγχωρεῖ τῷ λογισμῷ συνεστάναι λοιπόν;

Else must I needs mourn, with constant tears, nor shall I be able to pass the residue of my days in peace. For while the people of God, whose fellow-servant I am, are thus divided amongst themselves by an unreasonable and pernicious spirit of contention, how is it possible that I shall be able to maintain tranquillity of mind?

There is undoubtedly some rhetorical overstatement in the Emperor's letter, even though he does not seem to show any willingness to undertake any significant measures in response to the dispute. He appears to be convinced of the force of his persuasion and the eventual effect of the letter on the settlement of the controversy.

ἵνα δὲ τῆς ἐπὶ τούτῳ λύπης τὴν ὑπερβολὴν αἴσθησθε· πρώην ἐπιστὰς τῇ Νικομηδέων πόλει παραχρῆμα πρὸς τὴν ἑῴαν ἠπειγόμην τῇ γνώμῃ. σπεύδοντι δή μοι ἤδη πρὸς ὑμᾶς καὶ τῷ πλείονι μέρει σὺν ὑμῖν ὄντι ἡ τοῦδε τοῦ πράγματος ἀγγελία πρὸς τὸ ἔμπαλιν τὸν λογισμὸν ἀνεχαίτισεν, ἵνα μὴ τοῖς ὀφθαλμοῖς ὁρᾶν ἀναγκασθείην, ἃ μηδὲ ταῖς ἀκοαῖς προαισθέσθαι δυνατὸν ἡγούμην. ἀνοίξατε δή μοι λοιπὸν ἐν τῇ καθ' ὑμᾶς ὁμονοίᾳ τῆς ἑῴας τὴν ὁδόν, ἣν ταῖς πρὸς ἀλλήλους φιλονεικίαις ἀπεκλείσατε, καὶ συγχωρήσατε θᾶττον ὑμᾶς τε ὁμοῦ καὶ τοὺς ἄλλους ἅπαντας δήμους ἐπιδεῖν χαίροντα, καὶ τὴν ὑπὲρ τῆς κοινῆς ἁπάντων ὁμονοίας καὶ ἐλευθερίας ὀφειλομένην χάριν ἐπ' εὐφήμοις λόγων συνθήμασιν ὁμολογῆσαι τῷ κρείττονι.

And I will give you a proof how great my sorrow has been on this behalf. Not long since I had visited Nicomedia, and intended forthwith to proceed from that city to the East. It was while I was hastening towards you, and had already accomplished the greater part of the distance, that the news of this matter reversed my plan, that I might not be compelled to see with my own eyes that which I felt myself scarcely able even to hear. Open then for me henceforward by your unity of judgment that road to the regions of the East which your dissensions have closed against me, and permit me speedily to see yourselves and all other peoples rejoicing together, and render due acknowledgment to God in the language of praise and thanksgiving for the restoration of general concord and liberty to all.

These sentences are fairly odd: if the dispute revolved around trivial matters, as Constantine had stated before, why would he postpone his planned journey? We know from some other sources that the Emperor would set out on such a journey in the following year, despite the fact that the Arian controversy had been by no means resolved. He finished his tour at Rome amid the grand celebrations of the *vicennalia* of his reign. The Emperor's statement referring to the postponement of the journey may be a rhetorical exaggeration. On the other hand, we know that Constantine arrived at Nicomedia in late September, after the defeat of Licinius. Was he going to set out on his journey to the East with the winter season so close at hand?

As we can see, the letter does not make it clear what was the actual cause of the dispute between the bishop and his presbyter; nor does it imply that the author had ever heard of any synod at which Arius would have been excommunicated. All that he is aware of is the dispute which had caused a split within the Church, not just within the local church of Alexandria, but in the entire East. It would be difficult to assume that the Emperor had written the epistle *manu propria* and *propria mente*. As far as the dispute is concerned, he had certainly known only as much as his advisors, most probably especially Hosius, perhaps also Eusebius of Nicomedia, communicated to him, with the reservations stated at the beginning of this chapter as regards Eusebius' relations with Licinius, which must have put the former in a somewhat suspect position in Constantine's eyes. Is it possible then that the two advisors had also ignored Alexander's disciplinary measures taken against Arius? It is known that Arius had complained about the situation in his letter to Eusebius, Alexander publicized the whole affair, and Eusebius stood up for Arius! As a matter of fact, it was the scandalous contention itself, so harmful to the unity of the Church, not any doctrine-related issue, that the Emperor saw as a cause for concern. The veiled contents of the letter imply that it is concerned in fact with some broader issues and was apparently addressed to the synod at Antioch.[43] Perhaps not necessarily to that particular synod, yet it is evident that the epistle is concerned with more than just a dispute between the two clergymen from Alexandria. In all probability, there was something more on the Emperor's mind, and the impression is all the stronger in view of the messenger's high rank. These circumstances indicate the unusual nature of the delivery (common messengers would have sufficed on ordinary errands).

Eusebius goes on to note that the Emperor's letter brought no result and "the acrimony of the contending parties continually increased" (VC II, 73) throughout the East. He also says that the conflict caused at Alexandria led to a schism between Alexandria and Thebes and "in every city bishops were engaged in obstinate conflict with bishops, and people rising against people; and almost like the fabled Symplegades, coming into violent collision with each other. Nay, some were so far transported beyond the bounds of reason as to be guilty of reckless and outrageous conduct,

---

[43] Cf. S.G. Hall, *Some Constantinian Documents in the Vita Constantini*, 86-103.

and even to insult the statues of the emperor. This state of things had little power to excite his anger, but rather caused in him sorrow of spirit; for he deeply deplored the folly thus exhibited by deranged men." (VC III, 4) He goes to recount the problems connected with the controversy over the date of Easter and concludes: "as soon as he [Constantine] was made acquainted with the facts which I have described, and perceived that his letter to the Alexandrian Christians had failed to produce its due effect, he at once aroused the energies of his mind, and declared that he must prosecute to the utmost this war also against the secret adversary who was disturbing the peace of the Church." (VC III, 5) It would be then that he called a general synod to Nicaea.

Eusebius composed his work after Constantine's death, i.e., 12 years after the events in question. Did he recall all the dates with accuracy? What was the said schism between Alexandria and Thebes? He may have possibly alluded to Lycopolis in Thebaid I, Meletius' episcopal see, from which we could infer that the reference is in fact to the Meletian schism. In consequence, there arises a question of the existence of a possible connection, in the opinion of Constantine and his advisors, between the Meletian schism and the controversy involving Alexander and Arius. If that had indeed been the case, it would have been conceivable that the Emperor was calling on the two to become reconciled, as the ongoing dissension would only aggravate the state of the affairs in the Church caused by the schism. It seems to follow from Eusebius' account that the schism in question was the Emperor's greatest concern. Let us also recall that Hosius had attended the synod of Alexandria, where this particular matter was submitted for consideration.[44]

According to Sozomen,[45] Arius had been associated with Meletius in the period of Bishop Peter's episcopate. However, he deserted Meletius, and thereafter Peter made him a deacon. Subsequently, he would criticize the bishop for his anti-Meletian decrees (too strict, in Arius' view), for which he would be excluded from the Church. Pardoned once again (this time, by Bishop Achillas), he was ordained a presbyter. As experience shows that frequent changes of party affiliations do not make friends, it may be true after all that Meletius had informed Alexander of Arius' unorthodox statements, as Epiphanius puts it in his *Panarion.*[46]

By way of recapitulation, let us venture the following hypothetical reconstruction of the events:

The Emperor Constantine endeavoured to ensure the religious peace

[44] Cf. SCL 1, 82.

[45] Sozomen, *h.e.* I, 15.

[46] Epiphanius, *Panarion* 69, 3.

in the Empire, which did not amount, in his view, to any form of religious unification. Christianity became incorporated in the body of the religions protected by law and came under his pontifical tutelage. In consequence, he considered himself as its superior authority. He was concerned about the Donatist schism in Africa and the Meletian schism in Egypt, and he wished to restore the unity of the Church. The information on the dispute between Alexander and Arius, which he had most probably received only after his return from the war against Licinius (in September 234), convinced him that the problems in Egypt had been getting even worse and induced him to write a letter which was to be publicized in the East. Although he treated this doctrinal controversy in terms of a debate in a school of philosophy, that is, a question of little practical significance, he realized, or was made aware of, that the problems arising from the schism compounded by the new dispute thwart his hopes for achieving a lasting peace. Therefore, he sent Hosius on a mission to mitigate the contention and ensure a settlement of the problems. It is difficult to imagine that he could have possibly decided on calling a general synod of the bishops to Nicaea for the summer of 325 only after having received the news of the failure of Hosius' mission from Alexandria, as there would have been apparently no time for that. Beginning from 12 November, there was no longer any navigation on the Mediterranean and it would not have been possible for the Emperor to send out invitations so that all the bishops concerned could have received them on time, i.e. before Easter, which had fallen on 18 April in that year (as per the Alexandrian calculation) and made it to Nicaea. The conciliatory tone of the letter seems to point out that the Emperor had believed Hosius' mission would be successful and lead to a reconciliation between Alexander and Arius, as well as alleviate the contentious attitudes in the East. If it had been the case indeed, and the invitations to the council would have been dispatched as early as in the autumn of 324, it is not evident that the Arian controversy had been the reason for the calling of the council.

Such an interpretation of the events is at odds with the commonly accepted view that the council was summoned only after the Emperor had found out about the failure of Hosius' mission. It appears to follow from these excerpts of Eusebius' account:

ὃς ἐπειδὴ τὴν τῶν λεχθέντων διέγνω ἀκοὴν τό τε καταπεμφθὲν αὐτῷ γράμμα τοῖς κατὰ τὴν Ἀλεξάνδρειαν ἄπρακτον ἑώρα, τότε τὴν αὐτὸς ἑαυτοῦ διάνοιαν ἀνακινήσας,	As soon as he was made acquainted with the facts which I have described, and perceived that his letter to the Alexandrian Christians had failed to produce its due effect, he at once aroused the energies of his mind,

ἄλλον τουτονὶ καταγωνιεῖσθαι δεῖν
ἔφη τὸν κατὰ τοῦ ταράττοντος τὴν
ἐκκλησίαν ἀφανοῦς ἐχθροῦ πόλεμον.
6. Εἶθ' ὥσπερ ἐπιστρατεύων αὐτῷ
φάλαγγα θεοῦ σύνοδον οἰκουμενικὴν
συνεκρότει, σπεύδειν ἀπανταχόθεν
τοὺς ἐπισκόπους γράμμασι τιμητικοῖς
προκαλούμενος.

and declared that he must prosecute to the utmost this war also against the secret adversary who was disturbing the peace of the Church.
6. Then as if to bring a divine array against this enemy, he convoked a general council, and invited the speedy attendance of bishops from all quarters, in letters expressive of the honorable estimation in which he held them.[47]

I would like to note that this interpretation (a correct one, after all) may be construed in terms of the outcome, i.e., perceiving the summoning of the council as the result of the inefficiency of the Emperor's letter addressed to Alexander and Arius. Nonetheless, a different circumstance is possible as well: Constantine decided to counter the crisis spreading throughout the Church, beginning from Alexandria, and his summons for a general council, previously dispatched to the bishops from all quarters, had offered a great opportunity to do so. In consequence, the burgeoning Arian movement did not have to be the main cause for inviting the bishops to attend, just one of a certain number of other issues to be debated there, and the actual reasons for the convocation were different. It is affirmed by the fact that Eusebius passes over this particular subject in his panegyrical work containing an account of the proceedings of the council. Likewise, the Emperor does not even make a mention of this issue in his post-synodal epistle to all the bishops, something that would have been utterly inconceivable had the Arian controversy been the main reason for the convocation of this council. We shall have a closer look at Constantine's post-synodal letter further on.[48]

[47] Eusebius of Caesarea, *v.C.* III, 5-6 (NPNF 2,1).
[48] Cf. Ch. 8.

IV

THE CONVOCATION AND PROCEEDINGS
OF THE COUNCIL OF NICAEA

In the previous chapter, we were concerned with Constantine's letter from which it followed that even in late September 324 the Emperor regarded the dispute between Alexander and Arius as a scandalous occurrence that ought to be censured, but is of no major significance. The Emperor expressed his hopes the opponents would become reconciled and the problem would be resolved.

It is commonly believed that Hosius' efforts at Alexandria brought no result at all, and therefore he returned to Nicomedia and persuaded the Emperor to convoke a general council, as he had realized the doctrinal significance of Arianism.[1] However, there was not enough time to do so. As we have seen, Hosius could have departed from Nicomedia only in late September or even in October 324, that is, almost at the last possible moment for a sea journey to Alexandria and thus he could not have hoped he would be able to return still before the following spring. Likewise, he had no possibility to dispatch a letter to the Emperor and inform him whether the mission was successful or not.[2] Therefore, his mission must have been of a more general nature, especially as Hosius would be present at Antioch in the spring of 325, which I shall yet discuss further on.

Athanasius makes a passing mention of Hosius' participation in some synod held at Alexandria, dealing with the Meletian question. Evidently, he had been entrusted with handing over the letter as well as somehow taking care of the issue of the Meletian controversy.[3] He must have been certainly preoccupied with something, as he had found himself staying there for the winter. For, in all probability, he must have stayed there. Barnes seems to believe in a near-miraculous pace of Hosius' journey; he would have arrived at Alexandria in late autumn, and stayed there for an unknown period of time. Subsequently, he would have returned to Nicomedia and, upon the news of the death of the Bishop of Antioch, departed for Antioch, just in

---

[1] E.g., M. Simonetti, *La crisi ariana*, 37.

[2] Although many scholars agree with this view; in consideration of the difficulties involved in arguing for Hosius' journey to Nicomedia over the winter season, they at least surmise that a letter to the Emperor would have been sent around February, see CH. M. Odahl, *Constantine and the Christian Empire*, 169-170.

[3] Athanasius, *Apologia contra Arianos* 74.

time for the synod before the Easter.[4] Similar views can be found in Odahl[5] and a number of various textbooks. No schedule of maritime travel in the Mediterranean or the postal service system operating on land could have possibly withstood such a swift travelling regimen.

According to Philostorgius, the Arian historian living at the turn of the fourth century,[6] Hosius returned to Nicomedia after his visit at Alexandria, followed by Arius and Alexander in order to meet with him there: Arius made his journey by land, while Alexander chose to go by ship. This is most likely some sort of "shortening" of the timeline perspective. Why should they have followed him almost immediately after having parted with him? Besides, Philostorgius does not say for how long Hosius had been staying at Alexandria. Secondly, the two Alexandrian clergymen had not been on good terms with each other and obviously unwilling to travel together. But there must have been some more important reasons for his decision to make a several-month-long journey by land, instead of travelling by ship, which would have taken only a few weeks, at the most. For instance, something very important to take care of on his way. Moreover, it must have been necessary to leave in advance accordingly, so that the opponent could not have too much of an advantage. What is it that Arius had to attend to on the way, considering how much inconvenience such a journey must have involved, and why would he have wished to meet with Hosius again? And would he have decided to go to Nicomedia by land in the course of the winter season? Let us not forget the rugged mountainous terrain.

Hypothetically speaking, the following course of the events may have been possible: Hosius' arrival at Alexandria took place as part of the mission in the East entrusted to him by the Emperor, which had comprised at least three issues: settlement of the problem of the Meletian schism, determination of the date of Easter, and reconciliation between Alexander and Arius. As regards the latter problem, he delivered the Emperor's epistle, probably spoke with the two addressees, yet failed to mitigate the contention itself. Concerning the Meletian schism, he participated in at least one synod, most likely negotiated with those involved in the controversy, made efforts to resolve the problem, though we do not know if he managed to obtain any result. As for determining the date of Easter, we know that he was to negotiate on the matter as well.[7]

---

[4] T.D. Barnes, *Athanasius and Constantius*. 16.

[5] Ch. M. Odahl, *Constantine and the Christian Empire*, 170.

[6] Philostorgius, *h.e.* I, 7.

[7] Sozomen, *h.e.* I, 16. See A. Di Berardino, *L'imperatore Costantino e la celebrazione della Pasqua*, w: *Costantino il Grande dall'antichità all'umanesimo*. Colloquio sul Cristianesimo nel mondo antico, Macerata 18-20 Dicembre 1990, vol. I, eds. G. Bonamente e Franca Fusco, Università degli Studi di Macerata 1992, 363-384.

As the question of this date will be reappearing time and time again, let us now discuss it in a little more detail.

The Church had been already faced with this particular problem for a long time. There had been two traditions followed since the very beginning. The Judeo-Christians saw no reason to celebrate Easter on any day other than that determined by the Jewish calendar, i.e., on the 14th day of the month Nisan, regardless of the week-day. On the other hand, the Gentile Christians, i.e., the faithful from all the other ethnic communities, celebrated Easter on the Sunday after that date, namely following the first spring full moon, in commemoration of Christ's resurrection "after the Sabbath."[8] Already in the second century, Pope Victor attempted to persuade the faithful in Asia to celebrate Easter on Sunday, and Bishop Polycarp of Smyrna even met with Victor to discuss this issue. No resolution was achieved, even though the talks between the two ended in a peaceful atmosphere. Irenaeus defended the validity of the Eastern practice as well. Apart from the Judeo-Christian communities, it became customary for the Bishop of Alexandria to inform the entire Christian world of the Easter date in a given year. Apparently, the Egyptian astronomers were commonly considered to be trustworthy. By the early fourth century, however, the nature of the problem had changed. There had still existed some Judeo-Christian communities, of course, but their numbers had dwindled so much by then that the Emperor could have well afforded to overlook their position on the issue. A much greater cause for concern was that the principal sees of Christendom, i.e., Alexandria and Rome, were not able to reach any consensus in the matter. In Egypt, the Passover date was calculated to the best of their knowledge and abilities, ignoring the fact that the date would at times fall past 21 April. At Rome, on the contrary, it was absolutely unacceptable: notably, it was the day (the date of the foundation of the City) marking the beginning of the year at times. In consequence, should Easter ever fall after that date, there would be no Easter day at all in one year and two Easters in the other. In his post-synodal letter addressed to the Churches, the Emperor writes: "Surely we should never suffer Easter to be kept twice in one and the same year!"[9] It would apply also to the Judeo-Christian Passover, as it might fall either before or after 21 April, and sometimes even prior to the spring equinox. Jews would not rely on astronomical observations, as they followed the established lunar calendar, in which the year was divided into 12 months, 29 or 30 days each, with a total of 354 days. Therefore, a new lunar month would be added to the year every three years in order to make it draw level with the solar year.

---

[8] On the complicated calculations of the date of Easter, cf. J. Naumowicz, *Geneza chrześcijańskiej rachuby lat*, Wydawnictwo Benedyktynów, Kraków 2000, 82ff.

[9] The letter as cited in: Socrates, *h.e.* I, 9 (NPNF 2,2).

As a result, it caused that the 14th day of the lunar month Nisan, i.e. the time of the Jewish Passover, could sometimes fall on a date prior to the equinox.[10]

It is noteworthy that the Church had managed to carry on despite those differences. Nonetheless, the Emperor could not have afforded to leave the question unresolved. In his capacity as the *Pontifex Maximus*, he was responsible for determining the calendar of feast days for all the religions in the Empire.[11] Consequently, in 321, he established Sunday as a holiday,[12] and even composed a prayer to be said by legionaries.[13] He also wished, or felt he really had to, establish the date of Easter to be celebrated throughout the Empire, in order to make it a truly once-in-a-year feast day. Previously, he had already attempted to urge the bishops assembled at the synod of Arles (314) to determine the date, unfortunately with no definite resolution achieved, since the bishops had only expressed their will that all the Churches celebrate Easter on the same day.[14]

The further course of the events points out that the Alexandrians may have only communicated to Hosius their firm position on how they calculated the date of Easter and their outright disinterest in following any other practice, and quite predictably so. If he were thus expected to attain any result on the issue, it would be only natural to assume that his mission was not limited to Alexandria.

If, at that point, Hosius had wished to return to Nicomedia, there must have been the "open sea" period again, i.e., at least March 10, 325, provided that he was willing to take the risk and managed to procure a vessel fit for the journey.[15] Decent people and cautious sailors would not set out into the high seas before 25 May, in a period just after the springtime stormy weather spells, perhaps only possibly along the coastline. In that case, it would have been much too late for reporting to the Emperor so as to make it possible for him to have sent out his invitations to the bishops to arrive at a synod to be held in June of that year (in the hopes that the invitations would be delivered in due time and the invited bishops make it to the venue of the

---

[10] J. Naumowicz, *Geneza*, 91-104; D. Vigne, *Une Église, plusieurs dates de Pâques?* in BLE 102(2001), 250.

[11] Cf. J. Guillen, *Urbs Roma. Vida y costumbres de los Romanos*, III, Ed. Sigueme, Salamanca 1980, 303ff. Cf. Livy, *History of Rome* I, 20.

[12] Iustinianus, *cod.* III, 12, 2.

[13] *v. C* IV, 19s.

[14] Council of Arles (314), c. 1; SCL 1, 71. Cf. A. Di Berardino, *L'imperatore Costantino e la celebrazione della Pasqua*, 364ff.

[15] Of course, there are scholars who believe that Hosius had managed to make it back to Nicomedia *via* Antioch to inform the Emperor of the problem. Cf. J. Behr, *The Nicene Faith*, St. Vladimir's Seminary Press, Crestwood, New York 2004, I, 66-67.

synod). In addition, Hosius had presided over the synod at Antioch and then managed to make it to the council at Nicaea, just as the other bishops had. To travel the distance by sea, one had to sail from Antioch to Byzantium or Nicomedia, thence on to Nicaea, three weeks in all. In turn, travelling by land, with the assistance of the Imperial postal system, as Constantine had recommended to the bishops,[16] would normally take two months. Therefore, we must assume that Hosius had departed from Alexandria only to head straight for Antioch, and not back to Nicomedia, as part of the continuation of his mission in the East.[17] He may have reached there before the Easter, i.e., 18 April, according to the Alexandrian calculation. By that time, there might have perhaps still existed some communities in Asia celebrating the Passover according to the Jewish calendar, but they had definitely become marginalized in the Church. Philostorgius' account begins to make sense: Alexander and Arius wanted to meet with Hosius, as they were aware he would report to the Emperor not just on his visit to Alexandria (they needed no further information about it), but also on the proceedings of the synod at Antioch. To both of them, it must have been very important indeed. As Arius may have been particularly interested in meeting with his friend Eusebius of Caesarea in the first place, he decided to make a more time-consuming land journey through Palestine. It was most probably the inaccurately transmitted information on this voyage that would be also used by Epiphanius, in whose account Arius went to Caesarea after he had been excommunicated by Alexander.[18]

This allows us to propound a new hypothetical reconstruction of the sequence of the events related to the dispute between Alexander and Arius as well as those connected with Bishop Hosius' mission:

1) A public debate took place at which the participants disagreed on interpreting a certain passage of the Scriptures. Arius, whose views were anti-Monarchian, would firmly emphasize the distinction between the Father and the Son, which made some people contest his position and resort to the arguments similar to those once used against Dionysius of Alexandria. Having considered the question, Bishop Alexander agreed with Arius' opponents and called on him to state his position in writing. The news of the dispute spread around and aroused a general discussion.

2) Arius and his followers addressed Alexander in a letter, where Arius stated his views on the created being of the Son ("but not like other created beings").

[16] Eusebius of Caesarea, *v.C.* III, 6.

[17] A.H.B. Logan, *Marcellus of Ancyra and the Councils of AD 325: Antioch, Ancyra and Nicaea*, in JThSt 43 (1992), 428-446.

[18] Epiphanius, *Panarion* 69, 3.

3) Alexander summoned a synod at which he (and the one hundred bishops in attendance) condemned the letter and its signatories in the same order in which they had incautiously endorsed it.

4) Arius wrote a letter to Eusebius of Nicomedia, in which he depicted Alexander as someone sympathetic with the Monarchian-oriented heretics.

5) Eusebius gave Arius credence, or at least took advantage of the controversy to publicize the allegations of Alexander's unjust conduct.

6) Hosius and Constantine were informed of the events; as part of the already planned mission to the East, the Emperor bid Hosius to make the both parties agree to a reconciliation and addressed the two Alexandrian clergymen in a letter.

7) Hosius' efforts failed to produce any result; with the rest of the entrusted matters settled (or not), he proceeded to Antioch in early spring.

The above analysis eventually leads us to ask the following question: what was the time for the Nicene synod to take place, as specified by the Emperor? The spring of 325 would have been too late, as almost none of the invited bishops could have made it there on time. Therefore, he must have taken care of it beforehand, so that the letters would have been taken by the last ships to sail off in 324 or delivered by means of the Imperial postal service (this latter option taking definitely much more time). It would follow then that the idea of inviting the bishops to attend a synod had preceded the plan to send Hosius on a mission to the East, or, possibly, had been parallel to that plan. Since no one sends out an arbitrator with the assumption that his mission would prove to be a failure anyway, Constantine must have expected Hosius to settle all the issues entrusted to him, i.e., the Arian controversy, the Meletian schism, and the question of the date of Easter. So why should he convoke a general synod at all? Let us leave this question unanswered for the time being.

Already more than half a century ago, J. R. Nyman noted that there had been not enough time to convoke a synod to Nicaea in the winter of 324 – 325.[19] He concluded then that the council would have been evidently convoked to Ancyra at an earlier date, and only transferred to Nicaea later on, at Hosius' incentive. As that must have occurred, however, at some earlier date as well, he propounded that the synod at Antioch be dated back to 324. Unfortunately, this assertion does not tally with the chronology given by Eusebius of Caesarea, which none of the contemporary authors ever questioned.

As I have already noted above, a number of letters were written and sent in connection with the controversy over Arius. Alexander addressed

[19] J.R. Nyman, *The Synod at Antioch (324-325) and the Council of Nicaea*, Studia patristica. - Vol. 4, P. 2 (1961). - (Texte und Untersuchungen 79) 483-489.

his circular letter against him, whereas Eusebius of Nicomedia would address his letter to "all" the bishops. It gives us some reason to believe that a local dispute had turned into a general problem affecting the entire Church and the whole controversy had been already going on for a few years before the council. Nonetheless, we could still wonder why the Emperor would have continued to regard the contention as a local affair in September or October 324. How can it be explained? Notably, let us turn in this context to the following passage from the above-mentioned circular letter of Alexander. In his words: "I felt imperatively called on to be silent no longer, knowing what is written in the law, but to inform you of all of these things, that ye might understand both who the apostates are, and also the contemptible character of their heresy, and pay no attention to anything that Eusebius should write to you."[20] As it appears, Alexander had already received Eusebius' letter, or was at least informed that the other bishops would receive it as well (although, perhaps, not as yet). It would have meant that the both bishops addressed those letters to their colleagues at approximately the same time, as if trying to vie with each other. At this point, we might want to investigate the matter further and ask about the possible "motive." Why should they have been so much preoccupied with their endeavours to persuade, so swiftly, all the bishops to accept their view? I understand Arius' decision (immediately following the synod which had condemned him) to address his letter to Eusebius of Nicomedia, whom he considered as his ally. It is just as easy to understand that Eusebius would stand up for Arius. I cannot see, however, why he would have decided to give the dispute so much "publicity," thus helping to turn it into a matter of general concern throughout the Church. It could have been easily foreseen that many (bishops) would side with the metropolitan Alexander rather than with the presbyter Arius. Alexander would have certainly had the reasons to spread the word of the synodal verdict (an ordinary practice, after all). But why would Eusebius have been the first one to do so?

The Synod at Antioch

There are two extant documents (composed in Syriac) which shed some more light on this question, yet at the same time make things somewhat more complicated. The first one is the Emperor Constantine's letter, from which it follows that he first invited the bishops to Ancyra, but would subsequently relocate the venue to Nicaea.[21] The other document is a letter addressed by the fifty-nine participants of the synod at Antioch, assembled

[20] Cf. Alexander, *Letter to All the Bishops*, 4.
[21] Opitz, 20, p. 41f.

at the time following the invitation to Ancyra but prior to the relocation of the proceedings to Nicaea.[22] It was connected with the election of a new bishop, Eustatius.[23]

The synodal letter is addressed to Alexander, Bishop of "the new Rome." The expression looks like a reference to Constantinople, but the City of Constantinople had yet to be founded, and nobody would have thought of referring to Byzantium as "the new Rome." The bishop of that city had been indeed named Alexander, yet unfortunately we only know very few facts about him. Therefore, why would the bishops assembled at Antioch have addressed their synodal relation to him, the bishop of a pleasantly situated, yet still relatively not very significant, city? Again, there is some room for speculation here.

Was the letter supposed to be shown to the bishops travelling to attend the council and crossing the Bosphorus at Byzantium? Did the Syrian copyist make a mistake while copying the address? Can the address possibly refer to some other figure named Alexander? We could ask even more questions. It is conceivable that Hosius may have intended to have the letter delivered to the Emperor as soon as possible; incidentally, the first ship to depart would have been bound for Byzantium (a journey of three weeks' time[24]), sufficiently close to Nicomedia to make the delivery of the letter possible. All of this is merely speculation. Instead, let us stick to the contents of the letter, independent of the actual identity of the addressee.

It is notable that Hosius' presidency of the synod has been deduced on the basis of a certain error: the text records the name Eusebius, even though we do know that there was no figure named Eusebius in the vicinity with the authority to make him eligible to preside over a synod in a different city. And secondly, there is some evidence that points to the Syriac transcription of the name Hosius as Eusebius. Indeed, although bishops Eusebius of Caesarea and Eusebius of Nicomedia were important figures, the former had been called on, at the synod, to revise some of his previous statements, whereas the latter apparently did not attend the synod.[25] On the contrary, De Decker is almost certain that it was Eusebius of Nicomedia who had presided over that synod, due to his position as the most important bishop

[22] Opitz, 18, p. 36ff.

[23] For a brief and fairly conventional depiction of the synod, see L. Ayres, *Nicaea and Its Legacy*, 18.

[24] Cf. T. Lewicki, *Les voies maritimes de la Méditerranée dans le Haut Moyen Age d'apres les sources Arabes*, in : *La navigazione mediterranea nell'Alto Mediovo*, Spoleto 1978, 451.

[25] Cf. H. Chadwick, *Ossius of Cordova and the Presidency of the Council of Antioch, 325*, in JThSt 9 (1958), 295; M. Simonetti, *La crisi ariana*, 38, n. 26.

in the East.[26] In my opinion, the scholar overstates the significant role of that bishop. Moreover, we do know that Hosius, not Eusebius, was the one who had been entrusted with a mission in the East. Secondly, as we shall see, the text of the preserved synodal letter is clearly very anti-Arian, which would have been surely prevented by Eusebius, had he indeed possessed the authority attributed to him by De Decker.

Before I proceed to discuss the content of the synodal letter, I would like to take note of one particularly significant fact: as far as one can tell, it is the first testimony of a profession of faith determined by a synod and signed by the bishops. Until then, each Church had adhered to its own *credo*; it was taught to catechumens and passed to them before being baptized. There were more or less apparent differences among those various creeds, yet there is no document that would suggest the Church felt any need to formulate some sort of a general-purpose profession of faith. Who then would have come up with the idea of formulating such a creed at Antioch, on the eve of a general synod? What is the reason for such a sudden emergence of this necessity? It does not suffice to say that it was all about condemning the Arian teachings, considering that many of the earlier synods had excommunicated various figures and no new creed had ever been signed (for instance, at Alexandria, where Demetrios condemned Origen in *ca.* 230,[27] or even at Antioch in 268, when Paul of Samosata was condemned[28]). Yet this time, let us note, the bishops resort to formulating a creed, followed by a long series of synods, bringing a succession of newly worded formulas, with the participants striving to prove that the new one is superior to all the previous creeds.

The only evident answer, in my view, is related to the fact that all the synods had submitted their creeds to the emperors: the Council of Nicaea to Constantine, Antioch (341)[29] and Sardica (343)[30] to Constans, Sirmium (357)[31] to Constantius, *etc.* Who really needed then a general creed of the Christian faith: the Church or the emperor? Supposedly, had the Church required such a creed, it would have been formulated sooner.

As I have already noted, one of the principal duties of the *Pontifex Maximus* was to preserve the holy formulae of all the religions and ensure that the faithful conform to their appropriate formula. Until then, there had been no Christian texts in those much-venerated Pontifical Books. How was the

---

[26] D. De Decker, *Eusèbe de Nicomédie*, 133-134.

[27] Cf. Eusebius of Caesarea, *h.e.* VI, 23, 4; Photius, *Bibliotheca* 118.

[28] Cf. Council of Antioch (268/269), SCL 1, 44-47.

[29] Council of Antioch (341), SCL 1, 129-142.

[30] Council of Sardica (343), SCL 1, 143-147.

[31] Council of Sirmium (357), SCL 1, 208-209.

Emperor, as the *Pontifex Maximus,* to watch over the proper implementation of the Christian worship? On what basis could he decide whether a certain religious conduct was permissible or not? Each bishop would first take the *credo* of his own Church into consideration. The Emperor needed a more generally formulated document. It is conceivable that this is exactly the reason why he had convoked the bishops to Nicaea, especially in view of the fact that a new creed was indeed promulgated there. As a matter of fact, Nicaea was a second attempt, as the first one had taken place at Antioch in the spring of 325. Therefore, could it be that Constantine had also entrusted Hosius with the task of formulating a new *credo* as part of his mission in the East? Apparently, yes. There is unfortunately no clear way we could answer the question why the Emperor would have required that the Christians provide their own creed, and not just worship formulae, as was the case with all the other religions. I surmise he may have been told that the *credo* is a kind of text used during the rites of Christian initiation, i.e., baptism; as a result, the Emperor may have perceived it as tantamount to initiation formulae. It may be then presumed that Hosius had presented the attendees of the Antiochene synod with the Emperor's wish and the bishops undertook to fulfil it. One cannot help but get the impression that the Emperor had aimed to resolve all the urgent questions still before the general synod at Nicaea.

As it appears, the Council of Nicaea did not discuss the aforementioned Antiochene creed at all. The Emperor and his advisors at the court must have been dissatisfied with it. Let us now have a closer look at it.[32]

A Copy of the Decisions of the Synod at Antioch to Alexander, Patriarch of the New Rome[33]

(1) To the eminent, dear, and like-minded brother and fellow-servant Alexander, Eusebius/Hosius, Eustatios, Amphion, Bassianos, Zenobius, Piperius, Salamanes, Gregory, Magnus, Peter, Longinus, Manitius, Mokimos, Agapios, Macedonius, Paul, Bassianos, Seleukos, Sopatros, Antioch, Macarius, Jacob, Hellanikos, Nicetas, Archelaos, Macrinus, Germanos,

---

[32] For the Syriac text and a Greek rendition thereof (Opitz, *Athanasius Werke* III/1, 36-41), see in SCL 1, 83-90.

[33] Opitz, *Athanasius Werke* III/1, 36-41 (the Syriac text and a Greek retroversion); F. Nau, in *Revue de l'Orient Chrétien* 4 (1909) 12-16 (a French translation), 17-24 (the Syriac text); M. Simonetti, *La crisi ariana,* 38-40; L. Abramowski, *The Synod of Antioch 324/25 and Its Creed,* in: *Formula and Context. Studies in Early Christian Thought,* Variorum, London 1992, note 3; the creed of the Antioch synod, in: *A New Eusebius. Documents Illustrating the History of the Church to AD 337,* J. Stevenson (ed.), SPCK, London 1990.

Anatolus, Zoilos, Kirillos, Paulinus, Aetius, Moses, Eustatios, Alexander, Eirenaios, Rabboulas, Paul, Lupus, Nikomach, Philoxenos, Maximus, Marinus, Euphrantion, Tarkondimantos, Eirenikos, Peter, Pegasius, Eupsychios, Asklepeios, Alpheios, Bassos, Gerontios, Hesychius, Auidius, Terentius [send] their greetings in the Lord.

In the Syriac version of the letter, the first of the enumerated names may be construed as either Eusebius or Hosius. However, in the final section of the document, Eusebius is mentioned as a follower of Arius; he is censured, not to say condemned, yet it appears that no definite verdict was passed, pending resolution to be made at the already summoned council (please refer to the relevant commentary above).

(2) The Catholic Church is one body[34] in all the places, just as the seats of all those assembled here together are in various places, like parts of the entire body, one ought to know the things that I, and our pious and like-minded brethren and fellow-servants, have undertaken and done, so that you, too, present in your spirit with us, could prudently speak, in common ministry, of the things we have determined and done in accordance with the law of the Church. (3) Having arrived in the Church of Antioch, as I had seen the Church much perturbed because of the weeds of the teachings[35] of some and the dispute, it appeared righteous to me that not only should I myself reject and resist it, but that the brothers in common spirit, our fellow-servants, nearest to us, in the face of the urgent and necessary cause, should encourage our brothers in Palestine and Arabia, in Phoenicia, in Lower Syria and Cilicia, and Cappadocia, so that we could jointly examine and establish the matters of the Church in a final form. For many righteous men dwell in the city.[36]

The author appears to be convinced that the addressee is aware of the whole dispute and that there is no reason to discuss it in detail. He goes on to refer very clearly to the Arian controversy, which, as we can see, had already reached Antioch.

(4) When therefore the grace of God assembled us in the community at Antioch, we investigated and busied ourselves with a policy common, helpful and beneficial for the Church of God. We found a great deal of disorder, the chief reason being that the law of the Church had been in so

[34] Cf. *Eph.* 3:4.
[35] Cf. *Mt.* 13:25.
[36] Cf. *Gen.* 18:23ff.

many respects slighted and despised, and the canons had in the meantime been wholly invalidated by worldly men.

(5) Since the holding of a synod of bishops had been hindered in these parts our first care was to investigate a topic that is most important of all and surpasses all others – in fact it comprises the whole mystery of the faith that is in us – I mean what concerns the Saviour of us all, *the Son of the Living God.*[37]

It would be difficult to guess what were the specific problems of the Church of Antioch at the time. We have got the information on the death of Bishop Philogonius, whom Arius, in his letter to Eusebius of Nicomedia, described as an ignorant heretic, along with some men named Ellanikos and Macarius. In his words, "some of them say that the Son is an eructation, others that He is a production, others that He is also unbegotten."[38] It is not known if they all professed those views in common, or if each one of them subscribed to just one of those teachings, respectively. If that had been the case, Philogonius would have espoused a Christological interpretation of Ps 44:2, saying that the word flows out of the heart, and rather would not have been a follower of Origen, since the latter regarded referring to the Son as to be precarious and suggestive of the Logos' existence as the non-personal intellect in God.[39] It also seems that the said breach of the law is somehow linked to the Christological doctrinal issues. If so, it may have been possible that the Antiochians had not paid very much attention to the condemnation of Arius and his followers at Alexandria, and remained in communion with them (or some of them) in contravention of the synodal decrees.[40]

(6) For since our brother and fellow servant, the honoured and beloved Alexander, Bishop of Alexandria, had excommunicated some of his presbyters, i.e. Arius and his friends, for the blasphemy which they directed against our Saviour, though they were able by their impious teaching to cause some to stray to such an extent that they were received into communion by them, the holy synod decided to investigate this question first, in order that after a solution had been reached of the supreme points in the mystery as far as lay in our power, so the remaining questions could be investigated in turn individually.

[37] Cf. *Mt.*16:16.

[38] Arius, *Letter to Eusebius of Nicomedia* 3 (see above).

[39] Origenes, *CIo.* I, 24, 151.

[40] Cf. Council of Elvira (306), c. 53 (SCL 1, 57); Council of Arles (314), c. 17 (SCL 1, 73); *Can, App.* 9-12 (SCL 2, 275).

Once again, the author (authors) of the letter asserts that the most important question is the mystery of the faith in the Saviour. I would like to highlight this point, since it has become customary to define Arianism in terms of a Trinitarian controversy, as opposed to the later Christological ones: Apollinarianism, Nestorianism, and Monophysitism, to name just a few of the most prominent. It may have happened because Athanasius of Alexandria, who is mostly responsible for the eventual shape of the notions about Arianism, had spoken primarily of the Father-and-Son relation in this context. But since the participants of the synod, with Hosius as a leading figure among them, state that the question was concerned with the Saviour Himself, not with His generation from the Father, it is due to be taken into consideration. Of course, the thing may be a difference in aspects only, but it is here the starting-point that is of concern. It may be then worth contemplating if the issue of Christ's mutability should not be given more attention than that of his descent. We have already seen that Arius would deal with the question of mutability/immutability at some length, for instance, in his *Letter to Alexander.*

(7) At our meeting, and in the presence of some brethren learned in the Church's faith which we were taught by the Scriptures and the apostles and which we have received from the fathers, we held a full discussion. We kept before us what Alexander, Bishop of Alexandria, had done against Arius and his friends, that if any clearly were tainted with teaching opposed to these actions, they too should be expelled from the Church, to prevent them by their continuous presence from being able to seduce some of the simpler brethren.

Theoretically speaking, Alexander had undertaken to propagate his own position. It was evidently not much of a success, though, as another, more detailed, statement was in order. But, by the way, are circular letters approached with more attention these days?

[*Credo* of the Synod at Antioch]

(8) The faith is as follows, passed down by the holy men, as to whom it is of little significance that they had lived and understood in the body, but it is [of consequence] that they had been educated in the spirit of the divinely inspired scriptures: to believe in one God, Father almighty, incomprehensible, immutable and unchangeable, providential ruler and guide of the universe, just, good, maker of heaven and earth and of all the things in them, Lord of the law and of the prophets and of the new covenant;

(9) and in one Lord Jesus Christ, only begotten Son, begotten not from that which is not but from the Father, not as made but as properly an

offspring, but begotten in an ineffable, indescribable manner, because only the Father who begot and the Son who was begotten know (for *no one knows the Father but the Son, nor the Son but the Father*),[41] who exists everlastingly and did not at one time not exist.

(10) For we have learned from the Holy Scriptures that he alone is *the sole image*,[42] not (plainly) as if he might have remained unbegotten from the Father, nor by adoption (for it is impious and blasphemous to say this); but the Scriptures described him as validly and truly begotten as Son, so that we believe him to be immutable and unchangeable, and that he was not begotten and did not come to be by volition or by adoption, so as to appear to be from that which is not, but as befits him to be begotten; not (a thing which it is not lawful to think) according to likeness or nature or commixture with any of the things which came to be through him, but in a way which passes all understanding or conception or reasoning

(11) we confess him to have been begotten of the unbegotten Father, God the Word, true light,[43] righteousness,[44] Jesus Christ, Lord and Saviour of all. For he is *the image*, not of the will or of anything else, but of his Father's *very substance* (*hypostasis*).[45]

As we can see, the document contains a number of references to the immutability and unchangeability of God and the Son. There is also a contrast made between the creation, as related to a work, and the begetting, which is soon to be enshrined in the Nicene *credo*. There is no mention at all of the views ascribed to Philogonius and his friends by Arius, i.e., some form of emanation, or even being co-unbegotten. Also noteworthy is the rejection of referring to the Son as a work made (ποίημα). It was characteristic of the whole tradition drawing on the legacy left by Philo of Alexandria, who held that the creation of the Logos was expressed in the words of the first verse of the Bible, where "at the beginning, God made heaven and earth" - ἐποίησεν ὁ θεὸς.[46] This particular assertion was not questioned by Origen and his disciple Dionysius of Alexandria,[47] yet it was vehemently opposed

---

[41] Cf. *Mt.* 11:27; *Lc.* 10:22.

[42] Cf. *2 Cor.* 4:4.

[43] *Io.* 1:9.

[44] *1 Cor.* 1:30.

[45] Cf. *2 Cor.* 4:4; *Hbr.*1:3.

[46] Cf. Philo of Alexandria, *De opificio mundi*, *passim*.

[47] Cf. Athanasius of Alexandria, *De sententia Dionysii*; H. Pietras, *Jedność Boga, jedność świata i jedność Kościoła. Studium fragmentów Dionizego Aleksandryjskiego*, WF TJ, Instytut Kultury Religijnej, Kraków 1990 (see ch. I).

by Dionysius of Rome and his synod.[48] It is therefore possible that Hosius himself, as a representative of the West, may have been responsible for this insertion in the document.

(11 cont.) This Son, God the Word, having been born in flesh from Mary the Mother of God and made incarnate, having suffered and died, rose again from the dead and was taken up into heaven, and sits on the right hand of the Majesty most high, and is coming to judge the living and the dead.

(12) Furthermore, as in our Saviour, the holy Scriptures teach us to believe also in one Spirit, one Catholic Church, the resurrection of the dead and a judgement of requital accordingly to whether a man has done well or badly in the flesh.[49]

This particular passage appears to be the most "occidental" in the whole *credo* and strangely reminiscent of the end of the Apostles' Creed, not verbatim and *en bloc*, of course, but let us not forget that the earliest evidence of the Apostles' Creed is of a somewhat later date. This may have been another contribution on Hosius' part.

(13) And we anathematize those who say or think or preach that the Son of God is a creature or has come into being or has been made and is not truly begotten, or that there was when he was not. For we believe that he was and is and that he is light.[50] Furthermore, we anathematize those who suppose that he is immutable by his own act of will, just as those who derive his birth from that which is not, and deny that he is immutable in the way the Father is. For just as our Saviour is the image of the Father[51] in all things, so in this respect particularly he has been proclaimed the Father's image.

In terms of its condemnation, the above anathematism puts three notions on par, while settling for just one. Namely, it condemns "creating," "coming into being," and "making," which, as per the Greek retroversion, should correspond to the terms κτίσμα, γενητόν, ποιητόν, but allows just γέννημα. If we juxtapose it with the creed and anathematism of the Council of Nicaea,[52] certain similarities are plain to see. Therein, it reads γεννηθέντα οὐ ποιηθέντα, while κτίσμα can be found in the anathematism versions dependent on Athanasius. Moreover, the both make a mention of mutability/immutability and refer to condemning those who preached "that there was when he [the

---

[48] Cf. Council of Rome (*ca.* 263), SCL 1, 42, as in: Athanasius of Alexandria, *De decretis Nicaenae synodi* 26, 4.

[49] Cf. *Sir.* 12:14; *Ier.* 42:6; *Mt.* 16:27; *2 Cor.* 5:10.

[50] Cf. *Io.* 1:9.

[51] Cf. *2 Cor.* 4:4; *Col.* 1:15.

[52] Cf. Council of Nicaea (325), DSP 1, 24.

Son] was not." It is difficult to say what it may imply, but there are certainly many similarities. Is it likely then that the anathematism of Nicaea would have turned out to be a thoroughly revised Antiochene formula?

(14) This faith was proposed and the whole of the holy synod agreed and confessed that this is the apostolic and saving teaching. All our fellow ministers were unanimous, except for Theodotus of the church of the Laodiceans (i.e. Laodicea in Syria), and Narcissus of Neronias (in Cilicia) and Eusebius of Caesarea in Palestine who as though forgetful of the Holy Scriptures and the apostolic teaching (though they tried to evade discovery in diverse manners and to conceal their errors by untrue subterfuges) manifestly introduced opposing views. For clearly, from our questions and theirs, they were proved to have the same views as Arius, and hold to opposite views to the above mentioned ones. Through their excessive obtuseness and failure to reverence the holy synod, which rejected their views and regarded them with aversion, we all, fellow ministers in the synod, have judged that we should not communicate with them, and that they are not worthy to communicate with us as their faith is foreign to the Catholic Church.

(15) We are writing to you to let you know that you should be on your guard against communicating with them, against writing to them and against receiving letters of communion from them. And know this also that through the great love of the brethren felt by the synod we have given them the great and priestly synod at Ancyra as a place of repentance and recognition of the truth.[53] Make therefore every effort to communicate this to all the brethren of one spirit, so that they too could get to know the matter, which is, who amongst them are apostates, separated from the Church. Send greetings to all your brethren. All those present here send you their greetings in the Lord.

As we can see, three bishops had reportedly opposed such a definition of faith. Theodotus is said to have deserved Eusebius' praise for the healing of bodies of souls;[54] we also know that he was censured by this synod and previously condemned elsewhere (unjustly, as Arius states in his letter to Eusebius of Nicomedia). As regards Narcissus, he is reported to have opposed the condemnation of Arius, subscribed to the creed affirmed at Nicaea, and subsequently actively opposed Eustatius and Athanasius. In turn, Eusebius of Caesarea is a well-known figure, his views rather not inclined

---

[53] Cf. *Kaiser Konstantins Schreiben zur Einberufung der nicänischen Synode*, Opitz, *Athanasius Werke* III/1, 41-42, Urkunde 20.

[54] Eusebius of Caesarea, *h.e.* VII, 32, 23.

towards Arianism.[55] Perhaps, their only fault was to "attempt to make light of the question and conceal the error under the guise of false arguments." We could also ask if they had actually intended to lend their support to any heresy. Or did they perceive the whole issue as perhaps too trivial to castigate and condemn anybody? We read that they were not bothered about the judgement passed by the others, became hardened and were not afraid of the condemnatory verdict. Could their self-confident attitude and the apparent trivialization of the problem have been inspired by the Emperor's letter to Alexander and Arius? It would be possibly yet another argument in support of the thesis that Arianism had nothing to do with the convocation of a general council first to Ancyra, then to Nicaea. Eusebius was aware of the fact that Constantine did not attach much importance to the controversy (despite his opinion of its scandalous character), and therefore was not afraid, in the Emperor's presence, of any harm that might befall him there. Could all the trivializing have meant that the three bishops had not wanted to sign their names under that creed? The only thing that may have deterred a figure like Eusebius was the proscription of the term κτίσμα, which should have been deemed as acceptable on account of its Biblical presence.

Another circumstance proving that the decisions of that synod had been completely rejected even before the bishops assembled at Nicaea may be the fact that no one was really bothered about the condemnation of Eusebius of Caesarea, which was a very peculiar condemnation indeed. It is true that the bishops communicated that they had ceased to be in communion with those condemned, and dissuaded others from continuing to remain in it, but they also made reference to a general synod, which was yet to take place, as they believed at the time, at Ancyra. Had it been a "genuine" synodal condemnation, those three bishops would have been banned from attending any synod. And Eusebius of Caesarea reputedly had the honour to make a formal address to the Emperor at the beginning of the proceedings, at least according to Sozomen's account.[56] This may be, however, one of his numerous unsubstantiated, and perhaps untrue, items of information. Nonetheless, there is another, and generally attested, statement made by Eusebius, with the bishops and the Emperor present, when he put forward a profession of faith in front of the assembled Fathers, which is widely understood as a proposition for a creed of the Church of Caesarea to be

---

[55] Quite recently, I have been "accused" of ascribing Arianism to Eusebius, cf. R. Toczko, *O arianizmie Euzebiusza z Cezarei*, in: *U schyłku starożytności, Studia Źródłoznawcze* 8 (2009), 101. Nonetheless, this is an otherwise "almost" good article.

[56] Sozomen, *h.e.* I, 19.

acknowledged by the Council.[57] Although his proposal was not carried through, the newly approved *credo* differed from that formulated at Antioch – it was definitely not that anti-Arian. Even following the Council, Eusebius continued to enjoy the Emperor's favour; he was even charged with the honourable task of preparing the holy books for the churches of the new city of Constantinople.[58] As for Hosius, the situation appears to have been just the opposite. Nothing is known of his role at the Council. Eusebius takes on an apparently slightly scathing tone as he says: "Even from Spain itself, one whose fame was widely spread took his seat as an individual in the great assembly."[59] His name is present among the signatories of the Council, but he departs for the West afterwards, as if his role of the Emperor's counsellor in ecclesiastical matters were definitively concluded. Was the Emperor so dissatisfied with the apparent failure of Hosius' "mission in the East"? We have already seen that Constantine dispatched him to Alexandria in order to bring a settlement of the serious problem of the Meletian schism as well as the dispute between Alexander and Arius (the latter question being of much less importance, in the Emperor's view). Hosius was also entrusted with ensuring an agreement on the date of Easter and, in all likelihood, bringing over a valid profession of faith. Hosius' mission failed to produce satisfactory results and it was necessary to address those issues again.

At this point, let us return to considering the reason why the Emperor had called on the bishops to come to a general synod.[60]

It is said in the prologue of Constantine's convocation letter (preserved in Syriac) that the Emperor invites the bishops to arrive on the 19th of June in the 20th year of his reign (*vicennalia*). This is the only expressly stated circumstance.[61] In his *Vita Constantini* (III, 8), Eusebius commends the ruler as follows: "Constantine is the first prince of any age who bound together such a garland as this with the bond of peace, and presented it to his Saviour as a thank-offering for the victories he had obtained over every foe, thus exhibiting in our own times a similitude of the apostolic company."[62] It is as if the author had wished to say that various rulers had different ways of offering thanks for their victories, but Constantine

---

[57] Cf. Eusebius of Caesarea, *Letter of Eusebius of Caesarea to the People of His Diocese*, in: Socrates, *h.e.* I, 8.

[58] Socrates, *h.e.* I, 9.

[59] Eusebius of Caesarea, *v.C.* III, 7 (NPNF 2,1); Socrates, *h.e.* I, 8.

[60] It is almost generally believed that Arianism was the main issue, owing to the credence given to Athanasius' *Ad Afros Ep.* 2; SCL 1, 266. Cf. L. Ayres, *Nicaea and its Legacy*, 19. However, Athanasius wrote it only as late as 370.

[61] Cf. F. Nau, in *Revue de l'Orient Chrétien* 4 (1909) 5ff.

[62] Cf. Eusebius of Caesarea, *v.C.* III, 7 (NPNF 2,1); Socrates, *h.e.* I, 8.

convoked a council. The Emperor acceded to the throne in 306, and therefore the celebration of the 20th anniversary of his reign would have commenced in 325. Likewise, Diocletian began to celebrate his *vicennalia* in 303, at the beginning of his anniversary year, while Constantine himself celebrated his *decimalia* in 315, as affirmed by the relevant inscription on the Arch of Constantine at Rome.

Therefore, in view of all the above circumstances, i.e., Hosius' apparently unsuccessful mission in the East, the Emperor's *vicennalia* and his duties as the *Pontifex Maximus*, I would like to put forth a hypothesis that Constantine had invited the bishops to Nicaea to attend the inauguration of the *vicennalia* of his reign. On that solemn occasion, he was to announce the reconciliation of all the contending parties, the Paschal calendar as well as the fundamental creed of the Christian faith. It was as early as 1990 that Angelo di Berardino noted, albeit fairly tentatively, that Arianism had not been the reason for the convocation of the council.[63]

The Course of the Proceedings

The earliest sources on the council, composed very briefly after Constantine's death, is Eusebius of Caesarea's letter addressed to his own Church[64] as well as the *Vita Constantini* by the same author. This ostensibly trivial piece of information is somewhat more noteworthy in view of the observation that historians generally prefer quoting from Socrates, Sozomen, or Theodoret, rather than from Eusebius, regarding the latter author's account as biased, apparently for his alleged crypto-Arian affiliation. Nonetheless, let us notice that Eusebius' composition, irrespective of its panegyrical nature, is the only one of the above works that could have been read and contested by the members of the council. Would not Athanasius (ill-disposed towards Eusebius, who must have reciprocated the resentment) have certainly raised his voice in outrage if he had been able to prove Eusebius was a liar. Both of them, as we know, had taken part in the council. Interestingly, in the light of the extant evidence, no one had ever accused Eusebius of lies or forgery. If, then, this is indeed a panegyrical work, it would have been apparently, in the readers' opinion, a true depiction of the events, although some rhetorical exaggeration can be seen in the account as well. But everybody would have been familiar with rhetorical figures and such a manner of expression would not have been much of a surprise. I would take, therefore, at face value everything that Eusebius reports with respect to the course of the conciliar proceedings,

---

[63] See A. Di Berardino, *L'imperatore Costantino e la celebrazione della Pasqua*, 368.

[64] Cf. Ch. 6.

regardless of what would be written down over 100 years later by the other historians.[65]

There are two different dates of the inauguration of the council proceedings, i.e., the first official meeting with the participation of the Emperor, the bishops, and the other figures in attendance. According to Socrates, it took place on May 20,[66] whereas the previously cited Syriac document records the date June 19,[67] which is also further confirmed by the Council of Chalcedon. Some scholars have attempted to account for the two dates, assuming that the former date refers to the inauguration and the latter to the conclusion of the council. Unfortunately, this is impossible for two reasons. As I have noted before, the Mediterranean Sea would be closed for navigation from November 12 to March 10, but in actual fact only open from May 27 to September 14. Moreover, the Easter of 325 fell on April 18. In consequence, there was no possibility for anybody from overseas or the hinterland of Asia Minor to reach the destination by May 20. It was about 1,200 miles from Antioch to Nicaea via Roman roads, and the Imperial postal service would have taken about 60 days to cover such a long-distance route.[68] The other councils would pose the same difficulty. Theodosius II sent out his invitations to Ephesus for June 7, 431, and neither the papal legates nor John of Antioch (the latter travelling by land) were not able to make it there on time, as they could have departed on April 27, at the earliest, i.e., already at the time after Easter that had fallen on April 19 in that year. In turn, Marcian convoked a council to Nicaea for September 1, 451, thus offering a good chance to reach the venue on time.

The date of the council's conclusion is equally disputable. Eusebius writes that the ceremonious ending of the proceedings had coincided with the celebrations of the anniversary of the Emperor's reign.[69] The

[65] On the contrary, L. Ayres (*Nicaea and its Legacy*, 89) prefers to give credence to the later accounts and writes of Hosius' presiding at the synod as well as Marcellus of Ancyra and Eustatius of Antioch having actively participated in the synodal debates. Theodoret of Cyrrhus, *h.e.* I, 7, 10, writes of the latter figure's inaugural speech, yet the author's attitude is characterized by an explicitly anti-Arian bias.

[66] Socrates, *h.e.* I, 13. A number of scholars agree with the date, e.g., M. Simonetti, *La crisi ariana*, 38, G. Alberigo (ed.), *Storia dei concili ecumenici*, Quiriniana, Brescia 1990, 26. M. Starowieyski in his *Sobory Kościoła niepodzielonego*, Biblos, Tarnów 1994, 23, settles for May 25.

[67] The date affirmed by N. Tanner, *Decrees of the Ecumenical Councils I*, Sheed & Word and Georgetown Univ. Press 1990.

[68] Cf. R. Chevallier, *Voyages et déplacements dans l'Empire Romain*, 60.

[69] Eusebius of Caesarea, *v.C.* III, 21; cf. Sozomen, *h.e.* I, 25.

anniversary year commenced on July 25.[70] To sum up our discussion of the dates, it maybe assumed that the ecumenical council began on June 19 and was concluded on July 25, 325.

Eusebius describes those present at the council with some panegyrical emphasis:

In effect, the most distinguished of God's ministers from all the churches which abounded in Europe, Lybia, and Asia were here assembled. And a single house of prayer, as though divinely enlarged, sufficed to contain at once Syrians and Cilicians, Phœnicians and Arabians, delegates from Palestine, and others from Egypt; Thebans and Libyans, with those who came from the region of Mesopotamia. A Persian bishop too was present at this conference, nor was even a Scythian found wanting to the number. Pontus, Galatia, and Pamphylia, Cappadocia, Asia, and Phrygia, furnished their most distinguished prelates; while those who dwelt in the remotest districts of Thrace and Macedonia, of Achaia and Epirus, were notwithstanding in attendance.[71]

In addition to Hosius of Cordova, Rome was represented by two presbyters, Vitus and Vincent, who acted as the bishop's delegates.

Rafał Toczko is surprised at Eusebius' account of the proceedings; this sort of response is so symptomatic that I should take the opportunity to quote the relevant passage: "The entire description of the council is equally unexpected to the modern reader. Everybody who has read it must be surprised that instead of [referring to] Arius, the process of determining the *credo*, and his own role in the proceedings, Eusebius writes of the external aspects of the whole endeavour."[72] He goes on to try to justify Eusebius by saying that he did not need to write about everything and, moreover, the existence of the available acts of the council, in the late 330s, would not make it necessary to dwell on the details.[73] As far as I can tell, the problem is that the contemporary sources do not provide us with any specific information on the existence of such acts. Athanasius, with all his inclination to use citations to his advantage, offers no relevant quotes. In his book on the Council of Nicaea, he does not even allude to the existence of the acts. In all probability, therefore, the entire legacy of the council is contained in the profession of faith and the canons. Furthermore, the attendees of

[70] Cf. A.H.M. Jones, J.R. Martindale (eds.), *The Prosopography of the Later Roman Empire 1*, A.D. 260-395, Cambridge University Press 1971, 223; cf. Sextus Aurelius Victor, *A Book on Caesars* 40, 2-4; Eutropius, *Eutropi Breviarium ab urbe condita* X, 1-2.

[71] Eusebius of Caesarea, *v.C.* III, 7 (NPNF 2,1); cf. Sozomen, *h.e.* I, 8.

[72] Cf. R. Toczko, *O arianizmie Euzebiusza z Cezarei*, 110.

[73] Cf. R. Toczko, *O arianizmie Euzebiusza z Cezarei*, 111.

the council would have certainly noticed and commented on any possible misrepresentations on Eusebius' part. Socrates Scholasticus mentions a *Liber synodicus* by Athanasius, wherein the names of all the attendees of the council were purportedly recorded,[74] yet there is no evidence to substantiate this information. A list of the participants can be found in one of the manuscripts; it is included in the *Sources Chrétiennes* and contains 196 names.[75] It may be assumed then that Eusebius is more credible than others in this respect, i.e., his numbers are comparatively less exaggerated.

According to the sources, the Emperor had been officially greeted by one of the bishops: Eusebius of Caesarea (Sozomen) or Eustatius of Antioch (Theodoret).[76] Notwithstanding the sources, Daniel De Decker argues that it was certainly Eusebius of Nicomedia.[77] The scholar also says that Eusebius had been undoubtedly at the helm of the council, especially during its initial stage, referring to Philostorgius, Ambrose, and Theodoret of Cyrrhus, who do not state such an item of information at all.[78] Next, Constantine proceeded to speak, giving thanks to God for the possibility of such an assembly having been summoned and urging those present to cease all contentions. The notable elements of the speech, in my opinion, are referring to the bishops as "priests of Christ" and the Emperor's use of Latin, not Greek, even though he could speak the latter language (it was translated simultaneously, as only very few of the attendees would have a command of Latin).[79] It appears to me that the speech would have resembled the *Pontifex Maximus*' oratory to the College of Pontiffs. Traditional collegial bodies of priests, responsible for regulating matters of worship within each religion, had been still in existence at the time. Although Christianity had been recognized as a legitimate religion of the Empire, it did not have any officially established collegial body of priests or a calendar of religious feast days held as valid throughout the Empire. In consequence, Constantine had spoken as the *Pontifex Maximus*, using the formal language pertinent to this office, and proceeded to proclaim the episcopal assembly as a pontifical college of the Christian religion in order to promulgate the date of Easter.

---

[74] Socrates, *h.e.* I, 13.

[75] Socrates, *h.e.* I, 13, SCh 477, 154-165.,

[76] Theodoret, *h.e.* I, 7. The state of the scholarly debate on the subject is reported in a long note by the editors of SCh 501, 204-205.

[77] D. De Decker, *Eusèbe de Nicomédie*, 159-161.

[78] D. De Decker, *Eusèbe de Nicomédie*, 158: Philostorgius, *h.e.* I, 9 – refers to Eusebius as "the Great;" Ambrose, *De fide* 3, 15, writes that Eusebius' aversion to *homoousios* can be seen in his letter; Theodoret, *h.e.* I, 16, mentions Eusebius of Caesarea with no reference to the council.

[79] Eusebius of Caesarea, *v.C.* III, 12-13.

It is noteworthy that bishops, presbyters, and deacons would have been previously referred to as *sacerdotes* on very rare occasions only, basically in some exegetic contexts, e.g., when homiletic commentators would expound the Old-Testament texts concerning priests and attempt to express them in more up-to-date terms.[80]

Although it is true that Constantine was to announce a profession of faith as well as a Paschal calendar at this eminent assembly of bishops, he had no doubt foreseen that the participants would have taken the opportunity to discuss many other issues. For this reason, he had sent out his invitations one month in advance of the inauguration of the anniversary celebrations. As it would soon turn out, the bishops submitted a definitely excessive amount of questions to be dealt with. There had been reportedly so many petitions submitted in writing that the Emperor would finally have them all collected and burned, at least according to Socrates' account.[81] On the other hand, our main authority on the subject offers a more reserved depiction of the event: the bishops had been arguing and trying to outdo one another in submitting their proposals and petitions, while the Emperor would advise moderation and encourage the disputants to seek reconciliation. Ultimately, they agreed upon one established creed and one date of Easter to be celebrated in the entire Church. As we shall see in Eusebius' letter addressed to the Church of Caesarea, it would not have been achieved without certain difficulties, but, nevertheless, the participants had managed to reach an accord and signed their names on the documents of the council.

Socrates had known of several more events at the council thanks to his own sources of information. He mentions an attendee named Acecius, a Novatian bishop invited to the council, reportedly attempting to persuade the Emperor into acknowledging the Novatian practice (and theory) of regarding the clergymen guilty of a mortal sin as unworthy of administering the sacraments. The Emperor is said to have told him the following words: "Place a ladder, Acecius, and climb alone into heaven."[82] This is also the only author who makes a note of a discussion on a certain ardent participant's proposal to decree proscribing the higher-ranking clergy to remain in intimate relations with their wives. In response, Bishop Paphnutius of the Upper Thebaid had reportedly spoken, calling on the attendees to act prudently in this matter and abstain from imposing excessive burdens.[83] Nonetheless, his effort appears to have been rather unsuccessful, as the

---

[80] Cf. H. Pietras, *Od prezbiteratu do kapłaństwa: ewolucja pojęć i urzędu*, in *Studia Bobolanum* 3 (2002), 5-17.

[81] Socrates, *h.e.* I, 8.

[82] Socrates, *h.e.* I, 10 (NPNF 2,2).

[83] Socrates, *h.e.* I, 11.

council would go on to decree a canon forbidding clergymen "to keep a woman who has been brought in to live with him," except for their mothers, sisters, aunts, "or of any person who is above suspicion."[84] Wives are not mentioned at all.

Celebrations commenced on the anniversary day.[85] It does not mean that the Emperor had completed the 20th year of his reign then, as the *imperfectum* of πληρόω, as it is said in the text, may have pointed to the beginning of the course of that year, or, strictly speaking, a lapse of the time dedicated to the celebration of the *vicennalia*. And, as a matter of fact, it would have been the case indeed, because, as I have noted above, Constantine began his rule on July 25, 306. Following the lavish banquets, the Emperor would present all those in attendance with gifts whose value matched the merit of each person. Finally, he addressed his letter to the Churches, informing them of the recently concluded synod. Most certainly, in order to let everybody know the issues dealt with in the course of the proceedings. We shall be concerned with the contents of that letter further on.

To make our discussion complete, let us also take a note of the opinion that about three years later there would have reputedly taken place a second session of the Council of Nicaea, during which the Emperor would have changed his position and sided with Arius. This hypothesis is supported by De Decker, who draws on Luibhéid[86] and, even more thoroughly, on Schwartz. However, this is not substantiated by any evidence in the writings of the participants of the synodal proceedings, those of Eusebius of Caesarea, Athanasius, or anybody else.

[84] Canon 3, cf. Ch. 5.

[85] Eusebius of Caesarea, *v.C.* III, 15-16.

[86] D. De Decker, *Eusèbe de Nicomédie*, 162; C. Luibhéid, *The Alleged Second Session of the Council of Nicaea*, in *Journal of Ecclesiastical History* 34 (1983), 165-174.

V

CANONS OF THE COUNCIL

In a manner similar to the earlier synods, the Council of Nicaea determined a number of disciplinary canons that were to become a point of reference for many of the later synods.[1] Let us now turn to a brief overview of the canons. It seems that the bishops present at Nicaea held them to have been even more important than the *credo* itself. Likewise, from the perspective of the reception of the resolutions of the council, the canons definitely precede the creed, as the latter would not become adopted for many years, and only in 25 years after the conclusion of the council would Athanasius begin to expound and propagate it. According to one "conspiracy theory," almost all of the canons had been formulated in order to thwart Eusebius of Nicomedia.[2] I would like to note that I have decided to rely on the interpretation of the canons as put forward in Leclercq's commentary.[3] With his interpretative framework in mind (but without excessive reliance on it), we shall go through a general survey of the canons. According to Socrates' account, the bishops would bring along such a great number of propositions and motions to be submitted to the Emperor and the synod that Constantine had them burned, as it is clearly depicted on one of the wall paintings at the baptistery of the Basilica of St John Lateran.[4] If this is the case indeed, it can be assumed that these canons do not necessarily reflect the state of the bishops' awareness of the most pivotal problems of the Church, but rather deal with those issues which had been decided or resolved at all. There may have been possibly dozens of other, more pressing, questions awaiting consideration and decision, yet the time of the proceedings and the patience of the Emperor (obliged to ensure the maintenance of the whole assembly) had run out.

The canons are cited in their English rendition only,[5] because of the absence of any specific theological terminology in the original.

---

[1] Cf., for instance, dozens of references contained in the indexes to SCL 1 and SCL 4; canons of the Council of Nicaea, in: *Decrees of the Ecumenical Councils*, vol. 1, N.P. Tanner (ed.), Georgetown University Press 1990.

[2] D. De Decker, *Eusèbe de Nicomédie*, 148-154.

[3] Cf. K.J. Hefele, H. Leclercq, *Histoire des conciles d'après les documents originaux* I, Letourey et Ané Éditeurs, Paris 1907-.

[4] Socrates, *h.e.* I, 8.

[5] DSP 1.

Canon 1: *Concerning those who make themselves eunuchs and others who suffer the same loss at the hands of others*

If anyone in sickness has undergone surgery at the hands of physicians or has been castrated by barbarians, let him remain among the clergy. But if anyone in good health has castrated himself, if he is enrolled among the clergy he should be suspended, and in future no such man should be promoted. But, as it is evident that this refers to those who are responsible for the condition and presume to castrate themselves, so too if any have been made eunuchs by barbarians or by their masters, but have been found worthy, the canon admits such men to the clergy.

The canon affirms the custom whose first known formalized occurrence was the synod of 231, convoked by Bishop Demetrios of Alexandria against Origen.[6] The synod nullified the validity of Origen's presbyterial ordination, citing the circumstances such as the performance of his ordination by the Bishop of Caesarea, with no consent given by the Bishop of Alexandria, and his self-castration. This is how it is related by Photius,[7] whose account is based on Pamphilus, who had recounted the whole thing in Book II of his *Apology for Origen*. The information comes from Eusebius,[8] but it cannot be ascertained as the book in question is lost. Self-castration was the subject of the synod in Greece (250).[9] The point was to resist the views of the Gnostic sect of *Eunuchs*, who were known for propagating castration as a method of attaining perfection. The view that self-castration is something better than impurity is not Christian, as it had first emerged in the teachings of Philo of Alexandria (at the turn of the first century BC)[10] and Sextus Empiricus (second - third centuries AD),[11] a prominent teacher of Sceptic philosophy, for which they would be criticized by Origen.[12] Justin Martyr describes the case of a certain Christian from Alexandria, without saying if the man was a cleric or a lay person, who wished to obtain the prefect's permission for such an operation, but his request was turned down.[13] Epiphanius of Salamis[14] mentions numerous cases of self-castration. Moreover, one Syrian synod

---

[6] Council of Alexandria (231), SCL 1, 4.

[7] Photius, *Bibliotheca* 118.

[8] Eusebius of Caesarea, *h.e.* VI, 23, 4.

[9] Council of Achaia (250), SCL 1, 5.

[10] Philo of Alexandria, *Quod deterius potiori insidiari soleat* 176.

[11] Sextus Empiricus, *Sententiae* 13. 273.

[12] Origenes, *CMt.* XV, 3; cf. also *Contra Celsum* VII, 48.

[13] Justin, *Apologia* I, 29.

[14] Epiphanius, *Panarion, Expositio fidei* 13.

repeated the Nicene prohibition.[15] Such incidents must have happened fairly often, as by the fourth century it had become necessary to introduce a prohibition against castration in the Church laws, i.e., in this particular Nicene canon and in the *Apostolic Canons* 21-24.[16] The origin of the latter remains unknown, except for the fact that they had been incorporated into the body of the *Apostolic Constitutions* dated back to the late fourth century. It is possible then that they may have been inspired by that particular canon. They would also become part of *Decretum Gratiani*,[17] thus ensuring their continued validation until as late as the medieval period. As a result, I cannot see why the promulgation of this canon by the "great Church" would have been something unsubstantiated, as it is argued by De Decker.[18] In his view, it would have been a canon aimed against the Arian party at the Emperor's court, and thus indirectly against Eusebius, but there is no evidence to support it. I would like to note that there is no mention of any followers of Arianism here, only certain references to the increasing, or at least still strong, phenomenon of castration and the presence of eunuchs. It is no wonder then that some of them would try to become deacons, presbyters, and bishops, or their congregations simply wished to have them ordained. In my opinion, this specific precept has a character of a rescript referring, in its strict sense, to the proscription of the ordination of eunuchs, and having no connection with Arianism.

Canon 2: *Concerning those who are admitted to the clergy immediately after baptism*

Since, either through necessity or through the importunate demands of certain individuals, there have been many breaches of the church's canon, with the result that men who have recently come from a pagan life to the faith after a short catechumenate have been admitted at once to the spiritual washing, and at the same time as their baptism have been promoted to the episcopate or the presbyterate, it is agreed that it would be well for nothing of the kind to occur in the future. For a catechumen needs time and further probation after baptism, for the apostle's words are clear: "Not a recent convert, or he may be puffed up and fall into condemnation and the snare of the devil."[19] But if with the passage of time some sin of sensuality is discovered with regard to the person and he is convicted by two or three witnesses, such a one will be suspended from the clergy. If anyone

[15] Council of Saliq (410), c. 2, SCL 4, 172.

[16] SCL 2, 277-278.

[17] *Decretum Gratiani* D. LV, c. 8 (217); c. 4 (216).

[18] D. De Decker, *Eusèbe de Nicomédie*, 149.

[19] *1 Tim.* 3:6-7.

contravenes these regulations, he will be liable to forfeit his clerical status for acting in defiance of this great synod.

It appears from the canon that the catechumenate period had become significantly reduced by that time, although there are also some other aspects involved. Certain restrictive regulations concerning ordination had been already formulated before. It was determined at Neocaesarea (*ca.* 314) that individuals who had been baptized in illness (i.e., in a life-threatening situation), which made it necessary to shorten the catechumenate, should not be admitted to the presbyterate.[20] The synod at Sardica (*ca.* 343) made the Nicene regulation more specific by requiring candidates for bishop to complete all the clerical ranks,[21] and the synod at Laodicea would extend the requirement to all clergymen.[22] According to Daniel De Decker, it was Eusebius, filled with the spirit of intrigue, who would ordain great numbers of clergymen of questionable provenance in contravention of the church regulations. Unfortunately, he does not state any source for this particular information.[23]

Another question is the dismissal of clergymen who had committed a cardinal sin, as confirmed by two or three witnesses. In accordance with some other synodal regulations, usury (i.e., each instance of lending at interest) constituted such a cardinal sin. The extremely important character of this reason is reflected in the fact that the whole of canon 17 of the Council is devoted to this matter, as we shall see further on. As regards the issue of sexual conduct, it had already been acknowledged in 306 (the year of the earliest known record) that high-ranking clergymen must abstain from intimate relations with their wives,[24] and if they committed adultery, they would be divested and removed for life from the communion of the Church.[25] Let us take note of the strictness of the *Apostolic Canons*, providing for the dismissal of clergymen for the following transgressions: "striking of the faithful that offend (28), fornication, or perjury, or stealing (25), indulging in dice or drinking (42-43), eating flesh with the blood of its life, or that which is torn by beasts, or which died of itself (63), not partaking of flesh or wine on festival days (53), not fasting the fast of forty days (69), fasting on the Lord's day, or on the Sabbath-day (64), eating in a tavern,

---

[20] Council of Neocaesarea (314-319), c. 11-12; SCL 1, 77.

[21] Council of Sardica (343/344), c. 10, SCL 1, 152.

[22] Council of Laodicea (late 4th century), c. 3, SCL 4, 111.

[23] D. De Decker, *Eusèbe de Nicomédie*, 150-151.

[24] Council of Elvira (306), c. 33, SCL 1, 55; cf. Council of Arles (314), II/B, c. 29, SCL 1, 74. .

[25] Council of Elvira (306), c. 18, SCL 1, 52.

except at an inn upon the road (54), taking no care of the clergy or people (58), not receiving him that returns from his sin (52), baptizing improperly (49-50), acknowledging the baptism of the heretics (46-47), receiving a second ordination or ordaining for second time (68), going to the army (83), rebaptizing the baptized (47), keeping the festivals with the Jews (70), entering into a synagogue of the Jews or the church of the heretics (65), striking and killing someone (66), heresy (60), abuse of his bishop (55), abuse of the king or the governor (84)."[26]

The final sentence of the canon refers to obeying the synodal decisions, also on the pain of being dismissed. In a relatively short time following the council, the regulation would be repeated at the synods of Sardica,[27] Carthage,[28] and on a number of other occasions later on.[29] Apparently, the problem continued to exist.

Canon 3: *Concerning women who have been brought in to live with the clergy*

This great synod absolutely forbids a bishop, presbyter, deacon or any of the clergy to keep a woman who has been brought in to live with him, with the exception of course of his mother or sister or aunt, or of any person who is above suspicion.

As we can see, a clergyman's wife is not mentioned in the canon, although, as a general rule, a married man would be admitted to ordination. As I have noted in my comment on the previous canon, it was prohibited for a clergyman to remain in intimate relations with his wife after being ordained.[30] This particular canon concerned the three higher clerical ranks, whereas the others were allowed to cohabit with their wives. The reason for such a proscription can be found in c. 29 of the synod at Arles (see note 30 below): "because they perform the daily service." Therefore, it is evident that the crucial point here is the ritual cleanliness derived from the conviction that any sexual intercourse is unclean as such and must be avoided by those who officiate the Eucharist.

---

[26] Cf. *Apostolic Canons*, in: *Apostolic Constitutions* VIII, 47, 1-85 (ANF 7); SCL 2, 273-293. The above paragraph cites a brief passage from my article: *Dymisja ze stanu duchownego i jej skutki w starożytności chrześcijańskiej*, in: K. Dyrek (ed.), *Odejścia od kapłaństwa. Studium historyczno-psychologiczne*, WAM 2010, 7-19.

[27] Council of Sardica (343), c. 20, SCL 1, 157.

[28] Council of Carthage (348), c. 14, SCL 1, 199.

[29] Cf. the index in SCL 4, entry: "synods."

[30] Council of Elvira (306), c. 33, SCL 1, 55; cf. Council of Arles (314), II/B, c. 29, SCL 1, 74. .

The situation varied depending on a province/region. One item of evidence from Ancyra (the present-day Ankara, Turkey), dated 314, says that deacons are allowed to marry, and thus remain in intimate relations with their wives, on the condition that such an intent is communicated to the local bishop prior to the ordination.[31] The canon of Nicaea had to be repeated, nonetheless, at the synod of Rome (385).[32] At Carthage (397), the list of the women allowed came to include the wife or a female servant of a clergyman's son, certainly assuming that the son also lived with the father.[33] In a Syriac collation of the canons (410), the Nicene canon is restated almost verbatim and it also makes reference to all the clergy, unless the term "son of the covenant" used therein is construed as referring to an ascetic, not a junior clergyman.[34] Moreover, we know that in Africa lectors were not only allowed to marry, but they were also obliged to make a clear and definite choice: to marry or live in celibacy.[35]

Canon 4: *Of the number needed to appoint a bishop*

It is by all means desirable that a bishop should be appointed by all the bishops of the province. But if this is difficult because of some pressing necessity or the length of the journey involved, let at least three come together and perform the ordination, but only after the absent bishops have taken part in the vote and given their written consent. But in each province the right of confirming the proceedings belongs to the metropolitan bishop.

The synod of Arles (314) expressly prohibited the episcopal appointment by just one bishop, providing for the presence of seven, or at least three, bishops.[36] The emphasis on the odd numbers is most certainly dictated by the requirement of a voting procedure. The term used to refer to an episcopal appointment is χειροτονία, i.e., except for the Judeo-Christian communities, denoting an act of raising one's hand in order to vote for a given candidate. The laying on (imposition) of hands was used for baptizing, whereas Jews used it in office appointment ceremonies, as the tradition would go back to the Pentateuch. In Africa, the appointment of bishops would become a more formalized procedure over time, with written

[31] Council of Ancyra (314), c. 10, SCL 1, 65.

[32] Council of Rome (385), 12, SCL 4, 42.

[33] Council of Carthage III (397), IV, 16, SCL 4, 77.

[34] Council of Saliq (410), c. 3, SCL 4, 172 and the note.

[35] Council of Hippo (393), c. 2, SCL 4, 61, subsequently repeated several times.

[36] Council of Arles (314), c. 20, SCL 1, 73.

confirmations required.[37] Most probably, the situation in Africa demanded such a solution on account of the Donatist crisis and the possible risk of confusion involved in personal identification.

Canon 5: *Concerning the excommunicated, that they must not be received by others; and concerning the duty to hold synods twice a year*

Concerning those, whether of the clergy or the laity, who have been excommunicated, the sentence is to be respected by the bishops of each province, according to the canon which forbids those expelled by some to be admitted by others. But let an inquiry be held to ascertain whether anyone has been expelled from the community because of pettiness or quarrelsomeness or any such ill nature on the part of the bishop. Accordingly, in order that there may be proper opportunity for inquiry into the matter, it is agreed that it would be well for synods to be held in each province twice a year, so that these inquiries may be conducted by all the bishops of the province assembled together, and in this way by general consent those who have offended against their own bishop may be recognised by all to be reasonably excommunicated, until all the bishops in common may decide to pronounce a more lenient sentence on these persons. The synods shall be held at the following times: one before Lent, so that, all pettiness being set aside, the gift offered to God may be unblemished; the second after the season of autumn.

The institution of regular synods is represented here as a measure of appeal. Of course, a number of synods had already taken place before, but in this case the authors of the canon wished to prevent possible intentional postponements of synods as a result of the metropolitan's reluctance to confront the episcopal assembly. Arbitrariness of certain verdicts may have resulted in various situations where individuals would be wronged or erroneously rehabilitated somewhere else. Prior to the Council of Nicaea, there is only one known instance of a canon against admitting the excommunicated by others; notably, it comes from the Western part of the Roman Empire.[38] The regulation would be subsequently repeated by a number of other synods.[39] This particular canon also proves that Secundus and Theognis, the two bishops in favour of Arius, could not have signed any

---

[37] Council of Milevi (402), c. 89, SCL 4, 147.

[38] Council of Elvira (306), c. 53, SCL 1, 57; Council of Arles (314), c. 17, SCL 1, 73.

[39] Cf. Council of Antioch (341), c. 6, SCL 1, 132; Council of Sardica (343), c. 13, SCL 1, 154; Council of Carthage (390), 7, SCL 4, 50; Nîmes (396), 3, SCL 4, 69 *et al.*, see SCL 4, the index entries: "excommunication" and "excommunicated."

documents at Nicaea, as it would have constituted a breach of the canon. They had been excommunicated by Alexander of Alexandria, and that city was the only place where their rehabilitation would have been possible.

In reality, the obligation to hold synods twice a year would prove too much of a burden. In 397, a synod at Carthage ruled that a plenary synod of Africa, with three delegates per each province, be held once a year,[40] and in 419, another synod of Carthage referred to such a practice in terms of an implementation of the decisions of Nicaea.[41] The Syrians would take it even further: aware of the requirement stated in the Nicene canon, they would earnestly request the *Katholikos* to summon them once every two years.[42]

Canon 6: *Concerning the forms of primacy belonging to some cities; and the bishops may not be created without the consent of the metropolitan*

The ancient customs of Egypt, Libya and Pentapolis shall be maintained, according to which the bishop of Alexandria has authority over all these places, since a similar custom exists with reference to the bishop of Rome. Similarly in Antioch and the other provinces the prerogatives of the churches are to be preserved.

In general the following principle is evident: if anyone is made bishop without the consent of the metropolitan, this great synod determines that such a one shall not be a bishop. If however two or three by reason of personal rivalry dissent from the common vote of all, provided it is reasonable and in accordance with the church's canon, the vote of majority shall prevail.

The canon attempts to put several evidently contentious questions in order, yet in a clearly considerate manner. Its structure indicates that it is not concerned with providing a solution for the entire Church, for in that case it would have been proper to begin with the Bishop of Rome and ascertain the scope of his competence, considering the fact that his primacy, at least as regards the titular dignity, was not questioned by anyone.[43] The canon does not even specify the names of the provinces within the scope of his authority comparable to that of the Bishop of Alexandria. As it begins with Alexandria, it appears to signify that the bishop of this see is held to be the principal protagonist of the canon. His "superior" status in the provinces mentioned in the canon had been apparently never called into question by

---

[40] Council of Carthage (397), IV, 5, SCL 4, 74.

[41] Council of Carthage (419), c. 18, SCL 4, 264-265.

[42] Council of Saliq (410), c. 6, SCL 4, 173.

[43] Cf. H. Pietras, *Świadomość prymatu biskupa Rzymu w Kościele starożytnym*, in *Christianitas Antiqua* 2 (2009), 190-205.

anyone. It would seem that if it became necessary to bring up the names, it may have been done to point to the actual extent of his competence. We have already seen Bishop Alexander's very critical comments on Eusebius of Nicomedia, e.g., there are several in his *Ep. ad Episcopos* (cf. Chapter 1, which is concerned with the situation before the Council of Nicaea). It might have been perhaps Eusebius' idea to propose a canon intended to prevent the Bishop of Alexandria from interfering in affairs beyond his jurisdiction. Such inclinations would be also manifested by the bishops of this city later on, in consequence of their belief in the supreme position of the Church of Alexandria in the East. It was stated expressly in one of the canons of the First Council of Constantinople,[44] after Peter of Alexandria had attempted to install his protégé at the capital, Theophilus carried through John Chrysostom's condemnation to exile,[45] and Cyril of Alexandria acted to suppress Nestorius, even at Constantinople.[46] Antioch and "the other provinces" are duly mentioned as well, with a reference to their prerogatives derived from their senior status. From the standpoint of the apostolic primacy, the precedence of Alexandria over Antioch resembled that of a disciple over the teacher, i.e., Mark over Peter. This provision would entail some serious consequences, as after the foundation and erection of Constantinople (the capital city without any apostolic roots), neither Alexandria nor Rome wanted to recognize its primacy in the East, despite the canons promulgated at Constantinople and Chalcedon.[47] Incidentally, the city would have to wait for its recognition by Rome as the second-most important see (after Rome) until the year 519 and Hormisdas' pontificate.[48] De Decker is also of the opinion that this canon is aimed at the "patriarchal" claims of Eusebius of Nicomedia.[49]

Canon 7: *Concerning the bishop of Aelia [= Jerusalem]*

Since there prevails a custom and ancient tradition to the effect that the bishop of Aelia is to be honoured, let him be granted everything consequent upon this honour, saving the dignity proper to the metropolitan.

[44] Council of Constantinople I (381), DSP, 71.

[45] "Synod of the Oak" (403), SCL 4, 151-154.

[46] Cf. Council of Ephesus I (431), DSP 1, 109-159.

[47] Cf. Council of Constantinople I (381), c. 3, DSP 1, 73; Council of Chalcedon (451), c. 28, DSP 1, 251.

[48] Cf. A. Thiel, *Epistolae Romanorum Pontificum genuinae* I, Brunsbergae 1868, Epist. 76, 4, p. 873.

[49] D. De Decker, *Eusèbe de Nicomédie* 154.

The metropolitan see for Jerusalem, decreed to be called Aelia
Capitolina by the Emperor Aelius Hadrian, was Caesarea in Palestine,
with Eusebius of Caesarea as the metropolitan bishop at the time of
the Council of Nicaea. The regard for the apostolic status dictated the
acknowledgement of the dignity of this episcopal see, while the politically
and socially marginal significance would not allow the relinquishment of
the principle of accommodation, according to which the provincial capital
was simultaneously the metropolitan see in the Church. We know nothing
of any conciliar debates in connection with this canon. Likewise, we do not
know who would have submitted a canon proposal and why. Apparently, this
canon does not offer anything new to Jerusalem, as "there prevails a custom
and ancient tradition" in any case. Nevertheless, there must have been
some reason for its existence (and I have come to believe that there is no
synodal canon without a reason), namely in order to take care of a different
question: to defend the metropolitan status of Caesarea. Could anyone have
proposed establishing a separate metropolitan see at Jerusalem? It may have
been possible that Bishop Macarius lobbied for elevating the rank of the city
in the ecclesiastical hierarchy, in particular since he had managed to secure
some substantial support from the Emperor for the erection of a grand
basilica church.[50] Eusebius of Caesarea had been no less an influential figure
than his namesake of Nicomedia; the former succeeded in safeguarding
himself by means of this canon just as the latter would have perhaps done
by canon 6.

Canon 8: *Concerning the so-called Cathars*

Concerning those who have given themselves the name of Cathars, and
who from time to time come over publicly to the catholic and apostolic
church, this holy and great synod decrees that they may remain among the
clergy after receiving an imposition of hands. But before all this it is fitting
that they give a written undertaking that they will accept and follow the
decrees of the catholic church, namely that they will be in communion with
those who have entered into a second marriage and with those who have
lapsed in time of persecution, and for whom a period [of penance] has
been fixed and an occasion [for reconciliation] allotted, so as in all things to
follow the decrees of the catholic and apostolic church. Accordingly, where
all the ordained in villages or cities have been found to be men of this kind
alone, those who are so found will remain in the clergy in the same rank;
but when some come over in places where there is a bishop or presbyter
belonging to the catholic church, it is evident that the bishop of the church

---

[50] Cf. Eusebius of Caesarea, *v.C.* III, 30-31.

will hold the bishop's dignity, and that the one given the title and name of bishop among the so-called Cathars will have the rank of presbyter, unless the bishop thinks fit to let him share in the honour of the title. But if this does not meet with his approval, the bishop will provide for him a place as chorepiscopus or presbyter, so as to make his ordinary clerical status evident and so prevent there being two bishops in the city.

It can be seen that the canon provides for some fairly specific solutions, although the group in question is not clearly identified. There had existed several ones towards which such measures would have been adequate, as they would refuse to approve of second marriage[51] and opposed the readmitting of those who had lapsed in the time of persecution, or even those who fled to avoid it, back into the Church. The synods had been already concerned with this question for decades. Words of castigation and censure were directed at the Novatians,[52] Montanists,[53] Donatists,[54] and Meletians.[55] At the time of the Council of Nicaea, the strongest dissident groups were the Donatists in Africa and Meletians in Egypt. All the circumstances would then point out that the canon made reference to those groups in the first place, especially in view of the fact that the Emperor had been in favour of restoring them into the "great Church." Meletius had usurped the metropolitan's prerogatives at the time of the persecutions under Diocletian in the early fourth century and proceeded to appoint priests for the vacant parish churches, even when the vacancy was caused by the arrest of the local priest. Bishop Peter dedicated an entire treatise to the issue of readmitting such "lapsed" individuals back into the Church in response to the excessively rigorous attitude of the Meletians.[56] In his letter addressed to Alexander and Arius (see Chapter 3), Constantine clearly expressed both his concern about the peace in the Church and his discontent at the rise of the schisms. Bishop Hosius, who delivered the said letter to Alexandria in the late autumn of 324, would have been probably entrusted with undertaking to mediate between Alexander

---

[51] Cf. H. Crouzel, *Les digamoi visées par le concile de Nicée dans son canon 8*, in *Augustinianum* 18 (1978), 533-546.

[52] Cf. Council of Rome (251), Council of Carthage (251), SCL 1, 6-8, Council of Antioch (252), SCL 1, 12; Council of Alexandria (258), SCL 1, 41.

[53] Cf. Council of Hierapolis (ok. 150), SCL 1, 2; Council of Iconium (256), SCL 1, 46.

[54] Cf. Council of Rome (313), SCL 1, 62; Council of Arles (314), SCL 1, 68-74; Council of Carthage (348), SCL 1, 193.

[55] Cf. Council of Alexandria (306) and (324/325), SCL 1, 62 i 82.

[56] Cf. Peter of Alexandria, *Canons on Penitence*, in: Canons of the Greek Fathers, SCL 3, 11-22.

and the Meletians. According to Athanasius' account, Hosius had taken part in a synod convened to deal with this question.[57] Ten years after the Council, the synod at Tyre carried through the deposition of Athanasius in consequence of some charges levelled by the Meletians.[58] This somewhat confusing information can be found in Socrates Scholasticus. As we know, he composed his work one hundred years later, when Athanasius had already been regarded as a symbol of orthodoxy, held in great esteem and clearly portrayed in very positive terms. On principle, then, he must have been right, unlike those who had condemned him for his bad treatment of the Felicians, with Constantine's approval and additional sanction of banishment on top of the synodal verdict. As Socrates says, Athanasius did not want to attend the synod because of his apprehension that it would undertake to change the decrees of Nicaea. However, it appears that he had been condemned precisely for his failure to comply with them, since the Meletians could not have possibly counted on the Emperor's support (in view of the fact that he considered them as his achievement) otherwise, i.e., if Athanasius had conformed and they refused to comply. Presumably, the both parties had failed to play fair, but what is really of concern in the context of this canon, and the whole course of the events, is that the key points were the Meletian question and how to come to terms with them. Some further proof can be found in what the canon stipulates in the case when two clergymen make their claims to lead one and the same church. Situations like this had occurred exactly because the Meletians would have appointed their own clergy also for the churches remaining vacant even in the absence of anybody's fault or neglect, and only temporarily.[59]

Canon 9: *Concerning those who have been promoted to the rank of presbyter without examination*

If any have been promoted presbyters without examination, and then upon investigation have confessed their sins, and if after their confession men have imposed hands upon such people, being moved to act against the canon, the canon does not admit these people, for the catholic church vindicates only what is above reproach.

There are several canons worth mentioning in this context. At Elvira, it was determined that the guilty of committing adultery in his young

---

[57] Cf. Athanasius, *Apologia contra Arianos* 76.

[58] Cf. Council of Tyre (335), SCL 1, 91-92.

[59] See A. Camplani, *In margine alla storia dei meliziani*, in *Augustinianum* 30 (1990), 313-351.

age must not be appointed even a subdeacon, to prevent any further promotion, and if already appointed, he should be divested of his office.[60] Canon 9 of Neocaesarea provides that if a presbyter confessed to having committed a sin of fornication before his ordination, "he should not officiate the Eucharist, but can perform other duties connected with his rank, because, in accordance with the general opinion, the other sins are absolved through ordination. If he, however, fails to confess and so cannot be publicly reprimanded, he should be left to his own conscience."[61] The most interesting part is the reference to the commonly held opinion that ordination remits all sins, save those of sexual nature. The Nicene fathers modify this precept to a great extent, however, by referring to any sin, most certainly a cardinal one. The relevant Apostolic Canon stipulates that no person who is proven to have committed "fornication, or adultery, or any other forbidden action"[62] should be admitted to the clergy, which seems to agree with the Nicene canon. Needless to say, De Decker reckons this canon, as well as the next one, to have been aimed directly at Eusebius of Nicomedia, but offers no explanation again.[63]

Canon 10: *Concerning those who have denied the faith in persecution and have been promoted to the clergy*

If any among the lapsed have been promoted to ordination through the ignorance of their promoters or even with their connivance, this fact does not prejudice the church's canon; for once discovered they are to be deposed.

In spite of the clearly stated anti-Cathar position (see canon 8 above) and the readmittance of the lapsed into the Church after completion of the proper penance, they would not be admitted to ordination. For the first time, it can be seen in a post-synodal letter of Cyprian of Carthage, who also cites the Roman synod under Cornelius.[64] At Ancyra, the sole exception was made for those who had offered sacrifice to pagan idols under duress.[65]

---

[60] Council of Elvira (306), c. 30, SCL 1, 54.

[61] Council of Neocaesarea (314-319), c. 9, SCL 1, 76.

[62] *Can. App.* 61 (ANF 7), SCL 2, 288.

[63] D. De Decker, *Eusèbe de Nicomédie*, 152-153.

[64] Cf. Council of Rome (251), SCL 1, 6; Council of Carthage (254) V, SCL 1, 19 = Cyprian, *Letter* 67.

[65] Council of Ancyra (314), c. 3c, SCL 1, 63.

Canon 11: *Concerning those who have denied the faith and are numbered among the laity*

Concerning those who have transgressed without necessity or the confiscation of their property or without danger or anything of this nature, as happened under the tyranny of Licinius, this holy synod decrees that, though they do not deserve leniency, nevertheless they should be treated mercifully. Those therefore among the faithful who genuinely repent shall spend three years among the hearers, for seven years they shall be prostrators, and for two years they shall take part with the people in the prayers, though not in the offering.

The reservation that they already belong among the faithful means that catechumens are excluded from the practice (cf. canon 14). For a better understanding of the division into various categories of penitents, let us have a look at this fourth-century canon, attributed to Gregory Thaumaturgos. It is obviously anachronistic, as it includes a citation from a canon by Basil the Great:

Weeping takes place without the gate of the oratory; and the offender standing there ought to implore the faithful as they enter to offer up prayer on his behalf. Waiting on the word, again, takes place within the gate in the porch, where the offender ought to stand until the catechumens depart, and thereafter he should go forth. For let him hear the Scriptures and doctrine, it is said, and then be put forth, and reckoned unfit for the privilege of prayer.[66] Submission, again, is that one stand within the gate of the temple, and go forth along with the catechumens. Restoration is that one be associated with the faithful, and go not forth with the catechumens; and last of all comes the participation in the holy ordinances.[67]

Those who had to go out departed prior to the prayer of the faithful, and before they did, a special prayer would be said on their behalf for the forgiveness of their sins and conversion. An example of such a prayer dating from the fourth century can be found in the Apostolic Constitutions.[68] "Prostrators" were not literally required to lie prostrate through the whole liturgy. A different gesture of submission would have sufficed, for instance, kneeling, as it is stated in the canon above. These degrees of penance had

[66] Basil the Great, c. 75, *Canons of the Greek Fathers*, SCL 3, 57.

[67] Gregory Thaumaturgos, c. 11, *Canons of the Greek Fathers* (*Canonical Epistle* in: ANF 6), SCL 3, 10.

[68] *Apostolic Constitutions* VIII, 9, SCL 2, 229-230.

somehow corresponded to the degrees of catechumens' initiation and therefore it can be said that the expiatory practice consisted in, so to speak, relegating the penitent back to one of the degrees of initiation, as if to a "neo-catechumenate."

At Elvira, the rigorous bishops of Spain decreed that those who had offered sacrifices were to be removed from the Church without reprieve.[69] Those of the faithful who had voluntarily observed the offering of sacrifices were to be sentenced to ten years of penance.[70] Some time earlier, at St Cyprian's Carthage, the expiation would have been a practice for life, or at least until the penitent's grave illness, and this privilege would have been only allowed to those who had lapsed in prison or under torture.[71] Lifetime penance would be also proposed later on by Basil the Great, with the possibility to reduce the duration thereof, depending on the penitent's dedication.[72] The synod of Ancyra had introduced yet another category of the lapsed, namely those who had been coerced, but nonetheless complied without much resistance and even dressed up for the occasion. Such penitents must be "hearers" for one year, "prostrators" for three years, excluded from partaking of communion for two years, even though allowed to participate in prayers.[73] Those of the lapsed who had been additionally responsible for the fall of others had to face an even more stringent treatment: three years of "hearing," six years of "prostrating," and one year of exclusion from the Eucharist.[74]

Canon 12: *Concerning those who have made a renunciation and then returned to the world*

Those who have been called by grace, have given evidence of first fervour and have cast off their [military] belts, and afterwards have run back like dogs to their own vomit (cf. Prov 26, 11),[75] so that some have even paid money and recovered their military status by bribes – such persons shall spend ten years as prostrators after a period of three years as hearers. In every case, however, their disposition and the nature of their penitence should be examined. For those who through their fear and tears and perseverance and good works give evidence of their conversion by deeds and not by outward show,

[69] Council of Elvira (306), c. 1, SCL 1, 50.

[70] Council of Elvira (306), c. 59, SCL 1

[71] Cf. Council of Carthage (251) (252), SCL 1, 6-12

[72] Basil, c. 73-74, *Canons of the Greek Fathers*, SCL 3, 56.

[73] Council of Ancyra (314), c. 4, SCL 1, 63.

[74] Council of Ancyra (314), c. 9, SCL 1, 65.

[75] *Prov.* 26:11; *2 P.* 2:22.

when they have completed their appointed term as hearers, may properly take part in the prayers, and the bishop is competent to decide even more favourable in their regard. But those who have taken the matter lightly, and have thought that the outward form of entering the church is all that is required for their conversion, must complete their term to the full.

The Christian attitude to military service evolved and changed over time. The canon is noteworthy in respect of the fact that it had been decreed at the time when the Church had already come under the Emperor's protection. Before Constantine, military service entailed obligatory participation in sacrificial rites performed in order to ensure favour of the gods in addition to the ordinary martial duties connected with fighting and killing (the latter condemned by Christianity).[76] Later on, the situation would change and the synod of Arles, summoned by Constantine, decreed that the soldiers who deserted their service in times of peace would be excluded from communion.[77] In consequence of the growing numbers of Christians in the military, Constantine ordered that they should be allowed the time off necessary for their participation in the Eucharist on Sundays.[78] The situation would take a different turn again, however, when Licinius (*Augustus* in the East from 313 until his final defeat by Constantine at Chrysopolis in Bithynia on September 18, 324) embarked on an increasingly aggravating anti-Christian course. His armies did not fight under the aegis of the cross. This canon begins with μέν, i.e., "whereas," "namely," in reference to the previous one, dealing with the period of "the tyranny of Licinius." In the previous one, the renegades would have to face a term of five-year-long penance, while in this case the situation is more serious, as it treats of the Christians who had been initially devoted to their faith, but subsequently departed to pursue their military careers, and even trying very hard to make it happen. Nevertheless, the bishops are instructed to deal with the problem with caution and approach each case on an individual basis. It is stated that the bishop could relieve a penitent of their penance with the "prostrators," even to the full extent of seven years, after the three years spent among the "hearers."[79] The last sentence[80] refers to those opportunistic Christians who wished to return for the same reason that had made them leave the

---

[76] See W. Myszor, *Europa. Pierwotne chrześcijaństwo. Idee i życie społeczne chrześcijan II i III wieku*, UKSW, Warszawa 2000, 99-119; R. Burggraeve, M. Vervenne, *Swords into Plowshares: Theological Reflections on Peace*, Peeters, Louvain 1991, 149.

[77] Council of Arles (314), c. 3, SCL 1, 71.

[78] Eusebius of Caesarea, *v.C.* IV, 18.

[79] Cf. P. Galtier, *Les canons pénitentiels de Nicée*, in *Gregorianum* 29 (1948), 288-291.

[80] This last sentence is rendered inaccurately in our edition of DSP 1, 39.

Church before, i.e., they preferred to join the winner's party for strictly opportunistic motives and treated their adherence to the Church in a kind of self-serving manner. They should not be rejected, yet there is no reason to reduce the terms of their penance.

Canon 13: *Concerning those who seek communion at the point of death*

Concerning the departing, the ancient canon law is still to be maintained, namely that those who are departing are not to be deprived of their last, most necessary viaticum. But if one whose life has been despaired of has been admitted to communion and has shared in the offering and is found to be numbered again among the living, he shall be among those who take part in prayer only <until the term fixed by this great ecumenical synod has been completed>. But as a general rule, in the case of anyone whatsoever who is departing and seeks to share in the eucharist, the bishop upon examining the matter shall give him a share in the offering.

This canon also makes reference to the situation discussed before, with the modest δέ instead of the equivalent μέν used in the previous canon. And, once again, it speaks of those who had renounced their faith under Licinius. The Fathers refer to the tradition of granting communion, in the both senses of the term, i.e., the Eucharist as well as becoming reconciled with the community of the Church, to a penitent at the point of death.[81] The instruction that the restored penitent return to their penance, should they have recovered after being admitted to communion, appears to have been a general rule, seemingly in contradiction (although, obviously, with no intent to prejudice either canon) with one of Cyprian-led synods, stipulating that the communion once granted, though hastily, should not be withdrawn.[82] The last sentence seems to convey a more general statement and refers to admitting a moribund person to communion, whether they were penitents or not. The sole criterion is apparently whether they ask for it or not. If there is a need to share in communion, it means that the dying person is guilty of some sin which prevents him or her from participating in communion, e.g., they had denied their faith. In 313, the synod at Arles required that requests of those who would ask for admitting them to communion on their death-bed without having previously performed the necessary expiation be turned down.[83] It is evident then that the Fathers of the Council wished to

[81] Cf. Council of Carthage (252) I, SCL 1, 9; Council of Elvira (306), c. 32. 37. 69, SCL 1, 54. 55. 60; Council of Council of Ancyra (314), c. 6. 22, SCL 1, 64. 68.

[82] Council of Carthage (253) I, SCL 1, 12.

[83] Council of Arles (314), c. 22, SCL 1, 74.

mitigate the rigorous treatment of those who would seek communion at the point of death.[84]

Canon 14: *Concerning catechumens who have lapsed*

Concerning catechumens who have lapsed, this holy and great synod decrees that, after they have spent three years as hearers only, they shall then be allowed to pray with the catechumens.

This is the last canon concerned with those who had lapsed during the persecution under Licinius. It begins with δέ as well. A similar canon had been decreed at Neocaesarea several years before. It said that if a catechumen committed a sin, and his catechumenal status corresponded to the "kneeling" status (see canon 11), he was to be relegated to the rank of "hearers," and if already, or still, a "hearer," he should be deprived of his [catechumenal] status.[85]

Canon 15: *Concerning a cleric who transfers from city to city*

On account of the great disturbance and the factions which are caused, it is decreed that the custom, if it is found to exist in some parts contrary to the canon, shall be totally suppressed, so that neither bishops nor presbyters nor deacons shall transfer from city to city. If after this decision of this holy and great synod anyone shall attempt such a thing, or shall lend himself to such a proceeding, the arrangement shall be totally annulled, and he shall be restored to the church of which he was ordained bishop or presbyter or deacon.

It is one of those canons that would have been apparently more readily promulgated than respected in reality. From the pre-Nicene period, we know of such a canon decreed at Arles,[86] while following the Council of Nicaea, the question would be resumed by the synods of Antioch, Carthage, Rome,[87] etc. The great disturbance, referred to in the canon, may have taken place in connection with Eusebius of Nicomedia, who had been originally ordained bishop at Beirut. In his letter to the bishops, Alexander of Alexandria expressed his stern disapproval of the situation. I have already

[84] Cf. P. Galtier, *Les canons pénitentiels de Nicée*, in *Gregorianum* 29 (1948), 291-294.

[85] Council of Neocaesarea (314-319), c. 5, SCL 1, 76.

[86] Council of Arles (314), c. 2, SCL 1, 71.

[87] Council of Antioch (341), c. 3, SCL 1, 136; Council of Carthage (348), c. 5, SCL 1, 196; Council of Rome (376), c. 9, SCL 1, 286; *can. App.* 14, SCL 2, 275.

referred to canon 6 as, perhaps, Eusebius' "victory" over Alexander, because the canon reminded the latter that his place was in Egypt. But this time, it could be said that Alexander got his revenge and carried through a canon whose formulation would be aimed directly at his opponent. However, it would turn out to have been of very little use, as Eusebius would eventually go on to become the Bishop of Constantinople.[88]

Canon 16: *Concerning those who do not remain in the churches in which they were promoted*

Any presbyters or deacons or in general anyone enrolled in any rank of the clergy who depart from their church recklessly and without the fear of God before their eyes or in ignorance of the church's canon, ought not by any means to be received in another church, but all pressure must be applied to them to induce them to return to their own dioceses, or if they remain it is right that they should be excommunicated. But if anyone dares to steal away one who belongs to another and to ordain him in his church without the consent of the other's own bishop among whose clergy he was enrolled before he departed, the ordination is to be null.

This canon follows in the footsteps of the previous one, but it only deals with presbyters and the lower-ranking clergy. Similar regulations can be found among the canons of the Arles synod[89] as well as in the Apostolic Canons.[90] The matter must have been very difficult to resolve indeed, hence the necessity to revisit it so many times.[91] Evidently, from the very beginning, there had existed a certain margin of the clergy intent on taking advantage of their clerical duties for their own benefit.

Canon 17: *Concerning clerics who practise usury*

Since many enrolled [among the clergy] have been induced by greed and avarice to forget the sacred text, "who does not put out his money

---

[88] Cf. Socrates, *h.e.* II, 7.

[89] Council of Arles (314), c. 21. 27, SCL 1, 73. 74.

[90] *can. App.* 16, SCL 2, 276.

[91] In a note to *can. App.* 15, we have included some of the more important references: Councils of: Ancyra (314), c. 18 (SCL 1, 67); Arles (314) I, 2 (SCL 1, 70); II, c. 2. 21. 27 (SCL 1, 71. 73. 74); Nicaea (325) (oec. I), c. 15 et 16 (DSP 1, 40); Antioch (341), c. 3. 16. 21 (SCL 1, 136. 139. 141); Carthage (*ca.* 348), c. 5. 7 (SCL 1, 196); Rome (376/377), 9 (*Tomus Damasi*, SCL 1, 186); Chalcedon (451) (oec. IV), c. 5. 10. 20 (DSP 1, 230. 234. 242); *Quinisexta* (692), c. 17-18; Nicaea (787) (oec. VII), c. 10. 15 (DSP 1, 360. 366).

at interest" (Ps 14, 5),[92] and to charge one per cent [a month] on loans, this holy and great synod judges that if any are found after this decision to receive interest by contract or to transact the business in any other way or to charge [a flat rate of] fifty per cent or in general to devise any other contrivance for the sake of dishonourable gain,[93] they shall be deposed from the clergy and their names struck from the roll.

This is another situation where the incriminated practice happened so frequently that the regulation had to be repeated for many times throughout Antiquity and the Middle Ages.[94] In music, *himolia* – in the DSP, we have mentioned the Latin term, derived from the Greek *hemiolia* – denotes the ratio 3:2 and the term was apparently carried over to the banking vocabulary to designate 50% interests. However, the Fathers censure not just lending money at such an exorbitant interest, but any lending in order to make a profit. It was only as late as the fifteenth century that the founding of the so-called "banks of piety," *montes pietatis*, would be permitted. They were allowed to charge very low interests to cover their own operating costs, but without making a profit. It is worth having a look at the relevant decree of the Fifth Lateran Council (1512-1517) *De reformatione Montium pietatis*, with the following explanatory note in the DSP (of course, with the priority given to the content of the decree): *montes pietatis* were banks established in order to curtail the practice of usury. They lent money at very low interests or even at no interest at all. *Montes pietatis* first appeared in the fourteenth century.[95]

The operation of this institution in Poland, at the St. Rochus' Fraternity, Warsaw, is described by Jędrzej Kitowicz:[96]

Mons Pietatis is a store of the financial capital collected from various pious individuals. This capital has the following two, commendable and useful, purposes: the first one – giving alms to the poor who are ashamed of begging in public, the other – lending money to those who need it urgently, with no commission involved. But the person asking for a loan must provide

---

[92] *Ps.* 14:5.

[93] Cf. *Tit.* 1:11; *1 P.* 5:2.

[94] Cf. Councils of: Elvira (ca. 306), c. 20 (SCL 1, 53); Arles (314), c. 13 (SCL 1, 72); Nicaea (325) (oec. I), c. 17 (DSP 1, 42); Carthage (343-348), c. 13 (SCL 1, 199); *Canones Basilii* 14 (SCL 3, 40); Laodicea (late fourth century), c. 4; SCL 4, 111); *Quinisexta* (692), c. 10; *Decretum Gratiani*, D. XLVII, c. 1 (169).

[95] Cf. Velia Bellagamba, *Monti di Pietà*, in: AA. VV. *La Marca e le sue istituzioni al tempo di Sisto V*, Ministero per i Beni Culturali e Ambientali, Roma 1991, 291-302; D. Montanari (ed.), *Monti di Pietà e presenza ebraica in Italia (secoli XV-XVIII)*, "Quaderni di Cheiron", 10 (1999) 215-244.

[96] J. Kitowicz, *Opis obyczajów i zwyczajów za panowania Augusta III*, M. Dernałowicz (ed.), PIW, Warszawa 1985, *O bractwach*, 36.

a warranty at twice the value of the loaned amount. The missionary prefect of the *Montis Pietatis* is responsible for the evaluation of the security being offered by calling on experts able to make a proper evaluation of the bond. Should the security not have been retrieved by the end of the year, it shall be entered *in fiscum Montis Pietatis*. After the bond has been sold, if the sale yields an amount higher than the value of the loan, the surcharge is returned to the borrower, that is, the owner of the bond. If less, the Mount of Piety shall be at loss. To prevent the Mount from being diminished and turning into a monad, the capital is hedged with commissions and after the services rendered solely the commission shall circulate. Consequently, it is not able to satisfy greater needs, but only the lesser ones.[97]

Similar banking institutions had been previously established by Piotr Skarga.

Canon 18: *That deacons should not give the eucharist to presbyters or be seated above them*

It has come to the attention of this holy and great synod that in some places and cities deacons give communion to presbyters, although neither canon nor custom allows this, namely that those who have no authority to offer should give the body of Christ to those who do offer. Moreover it has become known that some of the deacons now receive the eucharist even before the bishops. All these practices must be suppressed. Deacons must remain within their own limits, knowing that they are the ministers of the bishop and subordinate to the presbyters. Let them receive the eucharist according to their order after the presbyters from the hands of the bishop or the presbyter. Nor shall permission be given for the deacons to sit among the presbyters, for such an arrangement is contrary to the canon and to rank. If anyone refuses to comply even after these decrees, he is to be suspended from the diaconate.

The position of deacons in the Churches was varied, depending on the time and place. The canons of the Arles synod tell us that some deacons had officiated the Eucharist at certain locations; the synod had strictly forbidden the practice,[98] yet without discussing the question of the "validity" of such a mass. At some places, it was believed that a local Church should possess

---

[97] Council of Lateranum V (1512-1517), session 10, DSP 4, 108-109.

[98] Council of Arles (314), c. 16, SCL 1, 73. Cf. I. Grife, *A propos de trois canons du concile d'Arles de 314*, in BLE 54 (1953), 75-83.

seven deacons, following the example set by the Apostles at Jerusalem.[99] According to the *Apostolic Constitutions*, the number of deacons must be in proportion to the number of the faithful,[100] but the synod at Neocaesarea decreed that there ought to be seven.[101] The same number had been maintained at Rome, at least since the pontificate of Pope Fabian (236-250), who had divided the city into seven quarters, each one entrusted to the care of one deacon and a subordinate subdeacon.[102] Whatever the actual scope of the latter cleric's duties,[103] he was subordinate to the deacon. The Roman deacons must have held themselves in high regard, since the synod at Arles determined as follows: "Concerning the city deacons, that they take not so much upon themselves but preserve to the presbyters their order, that they do no such thing (e.g. baptizing or preaching) without the presbyters' knowledge."[104] Unfortunately, the canon does not specify what "such thing" really refers to. Could it have been stated in reference to canon 16, whereby it would be forbidden for them to officiate the Eucharist? Quite possibly, the canon in question is mostly concerned with the Church of Rome, because it had been only there (?) that the deacons were superiors *de facto* of the presbyters in their area. Immediately following Fabian's pontificate, i.e. in 251, the city of Rome had 46 presbyters, 7 deacons, 7 subdeacons, 42 acolytes, 52 exorcists, lectors, and *ostiarii*, as well as more than 1,500 widows and paupers supported by the Church, as listed in Pope Cornelius' letter cited by Eusebius of Caesarea,[105] and the deacons had been the most important of all for reasons of formal ecclesiastical organization. Perhaps this is why they considered themselves as so important and accentuated the fact in the liturgy as well.

Some evidence of the confusion over determining the hierarchy of the particular clerical ranks can be also found in the *Apostolic Constitutions*. They reflect the situation in the Syrian Church in the late fourth century (we do not really know to what extent similar situations may have existed elsewhere), stating that the deacon comes second after the bishop, and he ought to stand by the bishop just as Christ does by God the Father, whereas

---

[99] Cf. *Act.* 6:1ff.

[100] *Apostolic Constitutions* III, 19, 1, SCL 2, 94.

[101] Council of Neocaesarea (314-319), c. 15, SCL 1, 77.

[102] Cf. *Liber Pontificalis* XXI, 2.

[103] See *Apostolic Constitutions* VIII, 21, SCL 2, 253-254, where it is stated that he is allowed to touch the holy utensils.

[104] Council of Arles (314), c. 18 (in: *A New Eusebius. Documents Illustrating the History of the Church to AD 337*, J. Stevenson (ed.), SPCK, London 1990), SCL 1, 73.

[105] Eusebius of Caesarea, *h.e.* VI, 43, 11.

presbyters are successors to the Apostles.[106] The entire work is a compilation of various earlier ecclesiastical works, with the *Apostolic Didascalia* at the beginning, so it is no surprise that without much regard for consequences it proceeds to define, further on, the deacon's liturgical duties in assisting the bishop during dispensation of the Eucharist: "And let the bishop give the oblation, saying, The body of Christ; and let him that receives say, Amen. And let the deacon take the cup; and when he gives it, say, The blood of Christ, the cup of life; and let him that drinks say, Amen."[107] Did deacons hand over the cup to presbyters as well? Probably not, as it is said further on: "A deacon does not bless, does not give the blessed gift, but receives it from the bishop and presbyter: he does not baptize, he does not offer; but when a bishop or presbyter has offered, he distributes to the people, not as a priest, but as one that ministers to the priests."[108] It is very similar to the above Nicene canon.

The canon forbids deacons to take their seats among presbyters at liturgical services. Being seated alongside bishops had been equally subject to censure.[109]

Canon 19: *Concerning the followers of Paul of Samosata who come over*

Concerning the former Paulinists who seek refuge in the catholic church, it is determined that they must be rebaptised unconditionally. Those who in the past have been enrolled among the clergy, if they appear to be blameless and irreproachable, are to be rebaptised and ordained by the bishop of the catholic church. But if on inquiry they are shown to be unsuitable, it is right that they should be deposed. Similarly with regard to deaconesses and all in general whose names have been included in the roll, the same form shall be observed. We refer to deaconesses who have been granted this status, for they do not receive any imposition of hands, so that they are in all respects to be numbered among the laity.

Since it was determined that the followers of Paul must be baptized, it was recognized that his views had been too far apart from the faith of the Church. Let us recall that no such precept had been adopted in regard to any other group, e.g., the *Catharoi* of canon 8. Paul of Samosata, Bishop of Antioch in the 260s, professed that Jesus, the Son of Mary, became the Son of God, as if by adoption, upon being conjoined with the Divine

---

[106] *Apostolic Constitutions* II, 26, 5-7, SCL 2, 44.

[107] *Apostolic Constitutions* VIII, 13 (ANF 7, revised), SCL 2, 248.

[108] *Apostolic Constitutions* VIII, 28 (ANF 7, revised), SCL 2, 257.

[109] Cf. *Punishments of the Holy Apostles for the Lapsed* 6; SCL 2, 298.

Logos. Hence, it is Jesus, born at a definite time, not the Logos, who is the
everlasting Son. We can speak of the Son of God, therefore, that "there was
a time when he was not," as only the God Himself has existed since always. I
would like to quote the following excerpt from my *Początki teologii Kościoła*
("The Origins of the Church Theology"): "Therefore, there is only one Son
of God, a man, Jesus of Nazareth. This oneness appears to depend on the
oneness of birth: the Son of God was born only once, of Virgin Mary. He is
inseparably conjoined with the Divine Wisdom; however, the Wisdom is not
a hypostasis (or a person), but only the power inherent to God. Therefore,
Paul questioned speaking of the Logos as having been begotten before
there was time, as Justin and other apologists said in reference to the stadia
of His existence, as Tertullian and Clement of Alexandria envisaged, or of
His distinct and everlasting *hipostasis* or *ousia*, as Origen and his disciples
professed. According to his view, all of that would lead to a risky statement
that the one born of the Father (Divine Logos) was not the same as the
one born of Mary (the man named Jesus), and that, in consequence, there
would be two Sons of God and two Christs."[110] Paul had been condemned
for several times at the synods of Antioch in the years 263-268, and even
removed from the Church.[111] There must have been, however, something
appealing in his doctrine, as many new followers kept coming to embrace it,
and their sheer numbers made it necessary for the great synod to settle the
question of admitting them to the Church. Moreover, the Paulinists would
be further condemned at Antioch in 341,[112] and subsequently referred to by
the bishops of the East assembled at Sardica,[113] another synod at Antioch
(344),[114] Athanasius in his letter to the Antiochenes,[115] and even as late as
the synod of Rome in 430.[116] His name would even become synonymous with
heresy. As a result, his former adherents coming over to the Church ought
to be rebaptized.

The instructions concerning the clergy are noteworthy. Unlike in the
case of baptism, their ordinations are to be held as valid. If a cleric proved
to be unworthy, he ought to be deposed from the office he held. If he
proves worthy, the bishop is to "impose his hands" on him, or, to put it
more strictly, point at him in a kind of confirming gesture, as the term

---

[110] H. Pietras, *Początki teologii Kościoła,* 3.3.1.4 "«Antiocheńskie» wątpliwości Pawła
z Samosaty," WAM, Kraków 2007.

[111] Councils of Antioch (*ca.* 263/264), (*ca.* 266/267), (268/269), SCL 1, 43-47.

[112] Council of Antioch (341), I C, SCL 1, 133.

[113] Council of Sardica (343), VII, 2. 4. 27, SCL 1, 171. 173.182.

[114] Cf. Council of Antioch (344/345), IV, 2, SCL 1, 186.

[115] Council of Alexandria (362), 3, SCL 1, 251.

[116] Council of Rome (430), 8, SCL 4, 337.

used herein is χειροτονέω – "to raise one's hand," "to vote." After all, this is the term that was used to refer to the ordination of the clergy. Another one, though rendered just the same, is used in reference to deaconesses, namely χειροθεσία, meaning such an imposition of hands as performed during baptism or prayer over the sick. To make this important distinction between the two terms clearer, especially in the context of this particular canon, let me cite a couple of passages from a commentary in our edition of the *Apostolic Constitutions* (eds. Henryk Pietras, Arkadiusz Baron).

The verb χειροτονέω (the noun χειροτονία denotes raising one's hand to vote, electing, appointing, nominating); herein, it refers to the appointing of the high priest in the Old Testament era; at *ConstApost* II, 2, 3 – to ordaining a cleric in the Church; at V, 20, 11 and VII, 16 – to establishing the Roman empire and the emperor's investiture; at III, 9, 3 – to appointing priestesses for pagan deities; at II, 43, 3 – to electing/appointing persecutors of the Church by the devil.[117]

The Greek noun χειροθεσία (verb: χειροθετέω) denotes "operating by hand, e.g., as referring to an instrument," "fingering." Here, it is used in reference to the liturgical gesture of an imposition of hands: upon a catechumen, and subsequently on a candidate for baptism (cf. *ConstApost* III, 16, 3; VII, 39, 4; 44, 3); on a penitent (cf. II, 18, 7; 41, 2; 43, 1); on the faithful during benediction (cf. VIII, 37, 4; 39, 1). The laity were forbidden to use this gesture (cf. III, 10, 1). It was to be distinguished from the gesture of appointing clergymen (cf. III, 16, 3; VIII, 28, 2. 3). M. Metzger states that the nomenclature connected with the laying of hands had evolved overtime and, beginning from the eighth century, the expression χειροτονία would have been used in regard to ordaining bishops, presbyters, and deacons, while the term χειροθεσία – to ordaining the lower-ranking clergy (SCh 329, 77 no. 360); cf. "Χειροτονία, χειροθεσία, ἐπίθεσις χιερῶν", in: JThS 24 (1922-1923), 496-534.[118]

Clerics require a certain "confirmation" in their office, whereas deaconesses are not taken into account because of the absence of any imposition of hands. According to the *Apostolic Constitutions*, deaconesses ought to be appointed by receiving an imposition of hands,[119] and the Council of Chalcedon would maintain the practice as well.[120] Perhaps, the bishops at Nicaea might have known that deaconesses had not received any imposition of hands among the Paulinists.

[117] *Apostolic Constitutions* II, 27, SCL 2, 45*.

[118] *Apostolic Constitutions* II, 33, SCL 2, 49*.

[119] *Apostolic Constitutions* VIII, 19, SCL 2, 253.

[120] Council of Chalcedon (451), c. 15, DSP 1, 239.

Canon 20: *That one must not kneel on Sundays or during the season of Pentecost*

Since there are some who kneel on Sunday and during the season of Pentecost, this holy synod decrees that, so that the same observances may be maintained in every diocese, one should offer one's prayers to the Lord standing.

The kneeling position was mostly related to the second stage of catechumenate and expiatory observances. It appears that there is only one authority that we could refer to in order to provide some evidence for the practice of not kneeling on Sundays, namely a canon derived from a certain epistle, perhaps a Paschal one, by Peter of Alexandria.[121] On this occasion, we can also find out that the prescribed days of penance were Wednesday and Friday, in commemoration of the decision to deliver Christ to authorities and His passion, respectively. On these particular days, prayers were certainly supposed to be said kneeling.

---

[121] Peter of Alexandria, c. 15; CanPG, SCL 2, 22.

VI

LETTER OF EUSEBIUS OF CAESAREA
TO THE PEOPLE OF HIS DIOCESE[1]

Eusebius composed this letter after the Council, intending perhaps to stay longer at the Emperor's court. As a dedicated historian, he must have been concerned with everything that had taken place at Nicaea. The epistle is the earliest known account of the proceedings of the Nicene synod, its value all the greater in that we know it from Athanasius' *De decretis* ..., where the author cites the document in its entirety. As there were no friendly relations between Athanasius and Eusebius, any misrepresentation in the contents of the letter would have been surely noticed by Athanasius. There is no such thing, however, and I reckon that the inclusion of the letter in Athanasius' work is thus the strongest evidence of its credibility.

1. Τὰ περὶ τῆς ἐκκλησιαστικῆς πίστεως πραγματευθέντα κατὰ τὴν μεγάλην σύνοδον τὴν ἐν Νικαίᾳ συγκροτηθεῖσαν εἰκὸς μὲν καὶ ὑμᾶς, ἀγαπητοί, μεμα θηκέναι, τῆς φήμης προτρέχειν εἰωθυίας τὸν περὶ τῶν πραττομένων ἀκριβῆ λόγον.

1. What was transacted concerning ecclesiastical faith at the Great Council assembled at Nicæa, you have probably learned, Beloved, from other sources, rumour being wont to precede the accurate account of what is doing.

It would suggest that Eusebius wrote the letter at some time afterwards, when the other attendees would have already been gone. Let us remember that the rate of travelling of both correspondence and people had been the same at that time: the *cursus publicus* served as a carrier for both mail and travellers, should the latter have been authorized to use it.[2] Consequently, despite the earliest attested origin of this particular "report," there may have already elapsed even up to several months since the conclusion of the proceedings. I cannot really tell, of course, why Eusebius had not returned to his diocese at the time. Considering the fact that the Emperor had entrusted him with a honourable duty of preparing sets of the holy books for the churches to be erected at

---

[1] Cf. Athanasius, *Letter of Eusebius* (NPNF 2,4); DSP 1, A. Baron, H. Pietras (eds.), ŹMT 24, WAM, Kraków 2001, 55-61. See Eusebius of Caesarea, in: PG 20, 1535-1544; Socrates, *h.e.* I, 8; Theodoret, *h.e.* I, 12; Opitz 22, p. 42. Cf. also M. Simonetti, *Il Cristo*, II, 104-112.

[2] Cf. D. Gorce, *Les voyages l'hospitalité et le port des letters. Dans le monde chrétien des IV et V siécles*, Paris 1925, s. 49; M. Ożóg, *Podróże mnichów i duchownych w świetle pism świętego Hieronima*, in *Vox Patrum* 57 (2012), 453-468.

the future capital city of Constantinople,[3] it can be assumed that he had been among those in good graces at the court.

Ἀλλ᾿ ἵνα μὴ ἐκ μόνης τοιαύτης ἀκοῆς τὰ τῆς ἀληθείας ἑτεροίως ὑμῖν ἀπαγγέλληται, ἀναγκαίως διεπεμψάμεθα ὑμῖν πρῶτον μὲν τὴν ὑφ᾿ ἡμῶν προτεθεῖσαν περὶ τῆς πίστεως γραφὴν, ἔπειτα τὴν δευτέραν, ἣν ταῖς ἡμετέραις φωναῖς προσθήκας ἐπιβαλόντες ἐκδεδώκασι.

2. Τὸ μὲν οὖν παρ᾿ ἡμῶν γράμμα, ἐπὶ παρουσίᾳ τοῦ θεοφιλεστάτου ἡμῶν βασιλέως ἀναγνωσθὲν, εὖ τε ἔχειν καὶ δοκίμως ἀποφανθὲν, τοῦτον ἔχει τὸν τρόπον·

3. Καθὼς παρελάβομεν παρὰ τῶν πρὸ ἡμῶν ἐπισκόπων, καὶ ἐν τῇ κατηχήσει, καὶ ὅτε τὸ λουτρὸν ἐλαμβάνομεν, καὶ καθὼς ἀπὸ τῶν θείων γραφῶν μεμαθήκαμεν, καὶ ὡς ἐν τῷ πρεσβυτερίῳ, καὶ ἐν αὐτῇ τῇ ἐπισκοπῇ ἐπιστεύσαμέν τε καὶ ἐδιδάσκομεν, οὕτω καὶ νῦν πιστεύοντες, τὴν ἡμετέραν πίστιν ὑμῖν προσαναφέρομεν. Ἔστι δὲ αὕτη·

But lest in such reports the circumstances of the case have been misrepresented, we have been obliged to transmit to you, first, the formula of faith presented by ourselves, and next, the second, which [the Fathers] put forth with some additions to our words.

[2.] Our own paper, then, which was read in the presence of our most pious Emperor, and declared to be good and unexceptionable, ran thus:

3. As we have received from the Bishops who preceded us, and in our first catechisings, and when we received the Holy Laver, and as we have learned from the divine Scriptures, and as we believed and taught in the presbytery, and in the Episcopate itself, so believing also at the time present, we report to you our faith, and it is this:

It does not have to be necessarily understood as plural, as if Eusebius were writing on behalf of someone else as well, though we cannot rule it out. Literally, it reads *en plus dativus* in singular: *en to presbiterio, en te episkope*, which translates as "in the presbytery, and in the episcopate," i.e., "being a presbyter, and a bishop."

4. Πιστεύομεν εἰς ἕνα Θεὸν, Πατέρα παντοκράτορα, τὸν τῶν ἁπάντων ὁρατῶν τε καὶ ἀοράτων ποιητήν· καὶ εἰς ἕνα Κύριον Ἰησοῦν Χριστὸν, τὸν τοῦ Θεοῦ Λόγον, Θεὸν ἐκ Θεοῦ, φῶς ἐκ φωτός, ζωὴν ἐκ ζωῆς, Υἱὸν μονογενῆ, πρωτότοκον πάσης κτίσεως, πρὸ πάντων τῶν αἰώνων ἐκ τοῦ Θεοῦ Πατρὸς γεγεννημένον· δι᾿ οὗ καὶ ἐγένετο τὰ πάντα,

4. We believe in One God, the Father Almighty, the Maker of all things visible and invisible. And in One Lord Jesus Christ, the Word of God, God from God, Light from Light, Life from Life, Son Only-begotten, first-born of every creature,[4] before all the ages, begotten from the Father, by Whom also all things were made;[5]

[3] Cf. Theodoret of Cyrrhus, *h.e.* I, 16.

[4] *Col.* 1:15.

[5] Cf. *Io.* 1:3.

τὸν διὰ τὴν ἡμετέραν σωτηρίαν σαρκωθέντα, καὶ ἐν ἀνθρώποις πολιτευσάμενον· καὶ παθόντα, καὶ ἀναστάντα τῇ τρίτῃ ἡμέρᾳ· καὶ ἀνελθόντα πρὸς τὸν πατέρα, καὶ ἥξοντα πάλιν ἐν δόξῃ κρῖναι ζῶντας καὶ νεκρούς. Πιστεύομεν καὶ εἰς ἓν Πνεῦμα Ἅγιον.

5. Τούτων ἕκαστον εἶναι καὶ ὑπάρχειν πιστεύοντες, Πατέρα ἀληθῶς Πατέρα, καὶ Υἱὸν ἀληθῶς Υἱὸν, καὶ Πνεῦμα Ἅγιον ἀληθῶς Ἅγιον Πνεῦμα· καθὼς καὶ ὁ Κύριος ἡμῶν ἀποστέλλων εἰς τὸ κήρυγμα τοὺς ἑαυτοῦ μαθητὰς, εἶπε· "Πορευθέντες μαθητεύσατε πάντα τὰ ἔθνη, βαπτίζοντες αὐτοὺς εἰς τὸ ὄνομα τοῦ Πατρὸς, καὶ τοῦ Υἱοῦ, καὶ τοῦ Ἁγίου Πνεύματος". Περὶ ὧν καὶ διαβεβαιούμεθα οὕτως ἔχειν, καὶ οὕτω φρονεῖν, καὶ πάλαι οὕτως ἐσχηκέναι, καὶ μέχρι θανάτου οὕτω σχήσειν, καὶ ἐν αὐτῇ ἐνίστασθαι τῇ πίστει, ἀναθεματίζοντες πᾶσαν αἵρεσιν ἄθεον·

6. ταῦτα ἀπὸ καρδίας καὶ ψυχῆς πάντα πεφρονηκέναι, ἐξ οὗπερ ἴσμεν ἑαυτοὺς, καὶ νῦν φρονεῖν τε καὶ λέγειν ἐξ ἀληθείας, ἐπὶ τοῦ Θεοῦ τοῦ παντοκράτορος, καὶ τοῦ Κυρίου ἡμῶν Ἰησοῦ Χριστοῦ μαρτυρούμεθα· δεικνύναι ἔχοντες δι' ἀποδείξεων, καὶ πείθειν ὑμᾶς, ὅτι καὶ τοὺς παρεληλυθότας χρόνους οὕτως ἐπιστεύομέν τε καὶ ἐκηρύσσομεν ὁμοίως.

Who for our salvation was made flesh, and lived among men, and suffered, and rose again the third day, and ascended to the Father, and will come again in glory to judge the quick and dead. And we believe also in One Holy Ghost.

5. Believing each of these to be and to exist, the Father truly Father, and the Son truly Son, and the Holy Ghost truly Holy Ghost, as also our Lord, sending forth His disciples for the preaching, said, "Go teach all nations, baptizing them in the Name of the Father and of the Son, and of the Holy Ghost."[6] Concerning Whom we confidently affirm that so we hold, and so we think, and so we have held aforetime, and we maintain this faith unto the death, anathematizing every godless heresy.

6. That this we have ever thought from our heart and soul, from the time we recollect ourselves, and now think and say in truth, before God Almighty and our Lord Jesus Christ do we witness, being able by proofs to shew and to convince you, that, even in times past, such has been our belief and preaching.

This strong emphasis on the perseverance of the author's faith – "in times past" and to the death – may have been in connection with his condemnation, or at least censure, at Antioch. The latter sentence seems to point out that Eusebius may have felt compelled to offer a validation of his faith, as if in an attempt to clear himself of some accusations. Such news must have certainly reached Caesarea within a period from March by approx. August, i.e., when Eusebius had written that letter, and he may have received himself the news of some criticism aimed at him. The plural

---

[6] *Mt.* 28 :19.

reflexive pronoun *heautous*, meaning "ourselves," may be thus rendered as "since we have known one another," i.e., as we can see, "from the time we recollect ourselves." Therefore, this circumstance would also argue against assuming that Eusebius would have spoken on behalf of anybody else.

This particular creed is sometimes called "Caesarean," which means that it is inferred from Eusebius' incorporation thereof in his letter that it had been adopted by that church as a baptismal profession of faith.[7] Nonetheless, it seems strange. Why in a letter to his own church would Eusebius have quoted the content of the creed used there – so to speak – on a daily basis? And why, in addition, would he have assured his faithful with the following words: "being able by proofs to shew and to convince you, that, even in times past, such has been our belief and preaching," as we can see at the close of the above passage? I suppose that Eusebius cited the text of that *credo* because it had been unknown at Caesarea, and drawn up in an *ad hoc* manner by Eusebius, exactly because the Emperor had wished to submit for synodal approval some creed whose text would be acceptable to everybody. It would have been then a sort of artificially prepared text, nonetheless based on some orthodox creeds, as could be possibly proved. The last sentence could be therefore understood as follows: we can prove that the creed I have submitted agrees with everything we profess and teach daily, and with the contents of the individual creeds in our churches.

7. Ταύτης ὑφ' ἡμῶν ἐκτεθείσης τῆς πίστεως, οὐδενὶ παρῆν ἀντιλογίας τόπος. Ἀλλ' αὐτός τε πρῶτος ὁ θεοφιλέστατοςἡμῶνβασιλεὺς,ὀρθότατα περιέχειν αὐτὴν ἐμαρτύρησεν· οὕτω τε καὶ ἑαυτὸν φρονεῖν ἐμαρτύρατο, καὶ ταύτῃ τοὺς πάντας συγκαταθέσθαι, καὶ ὑπογράφειν τοῖς δόγμασι, καὶ συμφωνεῖν τούτοις αὐτοῖς παρεκελεύετο, ἑνὸς μόνου προσεγγραφέντος ῥήματος τοῦ "ὁμοουσίου."	7. On this faith being publicly put forth by us, no room for contradiction appeared; but our most pious Emperor, before any one else, testified that it comprised most orthodox statements. He confessed moreover that such were his own sentiments, and he advised all present to agree to it, and to subscribe its articles and to assent to them, with the insertion of the single word, One-in-essence,

Eusebius suggests that his creed had cleared him of any accusations and, moreover, the Emperor decided to adopt this particular profession of faith and submit it for approval by vote as obligatory to all. It remains to be resolved why he had the phrase "one-in-essence" ("consubstantial") incorporated therein. Possibly, there were some figures whose opinion of the creed had not been as favourable as that of the Emperor and they pointed to certain perceived shortcomings. If,

---

[7] Thus, e.g., in H. Denzinger, A. Schönmetzer, *Enchiridion Symbolorum, definitionum et declarationum de rebus fidei et morum*, 40, M. Simonetti, *La crisi ariana*, 83.

however, the text of this creed had been an "artificially" formulated document indeed (and I believe that was the case), as a matter of fact never previously used by any church, the Emperor himself might not have minded the situation, unlike the bishops. In the light of the Antioch document, in which such a heavy emphasis had been placed on the Son's immutability "by nature," the opposition may have been directed at Eusebius' perceived non-recognition of the consubstantiality (the common nature, or essence) of the Father and the Son. I assume that such an objection may have induced the Emperor to "come out" with the term *homoousios*. I would say "come out," because it takes someone rather not very familiar with theology to have suggested this particular term (a condition which the Emperor would have fulfilled entirely). According to De Decker's view, this is exactly the reason why the Emperor could not have been the initiator of the incorporation of that term, but he must have been definitely in favour as the expression itself may have evoked associations with the much-valued concept of the unity of the state, Church, and his dominion, i.e., *homonoia*.[8] However, those who venture to assume, like De Decker and Simonetti have done,[9] that the term had been certainly suggested by somebody else must deal with a very difficult problem of determining, even at a purely hypothetical level, who might have been that person. The question is that if any of the bishops had been indeed the originator of the idea, there would have been no reason for him at all to have relinquished it thereafter. More synods would ensue in the years to come, and some more creeds would be formulated as well, yet none of the attendees put forward such an idea, even at Sardica.[10] Incidentally, there is nothing to suggest the Occidental origin of the notion, despite certain assumptions to that effect.[11]

Let us recollect that the term had been (most likely) condemned within the context of the view formulated by Paul of Samosata, and perhaps that was the reason why Alexander had initially avoided using it in his dispute with Arius – as Sozomen recounts.[12] Eventually, he was to agree to accept it, but I do not think his approval had been something more than just a tactical move. We cannot really know, therefore, who might have possibly suggested the idea to the Emperor. He must have certainly known that in order to specify that two things are of the same nature (or essence), the term *homoousios*, in its most common meaning, should be applied. Therefore, it may have seemed to him a good complementary phrase, even though, as we shall see, it caused some considerable uproar among the bishops since

[8] D. De Decker, *Eusèbe de Nicomédie*, 140-141.

[9] Cf. M. Simonetti, *La crisi ariana*, 90-95.

[10] Council of Sardica (343), SCL 1, 143-145; Theodoret of Cyrrhus, *h.e.* II, 8.

[11] On this point, cf. X. Morales, *La théologie trinitaire d'Athanase d'Alexandrie* (Collection des Études Augustiniennes – Série Antiquité 180), Paris 2006, 242-243.

[12] Sozomen, *h.e.* I, 15.

hardly anybody would have evidently liked it even immediately prior to the Emperor's support for this term.[13] The myth of *homoousia* having been uniformly supported by all the "orthodox" clergy, as opposed to the Arians, is so well-entrenched that even now we can still encounter the view that at Nicaea Alexander, Athanasius, and others, had been firmly in favour of this expression,[14] although in fact the only contemporary text with a positive view towards the term is this particular letter by Eusebius. It cannot be found in any of Alexander's writings, whereas Athanasius used it only 25 years after the Council. Lewis Ayres notes that the word *homoousios* was chosen for theological reasons, with the awareness that Arius did not agree with it.[15] In my opinion, it still follows in the footsteps of the myth that the "orthodox" defended the consubstantiality and "Arians" opposed it. It is actually anachronistic (as any myth certainly is), projecting upon the Council of Nicaea the views that were to emerge in the Church only about 30 years after, and later on. Notably, the earliest extant synodal text where the consubstantiality is adopted, not rejected, is only the pronouncement of the Paris synod of 360,[16] while at Alexandria, where, according to the said myth, many of the followers of Athanasius had been in favour of *homoousia*, only in 362, in a post-synodal letter to the Antiochenes.[17]

Ὁ καὶ αὐτὸς ἡρμήνευσε λέγων, ὅτι μὴ κατὰ τὰ τῶν σωμάτων πάθη λέγοι τὸ "ὁμοούσιον," οὔτε οὖν κατὰ διαίρεσιν, οὔτε κατά τινα ἀποτομὴν ἐκ τοῦ πατρὸς ὑποστῆναι· μήτε γὰρ δύνασθαι τὴν ἄϋλον καὶ νοερὰν καὶ ἀσώματον φύσιν σωματικόν τι πάθος ὑφίστασθαι· θείοις δὲ καὶ ἀπορρήτοις ῥήμασι προσήκει τὰ τοιαῦτα νοεῖν. Καὶ ὁ μὲν σοφώτατος καὶ εὐσεβὴς ἡμῶν βασιλεὺς τοιάδε ἐφιλοσόφει· οἱ δὲ, προφάσει τοῦ "ὁμοουσίου", τήνδε τὴν γραφὴν πεποιήκασι.

which moreover he interpreted as not in the sense of the affections of bodies, nor as if the Son subsisted from the Father in the way of division, or any severance; for that the immaterial, and intellectual, and incorporeal nature could not be the subject of any corporeal affection, but that it became us to conceive of such things in a divine and ineffable manner. And such were the theological remarks of our most wise and most religious Emperor; but they, with a view to the addition of One in essence, drew up the following formula:

The Emperor's move to make it more specific must have been caused by someone's objection to the term in question, on account of its associations with

---

[13] I agree with De Decker on this point, cf. D. De Decker, *Eusèbe de Nicomédie*, 146.

[14] Cf. R. Toczko, *O arianizmie Euzebiusza z Cezarei*, 124.

[15] L. Ayres, *Nicaea and Its Legacy*, 90.

[16] Ciuncil of Paris (360/361), II/2, SCL 1, 247.

[17] Ciuncil of Alexandria (362), *Letter to the Antiochenes*, 5, SCL 1, 252.

the material world that might have led to treating God's essence as corporeal. In consequence, either the Emperor himself or somebody on his behalf must have acted to renounce any corporeal connotation of this notion. If we are to believe Eusebius, we would have to assume that the insertion of *homoousios* was not sufficient at all, and the attendees would proceed to introduce some more additions. Eusebius states that the Fathers of the Council had drafted a different document with the term "consubstantial" in the middle. There is a hypothesis that following the dismissal of the creed proposed by Eusebius, a profession of faith from some unidentified Syro-Palestinian city. Manlio Simonetti cites it tentatively (offering no arguments for or against it), referring to Kelly, among others.[18] With no source-based evidence to substantiate it, I think there is no need to discuss it further. As there is no information on the origin of this text, it may as well be assumed that Eusebius' formula was replaced by another, equally "artificial" and unfavoured, document, as it would become evident very soon.

8. Πιστεύομεν εἰς ἕνα Θεὸν Πατέρα παντοκράτορα, πάντων ὁρατῶν τε καὶ ἀοράτων ποιητήν· καὶ εἰς ἕνα Κύριον Ἰησοῦν Χριστὸν, τὸν Υἱὸν τοῦ Θεοῦ, γεννηθέντα ἐκ τοῦ Πατρὸς μονογενῆ, τουτέστιν ἐκ τῆς οὐσίας τοῦ Πατρός· Θεὸν ἐκ Θεοῦ, φῶς ἐκ φωτὸς, Θεὸν ἀληθινὸν ἐκ Θεοῦ ἀληθινοῦ· γεννηθέντα, οὐ ποιηθέντα·ὁμοούσιον τῷ Πατρί· δι' οὗ τὰ πάντα ἐγένετο, τά τε ἐν τῷ οὐρανῷ, καὶ τὰ ἐν τῇ γῇ· τὸν δι' ἡμᾶς τοὺς ἀνθρώπους, καὶ διὰ τὴν ἡμετέραν σωτηρίαν κατελθόντα, καὶ σαρκωθέντα, ἐνανθρωπήσαντα, παθόντα, καὶ ἀναστάντα τῇ τρίτῃ ἡμέρᾳ· ἀνελθόντα εἰς τοὺς οὐρανούς· ἐρχόμενον κρῖναι ζῶντας καὶ νεκρούς. Καὶ εἰς τὸ Πνεῦμα τὸ Ἅγιον. Τοὺς δὲ λέγοντας, "ἦν ποτὲ ὅτε οὐκ ἦν", ἢ "οὐκ ἦν πρὶν γεννηθῆναι", ἢ "ἐξ οὐκ ὄντων ἐγένετο", ἢ "ἐξ ἑτέρας ὑποστάσεως ἢ οὐσίας φάσκοντας εἶναι, <ἢ κτιστὸν>, ἢ τρεπτὸν, ἢ ἀλλοιωτὸν τὸν Υἱὸν τοῦ Θεοῦ", τούτους ἀναθεματίζει ἡ καθολικὴ καὶ ἀποστολικὴ τοῦ Θεοῦ ἐκκλησία.

8. We believe in One God, the Father Almighty, Maker of all things visible and invisible. And in One Lord Jesus Christ, the Son of God, begotten of the Father, Only-begotten, that is, from the essence of the Father; God from God, Light from Light, Very God from Very God, begotten not made, One in essence with the Father, by Whom all things were made, both things in heaven and things in earth; Who for us men and for our salvation came down and was made flesh, was made man, suffered, and rose again the third day, ascended into heaven, and cometh to judge quick and dead. And in the Holy Ghost. And those who say, 'Once He was not,' and 'Before His generation He was not,' and 'He came to be from nothing,' or those who pretend that the Son of God is 'Of other subsistence or essence,' or 'created' or 'alterable,' or 'mutable,' the Catholic Church anathematizes.

A commentary on this particular creed can be found in another chapter.

[18] M. Simonetti, *La crisi ariana*, 83; J.N.D. Kelly, *Early Christian Creeds*, Longman, London 1950, 217ff.

9. Καὶ δὴ ταύτης τῆς γραφῆς ὑπ' αὐτῶν ὑπαγορευθείσης, ὅπως εἴρηται αὐτοῖς τὸ "ἐκ τῆς οὐσίας τοῦ Πατρὸς", καὶ τὸ "τῷ Πατρὶ ὁμοούσιον", οὐκ ἀνεξέταστον αὐτοῖς καταλιμπάνομεν. Ἐπερωτήσεις τοιγαροῦν καὶ ἀποκρίσεις ἐντεῦθεν ἀνεκινοῦντο, ἐβασάνιζέν τε ὁ λόγος τὴν διάνοιαν τῶν εἰρημένων· καὶ δὴ καὶ τὸ "ἐκ τῆς οὐσίας" ὡμολόγητο πρὸς αὐτῶν, δηλωτικὸν εἶναι τοῦ ἐκ μὲν τοῦ Πατρὸς εἶναι, οὐ μὴν ὡς μέρος ὑπάρχειν τοῦ Πατρός·

10. ταύτῃ δὲ καὶ ἡμῖν ἐδόκει καλῶς ἔχειν συγκατατίθεσθαι τῇ διανοίᾳ, τῆς εὐσεβοῦς διδασκαλίας ὑπαγορευούσης ἐκ τοῦ Πατρὸς εἶναι τὸν υἱὸν, οὐ μὴν μέρος τῆς οὐσίας αὐτοῦ τυγχάνειν. Διόπερ τῇ διανοίᾳ καὶ αὐτοὶ συντιθέμεθα, οὐδὲ τὴν φωνὴν τοῦ "ὁμοουσίου" παραιτούμενοι, τοῦ τῆς εἰρήνης σκοποῦ πρὸ ὀφθαλμῶν ἡμῖν κειμένου, καὶ τοῦ μὴ τῆς ὀρθῆς ἐκπεσεῖν διανοίας.

9. On their dictating this formula, we did not let it pass without inquiry in what sense they introduced "of the essence of the Father," and "one in essence with the Father." Accordingly questions and explanations took place, and the meaning of the words underwent the scrutiny of reason. And they professed, that the phrase "of the essence" was indicative of the Son's being indeed from the Father, yet without being as if a part of Him.

10. And with this understanding we thought good to assent to the sense of such religious doctrine, teaching, as it did, that the Son was from the Father, not however a part of His essence. On this account we assented to the sense ourselves, without declining even the term "One in essence," peace being the object which we set before us, and steadfastness in the orthodox view.

According to Eusebius' view, "of the essence" is then tantamount to *homoousios*, provided that the incorporeal sense of the latter term is assumed. It is worth noting that exactly the same interpretation would be also propounded by Athanasius.[19]

11. Κατὰ τὰ αὐτὰ δὲ, καὶ τὸ "γεννηθέντα καὶ οὐ ποιηθέντα" κατεδεξάμεθα, ἐπειδὴ τὸ ποιηθὲν κοινὸν ἔφασκον εἶναι πρόσρημα τῶν λοιπῶν κτισμάτων, τῶν διὰ τοῦ Υἱοῦ γενομένων, ὧν οὐδὲν ὅμοιον ἔχειν τὸν Υἱόν· διὸ δὴ μὴ εἶναι αὐτὸν ποίημα, τοῖς δι' αὐτοῦ γενομένοις ὅμοιον· κρείττονος δὲ ἢ κατὰ πᾶν ποίημα τυγχάνειν οὐσίας, ἣν ἐκ τοῦ Πατρὸς γεγεννῆσθαι διδάσκει τὰ θεῖα λόγια, τοῦ τρόπου τῆς γεννήσεως ἀνεκφράστου καὶ ἀνεπιλογίστου πάσῃ γενητῇ φύσει τυγχάνοντος.

11. In the same way we also admitted "begotten, not made;" since the Council alleged that "made" was an appellative common to the other creatures which came to be through the Son, to whom the Son had no likeness. Wherefore, say they, He was not a work resembling the things which through Him came to be, but was of an essence which is too high for the level of any work; and which the Divine oracles teach to have been generated from the Father, the mode of generation being inscrutable and incalculable to every originated nature.

---

[19] Cf. Athanasius, *De Synodis* 35.

12. Οὕτω δὲ καὶ τὸ "ὁμοούσιον εἶναι τοῦ Πατρὸς" τὸν Υἱὸν ἐξεταζόμενος ὁ λόγος συνίστησιν, οὐ κατὰ τὸν τῶν σωμάτων τρόπον, οὐδὲ τοῖς θνητοῖς ζῴοις παραπλησίως· οὔτε γὰρ κατὰ διαίρεσιν τῆς οὐσίας, οὔτε κατὰ ἀποτομὴν, ἢ ἀλλοίωσιν τῆς τοῦ Πατρὸς οὐσίας τε καὶ δυνάμεως· τούτων γὰρ πάντων ἀλλοτρίαν εἶναι τὴν ἀγέννητον φύσιν τοῦ Πατρός·

13. παραστατικὸν δὲ εἶναι "τῷ Πατρὶ τὸ ὁμοούσιον", τὸ μηδεμίαν ἐμφέρειαν πρὸς τὰ γενητὰ κτίσματα τὸν Υἱὸν τοῦ Θεοῦ ἐμφαίνειν· μόνῳ δὲ τῷ Πατρὶ τῷ γεγεννηκότι κατὰ πάντα τρόπον ἀφωμοιῶσθαι, καὶ μὴ εἶναι ἐξ ἑτέρας τὲ ὑποστάσεως καὶ οὐσίας, ἀλλ᾽ ἐκ τοῦ Πατρός. Ὧι καὶ αὐτῷ τοῦτον ἑρμηνευθέντι τὸν τρόπον, καλῶς ἔχειν ἐφάνη συγκαταθέσθαι· ἐπεὶ καὶ τῶν παλαιῶν τινας λογίους καὶ ἐπιφανεῖς ἐπισκόπους καὶ συγγραφέας ἔγνωμεν, ἐπὶ τῆς τοῦ Πατρὸς καὶ Υἱοῦ θεολογίας τῷ τοῦ "ὁμοουσίου" συγχρησαμένους ὀνόματι.

12. And so too on examination there are grounds for saying that the Son is "one in essence" with the Father; not in the way of bodies, nor like mortal beings, for He is not such by division of essence, or by severance, no, nor by any affection, or alteration, or changing of the Father's essence and power (since from all such the unoriginate nature of the Father is alien),

13. but because "one in essence with the Father" suggests that the Son of God bears no resemblance to the originated creatures, but that to His Father alone Who begat Him is He in every way assimilated, and that He is not of any other subsistence and essence, but from the Father. To which term also, thus interpreted, it appeared well to assent; since we were aware that even among the ancients, some learned and illustrious Bishops and writers have used the term "one in essence," in their theological teaching concerning the Father and Son.

We do not really know whom Eusebius invokes here, i.e., who those "learned and illustrious" figures were. Unfortunately, it remains a mystery. Let us recall that the term *homoousios* was used, in a completely different sense, by Paul of Samosata. The term had been a subject of dispute even in the time of Dionysius of Rome and Dionysius of Alexandria. I have already referred to this question in my commentary on item 7.

14. Ταῦτα μὲν οὖν περὶ τῆς ἐκτεθείσης εἰρήσθω πίστεως, ᾗ συνεφωνήσαμεν οἱ πάντες οὐκ ἀνεξετάστως, ἀλλὰ κατὰ τὰς ἀποδοθείσας διανοίας, ἐπ᾽ αὐτοῦ τοῦ θεοφιλεστάτου βασιλέως ἐξετασθείσας, καὶ τοῖς εἰρημένοις λογισμοῖς συνομολογηθείσας·

14. So much then be said concerning the faith which was published; to which all of us assented, not without inquiry, but according to the specified senses, mentioned before the most religious Emperor himself, and justified by the forementioned considerations.

15. καὶ τὸν ἀναθεματισμὸν δὲ τὸν μετὰ τὴν πίστιν πρὸς αὐτῶν ἐκτεθέντα, ἄλυπον εἶναι ἡγησάμεθα, διὰ τὸ ἀπείργειν ἀγράφοις χρήσασθαι φωναῖς· διὸ σχεδὸν ἡ πᾶσα γέγονε σύγχυσίς τε καὶ ἀκαταστασία τῶν ἐκκλησιῶν. Μηδεμιᾶς γοῦν θεοπνεύστου γραφῆς τῷ "ἐξ οὐκ ὄντων", καὶ τῷ "ἦν ποτὲ ὅτε οὐκ ἦν", καὶ τοῖς ἑξῆς ἐπιλεγομένοις κεχρημένης, οὐκ εὔλογον ἐφάνη ταῦτα λέγειν καὶ διδάσκειν· ᾧ καὶ αὐτῷ καλῶς δόξαντι συνεθέμεθα, ἐπεὶ μηδὲ ἐν τῷ πρὸ τούτου χρόνῳ, τούτοις εἰώθαμεν χρῆσθαι τοῖς ῥήμασιν.

16. Ἔτι μὴν τὸ ἀναθεματίζεσθαι τὸ "πρὸ τοῦ γεννηθῆναι οὐκ ἦν" οὐκ ἄτοπον ἐνομίσθη, τῷ παρὰ πᾶσιν ὁμολογεῖσθαι εἶναι αὐτὸν υἱὸν τοῦ θεοῦ καὶ πρὸ τῆς κατὰ σάρκα γεννήσεως.

15. And as to the anathematism published by them at the end of the Faith, it did not pain us, because it forbade to use words not in Scripture, from which almost all the confusion and disorder of the Church have come. Since then no divinely inspired Scripture has used the phrases, "out of nothing," and "once He was not," and the rest which follow, there appeared no ground for using or teaching them; to which also we assented as a good decision, since it had not been our custom hitherto to use these terms.

16.[20] Moreover to anathematize "Before His generation He was not," did not seem preposterous, in that it is confessed by all, that the Son of God was before the generation according to the flesh.

Eusebius denounces the statement that "before His [the Son's] generation He was not," in the sense of the existence prior to his birth out of Mary ("before the generation according to the flesh"). Simonetti argues that he misconstrues its meaning, as it was concerned in fact with the eternal Divine generation, which was contradicted by Arius.[21] It may be possible, however, that the actual reason for the dispute was to contest the views of Paul of Samosata, who recognized the existence of the Son of God only from the point of His birth out of Mary.[22] I would like to add that Eusebius' letter was cited by Athanasius and he did not reproach the author for any distortion or misrepresentation.

Ἤδη δὲ ὁ θεοφιλέστατος ἡμῶν βασιλεὺς τῷ λόγῳ κατεσκεύαζε καὶ κατὰ τὴν ἔνθεον αὐτοῦ γέννησιν τὸ πρὸ πάντων αἰώνων εἶναι αὐτόν,

Nay, our most religious Emperor did at the time prove, in a speech, that He was in being even according to His divine generation which is before all ages,

---

[20] As per Socrates, h.e. 1, 8, the whole item 16 is missing.

[21] Cf. M. Simonetti, *Il Cristo*, vol. II, 556-557f.

[22] Cf. H. Pietras, *Le ragioni della convocazione del Concilio Niceno da parte di Costantino il Grande*, in: *Gregorianum* 82/1, (2001), 31.

ἐπεὶ καὶ πρὶν ἐνεργείᾳ γεννηθῆναι δυνάμει ἦν ἐν τῷ πατρὶ ἀγεννήτως, ὄντος τοῦ πατρὸς ἀεὶ πατρός, ὡς καὶ βασιλέως ἀεὶ καὶ σωτῆρος καὶ δυνάμει πάντα ὄντος, ἀεί τε καὶ κατὰ τὰ αὐτὰ καὶ ὡσαύτως ἔχοντος.

since [whereas?] before He was generated in energy, He was in virtue with the Father ingenerately, the Father being always Father, as King always, and Saviour always, being all things in virtue, and being always in the same respects and in the same way.

Arkadiusz Baron explains this passage as follows: "Our most religious Emperor did at the time prove, in a speech, that He was in being even according to His divine generation which is before all ages, Since even before He was generated in energy, He was in virtue (the Power) with the Father ingenerately, [the Son] of the Father, the Father being always Father, likewise as Lord always, and Saviour always, being the Power of all things, and being always in the same respects and in the same way." He assumes that the Son and His generation before all ages constitute the subject of the sentence. In my opinion, however, the passage is so abstruse exactly because Eusebius seems to be intent on concealing something rather than saying too much. In item 15, he says that he agreed to condemn the statement that "once He was not," and he goes on to say that "it had not been our custom hitherto to use these terms." He may have been reluctant to use such assertions because of their possible understanding in the sense imparted to them by Paul of Samosata, and not because he would think they should not have been applied at all. I suppose that the point is still the birth from the Virgin Mary, whereby the Son's existence could not have come into being (as Paul would argue), but which is solely the externalization (*energeia*) of the everlasting Power (*dynamis*), the realization of the salvation design of the Father, who is always the Lord and Saviour. The view that the Father is always and immutably Father may have been derived from Origen's theology.[23] I owe this interpretation of the text to Prof. Simonetti.[24]

17. Ταῦτα ὑμῖν ἀναγκαίως διεπεμψάμεθα, ἀγαπητοί, τὸ κεκριμένον τῆς ἡμετέρας ἐξετάσεώς τε καὶ συγκαταθέσεως φανερὸν ὑμῖν καθιστῶντες· καί, ὡς εὐλόγως, τότε μὲν καὶ μέχρι ὑστάτης ὥρας ἐνιστάμεθα, ὅθ' ἡμῖν τὰ ἑτεροίως γραφέντα προσέκοπτεν·

17. This we have been forced to transmit to you, Beloved, as making clear to you the deliberation of our inquiry and assent, and how reasonably we resisted even to the last minute as long as we were offended at statements which differed from our own,

[23] Cf. H. Pietras, *Argumentacja filozoficzna za wiecznością Syna Bożego u Orygenesa*, 89-97.

[24] Cf. M. Simonetti, *Il Cristo*, vol. II, 113.

τότε δὲ ἀφιλονείκως τὰ μὴ λυποῦντα κατεδεξάμεθα, ὅτε ἡμῖν εὐγνωμόνως ἐξετάζουσι τῶν λόγων τὴν διάνοιαν ἐφάνη συντρέχειν τοῖς ὑφ' ἡμῶν αὐτῶν ἐν τῇ προεκτεθείσῃ πίστει ὡμολογημένοις.

but received without contention what no longer pained us, as soon as, on a candid examination of the sense of the words, they appeared to us to coincide with what we ourselves have professed in the faith which we have already published.

I have already noted the significance of Athanasius' citation of the *Letter of Eusebius* without questioning the truthfulness of the author. It allows me to conclude that Eusebius' views are exactly as they are expounded in this letter, i.e., he comes to accept the expediency of subscribing the Nicene Creed along with the others. He also concurs with the opinion that a different one would have been better. Therefore, it is rather odd to think that he would continue to defend his non-Nicene doctrine until his death,[25] as if anybody had defended the Nicene one at the time. Athanasius himself would begin to do so only twenty years after the Council, having realized that nothing any better could be possibly formulated. The fact of Eusebius' opposition to the theological teachings of Marcellus of Ancyra (cf. Eusebius' *Ecclesiastica Theologia*) does not mean he had acted against the orthodox pro-Nicene doctrine,[26] but only that he would firmly oppose any teachings dangerously close, in his opinion, to the views espoused by Paul of Samosata.

[25] Cf. Dam R. Van, *The Roman Revolution of Constantine*, 284.

[26] Which is apparently assumed by R. Toczko in his *O arianizmie Euzebiusza z Cezarei*, 108-110, yet not without certain difficulties.

CREDO OF THE 318 FATHERS

There are so many different views, some of them fairly close to mere legend, concerning the creed of Nicaea that it takes a very disciplined and consistent approach in order to avoid falling into some well-trodden ruts left by the authorities of the past.

But let us first have a look at the sources.[1]

The earliest witness to the text of this creed is the *Letter of Eusebius of Caesarea to the People of His Diocese* (cf. Chapter 6). Let us recall it had been composed fairly soon after the conclusion of the synodal proceedings, following the departure of all the attendees to their churches. For some reasons of his own, Eusebius decided to stay on and write an epistle addressed to his own congregation.

The chronologically second source is that of Athanasius, with the reservation that it may be in fact the same text as the one provided by Eusebius, owing to Athanasius' inclusion of Eusebius' letter in an appendix to his brief work *De decretis.* In a letter to the Emperor Jovinian of 363,[2] where the text of the *Credo* is included as well, there is an addition ἢ κτιστὸν in the anathematism. It is a somewhat controversial question, nonetheless. According to Dossetti, the word can be found only in the creed present in the appendix to *De decretis,* in the creed as cited by Socrates (HE I, 8), as well as in Eusebius' letter. In Theodoret of Cyrrhus (HE I, 12), the same letter does not include the said addition. Opitz, in his edition of Eusebius' letter and the Symbol itself,[3] provides ἢ κτιστὸν, with no reservation made. It is the same in the *Thesaurus Linguae Graecae.* Hilarius of Poitiers, the most venerable of the Latin witnesses to the text, offers *convertibilem et demutabilem,* but not *creatum.*[4] So what is the conclusion? I do not know for sure, but I am afraid that Dossetti's opinion that the addition should be treated as an

---

[1] Athanasius, *Letter of Eusebius* (NPNF 2,4); G.L. Dossetti, *Il Simbolo di Nicea e di Costantinopoli.* Edizione critica, Herder, Roma 1967, 240.

[2] For the text and a translation, see SCL 1, 257-259.

[3] This edition is reproduced in M. Simonetti, *Il Cristo,* vol. II.

[4] Hilarius of Poitiers, *De synodis, seu de fide Orientalium* 84; cf. PL 10, 536; A. Hahn, *Bibliothek der Symbole und Glaubensregeln der alten Kirche,* Verlag von E. Morgenstern, Breslau 1897, 162.

Athanasian contribution to the Nicene Creed and thus simply dismissed,[5] seems to be too radical, after all. Somebody might have just as well omitted the word in question. Consequently, as far as the most crucial sources are concerned, the unfortunate ἢ κτιστὸν is either present or absent in the anathematism, depending on a specific manuscript.[6] Interestingly, in 1975, Prof. Simonetti[7] had relied on Dossetti, citing the text of the *Credo* without *creatum*, but in 1986 he followed Opitz and restored it in the *Credo* as well as in the *Letter*.[8]

There is still one more important thing to consider as regards this particular profession of faith. There is no trace of any evidence of anybody ever having used it, for any purpose, in the Church. It is worth discussing the history of its reception and interpretation, as much of the modern scholarly analysis of the subject tend to overlook or ignore opinions and views of the contemporary theologians. Of course, the latter were not in agreement on everything.

There is no doubt the great success of this creed was the Emperor Theodosius' decree[9] stating that everybody should adhere to the faith professed by Damasius of Rome and Peter of Alexandria. The bishops convoked by the Emperor (Constantinople, 381) had enshrined it in the text of canon 1, according to which the Nicene faith cannot be changed. And, very evidently, it had not been changed, as at Ephesus (431), or even at Constantinople (448) and the "Robber Council" of 449,[10] nobody would have heard of any alteration and the Fathers solely referred to this particular creed. Towards the close of this chapter, we shall have a look at the circumstances giving rise to the legend of the origin of this profession of faith at that specific synod.

The content of the *Creed* is as follows:

Πιστεύομεν εἰς ἕνα Θεὸν Πατέρα παντοκράτορα, πάντων ὁρατῶν τε καὶ ἀοράτων ποιητήν·	We believe in One God, the Father Almighty, Maker of all things visible and invisible.

---

[5] G.L. Dossetti, *Il Simbolo*, 256.

[6] Which would make me revise some of my previous annotations to the effect that the insertion is certainly of Athanasian origin, as, for instance, in the DSP 1, 25, as a result of my own reliance on Dossetti in this regard.

[7] M. Simonetti, *La crisi ariana*, 88.

[8] See M. Simonetti, *Il Cristo*, vol. II, 100 and 108.

[9] *CTh* XVI 1, 2 of 27 February 380.

[10] Cf. Councils of Ephesus (431), DSP 1, 166; Constantinople (448), SCL 6, 62-105; Ephesus (449), SCL 6, 144-172.

καὶ εἰς ἕνα Κύριον Ἰησοῦν Χριστόν, τὸν Υἱὸν τοῦ Θεοῦ, γεννηθέντα ἐκ τοῦ Πατρὸς μονογενῆ, τουτέστιν ἐκ τῆς οὐσίας τοῦ Πατρός· Θεὸν ἐκ Θεοῦ, φῶς ἐκ φωτός, Θεὸν ἀληθινὸν ἐκ Θεοῦ ἀληθινοῦ· γεννηθέντα, οὐ ποιηθέντα·ὁμοούσιον τῷ Πατρί· δι' οὗ τὰ πάντα ἐγένετο, τά τε ἐν τῷ οὐρανῷ, καὶ τὰ ἐν τῇ γῇ· τὸν δι' ἡμᾶς τοὺς ἀνθρώπους, καὶ διὰ τὴν ἡμετέραν σωτηρίαν κατελθόντα, καὶ σαρκωθέντα, ἐνανθρωπήσαντα, παθόντα, καὶ ἀνα- στάντα τῇ τρίτῃ ἡμέρᾳ· ἀνελθόντα εἰς τοὺς οὐρανούς· ἐρχόμενον κρῖναι ζῶντας καὶ νεκρούς. Καὶ εἰς τὸ Πνεῦμα τὸ Ἅγιον. Τοὺς δὲ λέγοντας, "ἦν ποτὲ ὅτε οὐκ ἦν", ἢ "οὐκ ἦν πρὶν γεννηθῆναι", ἢ "ἐξ οὐκ ὄντων ἐγένετο", ἢ "ἐξ ἑτέρας ὑποστάσεως ἢ οὐσίας φάσκοντας εἶναι, <ἢ κτιστὸν>, ἢ τρεπτὸν, ἢ ἀλλοιωτὸν τὸν Υἱὸν τοῦ Θεοῦ", τούτους ἀναθεματίζει ἡ καθολικὴ καὶ ἀποστολικὴ τοῦ Θεοῦ ἐκκλησία.

And in One Lord Jesus Christ, the Son of God, begotten of the Father, Only-begotten, that is, from the essence of the Father; God from God, Light from Light, Very God from Very God, begotten not made, One in essence with the Father, by Whom all things were made, both things in heaven and things in earth; Who for us men and for our salvation came down and was made flesh, was made man, suffered, and rose again the third day, ascended into heaven, and cometh to judge quick and dead. And in the Holy Ghost.

And those who say, 'Once He was not,' and 'Before His generation He was not,' and 'He came to be from nothing,' or those who pretend that the Son of God is 'Of other subsistence or essence,' or 'created' or 'alterable,' or 'mutable,' the Catholic Church anathematizes.

The text puts it in more precise terms that being begotten of the Father ought to be understood as being begotten of the Father's essence. Since I have discussed conceiving of the substance as *ousia* or *hypostasis* in one of my previous studies,[11] I shall only make a brief recapitulation of the most important aspects as well as elaborate a little on some of the relevant points.

The phrase referring to being begotten of the Father's essence is of significance in terms of understanding that essence. Origen had already been aware of possible misconceptions arising from the issue, knowing of certain potential ambiguities. In the context of his commentary on the fragment "give us today our supersubstantial bread," let us now quote the relevant passage from his composition concerned with prayer:

"*Ousia*, properly understood (κυρίως οὐσία), is regarded as incorporeal by the philosophers who insist that the pre-eminent reality is incorporeal (τῶν ἀσωμάτων ὑπόστασιν εἶναι). It has, then, for them an unchanging existence which admits neither increase not decrease. To admit either increase or decrease is the property of corporeal things which, because they are subject to change, need something to sustain and nourish them. If within a given time they acquire more than they lose, they increase; if less, they decrease.

---

[11] Cf. H. Pietras, *Pojęcie Bożej substancji w początkach Kościoła*, 122-140.

Again, it may happen that they receive nothing from outside, in which case they are, so to speak, in a state of pure decrease.[12]"

In the context of our discussion, the most important thing is that, in Origen's view, the properly understood *ousia* is the same as *incorporeal hypostasis*. According to Prof. Manlio Simonetti's very well known opinion, this *credo* is inclined towards Monarchianism due to this particular use of the terms *ousia* and *hypostasis* here as well as in the final anathematism. He had discussed it extensively for 40 years and his students reiterate that view in their works.[13] It follows from his assumption that *ousia* may have referred to both individual and generic substance, while *hypostasis* solely to the individual one. I shall try to demonstrate that this assumption is difficult to maintain.

Origen objected to speaking of the Son's origin from the Father's essence as he perceived some possible misconceptions arising from the fact that not everybody could conceive of *ousia* the way they should have, that is, exactly how he expounds in the text above. As he writes in Book XX of his *Commentary on John*, i.e., approximately, at the same time:

(157) Others, however, interpret the statement, "I proceeded from God," to mean, "I have been begotten by God." These must say consequently that the Son has been begotten of the Father's essence (ἐκ τῆς οὐσίας), as one might understand this also in the case of those who are pregnant, and that God is diminished and lacking, as it were, in the essence that he formerly had (οὐσία), when he has begotten the Son. (158) These people must also say, as a consequence, that the Father and the Son are corporeal, and that the Father has been divided. These are the doctrines of people who have not even dreamed of an invisible and bodiless nature (φύσιν ἀόρατον καὶ ἀσώματον) that is pure essence (οὖσαν κυρίως οὐσίαν).[14]

It follows from this text that *ousia* is not only identical with *incorporeal hypostasis*, but also with *incorporeal nature*. It is difficult to tell to whom Origen makes reference in this passage. Apparently, he is most shocked by putting "proceeding from God" on par with being "begotten by God." He perceives therein some hidden corporeal concept of God's *ousia*, and

[12] Origenes, *De oratione* 27, 8, in: *Ancient Christian Writers*, Newmann Press, New York 1954, vol. 19. Cf. H. Pietras, *Odpowiedź na Słowo. Najstarsi mistrzowie chrześcijańskiej modlitwy*, WAM, Kraków 1993.

[13] Cf., e.g., A. Segneri, *Introduzione*, in: Atanasio, *Lettera agli Antiocheni*, introduzione, testo, traduzione e commento a cura di Angelo Segneri, Biblioteca Patristica 46, EDB 2010.

[14] Origenes, *CIo.* XX, 18, 157f., in: *The Fathers of the Church*, The Catholic University of America, Washington 1993, vol. 89).

if corporeal, then also mutable, subject to being decreased or increased, as we have already seen above. And Origen would not agree to any mutability in God.[15] It is therefore not as if Origen had simply spoken of the Trinity as three *hypostases*, evading the term *ousia*. Another argument is his statement referring to the Divine Wisdom, which he had indisputably conceived of as the supreme *epinoia* of the Son, but also as existing substantially.[16] Origen defines its substantiality as *ousia*: οὐσία οὖσα ἡ τοῦ Θεοῦ σοφία.[17] The same term *ousia* is used then to refer to the substance of God the Father and the substance of God the Wisdom. In this situation, Origen's famous saying that the Son originates from the Father as the will from the intellect[18] lends itself to be legitimately rendered as "the Son's *hypostasis* originates from the *hypostasis* of the Father," or "the Son's *ousia* originates from the *ousia* of the Father." Notably, however, it ought not to be said that it "emerges" or "proceeds," as it would have entailed a change in God. It is nevertheless reconcilable with the everlasting subsistence/generation.

The formulation referring to the Son as being begotten "from the essence of the Father," as it is said in the Creed, had only one drawback: it was an extra-scriptural expression, and the contemporary bishops were very much sensitive to the application of such terms. It is confirmed, for instance, by the previously cited letter of Eusebius, where he notes that the expression required making it more specific, in such a way "that the phrase 'of the essence' is indicative of the Son's being indeed from the Father, yet without being as if a part of Him."[19] As a result, the interpretation that bothered Origen in his *Commentary on John* was precluded. I think there is no reason to reject such an explanation.

Further on, I would opt for the term "made" rather than "created" (Greek: *poiein*), as there is a difference between "make" and "create" (*ktidzein*). There may be not much of a difference as regards the material world, but not with reference to the Logos. In the Bible, the term "create" is used with reference to the Wisdom (Proverbs 8:22); as a result, it could not have been ruled out or dismissed. There is, however, a different story with *poiein*. Although Dionysius of Alexandria used that term in relation to the Son and was still able to counter the allegations of

---

[15] Cf. H. Pietras, *Argumentacja filozoficzna za wiecznością Syna Bożego u Orygenesa*, 89-97.

[16] Cf. M. Szram, *Chrystus - Mądrość Boża według Orygenesa*, RW KUL, Lublin 1997.

[17] Origenes, *Expositio in Proverbia* 17.185. Cf. the Latin text affirming the above in *De principiis* I, 2, 2; H. Pietras, *Pojęcie Bożej substancji w początkach Kościoła*, 130.

[18] Origenes, *De principiis* IV, 4; 1; H. Pietras, *Pojęcie Bożej substancji w początkach Kościoła*, 135-136.

[19] Eusebius, *Letter of Eusebius of Caesarea to the People of His Diocese* 5 (in: NPNF 2,4).

treating the Son as a created being,[20] there would have been nonetheless no scriptural grounds for this particular reference. Likewise, Eusebius refers to this question in his commentary on this profession of faith.[21]

The word *homoousios* comes next. It was first commented on by Eusebius and it can be used for reference.[22] Let us only note that in this case, as in explaining the origin *of the essence*, Eusebius categorically rules out any corporeal sense and also states that it is to mean that the Son does not come from any other *ousia* or *hypostasis*, save only from the Father. This particular phrase can be found in the anathematism of our *credo* and it led Prof. Simonetti to the idea of the Monarchian nature of the expression. Ordinarily, commentators discuss this point by writing separately of *ousia* and separately of *hypostasis* and analyze what the synonymy between them may consist in.[23] It is worth noticing, however, in what sense the blend of the two notions is employed, e.g., in Origen, where it is used to denote a real existence. In his *Contra Celsum*, he writes of Mnemosyne and Athena/ Minerva as not having a real existence, i.e., not having ὑπόστασιν καὶ οὐσίαν. It reads as follows:[24]

Δεικνύτω τοίνυν ὑπόστασιν καὶ οὐσίαν Μνημοσύνης γεννώσης ἀπὸ Διὸς τὰς Μούσας, ἢ Θέμιδος τὰς Ὥρας, ἢ τὰς Χάριτας ἀεὶ γυμνὰς παραστησάτω δύνασθαι κατ' οὐσίαν ὑφεστηκέναι. [...] Ἵνα δὲ καὶ τροπολογῆται καὶ λέγηται φρόνησις εἶναι ἡ Ἀθηνᾶ, παραστησάτω τις αὐτῆς τὴν ὑπόστασιν καὶ τὴν οὐσίαν, ὡς ὑφεστηκυίας κατὰ τὴν τροπολογίαν ταύτην.	Let [Celsus] establish, therefore, the existence of Mnemosyne, the mother of the Muses by Zeus; or of Themis, the parent of the Hours; or let him prove that the ever naked Graces can have a real, substantial existence. And to regard these myths in a figurative sense, and consider Minerva as representing prudence, let any one show what were the actual facts of her history, upon which this allegory is based.

The expression in the anathematism "of other subsistence or essence" ought to be rendered, in consequence, as "of other really existing" or "of other being," or perhaps somehow even more aptly. In any case, I cannot see any reason for concentrating on how to demonstrate the alleged

---

[20] Cf. Athanasius, *De sententia Dionysii* 4.

[21] Eusebius of Caesarea, *Letter of Eusebius of Caesarea to the People of His Diocese* 11.

[22] Eusebius of Caesarea, *Letter of Eusebius of Caesarea to the People of His Diocese* 12-13; see Ch. 6 and the commentary on item 7.

[23] Cf. X. Morales, *La théologie trinitaire d'Athanase d'Alexandrie*, 43.

[24] Origenes, *Contra Celsum* I, 23, 7 and VIII, 67, 1 (ANF 4); cf. H. Pietras, *Pojęcie Bożej substancji w początkach Kościoła*, 128.

Monarchian meaning of the term. The anathematism emphasizes that the Son is not originated from anything else, as the *Credo* affirms in *Very God from Very God*. In this way, it opposes Arius' teaching that He is from nothing and, likewise, the views of Paul of Samosata, according to whom the Son originates from Mary, as well as, obviously, all the Monarchians who would assert that He in fact is not originated from anything or anywhere, as He is identical with the Father. I would say that we should rather give credence to Eusebius and his clarification of the term *homoousios*, namely as he "suggests that the Son of God bears no resemblance to the originated creatures, but that to His Father alone Who begat Him is He in every way assimilated, and that He is not of any other subsistence and essence, but from the Father."[25] In other words, the resemblance to the Father, not to any creature, and the origin from the Father, not from any other being, are both present in Him.

It was to take Athanasius about 25 years to reach such an understanding of the concept of consubstantiality. It would be only in *ca.* 350, in his *De decretis*, that he seemed to construe the term precisely in this particular sense.

Athanasius puts this question, among other things, as follows:

"[they wrote] that the Son is 'one in essence' with the Father: by way of signifying, that the Son was from the Father, and not merely like, but the same in likeness, and of shewing that the Son's likeness and unalterableness was different from such copy of the same as is ascribed to us, which we acquire from virtue on the ground of observance of the commandments[26]"

Just like Eusebius, he links the origin from the Father with the resemblance to Him within the notion of consubstantiality. The sole difference is that Eusebius asserts the resemblance in every way, whereas Athanasius argues that the Son is "the same in likeness."

It is commonly known that hardly anybody would be willing to abide by this profession of faith after the Council. On the contrary, more and more creeds would be drafted and formulated in great abundance.[27] We know of as many as eighteen synods to have undertaken the effort. It is notable that in this general endeavour neither opponents nor followers of Athanasius had relied on, or referred to, the Nicene Creed. Even the synod of Sardica (343), with Athanasius attending, would not mention this creed at all. In

---

[25] Eusebius of Caesarea, *Letter of Eusebius of Caesarea to the People of His Diocese* 13. According to L. Ayres, the most important reason for the use of *homoousios* was Arius' objection to the term (*Nicaea and Its Legacy*, 90). It has become sort of customary indeed to assume this view, but the sources offer no evidence to confirm it.

[26] Athanasius, *De decretis* 20 [NPNF 2, 4].

[27] Cf. H. Pietras, *Spór o wyznanie wiary w IV w.*, 35-50.

addition, the key concept therein, i.e., *ousia*, had been found heretical.[28] Only around the year 350 did Athanasius come to the realization that the task of formulating new creeds, over and over again, is futile and begin to propagate the Nicene Symbol. The synod of Paris (360/361)[29] marks the appearance of the earliest information on this *credo* being gradually adopted in the Church. As I have said at the beginning of this chapter, the Emperor Theodosius promulgated his decree on the Catholic orthodoxy (380) and the synod of Constantinople affirmed it in its canon 1, forbidding any alteration in the said *credo*. I have already noted that the Council of Ephesus had decreed a similar prohibition. Let us now proceed to have a closer look at those proscriptions and the origin of the myth of the formulation of a profession of faith at the First Council of Constantinople.

Canon 1 of Constantinople I provides that:

"The profession of faith of the holy fathers who gathered in Nicaea in Bithynia is not to be abrogated, but it is to remain in force. Every heresy is to be anathematized and in particular that of the Eunomians or Anomoeans, that of the Arians or Eudoxians, that of the Semi-Arians or Pneumatomachi, that of the Sabellians, that of the Marcellians, that of the Photinians and that of the Apollinarians.[30]"

A similar decision was decreed at the synod of Iconium (376).[31]

Simultaneously, the Council of Constantinople decreed canon 3 on the supreme role of the Church of Constantinople in the East, as the second most-important see (after Rome). This canon clearly failed to garner much sympathy in the West and confronted a firmly negative response at Alexandria. We know it from the fact of the consistent omission of Constantinople in all the listings and enumerations of the sees and councils as well as from the equally consistent actions of the Bishops of Alexandria, since then up to as late as the Council of Chalcedon, undertaken to the detriment of the metropolitans of Constantinople (to note just a few examples: Theophilus vs. John Chrysostom, Cyril vs. Nestorius, Dioscorus vs. Flavian).

Canon 1 appears to have been generally accepted, as we do not hear of anybody having referred to a profession of faith other than the Nicene Creed at any synod of the period. In a somewhat mysterious manner, the present "Niceno-Constantinopolitan Creed" can be found in Epiphanius, at *Ancoratus* 121,[32] even though the author speaks only of the Nicene *credo*.

---

[28] Cf. SCL 1, 143.

[29] Council of Paris (360/361), SCL 1, 247.

[30] Council of Constantinople (381), c. 1; DSP 1, 71.

[31] Council of Iconium (376), 3, SCL 1, 283.

[32] Cf. Hefele-Leclercq, *Histoire des Conciles* II/1, 11f., n. 5.

Evidently, a copyist must have swapped creeds, providing the one that he believed would have been more suitable. In this context, this canon of the Council of Ephesus is of significance as well:

"It is not permitted to produce or write or compose any other creed except the one which was defined by the holy fathers who were gathered together in the holy Spirit at Nicaea. Any who dare to compose or bring forth or produce another creed for the benefit of those who wish to turn from Hellenism or Judaism or some other heresy to the knowledge of the truth, if they are bishops or clerics they should be deprived of their respective charges and if they are laymen they are to be anathematised.[33]"

With proscriptions like these, and 50 years after the synod of Constantinople, it would be indeed hard to imagine that the existence of some venerable creed might have been ignored by the Fathers. It is theoretically possible that the participants of this Council, all of them ill-disposed towards Constantinople, had passed over the Constantinopolitan formula on purpose and returned to the Nicene Symbol simply to spite the capital. It seems possible, but not very likely.

I would rather opt for a hypothesis of intentional falsification for the following reasons:[34] Harnack had already noticed a long time ago that something was missing there and suggested that the Council of Chalcedon had taken up some *credo* at random, apparently with some more reference to the Holy Spirit therein.[35] It appears, nonetheless, that a more likely hypothesis would be some deliberate misinformation intended to put pressure on Rome to recognize Constantinople in the Church. Canon 3 (381) used the argument of the capital status of Constantinople to bolster the claim to the principal position in the East.[36] This argument, however, was regarded as insignificant in the Church, as the Apostolic succession remained the crucial criterion. As the Council of Nicaea decreed: "the

---

[33] Council of Ephesus (431), c. 7, DSP 1, 165ff.

[34] I am aware that this opinion is perhaps not very common. Many scholars are still in favour of the authenticity of the "Constantinopolitan" *credo*, following in the footsteps of Kelly and his classic, fundamental work *Early Christian Creeds*, 296-331. See, e.g., J. Behr, *The Nicene Faith II*, 372-379; K. Anatolios, *Retrieving Nicaea. The Development and Meaning of Trinitarian Doctrine*, Baker Academy, Grand Rapids, Michigan 2011, 26-27

[35] M. Harnack, *Konstantinopolitanisches Symbol*, Real-Encyklopädie, 3rd ed., XI, 12-28.

[36] Council of Constantinople (381), c. 3; according to the canon, the Bishop of Constantinople ought to hold the honorary precedence after the Bishop of Rome, as Constantinople is the "New Rome."

prerogatives of the churches are to be preserved."[37] At Chalcedon, canon 3 of the First Council of Constantinople was reiterated, with its politically-motivated argumentation again, yet the situation made it appropriate to buttress it with some ecclesiastical argument for the benefit of Rome. Aside from the seniority question, the rank of the episcopal see was also determined by its position in the conciliar tradition. We can see it, for instance, in Pope Felix' letter to the clergy of Constantinople (484),[38] which mentions the councils of Nicaea, Ephesus, and Chalcedon. The *Decretum Gelasianum* (495) lists Rome, Alexandria, and Antioch (but not Constantinople) as the most important sees of the Church, precisely according to the requirement of the Apostolic succession. Although it does make a mention of *sanctam synodum Constantinopolitanam* further on (ch. IV), between Nicaea and Ephesus, all the manuscripts of the text are late enough to validate suspecting that one of the copyists may have added the "missing" synod thereto.[39]

Demonstrating a profession of faith formulated at Constantinople by a convocation of 150 Fathers, with all due respect for the Nicene Creed, but with the allegedly necessary addition on the Holy Spirit aimed against the Macedonians, was meant to serve the purpose of introducing Constantinople into the exclusive club of the most significant cities of Christendom, not just for the sake of its capital status but as one of the conciliar cities. It must be said that this particular manoeuvre had proved successful and, eventually, a report of Pope Hormisdas' Constantinople legates, dated 519, makes a mention of the four councils. As Thiel said in a note, Rome would have referred, since then, to four, not just three, ecumenical councils.[40]

But let us return for a while to the question of the *de facto* rejection, by the Church, of the Nicene Creed in favour of the new one. The crucial factors were, in my opinion, the Monophysite movement and the struggles for the recognition of the Council of Chalcedon in the course of the 470s that had coincided with the power struggle between the Emperor and Zeno and the usurper Basiliscus (475-477). The point of contention was not just the affirmation of the decisions of Chalcedon, but at the same time the recognition of Constantinople's supreme role, an unbearable prospect to both Antioch and Alexandria. As it happened, Basiliscus allowed

---

[37] Canon 6.

[38] Cf. A. Thiel, *Epistolae Romanorum Pontificum genuine* I, Brunsbergae 1868, Epist. 11, 4, p. 254.

[39] *I canoni dei concili della Chiesa antica*, a cura di A. Di Berardino, II/1, SEA 106, Roma 2008, 233. Cf. note in: Ernst Von Dobschütz, *Das „decretum gelasianum de libris recipiendis et non recipiendis"*, Texte und Untersuchungen zur Geschichte der Altchristlichen Literatur 38.4 (1912), 261f.

[40] A. Thiel, *Epistolae Romanorum Pontificum genuinae* I, Epist. 76, 4, p. 873

Peter the Fuller, known for his firm opposition to Chalcedon, to return from his exile.[41] The latter introduced the practice of saying the creed at Mass.[42] There is no information on which profession of faith he might have used, yet the supposition that it may have been the NC Creed is, I think, utterly implausible.[43] As a Monophysite, he could not have subscribed to anything affirmed at Chalcedon. It may have been, of course, some local creed, but I would rather assume the Nicene option. The Monophysites had ostentatiously deferred to the authority of the Council of Nicaea as well as the both Councils of Ephesus (341 and 449). At Nicaea, this particular creed was formulated, to be subsequently solemnly affirmed twice at Ephesus. By way of evidence, let us now have a look at a synodal letter by the adherents of Timothy Ailuros (the Cat), dating from the late 450s:

"[3] ... we preserve and protect the symbol and the faith of the three hundred and eighteen Fathers, who had assembled at Nicaea and spoken in the Holy Spirit, and (that) we add nothing thereto or alter anything therein.

[6] Since Your Grace bids us to make known our views on the synods, we hereby express our opinion, as the Church remains in communion with the synods of Ephesus. We do not know of any synod of the one hundred and fifty (bishops), but we know that, after the council, our holy Fathers and archbishops also assembled at the Church of Constantinople. Because the Church of the great Alexandria does not recognize the synod of Chalcedon.[44]"

Likewise, Basiliscus' circular letter defines the Nicene Creed as "the foundation and affirmation of human happiness" and prescribes it ought to "have, as the only one, the force of the law obligatory in all the most holy Churches of the orthodox people of God, being in fact the only formula of faith free from error and the norm sufficient for abolishing all heresy as well as achieving the closest union of the holy Churches."[45] In all probability, however, it had been the only liturgical application of this creed. I have not found any evidence to the contrary. There is, indeed, a certain text confirming another instance, but, in my opinion, it is mistaken in this respect. Namely, Theodore Lector records that Timothy, Bishop of Constantinople in the years 511-518, instructed that the creed of the 318

---

[41] Theodore Lector, *h.e.* I, 28, 30.

[42] Theodore Lector, *h.e.* II, 48.

[43] Cf. P. es. H. Paprocki, *Misterium Eucharystii*, WAM, Kraków 2010, 235.

[44] Alexandria (*ca.* 458), *Epistola quorundam episcoporum Aegyptiacae dioecesis...*, 6, SCL 6, 207-208. For some noteworthy comments on the intertwining of religious and political themes, see Monika Ożóg, *Teoderyk a schizma akacjańska*, Chrześcijaństwo u schyłku starożytności. *Studia Źródłoznawcze* 11 (2012), 107-126.

[45] Cf. Evagrius, *h.e.* III, 4; Nicephorus Calixt, *h.e.* XVI, 3.

Fathers be said in defiance of the Macedonians' teachings aimed against the Holy Spirit.[46] By that time, however, the NC Creed (perceived as the continuation of the Nicene one) had already been adopted as the one to be propagated further, in agreement with the arguments put forth at the Council of Chalcedon.

In consequence, the political and religious victory of the advocates of the two natures in Christ over those speaking of one nature turned out to be a victory of the 150 Fathers' creed over that of the 318 Fathers.

We can see one paradox after another: a creed formulated under pressure of Constantine the Great in 325, and actually desired by no one but himself, would go on to become, some fifty years later, the standard of orthodoxy thanks to Theodosius the Great. Another one hundred years later, the Monophysites would use it in their struggle against the Council of Chalcedon and it would ultimately come to suffer a defeat in Justinian's Empire. Interestingly, all these emperors were Great …

The fall of the Roman Empire in the West, the Visigoth incursion of the Iberian Peninsula, and their subsequent conversion to Catholicism, resulted in the growth of Spain's relations with Constantinople, as if over the head of Theoderic the Great. Consequently, Spain adopted the creed provided by Constantinople, which the Byzantine Empire would apparently employ as something of a propaganda resource, effectively used to legitimize the status of that Church within the Christian world. But this is a completely different story.

---

[46] Theodore Lector, *h.e.* II, 32; Nicephorus, *h.e.* XVI, 35, PG 147, 189.

POST-SYNODAL DOCUMENTS

Following the completion of the Council of Nicaea in July 325, the bishops remained surprisingly reticent about the course of its proceedings. As for the years immediately after that date, we have no testimony from any of the attendees, except for the aforementioned letter by Eusebius of Caesarea.[1] This earliest account is a very significant one for some other reasons as well. Eusebius treats of the doctrinal debates in connection with the profession of faith, yet he does not even make the slightest reference to the condemnation of Arius. It may be attributed to his friendship with Arius (he may have wished to keep the friend's name untarnished), but, incidentally, this particular letter has survived thanks to Athanasius (who was no friend of Arius and Eusebius), quoted in its entirety towards the end of his *De decretis Nicaenae synodi*. Notably, the epistle's partiality is by no means criticized.

I agree with Khaled Anatolios that the general belief in the triumph of the Athanasian orthodoxy over the Arian heresy at Nicaea is a purely invented proposition.[2]

Athanasius' well-known account dates from as late as 370 (his post-synodal *Ep. ad Afros*),[3] whereas some rudimentary information in *De decretis* can be dated back to *ca.* 350. His previous enunciations do not tell us much about the Council. The letter of the synod at Alexandria (338/339),[4] presided over by Athanasius, only says that Athanasius had spoken against Arius at the Council of Nicaea.[5] It is not known what might have been the occasion, as at the time he had not been a bishop (i.e., a fully eligible participant of the conciliar proceedings) yet. It was not deemed appropriate to have noted the purported condemnation of Arius at Nicaea, with the Emperor Constantine's consent, even though it would have been apparently very

---

[1] Cf. Ch. 4.

[2] Cf. K. Anatolios, *Retrieving Nicaea. The Development and Meaning of Trinitarian Doctrine*, 18. Frankly speaking, I do not concur with any of the other assertions of this author, as they do not contribute anything new to the discussion of the Council.

[3] Theodoret of Cyrrhus, *h.e.* I, 8, 7-16; Council of Alexandria (*ca.* 370), SCL 1, 265-275.

[4] Council of Alexandria (338/339), SCL 1, 93-109.

[5] Council of Alexandria (338/339), 6, 1; SCL 1, 97.

much on point. Two years later, at the synod of Rome, Pope Julius and the fifty bishops in attendance spoke in defence of Athanasius, who had been previously exiled from Alexandria. The post-synodal letter[6] does certainly reflect Athanasius' then-current view in everything concerning Arius. It says that the Arians were condemned by "all the participants of the great council at Nicaea,"[7] but it was stated only fifteen years following the Council, without any information on whether Arius had been condemned on the strength of a specially formulated decision or simply by an anathematism expressed in the *credo*. Five years before, at the synod of Jerusalem, the bishops opposed to Athanasius had written that "the Emperor [Constantine], dear to God, persuaded us, with his own letter, to do what ought to have been done, namely to eliminate all the hatred from the Church of God, eradicate from it all the envy that had once divided the Divine limbs, and, with the sincerity and peace in our hearts, to admit the followers of Arius, who had remained, for a certain time, beyond the Church as a result of the ignominious envy."[8] Athanasius describes them as Arians, of course, but this is his own opinion: it follows from the text that the bishops had restored the followers of Arius to communion of the Church, not that they had been his followers themselves. Charles Kannengiesser notes tentatively that a tragic possibility of the complete misunderstanding of Arius by Athanasius cannot be ruled out.[9] It seems to me that this is an understatement: Athanasius "used" Arius as a bogey-man and would call all his adversaries "Arius' maniacs." The point was not the theological views of the latter, but rather his own position. After many years, when he had come to realize that the time of deliberately mixing things up was through, he would proceed to expound the Nicene Creed, oddly in the "homoousian" spirit, i.e., according to the view of those whom he had called "maniacs" for such a long time. In his book *Nicaea and Its Legacy*, Lewis Ayres even speaks of "the creation of 'Arianism'" in the 340s.[10]

Apart from the previously cited *Letter of Eusebius of Caesarea to the People of His Diocese*, the only documents offering direct accounts of the proceedings at Nicaea are the following post-synodal epistles: *Letter of the Council of Nicaea*

---

[6] Council of Rome (340/341), SCL 1, 110-123. The letter as quoted by Athanasius in his *Apologia contra Arianos*, 21-35; PSP 21, 111-122.

[7] Council of Rome (340/341), 23, 1; SCL 1, 112.

[8] Council of Hierusalem (335), 21, 2; SCL 1, 92; the text as cited by Athanasius in *De synodis* 21, 2-7.

[9] CH. Kannengiesser, *Athanasius of Alexandria vs. Arius*, 212.

[10] L. Ayres, *Nicaea and Its Legacy*, ch. 5: "The Creation of 'Arianism': AD 340-350," 105-130.

to the Egyptians,[11] *Letter of Constantine to the Churches,*[12] *Letter of Constantine to the Church of Alexandria.*[13] We have known these documents for a very long time (cf., e.g., Socrates' *History*), with the second one preserved by Eusebius, and the first as well as the third one known from a collection of some documents discovered among the manuscripts containing Athanasius' writings. As a result, there appeared the opinion that the collection is a work of Athanasius himself,[14] which was then further consolidated by Opitz, who cited the letters as collected by Athanasius[15] (all the reference books tend to subscribe to that view). The Church historians such as Socrates, Sozomen, and Theodoret, draw on Eusebius and, most likely, this specific collection as regards the documents they quote.

In the present chapter, I would like to begin with the following question: how is it possible that Athanasius, a participant in the proceedings of the Council, and shortly thereafter the Bishop of Alexandria, had never quoted, to his own advantage, from any of those letters in one of the many writings he had produced in his self-defence? And he did like quoting! In his *Apologia contra Arianos* alone, he cites five epistles of Constantine (out of a total number of twenty).

Let us have a closer look at the letters in question and some of the inconsistencies they may possibly contain.

Letter of Constantine to the Church of Alexandria

Κωνσταντῖνος Σεβαστὸς, τῇ καθολικῇ Ἀλεξανδρέων ἐκκλησίᾳ. Χαίρετε ἀγαπητοὶ ἀδελφοί. Τελείαν παρὰ τῆς θείας προνοίας εἰλήφαμεν χάριν, ἵνα πάσης πλάνης ἀπαλλαγέντες, μίαν καὶ τὴν αὐτὴν ἐπιγινώσκωμεν πίστιν. Οὐδὲν λοιπὸν τῷ διαβόλῳ ἔξεστι καθ' ἡμῶν· πᾶν εἴ τι δ' ἂν κακοτεχνησά μενος ἐπεχείρησεν, ἐκ βάθρων ἀνῄρηται·

Constantine Augustus, to the Catholic church of the Alexandrians.
Beloved brethren, hail! We have received from Divine Providence the inestimable blessing of being relieved from all error, and united in the acknowledgment of one and the same faith. The devil will no longer have any power against us, since all that which he had malignantly devised for our destruction has been entirely overthrown from the foundations.

[11] Socrates, *h.e.* I, 9; Council of Nicaea (325), DSP 1, 46-53.

[12] Eusebius of Caesarea, *v.C.* III, 17ff.; Socrates, *h.e.* I, 9.

[13] *Letter of Constantine to the Church of Alexandria*, in: Socrates, *h.e.* I, 9 (NPNF 2,2).

[14] Cf. E. Schwartz, *Zur Geschichte des Athanasius*, Gesammelte Schriften III, W. de Gruyter, Berlin 1959, 73ff. (reprint z 1911).

[15] Cf. H.G. Opitz, *Athanasius Werke. Urkunden zur Geschichte des arianischen Streits*, W. de Gruyter, Berlin, 1934; G.L. Dossetti, *Il Simbolo*, 32-35.

τὰς διχονοίας, τὰ σχίσματα, τοὺς θορύβους ἐκείνους, καὶ τὰ τῶν διαφωνιῶν, ἵν' οὕτως εἴπω, θανάσιμα φάρμακα, κατὰ τὴν τοῦ Θεοῦ κέλευσιν, ἡ τῆς ἀληθείας ἐνίκησε λαμπρότης. Ἕνα τοιγαροῦν ἅπαντες καὶ τῷ ὀνόματι προσκυνοῦμεν, καὶ εἶναι πεπιστεύκαμεν. Ἵνα δὲ τοῦτο γένηται, ὑπομνήσει Θεοῦ συνεκάλεσα εἰς τὴν Νικαέων πόλιν τοὺς πλείστους τῶν ἐπισκόπων, μεθ' ὧν περ εἷς ἐξ ὑμῶν ἐγὼ, ὁ συνθεράπων ὑμέτερος καθ' ὑπερβολὴν εἶναι χαίρων, καὶ αὐτὸς τὴν τῆς ἀληθείας ἐξέτασιν ἀνεδεξάμην.

The splendor of truth has dissipated at the command of God those dissensions, schisms, tumults, and so to speak, deadly poisons of discord. Wherefore we all worship one true God, and believe that he is. But in order that this might be done, by divine admonition I assembled at the city of Nicæa most of the bishops; with whom I myself also, who am but one of you, and who rejoice exceedingly in being your fellow-servant, undertook the investigation of the truth.

Constantine rejoices at the acceptance of a common profession of faith, namely the Nicene Creed. According to his words, the primary objective of the convocation at Nicaea was precisely to formulate and adopt such a *credo*. It was one of the Emperor's duties, in his capacity as the *Pontifex Maximus*, to keep a record of important religious formulae for each religion recognized as legitimate in the Empire.[16] As we can see, there is no mention of any other possible reasons.

Ἠλέγχθη γοῦν ἅπαντα, καὶ ἀκριβῶς ἐξήτασται, ὅσα δὴ ἀμφιβολίαν ἢ διχονοίας πρόφασιν ἐδόκει γεννᾶν. Καὶ φεισάσθω ἡ θεία μεγαλειότης, ἡλίκα καὶ ὡς δεινὰ τὰ περὶ τοῦ μεγάλου Σωτῆρος, περὶ τῆς ἐλπίδος καὶ ζωῆς ἡμῶν, ἀπρεπῶς ἐβλασφήμουν τινες, τἀναντία ταῖς θεοπνεύστοις γραφαῖς καὶ τῇ ἁγίᾳ πίστει φθεγγόμενοί τε καὶ πιστεύειν ὁμολογοῦντες.

Accordingly, all points which seemed in consequence of ambiguity to furnish any pretext for dissension, have been discussed and accurately examined. And may the Divine Majesty pardon the fearful enormity of the blasphemies which some were shamelessly uttering concerning the mighty Saviour, our life and hope; declaring and confessing that they believe things contrary to the divinely inspired Scriptures.

It cannot be directly inferred from the Nicene Creed against which heretics it was formulated. Perhaps it was not meant to be directed against anybody, simply formulated in compliance with the Emperor's wish. It is noteworthy that none of the previous synods had ever drawn up a profession of faith. The sole exception was the synod at Antioch in the spring of

---

[16] Cf. H. Pietras, *List Konstantyna do Aleksandra i Ariusza a zwołanie Soboru Nicejskiego*, in *Vox Patrum* 26 (2006), vol. 49, 536f.

325,[17] where one of its prominent attendees, Hosius of Cordoba, acted to accomplish his mission and prepare a creed on the Emperor's orders. In turn, it clearly follows from the canons of the Council that the teachings and supporters of Paul of Samosata had been a subject of debate.[18]

Τριακοσίων γοῦν καὶ πλειόνων ἐπισκόπων, ἐπὶ σωφροσύνῃ τε καὶ ἀγχινοίᾳ θαυμαζομένων, μίαν καὶ τὴν αὐτὴν πίστιν, ἣ καὶ ταῖς ἀληθείαις καὶ ἀκριβείαις τοῦ θείου νόμου πέφυκε πίστις εἶναι, βεβαιούντων, μόνος Ἄρειος ἐφωράθη τῆς διαβολικῆς ἐνεργείας ἡττημένος, καὶ τὸ κακὸν τοῦτο πρῶτον μὲν παρ' ὑμῖν, ἔπειτα καὶ παρ' ἑτέροις ἀσεβεῖ γνώμῃ διασπείρας.

While more than three hundred bishops remarkable for their moderation and intellectual keenness, were unanimous in their confirmation of one and the same faith, which according to the truth and legitimate construction of the law of God can only be the faith; Arius alone beguiled by the subtlety of the devil, was discovered to be the sole disseminator of this mischief, first among you, and afterwards with unhallowed purposes among others also.

In contrast to the previous paragraph, where the heretics are referred to in plural, this one says that "Arius alone" had been in opposition. Let us also take note of the number of the attendees: "more than three hundred". In his *Vita Constantini*, Eusebius of Caesarea states that there had been over 250 in attendance.[19] Throughout this brief work, Eusebius puts many things in overstatement in order to aggrandize his protagonist even more. He would have gladly written there had been more participants, if he had not been well aware of the people's memory of the event. Eustathius of Antioch mentions the presence of 270 bishops.[20] Taking into account all the sources that we know, the number 300 appears for the first time in Pope Julius' post-synodal letter of 341,[21] which is cited in Athanasius' *Apologia contra Arianos*. This epistle represents a version of the events in agreement with that of the Bishop of Alexandria. Strangely enough, Constantine himself would write of 300 attendees of the Council, while Eusebius, a participant and

[17] Council of Antioch (325), 8-13; SCL 1, 86-88. See Ch. 4.

[18] Council of Nicaea (325), c. 19; DSP 1, 44.

[19] Eusebius of Caesarea, *v.C.* III, 8; ŹMT 44.

[20] Eustathius of Antioch, fr. 32; cf. M. Simonetti, *La crisi ariana*, 79. Prof. Simonetti has noted that the number of the attendees at the Council would have been somewhere between 150 and 200, but he offers no source for this estimate; cf. *Letteratura patristica*, a cura di A. Di Berardino, G. Fedalto, M. Simonetti, ed. San Paolo 2007, 1191.

[21] Council of Rome (340/341), 23, 2. 25, 1; SCL 1, 112. 114.

an unmistakable eulogist of the Emperor's achievements, with his evident inclination to exaggerate things, mentioned just 250.

Ἀναδεξώμεθα τοιγαροῦν, ἣν ὁ παντοκράτωρ παρέσχε γνώμην· ἐπανέλθωμεν ἐπὶ τοὺς ἀγαπητοὺς ἡμῶν ἀδελφοὺς, ὧν ἡμᾶς τοῦ διαβόλου ἀναιδής τις ὑπηρέτης ἐχώρισεν· ἐπὶ τὸ κοινὸν σῶμα, καὶ τὰ γνήσια ἡμῶν μέλη, σπουδῇ πάσῃ ἴωμεν. Τοῦτο γὰρ καὶ τῇ ἀγχινοίᾳ, καὶ τῇ πίστει, καὶ τῇ ὁσιότητι τῇ ὑμετέρᾳ πρέπει, ἵνα τῆς πλάνης ἐλεγχθείσης ἐκείνου, ὃν τῆς ἀληθείας εἶναι ἐχθρὸν συνέστηκεν, πρὸς τὴν θείαν ἐπανέλθητε χάριν.

Let us therefore embrace that doctrine which the Almighty has presented to us: let us return to our beloved brethren from whom an irreverent servant of the devil has separated us: let us go with all speed to the common body and our own natural members. For this is becoming your penetration, faith and sanctity; that since the error has been proved to be due to him who is an enemy to the truth, ye should return to the divine favor.

It is fairly difficult to understand the meaning of the Emperor's encouragement in this passage. It seems to me that he refers to some group gone astray, not any "alien" group, but those to whom the letter is addressed. Those who ought to return to the divine favour are referred to as "you," not "them." What is the point then? Could it be that the Emperor had spoken thus to the followers of Arius, who had been excluded at Alexandria back in *ca.* 323?[22] What is "the error" from which the addressees of the letter should withdraw? We have no information on Arius' followers gaining the upper hand in the Church of Alexandria, or relating to any major schism and Alexander's need to possess such a letter in order to be received back in his Church. Who were then those "beloved brethren" to whom one should return?

Ὁ γὰρ τοῖς τριακοσίοις ἤρεσεν ἐπισκόποις, οὐδὲ ἔστιν ἕτερον, ἢ τοῦ Θεοῦ γνώμη, μάλιστά γε ὅπου τὸ ἅγιον Πνεῦμα τοιούτων καὶ τηλικούτων ἀνδρῶν ταῖς διανοίαις ἐγκείμενον τὴν θείαν βούλησιν ἐξεφώτισεν.

For that which has commended itself to the judgment of three hundred bishops cannot be other than the doctrine of God; seeing that the Holy Spirit dwelling in the minds of so many dignified persons has effectually enlightened them respecting the Divine will.

[22] Council of Alexandria (ca. 323); SCL 1, 78-82.

Διὸ μηδεὶς ἀμφιβαλλέτω, μηδεὶς ὑπερτιθέσθω· ἀλλὰ προθύμως πάντες εἰς τὴν ἀληθεστάτην ὁδὸν ἐπάνιτε· ἵν᾽ ἐπειδὰν ὅσον οὐδέπω πρὸς ὑμᾶς ἀφίκωμαι, τὰς ὀφειλομένας τῷ παντεφόρῳ Θεῷ μεθ᾽ ὑμῶν ὁμολογήσω χάριτας, ὅτι τὴν εἰλικρινῆ πίστιν ἐπιδείξας, τὴν εὐκταίαν ὑμῖν ἀγάπην ἀποδέδωκεν. Ὁ Θεὸς ὑμᾶς διαφυλάξοι, ἀγαπητοὶ ἀδελφοί.

Wherefore let no one vacillate or linger, but let all with alacrity return to the undoubted path of duty; that when I shall arrive among you, which will be as soon as possible, I may with you return due thanks to God, the inspector of all things, for having revealed the pure faith, and restored to you that love for which ye have prayed. May God protect you, beloved brethren.

The author refers to the profession of faith again, stressing that it is a work of God. It looks as if the Emperor thought that from then on no other *credo* ought to be formulated. The tone of the letter should have effectively discouraged the addressees and everybody who would have known the Emperor's views from attempting to formulate any new creed. It was not to be like that, though. We do not know everything, but it is certain that four new formulae had been drawn up at Antioch,[23] two at Sardica, as far as the extant documents attest it, and no one there had even mentioned or referred to the Nicene *credo*.[24] We may ask again to whom the letter is actually directed, as the Emperor urges his addressees to return readily "to the undoubted path of duty."

The letter is definitely and unquestionably anti-Arian, and very strongly in favour of the Nicene Creed. It remains a mystery why the Emperor had chosen to make it so focused on one theme. And if he had, Athanasius would have certainly made use of such a letter through all his years of exile and trouble with the supporters of Arius.

Let us now turn to another important post-synodal document.

Letter of the Council of Nicaea to the Egyptians[25]

1. Τῇ ἁγίᾳ καὶ μεγάλῃ, χάριτι τοῦ θεοῦ, Ἀλεξανδρέων ἐκκλησίᾳ καὶ τοῖς κατὰ τὴν Αἴγυπτον καὶ Λιβύην καὶ Πεντάπολιν ἀγαπητοῖς ἀδελφοῖς, οἱ ἐν Νικαίᾳ συναχθέντες καὶ τὴν μεγάλην καὶ ἁγίαν σύνοδον συγκροτήσαντες ἐπίσκοποι ἐν κυρίῳ χαίρειν.

1. To the holy, by the grace of God, and great church of the Alexandrians, and to our beloved brethren throughout Egypt, Libya, and Pentapolis, the bishops assembled at Nicæa, constituting the great and holy Synod, send greeting in the Lord.

[23] Council of Antioch (341); SCL 1, 129-134.

[24] Council of Sardica (343); SCL 1, 144-147.

[25] Council of Nicaea (325), DSP 1, 46-53; cf. Socrates, *h.e.* I, 9 (NPNF 2,2); Theodoret of Cyrrhus, *h.e.* I, 9.

2. Ἐπειδὴ τῆς τοῦ θεοῦ χάριτος καὶ τοῦ θεοφιλεστάτου βασιλέως Κωνσταντίνου συναγαγόντος ἡμᾶς ἐκ διαφόρων ἐπαρχιῶν καὶ πόλεων ἡ μεγάλη καὶ ἁγία σύνοδος ἐν Νικαίᾳ συνεκροτήθη, ἐξ ἁπάσης τῆς ἱερᾶς συνόδου ἀναγκαῖον ἐφάνη καὶ πρὸς ὑμᾶς ἀποσταλῆναι γράμματα, ἵν' εἰδέναι ἔχοιτε τίνα μὲν ἐκινήθη καὶ ἐξητάσθη, τίνα δὲ ἔδοξε καὶ ἐκρατύνθη. πρῶτον μὲν ἐξητάσθη τὰ κατὰ τὴν ἀσέβειαν Ἀρείου ἐπὶ τοῦ θεοφιλεστάτου βασιλέως ἡμῶν Κωνσταντίνου,

2. Since, by the grace of God, a great and holy Synod has been convened at Nicæa, our most pious sovereign Constantine having summoned us out of various cities and provinces for that purpose, it appeared to us indispensably necessary that a letter should be written to you on the part of the sacred Synod; in order that ye may know what subjects were brought under consideration and examined, and what was eventually determined on and decreed. In the first place, then, the impiety and guilt of Arius and his adherents were examined into, in the presence of our most religious emperor Constantine.

3. καὶ παμψηφὶ ἔδοξεν ἀναθεμα-τισθῆναι τὴν ἀσεβῆ αὐτοῦ δόξαν καὶ τὰ ῥήματα καὶ τὰ νοήματα αὐτοῦ τὰ βλάσφημα οἷς ἐχρῆτο βλασφημῶν τὸν υἱὸν τοῦ θεοῦ, λέγων ἐξ οὐκ ὄντων εἶναι καὶ πρὶν γεννηθῆναι μὴ εἶναι καὶ εἶναί ποτε ὅτε οὐκ ἦν, καὶ αὐτεξουσιότητι κακίας καὶ ἀρετῆς δεκτικὸν τὸν υἱὸν τοῦ θεοῦ.

3. And it was unanimously decided that his impious opinion should be anathematized, with all the blasphemous expressions he has uttered, in affirming that 'the Son of God sprang from nothing,' and that 'there was a time when he was not'; saying moreover that 'the Son of God, because possessed of free will, was capable either of vice or virtue;' and calling him a creature and a work.[26]

4. ταῦτα πάντα ἀνεθεμάτισεν ἡ ἁγία σύνοδος, οὐδὲ ὅσον ἀκοῦσαι τῆς ἀσεβοῦς δόξης καὶ τῆς ἀπονοίας καὶ τῶν βλασφήμων ῥημάτων ἀνασχομένη. καὶ τὰ μὲν κατ' ἐκεῖνον οἵου τέλους τετύχηκεν ἢ ἀκηκόατε ἢ ἀκούσεσθε, ἵνα μὴ δόξωμεν ἐπεμβαίνειν ἀνδρὶ δι' οἰκείαν ἁμαρτίαν ἄξια τὰ ἐπίχειρα κομισαμένῳ.

4. All these sentiments the holy Synod has anathematized, having scarcely patience to endure the hearing of such an impious opinion, or, rather, madness, and such blasphemous words. But the conclusion of our proceedings against him you must either have been informed of already or will soon learn; for we would not seem to trample on a man who has received the chastisement which his crime deserved.

[26] The latter phrase present only in Socrates' work.

5. τοσοῦτον δὲ ἴσχυσεν αὐτοῦ ἡ ἀσέβεια ὡς καὶ παραπολαῦσαι Θεωνᾶν τὸν ἀπὸ Μαρμαρικῆς καὶ Σεκοῦνδον τὸν ἀπὸ Πτολεμαΐδος· τῶν γὰρ αὐτῶν κάκεῖνοι τετυχήκασιν. Ἀλλ᾿ ἐπειδὴ ἡ τοῦ θεοῦ χάρις τῆς μὲν κακοδοξίας ἐκείνης καὶ τῆς βλασφημίας καὶ τῶν προσώπων τῶν τολμησάντων διάστασιν καὶ διαίρεσιν ποιήσασθαι τοῦ εἰρηνευομένου ἄνωθεν λαοῦ ἠλευθέρωσε τὴν Αἴγυπτον, ἐλείπετο δὲ τὰ κατὰ τὴν προπέτειαν Μελιτίου καὶ τῶν ὑπ᾿ αὐτοῦ χειροτονηθέντων, καὶ περὶ τούτου τὰ δόξαντα τῇ συνόδῳ ἐμφανίζομεν ὑμῖν, ἀγαπητοὶ ἀδελφοί.

5. Yet so contagious has his pestilential error proved, as to drag into perdition Theonas, bishop of Marmarica, and Secundus of Ptolemaïs; for they have suffered the same condemnation as himself. But when the grace of God delivered us from those execrable dogmas, with all their impiety and blasphemy, and from those persons, who had dared to cause discord and division among a people previously at peace, there still remained the contumacy of Melitius [to be dealt with][27] and those who had been ordained by him; and we now state to you, beloved brethren, what resolution the Synod came to on this point.

Indeed, the phrases used in item 3 can be found in the anathematism included at the close of the Nicene Creed. It is however only this letter where it is said expressly that they are aimed directly at Arius. It also speaks clearly of the condemnation of Arius as if by a special sentence. The beginning of item 4 is a reiteration of the opening clause of item 3, whereas the beginning of item 5 tells us that Theonas and Secundus had joined Arius. It had already taken place at Alexandria prior to the Council,[28] and, in accordance with the contemporary practice, also affirmed at Nicaea,[29] the excommunicated in one Church could not be admitted at any other, or, in consequence, take part in synods. Let us recall that the synod at Sardica came to a halt because Athanasius and Marcellus, excommunicated in the East, attempted to participate in its proceedings.[30] Therefore, the absence of Theonas and Secundus among the signatories of the Nicene Creed would have been caused by the circumstance that they were not allowed to do so, not because they refused. It also appears that they would not have been rehabilitated at Nicaea; on the contrary, they had been supposedly sentenced to banishment. Further on, the text proceeds smoothly to deal with the problem of the Meletian schism and, thereafter, to the date of Easter. The passages treating of the Meletians are as follows:

---

[27] Melitius/Meletius, hence 'Melitian' or 'Meletian' schism.

[28] Council of Alexandria (ca. 323); SCL 1, 78-82.

[29] Council of Nicaea (325), c. 5; DSP 1, 30.

[30] Council of Sardica (343-344) VII, 4-7; SCL 1, 172-174.

6. ἔδοξε μὲν οὖν Μελίτιον, φιλαν-θρωπότερον κινηθείσης τῆς συνόδου (κατὰ γὰρ τὸν ἀκριβῆ λόγον οὐδεμιᾶς συγγνώμης ἄξιος ἦν), μένειν ἐν τῇ πόλει ἑαυτοῦ καὶ μηδεμίαν ἐξουσίαν ἔχειν μήτε προχειρίζεσθαι μήτε χειροθετεῖν μήτε ἐν χώρᾳ ἢ πόλει τινὶ φαίνεσθαι ταύτης τῆς προθέσεως ἕνεκεν, ψιλὸν δὲ τὸ ὄνομα τῆς τιμῆς κεκτῆσθαι.

7. τοὺς δὲ ὑπ' αὐτοῦ κατασταθέντας, μυστικωτέρᾳ χειροτονίᾳ βεβα-ιωθέντας, κοινωνηθῆναι ἐπὶ τούτοις ἐφ' ᾧ τε ἔχειν μὲν αὐτοὺς καὶ λειτουργεῖν, δευτέρους δὲ εἶναι ἐξ ἅπαντος τῶν ἐν ἑκάστῃ παροικίᾳ καὶ ἐκκλησίᾳ ἐξεταζομένων ὑπὸ τὸν τιμιώτατον καὶ συλλειτουργὸν ἡμῶν Ἀλέξανδρον προκεχειροτονημένων· ὡς τούτοις μὲν μηδεμίαν ἐξουσίαν εἶναι τοὺς ἀρεσκομένους αὐτοῖς προχειρίζεσθαι ἢ ὑποβάλλειν ὄνομα ἢ ὅλως ποιεῖν τι χωρὶς τῆς γνώμης τοῦ τῆς καθολικῆς καὶ ἀποστολικῆς ἐκκλησίας ἐπισκόπου τῶν ὑπὸ Ἀλέξανδρον·

8. τοὺς δὲ χάριτι θεοῦ καὶ εὐχαῖς ὑμετέραις ἐν μηδενὶ σχίσματι εὑρεθέντας, ἀλλ' ἀκηλιδώτους ἐν τῇ καθολικῇ καὶ ἀποστολικῇ ἐκκλησίᾳ ὄντας, ἐξουσίαν ἔχειν καὶ προχειρίζεσθαι καὶ ὄνομα ἐπιλέγεσθαι τῶν ἀξίων τοῦ κλήρου καὶ ὅλως πάντα ποιεῖν κατὰ νόμον καὶ θεσμὸν τὸν ἐκκλησιαστικόν.

9. εἰ δέ τινα συμβαίη ἀναπαύσασθαι τῶν ἐν τῇ ἐκκλησίᾳ, τηνικαῦτα συναναβαίνειν εἰς τὴν τιμὴν τοῦ τετελευτηκότος τοὺς ἄρτι προσλη φθέντας, μόνον εἰ ἄξιοι φαίνοιντο καὶ ὁ λαὸς αἱροῖτο, συνεπιψηφίζοντος αὐτοῖς καὶ ἐπισφραγίζοντος τοῦ τῆς καθολικῆς Ἀλεξανδρείας ἐπισκόπου.

6. It was decreed, the Synod being moved to great clemency towards Melitius, although strictly speaking he was wholly undeserving of favor, that he remain in his own city but exercise no authority either to ordain or nominate for ordination; and that he appear in no other district or city on this pretense, but simply retain a nominal dignity.

7. That those who had received appointments from him, after having been confirmed by a more legitimate ordination, should be admitted to communion on these conditions: that they should continue to hold their rank and ministry, but regard themselves as inferior in every respect to all those who have been ordained and established in each place and church by our most-honored fellow-minister, Alexander, so that they shall have no authority to propose or nominate whom they please, or to do anything at all without the concurrence of some bishop of the Catholic Church who is one of Alexander's suffragans.

8. On the other hand, such as by the grace of God and your prayers have been found in no schism, but have continued in the Catholic Church blameless, shall have authority to nominate and ordain those who are worthy of the sacred office, and to act in all things according to ecclesiastical law and usage.

9. When it may happen that any of those holding preferments in the church die, then let these who have been thus recently admitted be advanced to the dignity of the deceased, provided that they should appear worthy, and that the people should elect them, the bishop of Alexandria also ratifying their choice.

10. τοῦτο δὲ τοῖς μὲν ἄλλοις ἅπασι συνεχωρήθη· ἐπὶ δὲ τοῦ Μελιτίου προσώπου οὐκέτι ταῦτα ἔδοξε διὰ τὴν ἀνέκαθεν αὐτοῦ ἀταξίαν καὶ διὰ τὸ πρόχειρον καὶ προπετὲς τῆς γνώμης, ἵνα μηδεμία ἐξουσία αὐθεντίας αὐτῷ δοθῇ, ἀνθρώπῳ δυναμένῳ πάλιν τὰς αὐτὰς ἀταξίας ποιῆσαι.

11. ταῦτά ἐστι τὰ ἐξαίρετα καὶ διαφέροντα Αἰγύπτῳ καὶ τῇ ἁγιωτάτῃ ἐκκλησίᾳ Ἀλεξανδρείας. εἰ δέ τι ἄλλο ἐκανονίσθη ἢ ἐδογματίσθη, συμπαρόντος τοῦ κυρίου καὶ τιμιωτάτου [καὶ] συλλειτουργοῦ καὶ ἀδελφοῦ ἡμῶν Ἀλεξάνδρου, αὐτὸς παρὼν ἀνοίσει, ἅτε δὴ καὶ κύριος καὶ κοινωνὸς τῶν γεγενημένων τυγχάνων.

12. Εὐαγγελιζόμεθα δὲ ὑμᾶς καὶ περὶ τῆς συμφωνίας τοῦ ἁγιωτάτου ἡμῶν Πάσχα, ὅτι ταῖς ὑμετέραις εὐχαῖς κατωρθώθη καὶ τοῦτο τὸ μέρος ὥστε πάντας τοὺς τῆς Ἑῴας ἀδελφούς, τοὺς τὸ πρότερον μὴ ποιοῦντας σύμφωνα Ῥωμαίοις καὶ ὑμῖν καὶ πᾶσι τοῖς ἐξ ἀρχῆς φυλάττουσι τὸ Πάσχα, ἐκ τοῦ δεῦρο μεθ᾿ ὑμῶν ἄγειν.

13. χαίροντες οὖν ἐπὶ τοῖς κατορθώμασι καὶ ἐπὶ τῇ κοινῇ εἰρήνῃ καὶ συμφωνίᾳ καὶ ἐπὶ τῷ πᾶσαν αἵρεσιν ἐκκοπῆναι, ἀποδέξασθε μετὰ μείζονος τιμῆς καὶ πλείονος ἀγάπης τὸν συλλειτουργὸν ἡμῶν, ἐπίσκοπον δὲ ὑμῶν Ἀλέξανδρον, τὸν εὐφράναντα ἡμᾶς τῇ παρουσίᾳ καὶ ἐν ταύτῃ τῇ ἡλικίᾳ τοσοῦτον πόνον ὑποστάντα ὑπὲρ τοῦ εἰρηνεῦσαι τὰ παρ᾿ ὑμῖν.

10. This privilege is conceded to all the others indeed, but to Melitius personally we by no means grant the same license, on account of his former disorderly conduct, and because of the rashness and levity of his character, in order that no authority or jurisdiction should be given him as a man liable again to create similar disturbances.

11. These are the things which specially affect Egypt, and the most holy church of the Alexandrians: and if any other canon or ordinance has been established, our Lord and most-honored fellow-minister and brother Alexander being present with us, will on his return to you enter into more minute details, inasmuch as he has been a participator in whatever is transacted, and has had the principal direction of it.

12. We have also gratifying intelligence to communicate to you relative to unity of judgment on the subject of the most holy feast of Easter: for this point also has been happily settled through your prayers; so that all the brethren in the East who have heretofore kept this festival when the Jews did, will henceforth conform to the Romans and to us, and to all who from the earliest time have observed our period of celebrating Easter. 13. Rejoicing therefore in these conclusions and in the general unanimity and peace, as well as in the extirpation of all heresy, receive with the greater honor and more abundant love our fellow-minister and your bishop Alexander, who has greatly delighted us by his presence, and even at his advanced age has undergone extraordinary exertions in order that peace might be re-established among you.

εὔχεσθε δὲ καὶ ὑπὲρ ἡμῶν ἁπάντων, ἵνα τὰ καλῶς ἔχειν δόξαντα βέβαια μένοι διὰ τοῦ κυρίου ἡμῶν Ἰησοῦ Χριστοῦ, κατ' εὐδοκίαν γεγενημένα, ὥς γε πεπιστεύκαμεν, τοῦ θεοῦ καὶ πατρὸς ἐν πνεύματι ἁγίῳ· ᾧ ἡ δόξα εἰς τοὺς αἰῶνας τῶν αἰώνων, ἀμήν.

Pray on behalf of us all, that the things decided as just may be inviolably maintained through Almighty God, and our Lord Jesus Christ, together with the Holy Spirit; to whom be glory for ever. Amen.

It is noteworthy that this letter is the only (*sic!*) source of the information on the Council's decisions regarding the Meletians.[31] The text bears many similarities to canon 8 of the Council of Nicaea, which refers to those who call themselves 'Cathars'.[32] Nonetheless, the canon is concerned with any alleged 'Cathars', i.e., Montanists, Donatists, and Novatians. Perhaps even Meletians. The letter seemed to put canon 8 in more specific terms in relation to the problems that were to continue to exist in Egypt for a long time yet. In his *Apologia contra Arianos* 59 (NPNF 2,4), Athanasius states that the Arians had been condemned at the Council of Nicaea and "the Meletians on whatever grounds (for it is not necessary now to mention the reason) were received." It appears then that they had been readmitted, perhaps on account of some social, political, or possibly even opportunistic, reasons. Athanasius must have been discontented with the whole situation, yet without any deliberations over the fact, as there was nothing he could have done to prevent it. Had the letter in question been at his disposal, he would have possessed a very handy weapon against those who had charged him with attempting to enforce subordination of the Meletian clergy. He would have simply said that he had been following the directions stated in that post-synodal letter. Referring to the authority of this letter would have been also very much in order in the letter of the bishops of the West assembled at Sardica, in which they defended Athanasius against accusations levelled by the Meletians.[33] No such thing had happened, though. At item 9, it is said that upon the death of a bishop, he may be succeeded by one of the previously deposed clergy, provided that the Bishop of Alexandria should ratify the choice. And Athanasius had indeed followed the procedure, as attested by his lists of the deceased and newly appointed bishops as stated in the "paschal epistles" for 339 and 347.[34] It appears that Athanasius had worked out a certain *modus* of dealing with the Meletians and this specific

[31] Cf. E. Wipszycka, *La Chiesa nell'Egitto del IV secolo*, in: *Études sur le Christianisme dans l'Égypte de l'antiquité tardive*, SEA 52, Roma 1996, 145.

[32] Council of Nicaea (325), c. 8, see Ch. 7. Cf. A. Martin, *Athanase d'Alexandrie et l'Église d'Égypte au IVe siècle (328-373)*, École Française de Rome, 1996, 257.

[33] Council of Sardica (343-344) IV, 5; SCL 1, 164.

[34] Athanasius, *Epistulae festales*, PG 26, 1412-1414 and 1430.

practice is reflected in the letter. Annick Martin's article[35] on the conditions of the readmission of the Meletian clergymen to the ranks of the Catholic clergy, based entirely on the above letter, offers a very favourable view of Athanasius' achievements, but it misses the point as far as the Council itself is concerned.

Let us now turn to Constantine's letter addressed to all the Churches. Socrates cites it after Eusebius of Caesarea's *Vita Constantini* (III, 17ff.), an undeniably panegyrical work composed shortly after the Emperor's death, and not very long before Eusebius' death, i.e., in the years 337-339. The author could have hardly afforded to falsify any document of relevance, considering that they must have been indeed commonly known by then.

Constantine's Letter to the Churches[36]

17. Πεῖραν λαβὼν ἐκ τῆς τῶν κοινῶν εὐπραξίας, ὅση τῆς θείας δυνάμεως πέφυκε χάρις, τοῦτόν <γε> πρὸ πάντων ἔκρινα εἶναί μοι προσήκειν σκοπόν, ὅπως παρὰ τοῖς μακαριωτάτοις τῆς καθολικῆς ἐκκλησίας πλήθεσι πίστις μία καὶ εἰλικρινὴς ἀγάπη ὁμογνώμων τε περὶ τὸν παγκρατῆ θεὸν εὐσέβεια τηρῆται.
ἀλλ' ἐπειδὴ τοῦτο οὐχ οἷόν τ' ἦν ἀκλινῆ καὶ βεβαίαν τάξιν λαβεῖν, εἰ μή, εἰς ταὐτὸν πάντων ὁμοῦ ἢ τῶν γοῦν πλειόνων ἐπισκόπων συνελθόντων, ἑκάστου τῶν προσηκόντων τῇ ἁγιωτάτῃ θρησκείᾳ διάκρισις γένοιτο, τούτου ἕνεκεν πλείστων ὅσων συναθροισθέντων ᾽καὶ αὐτὸς δὲ καθάπερ εἷς ἐξ ὑμῶν ἐτύγχανον συμπαρών· οὐ γὰρ ἀρνησαίμην ἄν, ἐφ' ᾧ μάλιστα χαίρω, συνθεράπων ὑμέτερος πεφυκέναί,

17. Having had full proof, in the general prosperity of the empire, how great the favor of God has been towards us, I have judged that it ought to be the first object of my endeavors, that unity of faith, sincerity of love, and community of feeling in regard to the worship of Almighty God, might be preserved among the highly favored multitude who compose the Catholic Church. And, inasmuch as this object could not be effectually and certainly secured, unless all, or at least the greater number of the bishops were to meet together, and a discussion of all particulars relating to our most holy religion to take place; for this reason as numerous an assembly as possible has been convened, at which I myself was present, as one among yourselves (and far be it from me to deny that which is my greatest joy, that I am your fellow-servant),

[35] A. Martin, *Les conditions de la réadmission du clergé mélitien par le concile de Nicée*, in *Ancient Society* 20 (1989) 281-290.

[36] *Constantine's Letter to the Churches Respecting the Council at Nicaea*, in: Eusebius of Caesarea, *v.C.* III, 17ff (NPNF 2,1).

ἄχρι τοσούτου ἅπαντα τῆς προσηκούσης τετύχηκεν ἐξετάσεως, ἄχρις οὗ ἡ τῷ πάντων ἐφόρῳ θεῷ ἀρέσκουσα γνώμη πρὸς τὴν τῆς ἑνότητος συμφωνίαν εἰς φῶς προήχθη, ὡς μηδὲν ἔτι πρὸς διχόνοιαν ἢ πίστεως ἀμφισβήτησιν ὑπολείπεσθαι.

18. Ἔνθα καὶ περὶ τῆς τοῦ πάσχα ἁγιωτάτης ἡμέρας γενομένης ζητήσεως, ἔδοξε κοινῇ γνώμῃ καλῶς ἔχειν ἐπὶ μιᾶς ἡμέρας πάντας τοὺς ἀπανταχοῦ ἐπιτελεῖν. τί γὰρ ἡμῖν κάλλιον, τί δὲ σεμνότερον ὑπάρξαι δυνήσεται τοῦ τὴν ἑορτὴν ταύτην, παρ᾽ ἧς τὴν τῆς ἀθανασίας εἰλήφαμεν ἐλπίδα, μιᾷ τάξει καὶ φανερῷ λόγῳ παρὰ πᾶσιν ἀδιαπτώτως φυλάττεσθαι;
καὶ πρῶτον μὲν ἀνάξιον ἔδοξεν εἶναι τὴν ἁγιωτάτην ἐκείνην ἑορτὴν τῇ τῶν Ἰουδαίων ἑπομένους συνηθείᾳ πληροῦν, οἳ τὰς ἑαυτῶν χεῖρας ἀθεμίτῳ πλημμελήματι χράναντες εἰκότως τὰς ψυχὰς οἱ μιαροὶ τυφλώττουσιν. ἔξεστι γὰρ τοῦ ἐκείνων ἔθνους ἀποβληθέντος ἀληθεστέρᾳ τάξει, ἣν ἐκ πρώτης τοῦ πάθους ἡμέρας ἄχρι τοῦ παρόντος ἐφυλάξαμεν, καὶ ἐπὶ τοὺς μέλλοντας αἰῶνας τὴν τῆς ἐπιτηρήσεως ταύτης συμπλήρωσιν ἐκτείνεσθαι. μηδὲν τοίνυν ἔστω ὑμῖν κοινὸν μετὰ τοῦ ἐχθίστου τῶν Ἰουδαίων ὄχλου. εἰλήφαμεν γὰρ παρὰ τοῦ σωτῆρος ἑτέραν ὁδόν, πρόκειται δρόμος τῇ ἱερωτάτῃ ἡμῶν θρησκείᾳ καὶ νόμιμος καὶ πρέπων. τούτου συμφώνως ἀντιλαμβανόμενοι τῆς αἰσχρᾶς ἐκείνης ἑαυτοὺς συνειδήσεως ἀποσπάσωμεν, ἀδελφοὶ τιμιώτατοι.

and every question received due and full examination, until that judgment which God, who sees all things, could approve, and which tended to unity and concord, was brought to light, so that no room was left for further discussion or controversy in relation to the faith.

18. At this meeting the question concerning the most holy day of Easter was discussed, and it was resolved by the united judgment of all present, that this feast ought to be kept by all and in every place on one and the same day. For what can be more becoming or honorable to us than that this feast from which we date our hopes of immortality, should be observed unfailingly by all alike, according to one ascertained order and arrangement?
And first of all, it appeared an unworthy thing that in the celebration of this most holy feast we should follow the practice of the Jews, who have impiously defiled their hands with enormous sin, and are, therefore, deservedly afflicted with blindness of soul. For we have it in our power, if we abandon their custom, to prolong the due observance of this ordinance to future ages, by a truer order, which we have preserved from the very day of the passion until the present time. Let us then have nothing in common with the detestable Jewish crowd; for we have received from our Saviour a different way. A course at once legitimate and honorable lies open to our most holy religion. Beloved brethren, let us with one consent adopt this course, and withdraw ourselves from all participation in their baseness.

ἔστι γὰρ ὡς ἀληθῶς ἀτοπώτατον ἐκείνους αὐχεῖν, ὡς ἄρα παρεκτὸς τῆς αὐτῶν διδασκαλίας ταῦτα φυλάττειν οὐκ εἴημεν ἱκανοί. τί δὲ φρονεῖν ὀρθὸν ἐκεῖνοι δυνήσονται, οἳ μετὰ τὴν κυριοκτονίαν τε καὶ πατροκτονίαν ἐκείνην ἐκστάντες τῶν φρενῶν ἄγονται οὐ λογισμῷ τινι ἀλλ᾽ ὁρμῇ ἀκατασχέτῳ, ὅπῃ δ᾽ ἂν αὐτοὺς ἡ ἔμφυτος αὐτῶν ἀγάγῃ μανία; ἐκεῖθεν τοίνυν κἂν τούτῳ τῷ μέρει τὴν ἀλήθειαν οὐχ ὁρῶσιν, ὡς ἀεὶ κατὰ τὸ πλεῖστον αὐτοὺς πλανωμένους ἀντὶ τῆς προσηκούσης ἐπανορθώσεως ἐν τῷ αὐτῷ ἔτει δεύτερον τὸ πάσχα ἐπιτελεῖν. τίνος οὖν χάριν τούτοις ἑπόμεθα, οὓς δεινὴν πλάνην νοσεῖν ὡμολόγηται; δεύτερον γὰρ τὸ πάσχα ἐν ἑνὶ ἐνιαυτῷ οὐκ ἄν ποτε ποιεῖν ἀνεξόμεθα.

ἀλλ᾽ εἰ καὶ ταῦτα μὴ προὔκειτο, τὴν ὑμετέραν ἀγχίνοιαν ἐχρῆν καὶ διὰ σπουδῆς καὶ δι᾽ εὐχῆς ἔχειν πάντοτε, ἐν μηδενὸς ὁμοιότητι τὸ καθαρὸν τῆς ὑμετέρας ψυχῆς κοινωνεῖν δοκεῖν ἀνθρώπων ἔθεσι παγκάκων. <Πρὸς> τούτοις κἀκεῖνο πάρεστι συνορᾶν, ὡς ἐν τηλικούτῳ πράγματι καὶ τοιαύτῃ θρησκείας ἑορτῇ διαφωνίαν ὑπάρχειν ἐστὶν ἀθέμιτον. μίαν γὰρ ἡμῖν τὴν τῆς ἡμετέρας ἐλευθερίας ἡμέραν, τουτέστιν τὴν τοῦ ἁγιωτάτου πάθους, ὁ ἡμέτερος παρέδωκε σωτήρ, καὶ μίαν εἶναι τὴν καθολικὴν αὐτοῦ ἐκκλησίαν βεβούληται, ἧς εἰ καὶ τὰ μάλιστα εἰς πολλοὺς καὶ διαφόρους τόπους τὰ μέρη διῄρηται, ἀλλ᾽ ὅμως ἑνὶ πνεύματι, τουτέστι τῷ θείῳ βουλήματι, θάλπεται. λογισάσθω δ᾽ ἡ τῆς ὑμετέρας ὁσιότητος ἀγχίνοια, ὅπως ἐστὶ δεινόν τε καὶ ἀπρεπὲς κατὰ τὰς αὐτὰς ἡμέρας ἑτέρους μὲν ταῖς νηστείαις σχολάζειν, ἑτέρους δὲ συμπόσια συντελεῖν,

For their boast is absurd indeed, that it is not in our power without instruction from them to observe these things. For how should they be capable of forming a sound judgment, who, since their parricidal guilt in slaying their Lord, have been subject to the direction, not of reason, but of ungoverned passion, and are swayed by every impulse of the mad spirit that is in them? Hence it is that on this point as well as others they have no perception of the truth, so that, being altogether ignorant of the true adjustment of this question, they sometimes celebrate Easter twice in the same year. Why then should we follow those who are confessedly in grievous error? Surely we shall never consent to keep this feast a second time in the same year.

But supposing these reasons were not of sufficient weight, still it would be incumbent on your Sagacities to strive and pray continually that the purity of your souls may not seem in anything to be sullied by fellowship with the customs of these most wicked men. We must consider, too, that a discordant judgment in a case of such importance, and respecting such religious festival, is wrong. For our Saviour has left us one feast in commemoration of the day of our deliverance, I mean the day of his most holy passion; and he has willed that his Catholic Church should be one, the members of which, however scattered in many and diverse places, are yet cherished by one pervading spirit, that is, by the will of God. And let your Holinesses' sagacity reflect how grievous and scandalous it is that on the self-same days some should be engaged in fasting, others in festive enjoyment;

καὶ μετὰ τὰς τοῦ πάσχα ἡμέρας ἄλλους μὲν ἐν ἑορταῖς καὶ ἀνέσεσιν ἐξετάζεσθαι, ἄλλους δὲ ταῖς ὡρισμέναις ἐκδεδόσθαι νηστείαις. διὰ τοῦτο γοῦν τῆς προσηκούσης ἐπανορθώσεως τυχεῖν καὶ πρὸς μίαν διατύπωσιν ἄγεσθαι τοῦτο ἡ θεία πρόνοια βούλεται, ὡς ἔγωγε ἅπαντας ἡγοῦμαι συνορᾶν.

19. Ὅθεν ἐπειδὴ τοῦτο οὕτως ἐπανορθοῦσθαι προσῆκεν, ὡς μηδὲν μετὰ τοῦ τῶν πατροκτόνων τε καὶ κυριοκτόνων ἐκείνων ἔθνους εἶναι κοινόν, ἔστι δὲ τάξις εὐπρεπής, ἣν πᾶσαι αἱ τῶν δυτικῶν τε καὶ μεσημβρινῶν καὶ ἀρκτῴων τῆς οἰκουμένης μερῶν παραφυλάττουσιν ἐκκλησίαι καί τινες τῶν κατὰ τὴν ἑῴαν τόπων, οὗ ἕνεκεν ἐπὶ τοῦ παρόντος καλῶς ἔχειν ἅπαντες ἡγήσαντο, καὶ αὐτὸς δὲ τῇ ὑμετέρᾳ ἀγχινοίᾳ ἀρέσειν ὑπεσχόμην, ἵν' ὅπερ δ' ἂν κατὰ τὴν Ῥωμαίων πόλιν Ἰταλίαν τε καὶ Ἀφρικὴν ἅπασαν, Αἴγυπτον, Σπανίας, Γαλλίας, Βρεττανίας, Λιβύας, ὅλην Ἑλλάδα, Ἀσιανήν τε διοίκησιν καὶ Ποντικὴν καὶ Κιλικίαν μιᾷ καὶ συμφώνῳ φυλάττεται γνώμῃ, ἀσμένως τοῦτο καὶ ἡ ὑμετέρα προσδέξηται σύνεσις,
λογιζομένη ὡς οὐ μόνον πλείων ἐστὶν ὁ τῶν κατὰ τοὺς προειρημένους τόπους ἐκκλησιῶν ἀριθμός, ἀλλὰ καὶ ὡς τοῦτο μάλιστα κοινῇ πάντας ὁσιώτατόν ἐστι βούλεσθαι, ὅπερ καὶ ὁ ἀκριβὴς λόγος ἀπαιτεῖν δοκεῖ καὶ οὐδεμίαν μετὰ τῆς Ἰουδαίων ἐπιορκίας ἔχειν κοινωνίαν.

and again, that after the days of Easter some should be present at banquets and amusements, while others are fulfilling the appointed fasts. It is, then, plainly the will of Divine Providence (as I suppose you all clearly see), that this usage should receive fitting correction, and be reduced to one uniform rule.

19. Since, therefore, it was needful that this matter should be rectified, so that we might have nothing in common with that nation of parricides who slew their Lord: and since that arrangement is consistent with propriety which is observed by all the churches of the western, southern, and northern parts of the world, and by some of the eastern also: for these reasons all are unanimous on this present occasion in thinking it worthy of adoption. And I myself have undertaken that this decision should meet with the approval of your Sagacities, in the hope that your Wisdoms will gladly admit that practice which is observed at once in the city of Rome, and in Africa; throughout Italy, and in Egypt, in Spain, the Gauls, Britain, Libya, and the whole of Greece; in the dioceses of Asia and Pontus, and in Cilicia, with entire unity of judgment.
And you will consider not only that the number of churches is far greater in the regions I have enumerated than in any other, but also that it is most fitting that all should unite in desiring that which sound reason appears to demand, and in avoiding all participation in the perjured conduct of the Jews.

Ἵνα δὲ τὸ κεφαλαιωδέστατον συντόμως εἴπω, κοινῇ πάντων ἤρεσε κρίσει τὴν ἁγιωτάτην τοῦ πάσχα ἑορτὴν μιᾷ καὶ τῇ αὐτῇ ἡμέρᾳ συντελεῖσθαι. οὐδὲ γὰρ πρέπει ἐν τοσαύτῃ ἁγιότητι εἶναί τινα διαφοράν, καὶ κάλλιον ἕπεσθαι τῇ γνώμῃ ταύτῃ, ἐν ᾗ οὐδεμία ἔσται ἀλλοτρίας πλάνης καὶ ἁμαρτήματος ἐπιμιξία.

20. Τούτων οὖν οὕτως ἐχόντων, ἀσμένως δέχεσθε τὴν οὐρανίαν χάριν καὶ θείαν ὡς ἀληθῶς ἐντολήν· πᾶν γὰρ ὅτι δ᾽ ἂν ἐν τοῖς ἁγίοις τῶν ἐπισκόπων συνεδρίοις πράττηται, τοῦτο πρὸς τὴν θείαν βούλησιν ἔχει τὴν ἀναφοράν. διὸ πᾶσι τοῖς ἀπαγητοῖς ἡμῶν ἀδελφοῖς ἐμφανίσαντες τὰ προγεγραμμένα, ἤδη καὶ τὸν προειρημένον λόγον καὶ τὴν παρατήρησιν τῆς ἁγιωτάτης ἡμέρας ὑποδέχεσθαί τε καὶ διατάττειν ὀφείλετε, ἵνα ἐπεὶ δὰν πρὸς τὴν πάλαι μοι ποθουμένην τῆς ὑμετέρας διαθέσεως ὄψιν ἀφίκωμαι, ἐν μιᾷ καὶ τῇ αὐτῇ ἡμέρᾳ τὴν ἁγίαν μεθ᾽ ὑμῶν ἑορτὴν ἐπιτελέσαι δυνηθῶ καὶ πάντων ἕνεκεν μεθ᾽ ὑμῶν εὐδοκήσω, συνορῶν τὴν διαβολικὴν ὠμότητα ὑπὸ τῆς θείας δυνάμεως διὰ τῶν ἡμετέρων πράξεων ἀνῃρημένην, ἀκμαζούσης πανταχοῦ τῆς ἡμετέρας πίστεως καὶ εἰρήνης καὶ ὁμονοίας. Ὁ θεὸς ὑμᾶς διαφυλάξοι, ἀδελφοὶ ἀγαπητοί.

In fine, that I may express my meaning in as few words as possible, it has been determined by the common judgment of all, that the most holy feast of Easter should be kept on one and the same day. For on the one hand a discrepancy of opinion on so sacred a question is unbecoming, and on the other it is surely best to act on a decision which is free from strange folly and error. 20. Receive, then, with all willingness this truly Divine injunction, and regard it as in truth the gift of God. For whatever is determined in the holy assemblies of the bishops is to be regarded as indicative of the Divine will. As soon, therefore, as you have communicated these proceedings to all our beloved brethren, you are bound from that time forward to adopt for yourselves, and to enjoin on others the arrangement above mentioned, and the due observance of this most sacred day; that whenever I come into the presence of your love, which I have long desired, I may have it in my power to celebrate the holy feast with you on the same day, and may rejoice with you on all accounts, when I behold the cruel power of Satan removed by Divine aid through the agency of our endeavors, while your faith, and peace, and concord everywhere flourish. God preserve you, beloved brethren!"

As we can see, similar expressions can be found in the final part of the *Letter of Constantine to the Church of Alexandria*. And, likewise, this one carries words of encouragement, not to say of injunction, to conform to the decisions agreed as well as the hope that when the Emperor would come to visit the addressees, he should see unity, peace, and concord flourish everywhere. He also refers to the power of Satan being thwarted. However, the focus on a particular problem is different: in this letter, the Emperor speaks of the lack of the unity in faith, successively overcome by means of the adoption of the new creed, and the discrepancies in the dates of the Easter celebration, removed by the ultimate rejection of the Jewish calendar. In the other letter, the principal issue was Arianism. How can these differences be explained?

According to the commonly assumed textbook opinion, the actual reason for the convocation of this ecumenical council was, in the first place, the Arian controversy[37] and, secondarily, the date of Easter. Following in the footsteps of the ancient historians, especially Socrates and Sozomen, modern scholars tend to give credence to the Athanasian version of the events and dismiss Eusebius' account. But is this approach really the right one? It is true that Eusebius had been apparently partial to Arius and would not have been willing to speak ill of him. Yet it is true as well that Athanasius detested Arius and thus could not have played an impartial role in the dispute. Moreover, contrary to the opinion expressed by the bishops of the East, who specify the reasons for Athanasius' deposition in the so-called *Decree of the synod at Sardica of the Eastern bishops of the Arian party addressed to Africa*[38] – and those were disciplinary, not doctrinal, reasons – he was very much concerned with portraying himself as someone persecuted for his faith. Thus far, no one has proved that Eusebius had forged the documents. At the most, he may have been held liable for certain errors and misrepresentations in regard to the earlier period. His account of Constantine is exaggeratedly favourable, yet his citations are, simply and clearly, citations in consideration of the fact that he addressed those who had known the events in question just as well. Consequently, as far as the circumstances of the contemporary events are concerned, I am rather inclined to lend him credence. For the time being, then, I would rather assume that the most plausible reasons for summoning the council are those stated by Eusebius in 338, namely the questions of preserving the unity of faith and determining the date of Easter. But there is also no reason to doubt that the controversy over Arius had been a subject of debate. The proceedings were attended by Alexander of Alexandria, who had condemned him in *ca.* 323, and Eusebius of Nicomedia, who defended him, as well as by Hosius of Cordoba, who had brought the Emperor's letter concerning the dispute to Alexandria, entrusted with a mission to reconcile Alexander and Arius. Interestingly, Athanasius would refer on various occasions to the condemnation of Arius at Nicaea, yet he had not presented any conciliar text to that effect. The same thing can be applied to the Meletians. As we have already seen, he states that the Meletians had been

---

[37] See, e.g., M. Banaszak, *Historia Kościoła Katolickiego* 1, ATK, Warszawa 1986, 155 or the voluminous work (*History of the Church*) by Hubert Jedin (ed.); Italian edition: *Storia della Chiesa* II, *L'Epoca dei Concili*, Jaca Book, Milano 2002, 23ff. See Ch. 4.

[38] Council of Sardica (343-344) VII; SCL 1, 170-183.

"somehow" admitted to the community of the Church, without quoting any synodal letter referring explicitly to the conditions of such readmission.

The Falsification Hypothesis

The post-synodal letters addressed to the Church of Alexandria, had they really existed, must have been known to at least Athanasius. He would certainly have found them very useful: the *Letter of Constantine* in his struggle against the Arians and the *Letter of the Council of Nicaea* in the one against the Meletians. Athanasius had never used them at all, which would point to his very likely unfamiliarity with these epistles for as long as he lived. We know that since approximately 350, i.e. the supposed date of the composition of *De decretis*,[39] Athanasius had undertaken to propagate the Nicene Creed, which he had not done ever before. He would have to work for the success for a very long time indeed, practically until his death in 373. Unfortunately, he had not lived long enough to see canon 1 of the First Council of Constantinople (381): "The profession of faith of the holy fathers who gathered in Nicaea in Bithynia is not to be abrogated, but it is to remain in force. Every heresy is to be anathematized and in particular that of the Eunomians or Anomoeans, that of the Arians or Eudoxians, that of the Semi-Arians or Pneumatomachi, that of the Sabellians, that of the Marcellians, that of the Photinians and that of the Apollinarians."[40] Aside from the synods chaired by Athanasius, it appears that the first attempt to adopt the Nicene Creed was made at the synod of Rimini in 359, but it ended in failure.[41] In the following year, the synod of Paris, presided over by Hilarius of Poitiers, affirmed it.[42] The subsequent synods that were to subscribe to this creed took place at Antioch in 363,[43] at Tyana[44] and Rome in 365,[45] and, one year later, in Sicily.[46] The

---

[39] Opinions on the dating of *De decretis* are stated comprehensively by Enrico Cattaneo in his introduction to: Atanasio, *Il credo di Nicea*, Collana di Testi Patristici 160, Città Nuova 2001, 24-29.

[40] Council of Constantinople (381), c. 1 (in: *Decrees of the Ecumenical Councils*, vol. 1, N.P. Tanner (ed.), Georgetown University Press 1990); DSP 1, 71. The content of this canon casts doubt on the possibility of any new creed having been formulated at that synod. Cf. H. Pietras, *Spór o wyznanie wiary w IV w.*, 35-50.

[41] Council of Rimini (359) I; SCL 1, 226-227.

[42] Council of Paris (360/361) II; SCL 1, 246-249.

[43] Council of Antioch (363); SCL 1, 259-260.

[44] Council of Tyana (365); SCL 1, 260.

[45] Council of Rome (365/366); SCL 1, 261-263.

[46] Council of Sicilia (366); SCL 1, 263.

case was finally settled, when, after the confusion during Valens' reign,[47] the rulers of the Empire, led by Theodosius the Great, promulgated the decree on the Nicene faith on 10 January 381:[48]

"5, 6, 1. The throngs of all heretics must be restrained from unlawful congregations. The name of the One and Supreme God shall be celebrated everywhere; the observance, destined to remain forever, of the Nicene faith, as transmitted long ago by Our ancestors and confirmed by the declaration and testimony of divine religion, shall be maintained. The contamination of the Photinian pestilence, the poison of the Arian sacrilege, the crime of the Eunomian perfidy, and the sectarian monstrosities, abominable because of the ill-omened names of their authors, shall be abolished even from the hearing of men.[49] "

There is no reason to doubt that this decree provides the basis for canon 1 of the First Council of Constantinople, but afterwards as well it would have made no sense at all to produce a letter with such contents allegedly authored by the Emperor Constantine himself. If, therefore, the *Letter of Constantine to the Church of Alexandria* is a falsification indeed, it could have been possibly written in the years 373-380, i.e., following Athanasius' death and prior to Theodosius' decree.

It is more difficult to ascertain the date *ante quam* as regards the *Letter of the Council of Nicaea.* We know that some Meletian monasteries continued to exist for a long time, apparently at odds with the orthodox ones.[50] The Bishop of Alexandria may have faced some problems arising from that situation. For instance, canon 12 from the collected *Canons of Athanasius of Alexandria* begins with: "The singers shall not sing the writings of Meletius and of the ignorant, that sing without wisdom."[51] In turn, Shenute of Atripe (*ca.* 348-466)[52] castigated the practice of receiving communion several times

---

[47] Cf. Socrates, *h.e.* IV, 21-22. 24; Sozomen, *h.e.*, VI, 19-20; Theodoret of Cyrrhus, *h.e.*, VI, 22, 1-37.

[48] *Codex Theodosianus* XVI, 5, 6.

[49] *Codex Theodosianus* XVI 5,6 (in: C. Pharr (trans.), *The Theodosian Code and Novels and the Sirmondian Constitutions*, Princeton University Press, New York 1952).

[50] Cf. W.E. Crum, *Some Further Meletian Documents*, "Journal of Egyptian Archaeology" 13 (1927) 19-26; E. Wipszycka, *Études sur le Christianisme dans l'Égypte de l'antiquité tardive*, 319; A. Camplani, *In margine alla storia dei meliziani*, in *Augustinianum* 30 (1990), 327-329.

[51] Cf. c. 12, in: Wilhelm Riedel, *Canons of Athanasius of Alexandria*, 1904; SCL 3, 140; E. Wipszycka, *Études sur le Christianisme dans l'Égypte*, 249.

[52] See M. Starowieyski, *Słownik Wczesnochrześcijańskiego Piśmiennictwa Wschodu*, IW PAX, Warszawa 1999, 222-226.

a day by Meletian monks.[53] Both Arians and Meletians had reasons to be afraid of Athanasius on account of his very strong position in Egypt and beyond. It is worth noting that he had managed to consolidate it even with no recourse to either the anti-Arian *Letter of Constantine* or the anti-Meletian *Letter of the Council of Nicaea*. His successor was not to maintain an equally firm position. Designated by Athanasius, Peter would not command an authority comparable to that of his predecessor. Athanasius' opponents revolted, arrested Peter, and installed the homoiousian Lucius as Bishop of Alexandria. Lucius had been previously ordained at Antioch and, as Pierre Maraval nicely puts it, he would not have lasted more than forty-eight hours against Athanasius.[54] The sources describe acts of violence and bloody retribution, Peter's escape from captivity and his flight to Rome, as well as the persecution carried out with the Emperor Valens' support.[55] Theodoret quotes the fugitive bishop Peter's long letter recounting those terrible events.[56] Peter states that the calls for renouncing the Nicene faith were countered, among other things, by the following words: "our fathers throughout the world who assembled at Nicaea, and anathematized the false doctrine of Arius (...) laid down that the Son was not as you are now compelling us to say, of a different substance from the Father, but of one and the same (*ousia*). This their pious intelligence clearly perceived, and so from an adequate collation of divine terms they owned Him to be consubstantial (*homoousios*)."[57] This observation is noteworthy for its clear distinction between the condemnation of Arius and the criticism of the creed, the latter having been formulated, as it is recorded, following the condemnation. In his *De decretis* (3, 2), Athanasius himself states that the faith was laid down against them, which was endorsed by everybody. He makes no reference to any special decree or any other official act: the *credo* itself is portrayed as deliberately anti-Arian. Such a special condemnation is included, however, in the *Letter of the Council of Nicaea*. But on what grounds exactly?

[53] See T. Orlandi, *Coptic Literature*, in: B.A. Pearson, J.E. Goehring (ed.), *The Root of Egyptian Christianity*, Fortress Press, Philadelphia 1992, 68.

[54] *Histoire de christianisme* II, ed. J.-M. Mayeur, Ch. Pietri, L. Pietri, A. Vauchez, M. Venard, Desclée 1995, 893.

[55] Socrates, *h.e.* IV, 21-22. 24; Sozomen, *h.e.*, VI, 19-20; see E. Wipszycka, *Études sur le Christianisme dans l'Égypte*, 75.

[56] Theodoret of Cyrrhus, *h.e.* IV, 22, 1-37.

[57] Theodoret of Cyrrhus, *h.e.* IV, 19 (NPNF 2,3): οἱ γοῦν ἡμέτεροι κατὰ πᾶσαν τὴν οἰκουμένην πατέρες, [...] ἐν Νικαίᾳ συνελθόντες, ἀναθεματίσαντες τὴν Ἀρείου κακοδοξίαν, [...] οὐχ ἑτεροούσιον, [...] τὸν υἱὸν εἰρήκασι τοῦ πατρός, ἀλλ᾽ ἐκ τῆς αὐτοῦ οὐσίας· ὃ καλῶς μετ᾽ εὐσεβοῦς διανοίας νοήσαντες, ἐκ πολλῆς τῶν θείων ῥημάτων συλλογῆς ὁμοούσιον ὡμολόγησαν.

Let us notice that the above-mentioned expressions are very similar to some of the sentences in Athanasius' letter to the bishops of Africa.[58] It reads that the faith was passed down by the fathers assembled at Nicaea, who had arrived from throughout our civilized world (1), that they said the Son was from the Father's *ousia* (5), and that they subsequently collated statements from the Bible and ultimately pronounced that the Son was consubstantial with the Father (6). It seems to me that Peter, the author of the aforementioned letter on the disturbances at Alexandria, had been very well acquainted with Athanasius' letter, or he may have even had a copy at his disposal.

As I have already noted, Peter escaped from captivity and left for Rome to seek Pope Damasius' protection. Charles Pietri describes the situation as follows: Damasius got this "rude" individual for an advisor, a figure more adamant and undoubtedly less balanced than Athanasius. This dramatic episode completely changed the equilibrium in the ecclesiastical relations: the great Church of Alexandria, the last of the Nicene churches in the East, disappeared, and Rome would come to assume the full responsibility for the struggle.[59]

The years of the unfortunate episcopate of Peter, who was also to become known for his attempt to install Maxim the Cynic as Bishop of Constantinople,[60] seem to have been the time when both of the letters in question may have been produced. At that time, they would have come of great use to Peter and Damasius in their efforts to recover Alexandria from the homoiousian party. It is only the falsification hypothesis that makes me see what the calls for the return to concord and unity with the brethren (cf. *Constantine's Letter*) really refer to, and to whom the following words are directed: "For this is becoming your penetration, faith and sanctity; that since the error has been proved to be due to him who is an enemy to the truth, ye should return to the divine favor." The passage refers to the return of the Alexandrian faithful to the Nicene Church as represented by Peter.

Around the year 375, when none of the attendees of the Council of Nicaea would have been still among the living, Sabinus of Heraclea, a bishop affiliated with the Macedonians (and thus pro-homoiousian) had made a collation of the synodal documents.[61] Socrates refers to this particular collection on several occasions (unfortunately, the collection itself is now lost). He says that Sabinus commends the truthfulness of

[58] Council of Alexandria (*ca.* 370); SCL 1, 265-275. To a large extent, the letter is an assemblage of fragments from *De decretis* and *De synodis*.

[59] CH. Pietri, *Roma Christiana*, École Française de Rome, 1976, 803.

[60] Cf. Council of Constantinople (381), c. 4; DSP 1, 72.

[61] M. Simonetti, *La crisi ariana nel IV secolo*, 25.

Eusebius of Caesarea and depicts the participants of the Council, the authors of the *credo*, as simpletons,[62] that "of his own will, (he) rejects such an assessment of the decisions of the council" as Socrates had read in the *Constantine's Letter to the Church of Alexandria*,[63] and that he cites the letter of the synod at Antioch to Julius,[64] but not Julius' letter to Antioch,[65] because "he carefully introduces such letters as make no reference to, or wholly repudiate the term homoousion; while he purposely passes over in silence those of a contrary tendency."[66] He concedes, however, as if contradicting himself, that he draws the letter of the Antiochene synod from Sabinus, i.e., the letter in which the Nicene Creed, along with the term *homoousios*, is affirmed,[67] and that he [Sabinus] had written of the affirmation of that *credo* by the Macedonians in Sicily.[68] Socrates also reproaches him for deliberately passing over the crimes committed in connection with Peter's arrest at Alexandria and Lucius' ingress,[69] yet the charge is misdirected, as Sabinus had made a collection of the synodal acts, not a chronicle of various incidents.

It appears to me that it is possible, in view of the above opinions, to formulate a tentative conclusion that Sabinus' collation may have been a fairly good one after all. According to Socrates' view, however, it had a serious flaw in that it contained none of the two epistles in question, which were, in his opinion, authentic and definitely clear in all that referred to the condemnation of Arius and the praise of the Nicene Creed. In consequence, he charges Sabinus with having manipulated the material. I suppose that the latter bishop had not cited those documents simply because he had no knowledge of them. It may point to the time of their origin: shortly before Peter's return to Alexandria in 378. There are some accounts reporting that Peter had returned with Damasius' letter affirming the Nicene profession of faith.[70] Did he have any other document with him? Pope Damasius is known to have coped with even more difficult situations.

[62] Socrates, *h.e.* I, 8.

[63] Socrates, *h.e.* I, 9.

[64] Council of Antioch (341) II: SCL 1, 134ff.

[65] Rome (340/341); SCL 1, 110-123.

[66] Socrates, *h.e.* II, 17 (NPNF 2,2).

[67] Socrates, *h.e.* III, 25; Council of Antioch (autumn 363); SCL 1, 259-260.

[68] Socrates, *h.e.* IV, 12; Council of Sicily (366); SCL 1, 263.

[69] Socrates, *h.e.* IV, 22.

[70] Socrates, *h.e.* IV, 37; Sozomen, *h.e.*VI, 39.

CONCLUSION

In the nine chapters of this book I have attempted to analyze and discuss the fundamental documents related to the Council of Nicaea, and some myths around the event, and to propose interpretations of the material that may be different from those traditionally (i.e., for as long as 1,500 years) recognized as valid.

I shall now try to put them into one coherent story.

In Chapter 1, I have tried to take a closer look at some historical accounts on the beginnings of the controversy at Alexandria that was to turn into the main point of theological debates and discussions. We have seen Arius' letter to Alexander, also endorsed by his thirteen followers. In Alexander's letter to Arius, all of them are enumerated in the same order as anathematized, from which I infer that Arius' letter comes before the condemnation at Alexandria and all the other documents from the early stage of the controversy.

An unprecedented epistolar war broke out between Bishop Alexander of Alexandria, intent on ensuring support for the cause, and the presbyter Arius, who had obtained support from Eusebius of Nicomedia. This considerable increase in correspondence activity was brought about, I suppose, by the Emperor Constantine I's invitations addressed to the bishops, requesting them to arrive at his capital in order to take part in the festive celebrations of the inauguration of the anniversary year, i.e., *vicennalia*, marking the 20th year of his reign. It was a truly unprecedented opportunity for the bishops of the entire Christian world of the East to meet together at one general assembly, with the Emperor himself in attendance. Briefly before the great synod, the Emperor had written a letter addressed to Alexander and Arius, but seemingly intended for a wider dissemination in the East in order to make everybody see that the Emperor is opposed to disturbances or contentions, whereas theoretical debates should be resolved behind closed doors, with only feelings of concord and fraternity in public.

It seems that the attendees of the great synod were to triumphantly pronounce Constantine's victory over all the enemies, declare peace (the holy peace, so to speak), one profession of faith to be acknowledged as a sort of a measure of orthodoxy (and very likely to be incorporated in the *Liber pontificalis*), and the date of Easter common to the entire Christian world. Whether by opportunity or in agreement with the initiators' design, the council promulgated a body of twenty canons that were to be met with a very favourable reception in the Church. As based on the Emperor Constantine's letter addressed to all the churches, written at the occasion of the conclusion of the proceedings with a clear intention to impart the author's satisfaction with the outcome, the actual scope of the Council's achievements can be determined, namely a commonly accepted creed and the date of Easter to be observed by everybody on the same day (the date itself was not specified, but the reliance on the Jewish calendar was ruled out).

I have also discussed Eusebius of Caesarea's letter to his church, written very shortly after the Council. The author recounts the circumstances of the formulation of a new *credo* and the difficulties arising from considerable differences in the participants' opinions. Until then, each church would have possessed their own creed and none of the bishops felt it was necessary to draw up a compromise formula. Evidently, however, the Emperor did require such a profession of faith and persuaded the Fathers of the Council into formulating and affirming a creed, having reportedly suggested the insertion, into its text, of a statement referring to the consubstantiality of the Father and the Son, i.e., the Son's origin from the Father, not "from nothing." This item of information from Eusebius' letter seems to be very plausible, as Constantine must have been the only one, of those present at the Council, who was unaware of the past heretical connotations of the term.

The fact is that the *credo* was affirmed and subscribed. It was not endorsed by Eusebius of Nicomedia (for reasons unknown) and the two bishops, Secundus and Theonas, who had been previously condemned along with Arius at Alexandria. They arrived to take part in a convocation at Nicaea, but were most probably prevented from attending the synodal proceedings on account of their condemnation in Egypt. It would be confirmed further by one of the canons of Nicaea, expressly forbidding the participation of the excommunicated.

The two documents known as "post-synodal letters," i.e., allegedly Constantine's letter to the Church of Alexandria and the letter of the Council of Nicaea addressed to the Alexandrian Church as well, both appear to report on the proceedings of an ostensibly different synod, where the most important issues were the Arian controversy and the Meletian schism. It seems, however, that these are forgeries produced at the time of the unrest following the death of Athanasius in 373, when his successor Peter had barely managed to escape from his captivity at the city, subsequently leaving for Rome, while the previous opponents of Athanasius had effectively taken control over the See of Alexandria. These letters are therefore more a testimony to the situation in the Church of Alexandria in the latter half of the 370s rather than to the period immediately after the Council of Nicaea.

In my opinion, the myth of the anti-Arian Council of Nicaea had originated from those two letters, in the light of which Athanasius' writings would be subsequently construed and represented. A reflection of this legend can be also found in the myth of Athanasius as a fearless anti-Arian defender of the Nicene Creed. Very soon after his election to the See of Alexandria, or his appointment by the predecessor (his uncle), he came into conflict within the Church over his relentless position towards the Meletians, who were "somehow," as he would say, reconciled with the Church at Nicaea. He preferred, however, to have been regarded as someone persecuted for his faith and called all his opponents "Arius' maniacs." It did not make him an immediate advocate of the Nicene Creed, as he would not have spoken in defence of it for as long as about 25 years following the great synod. Only afterwards, perhaps having realized the unbeneficial effects of his endeavours, did he come to propagate this *credo*. Admittedly, he was successful in his effort, yet it would fail to prove of much use to the Nicene Creed, as it had to make way for the Chalcedonian profession of faith, to be known as the "Niceno-Constantinopolitan," yet it did have its glory days when the Emperor Theodosius had proscribed formulating any new creed, as affirmed by his convocation of the Eastern bishops in 381. (Incidentally, I would rather say "convocation," as it would not have been regarded as a significant synod until as late as 451 in the East, with a tremendous creed falsification committed at the occasion, and 519 in the West, which I have also referred to in the chapter on the *credo*).

The importance of the general synod of Nicaea – the First Ecumenical Council – as a great action undertaken by the Church in defence of the divinity of Christ appears to be, therefore, a mythical event, like, for instance, the Deluge or the crossing of the Red Sea. It is one of the founding myths of the Church, very much like those preserved by other communities. A venerable one, more ancient than King Arthur or the Battle of Grunwald, but, likewise, based upon an actual historical event. I believe that the realization of this fact will do no harm to the Church, just as Poland will not be harmed by the historical truth about the Teutonic Order.

BIBLIOGRAPHY

Sources:

Acta Synodalia (ab anno 50 ad annum 381), SCL 1, ed. A. Baron, H. Pietras, ŹMT 37, Kraków 2006.

Athanasius, *Apologia ad Constantium*, ed. with French trans. J.M. Szymusiak, SCh 56, pp. 88-132; (PG 25, cols. 596-641).

Athanasius, *Apologia contra Arianos (Apologia secunda)*, ed. H.G. Opitz, in: *Athanasius Werke* II,1,3-5, Berlin 1938-1940, pp. 87-168; (PG 25, cols. 248-409).

Athanasius, *De decretis Nicaenae synodi*, ed. H.G. Opitz, in: *Athanasius Werke* II,1,1, Berlin 1935, pp. 1-45; (PG 25, cols. 416-476).

Athanasius, *De sententia Dionysii*, ed. H.G. Opitz, in: *Athanasius Werke* II,1,2, Berlin 1935, pp. 45-67; (PG 25, cols. 480-521).

Athanasius, *De synodis Arimini in Italia et Seleuciae in Isauria*, ed. H.G. Opitz, in: *Athanasius Werke* II,1,6-7, Berlin 1940, pp. 231-278; (PG 26, cols. 681-793).

Athanasius, *Epistula ad Afros*, PG 26, 1029-1048; SCL 1, 265-275.

Athanasius, *Epistula ad episcopos Aegypti et Libyae*, ed. K. Tetzler, D. Hansen, K. Savvidis, in: *Athanasius Werke* I,1,1, Berlin 1996, pp. 1-64; (PG 25, 537-593).

Athanasius, *Tomus ad Antiochenos*, PG 26, 796-809; SCL 1, 249-255.

Canones Apostolorum, SCL 2.

Dionisius Alexandrinus, in: L. Feltoe, *The Letters and Other Remains of Dionysius of Alexandria*, Cambridge 1904.

Dokumenty Soborów Powszechnych ("Documents of the Ecumenical Councils"), vol. I, ed. A. Baron, H. Pietras, ŹMT 24, Kraków 2001.

Epiphanius, *Panarion*, ed. K. Holl, vol I-III, Leipzig 1915-1933; (*The Panarion of St. Epiphanius, Bishop of Salamis*, P. Amidon (trans.), OUP, New York – Oxford 1990).

Eusebius Caesariensis, *Historia ecclesiastica*, ed. E. Schwartz and T. Mommsen, GCS NF 6/1-3 (*Nicene and Post-Nicene Fathers*, Second Series, vol. 1: *Eusebius: Church History, Life of Constantine the Great, and Oration in Praise of Constantine*, reprint: Hendrickson Publishers, Peabody (Mass.) 1994).

Eusebius Caesariensis, *Vita Constantini*, PG 20, 905-1440, critical edition H.G. Opitz, *Athanasius Werke* III,1, Walter de Gruyter and Co, Berlin – Leipzig 1934, document 17, pp. 32ff.. (*Nicene and Post-Nicene Fathers*, Second Series, vol. 1: *Eusebius: Church History, Life of Constantine the Great, and Oration in Praise of Constantine*, reprint: Hendrickson Publishers, Peabody (Mass.) 1994).

Eutropius, *Eutropii Breuiarium ab urbe condita*, ed. C. Santini, BSGRT, Leipzig 1979.

Evagrius Scholasticus, *Historia Ecclesiae, The Ecclesiastical History of Euagrius with the Scholia*, ed. J. Bidez, L. Parmentier, London 1898 (repr. 1979).

Justin, *Dialogus cum Triphone, A Dialogue with Trifon*, in *The Ante-Nicene Fathers*, vol. 1: *The Apostolic Fathers – Justin Martyr – Irenaeus*, reprint: WM. B. Eerdmans Publishing Company, Gran Rapids (Michigan) 1979.

Origenes, *Contra Celsum*, introduction, texte critique, traduction et notes par Marcel Borret, SCh 132,136,147,150,227, Paris: Cerf 1967-1976.

Origenes, *De principiis*, ed. with French trans. H. Crouzel, M. Simonetti, SCh 252; SCh 268; Greek and Latin fragments, commentary and index SCh 253; SCh 269; SCh 312.

Origenes, *Commentarium in evangelium Joannis*, ed. with French trans. C. Blanc, SCh 120; SCh 157; SCh 222; SCh 290; SCh 385 (*The Fathers of the Church*, The Catholic University of America, Washington 1989, vol. 80).

Philo Alexandrinus, *De Opificio Mundi*, in: *Philo in ten volumes* (and two supplementary volumes) / with an english translation by F.H. Colson, G.H. Whitaker, London : Heinemann Cambridge (MA); London: Harvard University Press, 1968-1987, vol I.

Ruphinus, *Historia ecclesiastica*, in: *Eusebius Werke* II, GCS, ed. Th. Mommsen, Leipzig 1903-1909.

Sextus Aurelius Victor, *De caesaris*, edited by P. Dufraigne, BL, Paris 1975 (with a French trans.).

Socrates Scholasticus, *Histoire Ecclesiastique*, vol. I, introduction and edition P. Maraval. SCh 477, Paris 2004 (*Nicene and Post-Nicene Fathers*, Second Series, vol. 2: *Socrates, Sozomenus: Church Histories*, reprint: Hendrickson Publishers, Peabody (Mass.) 1994).

Sozomen, *Histoire Ecclesiastique*, vol. I (Livres I-II), ed. G. Grillet, G. Sabbah, A.-J. Festugiere, SCh 306, Paris 1993 (*Nicene and Post-Nicene Fathers*, Second Series, vol. 2: *Socrates, Sozomenus: Church Histories*, reprint: Hendrickson Publishers, Peabody (Mass.) 1994).

Theodor Lector, *Excerpta ex Ecclesiastica Historia*, PG 86, 165-228.

Theodoret, *Historia Ecclesiastica*, ed. L. Parmentier, Leipzig 1911 (new revised edition F. Scheidweiler, GCS, Berlin 1954), with a French trans., ed. J. Bouffartique, P. Canivet, C. Fraisse, A. Martin, L. Pietri, F. Thelamon, SCh 501, Paris 2006 (*Nicene and Post-Nicene Fathers*, Second Series, vol. 3: *Theodoret, Jerome, Gennadius, Rufinus: Historical Writings, etc.*, reprint: Hendrickson Publishers, Peabody (Mass.) 1994).

Philostorgius, *Historia Ecclesiastica*, 3rd edition (revised) J. Bidez, F. Winkelmann, GCS, Berlin 1981.

Studies:

Anatolios K., *Retrieving Nicaea. The Development and Meaning of Trinitarian Doctrine*, Baker Academic, Grand Rapids, Michigan 2011.

Ayres L., *Nicaea and Its Legacy, an Approach to Fourth-Century Trinitarian Theology*, Oxford Univ. Press, 2004.

Bardy G., *Recherches sur S. Lucien d'Antioche*, Beauchesne, Paris 1936.

Barnes T., *Athanasius and Constantius. Theology and Politics in the Constantinian Empire*, Harvard University Press, Cambridge (Mass.) – London (England) 1994 (2nd ed.).

Barnes T., *The Exile and Recalls of Arius*, JThS 60 (2009), 109-129.

Behr J., *The Nicene Faith II*, St. Vladimir's Seminary Press, Crestwood, New York 2004.

Di Berardino A., *L'imperatore Costantino e la celebrazione della Pasqua*, in: *Costantino il Grande dall'antichità all'umanesimo. Colloquio sul Cristianesimo nel mondo antico, Macerata 18-20 Dicembre 1990*, vol. I, edd. G. Bonamente-F. Fusco, Università degli Studi di Macerata 1992, 363-384.

Cataudella M. R., *Costantino „episcopos" e l'„Oratio ad Sanctorum coetum"*, in: *Politica retorica e simbolismo del primato: Roma e Costantinopoli, secoli 4.-7. Atti del Convegno internazionale, Catania, 4-7 ottobre 2001*, a cura di F. Elia, Catania 2002, 263-280.

Boularand E., *L'hérésie d'Arius et la foi de Nicée*, Letouzey et Anè, Paris 1972.

Chadwick H., *Ossius of Cordova and the Presidency of the Council of Antioch, 325*, JThS 49 (1948), 27-35.

Chevallier R., *Voyages et déplacements dans l'Empire Romain*, Armand Colin, Paris 1988.

Dal Covolo E., *Il Credo di Nicea. A proposito di un libro recente*, in: *Salesianum* 65 (2003), 769-778.

DeClercq V. C., *Ossius of Cordova, a Contribution to the History of the Constantinian Period*, Cath. Univ. of America Pr., Washington 1954.

De Decker D., *Eusèbe de Nicomédie, pour une réévaluation historique critique des avatars du Premier Concile de Nicée*, in: *Augustinianum* 45 (2005), 95-170.

Dossetti G.L., *Il Simbolo di Nicea e di Costantinopoli*. Herder, Roma 1967.

Elliott Th. G., *Constantine's Preparations for the Council of Nicaea*, in: *The Journal of Religious History* 17 (1992), 127-137.

Farina R., *L'Impero e l'Imperatore cristiano in Eusebio di Cesarea. La prima teologia politica del cristianesimo*, Pas Verlag, Zürich 1966.

Ferguson Th. C., *The Past is Prologue: the Revolution of Nicene Historiography*, Suppl. to Vigiliae Christianae, Brill, Leiden – Boston 2005.

Gliściński, J., *Współistotny Ojcu*, Diecezjalne Wydawnictwo Łódzkie, Łódź 1992.

Gorce D., *Le voyages, l'hospitalité et le port des lettres dans le monde chrétien des IV et V siècles*, Librairie Auguste Picard, Paris 1925.

Griggs C.W., *Early Egyptian Christianity from its Origins to 451 C.E.*, vol. 2, ed. M. Krause, E. J. Brill, Leiden 1990 (Coptic Studies).

Gonnet, D., *La réception de Nicée I par Athanase: quels types de langage utilise-t-il pour parler du Verbe?* in: *Christus bei den Vätern. Forscher aus dem Osten und Westen Europas an den Quellen des gemeinsamen Glaubens*, edd. Y. de Andia-P.L. Hofrichter, Pro-Oriente, Wien 2003, 134-139.

Gonzalez, C. I., *Antecedentes de la cristologia ariana el el siglo III*, in: *Medellin* 63 (1990), 315-361.

Hall S. G., *Some Constantinian Documents in the Vita Constantini*, in: *Constantine. History, Historiography and Legend*, ed. S. N. C. Lieu-D. Montserrat, Routledge, London-New York 1998, 86-103.

Hanson R. P. C., *The Search for the Christian Doctrine of God (The Arian Controversy 318-381)*, Edinburgh 1988.

Athanasius von Alexandrien, De sententia Dionysii, ed. U. Heil, Walter de Gruyter, Berlin-New York 1999 (Patristische Texte und Studien 52).

Iborra M. M., *El Concilio di Constantinopla y el simbolo di fe niceno-constantinopolitano*, in: *I Padri e le scuole teologiche nei concili. Atti del VII simposio internazionale nella Facolta di teologia, Roma 6-7 marzo 2003*, a cura di J. Grohe-J. Leal-V. Reale, Lib. Ed. Vat 2006, 341-356.

Jaczynowska M., *Religie świata rzymskiego*, PWN, Warszawa 1987.

The Prosopography of the Later Roman Empire, vol. I, *AD 260-395*, edd. A. H. M.Jones-J. R. Martindale, Cambridge University Press 1971.

Kannengiesser Ch., *Alexander and Arius of Alexandria: the Last Ante-Nicene Theologians*, in: *Miscelanea En Homenaje Al P. Antonio Orbe*, ed. E. Romero-Pose, (*Compostellanum*, vol. 35), Santiago de Compostela 1990, 391–403; *Arius and Athanasius: Two Alexandrian Theologians*, Variorum, London 1991, (Collected Studies Series 353), art. IV.

Kannengiesser Ch., Athanasius of Alexandria vs. Arius: The Alexandrian Crisis, in: *The Roots of Egyptian Christianity*, ed. Birger A. Pearson-J. E. Goehring, Fortress Press, Philadelphia 1986, (*Studies in Antiquity and Christianity*), 204–215; *Arius and Athanasius : Two Alexandrian Theologians*, Variorum, London 1991, (Collected Studies Series 353), art. XII.

Kannengiesser Ch., *Les Blasphèmes d'Arius (Athanase d'Alexandrie, De Synodis 15): un écrit néo-arien, Mémorial André-Jean Festugière: antiquite païenne et chrétienne*, ed. E. Lucchesi-H.D. Saffrey, Genève 1984, 143-151.

Kannengiesser Ch., *Nicée 325 dans l'histoire du christianisme*, in: *Concilium: Revue internationale de théologie* 138 (1978), 39-47.

Kotłowska A., *Obraz dziejów w* Chronici Canones *Euzebiusza z Cezarei*, Wydawnictwo Poznańskie 2009.

Lettieri G., *Passione e/o impassibilità di Dio nella controversia ariana*, in: *Croce e identità cristiana di Dio nei primi secoli*, ed. F. Taccone, Edizione OCD, Roma 2009, 37-57.

Logan A. H. B., *Marcellus of Ancyra and the Councils of AD 325: Antioch, Ancyra and Nicaea*, in: JThSt NS 43 (1992). 428-446.

Longosz S., Św. Atanazy Aleksandryjski i biskupi Rzymu, in: VoxP 24 (2004), 163-191.

Löhr W., *Arius Reconsidered* (part 1), in: *Zeitschrift für Antikes Christentum* 9 (2006), 524-560,

Löhr W., *Arius Reconsidered* (part 2), in: *Zeitschrift für Antikes Christentum* 10 (2006), 121-157.

Loose U., *Zur Chronologie des arianischen Streites*, in: ZKG 101 (1990), 88-92.

Luibhéid C., *The Council of Nicaea*, Officina Typographica, Galway 1982.

Luibhéid C., *The Alleged Second Session of the Council of Nicaea*, in: *Journal of Ecclesiastical History* 34 (1983), 165-174.

Martin A., *Les conditions de la réadmission du clergé mélitien par le concile de Nicée*, in: *Ancient Society* 20 (1989), 281-290.

Histoire du christianisme, vol. 1-3, edd. J.-M. Mayeur-Ch. Pietri-L. Pietri-A. Vauches-M. Venard, Desclée 1995-1998.

Molland D. L., *Die Synod von Antiochien*, 324-5, in: ZKG 81 (1970), 163-181.

Morales X., *La théologie trinitaire d'Athanase d'Alexandrie*, Paris 2006 (Collection des Études Augustiniennes – Série Antiquité 180).

Moroziuk R. P., *Origen and the Nicene Orthodoxy*, in: *Origeniana Quinta. Papers of the 5th International Origen Congress, Boston College, 14-18 August 1989*, ed. P. Daly, Peeters Publishers 1992, (Bibliotheca Ephemeridum Theologicarum Lovaniensium 105), 488-493.

Naumowicz J., *Geneza chrześcijańskiej rachuby lat*, Wydawnictwo Benedyktynów, Kraków 2000.

Navascués P. de, *Pablo de Samosata y sus adversarios. Estudio histórico-teológico del cristianismo antioqueno en el s. III*, Augustinianum, Roma 2004 (SEA 87).

Nyman J. R., *The Synod at Antioch (324-325) and the Council of Nicaea*, in: *Studia Patristica* 4/2 (1961), 483-489.

Odahl Ch. M., *Constantine and the Christian Empire*, Routledge, Taylor & Francis Group, London-New York 2004.

Ortiz de Urbina I., *El Simbolo Niceno*, Consejo Superior de Investigaciones Cientificas, Madrid 1947.

Ortiz de Urbina I., *Nicée et Constantinople*, Éditions de l'Orante, Paris 1982 (Histoire des Conciles Oecumeniques 1).

Ożóg M., *Podróże mnichów i duchownych w świetle pism świętego Hieronima*, in *Vox Patrum* 57 (2012), 453-468.

Ożóg M., *Teoderyk a schizma akacjańska*, in: *Chrześcijaństwo u schyłku starożytności* 11 (2012), 107-126.

Pietras H., *Argumentacja filozoficzna za wiecznością Syna Bożego u Orygenesa*, in: *Ojcowie Kościoła wobec filozofii i kultury klasycznej. Zagadnienia wybrane*, edd. F. Drączkowski, J. Pałucki, M. Szram, Polihymnia Lublin 1998, 89-97.

Pietras H., *Jedność Boga, jedność świata i jedność Kościoła. Studium fragmentów Dionizego Aleksandryjskiego*, Wydział Filozoficzny Towarzystwa Jezusowego, Kraków 1990 (Instytut Kultury Religijnej, Studia i Materiały I).

Pietras H., *Le ragioni della convocazione del Concilio Niceno da parte di Costantino il Grande. Un'investigazione storico-teologica*, Gregorianum 82/1 (2001), 5-35.

Pietras H., *List Konstantyna do Aleksandra i Ariusza a zwołanie Soboru Nicejskiego*, VoxP 26 (2006) vol. 49, 531-547.

Pietras H., *Lettera di Costantino alla Chiesa di Alessandria e Lettera del sinodo di Nicea agli Egiziani (325) – i falsi sconosciuti da Atanasio?*, Gregorianum 89/3 (2008), 727-739.

Pietras H., *L'unità di Dio in Dionigi di Alessandria*, Gregorianum 72 (1991), 459-490.

Pietras H., *Początek „kontrowersji ariańskiej"*, in: *Chrześcijaństwo antyczne*, ed. J. Drabina, Państwowe Wydawnictwo Naukowe 2006, (Zeszyty naukowe Uniwersytetu Jagiellońskiego. Studia Religiologica 39), 57-79.

Pietras H., *Początki teologii Kościoła*, Wydawnictwo WAM, Kraków 2007 (2 ed.).

Pietras H., *Pojęcie Bożej substancji w początkach Kościoła*, in: *Metafizyki i teologia. Debata u podstaw*, ed. R. Woźniak, Wydawnictwo WAM, Kraków 2008, (Myśl Teologiczna 62), 122-140.

Prinzivalli E., *L'arianesimo: la prima divisione fra i romani e la prima assimilazione dei popoli migranti*, in: *Cristianità d'occidente e cristianità d'oriente. Secoli VI-XI*, vol. 1, Centro Italiano di Studi sull'Alto Medioevo, Spoleto 2004, (Settimane di Studio del Centro Italiano di Studi sull'Alto Medioevo 51), 31-61.

Riedmatten H. de, *Les actes du procès de Paul de Samosate, Etude sur la cristologie du IIIe au Ive siècle*, Friburg en Suisse 1952.

Rousseau A., R. Lafontaine, *Athanase d'Alexandrie: les Trois Discours Contre les Ariens*, Brussel 2004 (Donner raison 15).

Sibilio V., *Constantino il Grande e la Chiesa. Una complessa relazione tra dogma, diritto e politica*, in: Nicol 33/1 (2006), 301-319.

Simonetti M., *Le origini dell'arianesimo*, in: *Rivista di Storia e Letteratura Religiosa* 7 (1971), 317-330.

Simonetti M., *La crisi ariana nel IV secolo*, Augustinianum, Roma 1975 (SEA 11).

Simonetti M., *Ancora su Homoousios a proposito di due recenti studi*, in: *Vetera Christianorum* 17 (1980), 85-98.

Simonetti M., (ed.) *Il Cristo*, vol. 2, *Testi teologici e spirituali in lingua greca dal IV al VII secolo*, , Fondazione Lorenzo Valla 1986.

Simonetti M., *Aspetti della cristologia del III secolo: Dionigi di Alessandria*, in: *Bessarione*, Roma 1989, (Quaderno 7), 37-65.

Spada D., *Le formule trinitarie da Nicea a Costantinopoli*, Pont. Univ. Urbaniana, Roma 1988 (Subsidia Urbaniana 32).

Speeten J. van der, *Le dossier de Nicée dans la Quesnelliana*, in: *Sacris erudiri* 28 (1985), 383-450.

Stead Ch., *Arius in Modern Research*, in: JThS 45 (1994) 24-35.

Stead Ch., *Was Arius a Neoplatonist?*, in: *Studia Patristica* 32 (1997), 39-52.

Tammaro C., *La giurisdizione episcopale nell'alto medioevo. Riflessioni sul principio „un solo vescovo per città" sancito dal can. VIII del Consilio di Nicea I (325)*, in: *Ius Canonicum* 92 (2006), 623-636.

Udovitch A. L., *Time, the Sea and Society: duration of commercial voyages on the southern shores of the Mediterranean during the high Middle Ages*, in: *La navigazione mediterranea nell'alto Medioevo*, Centro Italiano di Studi sull'Alto Medioevo, Spoleto 1978, (Settimane di Studio 25), 503-546.

Van Dam R., *The Roman Revolution of Constantine*, Cambridge University Press 2008.

Van Nuffelen P., *Arius, Athanase et les autres: enjeux juridiques et politiques du retour d'exil*, in: *Exil et relégation, les tribulations du sage et du saint dans l'Antiquité romaine et chrétienne (IIe avt-VIe s. ap. J.-C.)*, edd. P. Blaudeau-F. Prévot, Paris 2007.

Vigne D. *Une Église, plusieurs dates de Pâques?*, in: BLE 102 (2001), 247-264.

Williams R., *Arius, Heresy and Tradition*, Darton, Longman and Todd, London 1987.

Wipszycka E., *La Chiesa nell'Egitto del IV secolo*, in: Études *sur le Christianisme dans l'Égypte de l'antiquité tardive*, Studia Ephemeridis Augustinianum 52, Roma 1996,

Zieliński T., *Religia Rzeczypospolitej Rzymskiej*, Wydawnictwo J. Mortkowicza i Towarzystwo Wydawnicze w Warszawie, Warszawa-Kraków 1934.

Zygner L., *Formuła Światłość ze światłości w okresie przednicejskim*, in: VoxP 13-15/24-29 (1993-1995), 323-327.

INDEX BIBLICUS

INDEX FONTIUM

INDEX

Finito di stampare nel mese di aprile 2022
presso Scuola Tipografica s. Pio X - Roma